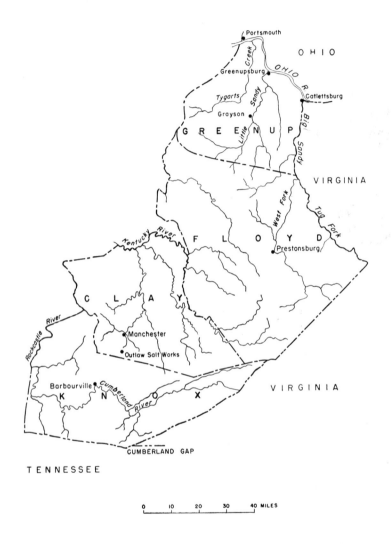

EASTERN AND SOUTHEASTERN KENTUCKY, 1809

C. M. Kozee, Sr., 1956

PIONEER FAMILIES

OF

EASTERN and SOUTHEASTERN KENTUCKY

By

WILLIAM C. KOZEE, A.B., LL.B.

REFERENCE

GENEALOGICAL PUBLISHING CO., INC.
BALTIMORE   1973

Originally Published
Huntington, West Virginia [1957]

Reprinted
Genealogical Publishing Co., Inc.
Baltimore, 1973

Library of Congress Catalogue Card Number 73-9090
International Standard Book Number 0-8063-0576-2

PUBLISHER'S NOTICE

At the time *Pioneer Families of Eastern and Southeastern
Kentucky* and *Early Families of Eastern and Southeastern Kentucky* were originally compiled, the apparent intention of the
author was to offer them as a set. As there may now be an
interest in only one of the two volumes, we are offering them
separately.

PREFACE

These two volumes pertain almost exclusively to people—the early adventurers, explorers, hunters, surveyors and the pioneer families and their descendants of the section of Kentucky that was originally embraced by the Counties of Floyd (1799), Knox (1799), Greenup (1803) and Clay (1806), as formed by the General Assembly of Kentucky, which is the section of the state east and south of a line roughly drawn from a point on the Ohio River, the northwestern corner of present Greenup County, along the western boundary line of that County to the boundary line of present Rowan (then Fleming) County; thence with the eastern boundary line of Rowan County and onward a southwesterly course to the northwest corner of present Whitley County; thence with the western boundary line of Whitley County, a southerly course, to the Tennessee state line—the "Kentucky Highlands" or mountain section.

In the preparation of the books all known available source materials were examined which necessitated extensive research in person in large areas of Kentucky and Virginia and in the National Archives, the Library of Congress and other libraries in Washington, D. C.; also it was necessary to contact a great number of descendants of these pioneer families for data relating to their respective families.

No similar book or books covering the whole mountain section of the state have been published. However, several excellent regional and county histories, some of which include genealogies, have been published. Among others are Ely's *The Big Sandy Valley*, 1887; Jillson's *The Big Sandy Valley*, 1923; Hall's *Johnson County*, 1928; and Biggs' and Mackoy's *History of Greenup County*, 1951.

I desire to express my thanks to the various county court clerks of the mountain section of Kentucky and of certain counties of Virginia and to those in charge of the National Archives and the Library of Congress, Washington, D. C., for courtesies shown while doing research in their respective offices; and I sincerely thank the many friends for their encouragement and interest and particularly for preparing and furnishing valuable biographical and genealogical data relating to their respective families.

WILLIAM CARLOS KOZEE
Author-Editor-Compiler.

Washington, D. C. and
Cove Point Beach, Md.
June 1, 1956.

CONTENTS

CHAPTER XV

CHAPTER XVI

CHAPTER I

EARLY ADVENTURERS, EXPLORERS, HUNTERS AND SURVEYORS

THE STORY of the mountain region of Kentucky falls naturally into successive periods — adventure and exploration, hunter, hunter-settler and homesteader. Each class made its own contribution and then passed on or was merged into the next evolution.

FIRST EXPLORATIONS

About 1763 Englishmen from the Crown colony of Virginia, under the patronage of Colonel Abraham Wood, whose fort stood at tidewater on the James River, were toiling through the Appalachian and the Blue Ridge Mountains in search of a short trading route to the west. In the year 1671, Captain Thomas Batts and Robert Fallam had pushed their way over the great Appalachian divide and had discovered the middle waters of the Kanawha River in present West Virginia. They returned to the east flushed with their success, and Colonel Wood, sensing the possibilities of a companion tour of exploration directed in a more southwesterly direction, sent out in 1763 James Needham and Gabriel Arthur who penetrated to the headwaters of the Tennessee River. Needham was killed by the Indians and Arthur, while accompanying a warring party of Cherokee Indians in 1764, was wounded and taken captive by a band of Shawnees between the mouths of the Big Sandy and Little Sandy Rivers. He was taken northward across the Ohio River to the Shawnee town on the lower Scioto River and was there adopted by the tribe who, when his wounds had healed, released him to return to the Cherokees in eastern Tennessee. After crossing the entire eastern part of Kentucky, apparently over the Warriors Trail, he rejoined the Cherokee tribesmen and finally made his way back to the home of his patron, Colonel Wood.[1]

THE OHIO COMPANY

In 1748 George II granted to a number of wealthy Virginians, organized as the Ohio Company, a tract of 500,000 acres of land on the Ohio River of which 200,000 acres were to be located on the south side of the Ohio between the Kanawha

1

and Monongahela Rivers, and 300,000 acres on the waters of the Ohio lower down, on either side. Thomas Lee was the projector of the Company but its affairs were later conducted by Lawrence Washington, half-brother of George. Other copartners were the then Governor of Virginia, Robert Dinwiddie, Augustine Washington, another half-brother of George, Arthur Dobbs, Samuel Smith, James Wardrop, Chapel Hanbury, John Taylor, Presley Thornton, Nathaniel Chapman, Jacob Giles, Thomas Cresap, John Mercer, James Scott, Richard Lee, Robert Carter and George Mason who was Treasurer. The area was extended from time to time and the Company finally, in 1773, merged into the Walpole grant under the name of the Great Ohio Company which included within its limits all that part of Kentucky east of the Kentucky River. The conditions of the grant were that 100 families should be settled on it, a fort built and a garrison maintained.

Christopher Gist was selected by the Company to explore and locate its lands. He set out from the Potomac, October 3. 1750, and passing over the Forbes Road to Ft. Pitt (now Pittsburgh), he came through Ohio and down the Scioto River to its mouth and swam his horses across the Ohio there, entering Kentucky at the northern terminus of the Warriors Trail. The night of Tuesday, March 12, 1751, he slept in an old Indian cabin on the site of present Fullerton, Greenup County. Turning to the west the next morning, he traversed the present counties of Lewis, Mason, Harrison, Nicholas, Bourbon, Scott, Franklin, Shelby, Woodford, Fayette and Clark. Turning southeast, he probably took up an old Indian trail near present Mt. Sterling which led him through Indian Valley into eastern Menifee County to the upper waters of Red River in central Wolfe County; thence crossing the watershed, he came onto the waters of the North Fork of the Kentucky River, along which he followed a very difficult Indian trail, passing through the site of present Jackson, Hazard and Whitesburg; then he crossed over Pine Mountains through Pound Gap and made his way back to his home in the Yadkin River valley in North Carolina.[2]

Colonel Gist, surveyor, farmer, diplomat to Indians, and brave soldier, was of English extraction and a native of Maryland. his grandfather having immigrated to that colony from England. He had retired and removed to the Yadkin River, North Carolina, where he was a friend and neighbor of Daniel Boone.

Colonel Gist left many distinguished descendants.

The Loyal Land Company

In 1749 the Loyal Land Company was chartered in London, England, under royal grant, to survey and locate 800,000 acres north of latitude 36° 30' in the territory of Kentucky, then a part of Fincastle County, Virginia.

On December 12, 1749, Dr. Thomas Walker of Castle Hill, Albemarle County, Virginia, contracted with the land company "to go to the westward," for the purpose of discovering a proper place for settlement. Leaving his home at Castle Hill, March 6, 1750, Dr. Walker, accompanied by a party of five: Ambrose Powell, William Tomlinson, Colby Chew, Henry Lawless and John Hughes, crossed the valleys of the Clinch and Holston Rivers and going down the Powell River came to the present Cumberland Gap on the 13th, which Dr. Walker called "Cave Gap." He called the mountain "Steep Ridge." Proceeding through the gap, they discovered and Dr. Walker named the Cumberland River in honor of William Augustus, Duke of Cumberland, son of George II and Queen Caroline, who, on the 16th of April, 1746, in the battle of Culloden, defeated with great slaughter the Highland forces which supported the cause of the Young Pretender. Proceeding down the Cumberland they crossed that stream on the 23rd at a place called "Swans Pond," about four miles from present Barbourville. Dr. Walker proposed that with two of the company he would proceed and that the other three should remain there until his return, which proposition was agreed to; and lots being drawn as to who should proceed, Ambrose Powell and Colby Chew were the fortunate ones, and the other three remained and built a small, rude structure just eight by twelve feet, cleared and broke up some ground, and planted corn and peach stones. This was the first house built in Kentucky by white men of which there is any record. It was occupied, with additions, until 1835. Lands including the site of the settlement have been set aside as the Walker State Park and a replica of the original log cabin erected on the site.

Dr. Walker, Powell and Chew continued the exploration northwest and "westerly" for about 35 miles when Dr. Walker concluded to return to the settlement which was reached on the 28th. After remaining at the settlement a short time, Dr. Walker and companions proceeded to Flat Lick and took the well marked Warriors Path northward to the vicinity of Red River. Despairing of finding good open meadow land, though being unknowingly near it, they then turned to the east and at length found an old trail, probably in the vicinity of Hazel Green in present Wolfe County. This prehistoric route they took to the east, past the site of present Salyersville to an old Indian rendezvous at Mud Lick and Paint Lick, which were then notable primeval places, close to present Paintsville, Johnson County. Continuing east they came to and crossed the middle waters of the west fork of the Big Sandy River, spending the period June 6-19, 1750, in exploring the valley. Dr. Walker, on Thursday, June 7, 1750, named the main or west fork of the Big Sandy, the "Louisa River," according to his diary. Continuing and passing over the divide to the waters of the Tug Fork they encountered the age-old Big Sandy Trail and thus returned to their homes in Virginia.[3]

Doctor Thomas Walker, physician, surveyor and a gentleman of wealth and culture, was born in Kings and Queens County, Virginia, January 25, 1715, and died at his home "Castle Hill," Albemarle County, Virginia, November 9, 1794. He was of English descent, his first American ancestors coming from Staffordshire, England, and settling in tidewater Virginia at an early date. The inference is that he attended William and Mary College. In 1741, at the age of 26, he married a lady who brought him an estate of 15,000 acres of land—a young widow, several years older than himself, Mrs. Nicholas Meriwether nee Mildred Thornton, a second cousin to President Washington. On this estate, east of Charlottesville, he afterward built his home, Castle Hill. Dr. Walker was the ancestor of many prominent families in Virginia and Kentucky.

Ambrose Powell was a surveyor and prominent citizen of Culpepper County, Virginia. He· was great-grandfather of General Ambrose Powell Hill, noted officer of the Confederate States Army. A son, Ambrose Powell, was an officer in the Revolutionary War; and a descendant of the same name was a judge of the County Court of Jackson County, Kentucky; another represented that county in the Kentucky Legislature.

Colby Chew was a lieutenant in the French and Indian War (1755-63) and was killed.

William Tomlinson moved to Kentucky and settled at Bryan's Station.

Henry Lawless served in the "Big Sandy Expedition" against the Indians (1756) under General Andrew Lewis and was killed by Indians in the next year.

SWIFT'S SILVER MINES

According to tradition commonly found throughout eastern and southeastern Kentucky and the adjacent Appalachian states of Pennsylvania, West Virginia, Virginia, Tennessee and the Carolinas, an English gentleman of education and means, John Swift, came into eastern and southeastern Kentucky annually, from 1760 to 1769, at the head of a company of Englishmen, Frenchmen and Shawnee Indians, for the purpose of operating certain silver mines.

It is asserted that Swift kept a journal of his activities in Kentucky which in his old age came into the possession of a Mrs. Renfro of Bean's Station in eastern Tennessee. The movements of Swift and his companions were well known to his contemporaries, and subsequent to his death many copies of his journal were made, from time to time, by those who sought to trace out his reported mines and caches of precious metal. As might be expected, not one of these copies of the journal agrees with any of the others, each apparently being an abbreviated interpretation of the original or some other copy. Of all of these, one copy which belonged to one Robert Alley, a native of eastern Tennessee, and long a resident of Johnson County, Kentucky, had the appearances of the original Swift document from certain parts of which it appears that Swift and five men—Hazlitt, Ireland, Blackburn, McClintock and Staley, made a first preliminary journey into eastern Kentucky in the spring of 1760 to make arrangements to operate the silver mines supposed to be in that region. They built a furnace, burned charcoal, and operated somewhere near the "Breaks of the Big Sandy"; and after proceeding southwestwardly along the base of the Pine Mountains where they made other mineral investigations, they returned to Alexandria, Virginia, on December 10, 1760. It appears that they had connections in Virginia with a Mr. Montgomery, who owned and operated sailing vessels to the Spanish Seas and was further engaged in the work of engraving and cutting dies for the coinage of silver and gold, he being an expert in that trade having formerly worked in the Royal Mint in the Tower of London.

The company was organized along partnership lines with fifteen members or participants. Taking out a large pack train from Alexandria on June 25, 1761, and following the Indian trails west, Swift and party arrived finally at the forks of the Big Sandy, the site of the present-day Louisa, where the party was divided into two parts—one going to each of the locations selected during the previous year. Being successful in the undertaking, and leaving some of the party to continue the development, Swift, accompanied by some companions, returned to Alexandria on December 2, 1761, and found the vessels had returned from the Spanish Seas after a profitable cruise; and after enlarging this part of the enterprise by the acquisition of five new ships, they returned to the interior in the last week of March, 1762, going over the Nemicolon Path or Braddock's Trail to Fort Pitt (now Pittsburgh), where a large pack train was taken out. Arriving at the forks of the Big Sandy they cast lots to determine who should go to the various places to work their properties. Continuing on separately, they found that much had been accomplished in their absence, but that the men were discouraged with living conditions in the wilderness. Swift and some others returned to Virginia, September 1, 1762, and again found that their shipping business had been profitable.

Each succeeding year up to and including 1769, when it was finally determined to close down operations and go out of business, Swift and party made trips into Kentucky ostensibly for the purpose of operating silver mines.

Reports of existence of these mines have been credited to different counties in eastern Kentucky from Bell in the south to Carter in the north; on the northwest side of Log Mountain, only a few miles from Cumberland Ford, now Bell county; in Wolfe County; at the three forks of the Kentucky River; and in Johnson, in Floyd and in Pike counties.

It is held that these stories of silver mines were really invented by Swift to cover up his operations while he and his fellows were engaged in the spurious minting of silver and gold bullion into English currency, which bullion was the result of their piratical sailing adventures on the Spanish Seas.

Swift and companions left the mines on the 9th of October, 1769, going by way of Big Sandy and Fort Pitt, and arriving at Alexandria on the 11th day of December, that year. They closed out their seafaring operations and it was written in the journal: "So, we end the labor of 10 years on sea and land, praising God that it has been successful." The journal ends with specific directions for finding the treasure left in all parts of the wilderness and for the discovery of the mines:

On the 1st day of September, 1769, we left between 22,000 and 30,000 dollars and crowns on a large creek running near a south course. Close to the spot we marked our names (Swift, Jefferson,

Mundy and others) on a beech tree with a compass, square and trowel. * * * * No great distance from this place we left $15,000 of the same kind, marking three or four trees with marks. Not far from these, we left the prize, near a forked white oak and about three feet underground, and laid two long stones across it, marking several stones close about it. At the forks of Sandy, close by the fork, is a small rock house with a spring in one end of it. Between it and a small branch we laid a prize under the ground; it was valued at $6,000. We likewise left $3,000 buried in the rocks of the rock house.[4]

WASHINGTON'S REPUTED SURVEYS IN THE BIG SANDY AND THE LITTLE SANDY VALLEYS

No other great figure in history has had to live down such a mass of tradition and legends as has Washington, notwithstanding his diaries, methodical records, etc., left for the examination and perusal of the general public.

The historian, Lewis Collins, in 1874, in his *Historical Sketches of Kentucky*, with no basis of fact whatever, states that Washington, in 1770, surveyed on the Big Sandy, including the site of the present city of Louisa, Lawrence County, and on the Little Sandy, eleven miles from its mouth in present Greenup County, tracts of land for John Fry. It appears a survey was made for John Fry under the proclamation of 1763 of a tract of 2,084 acres located on both sides of the Big Sandy embracing the present city of Louisa for which land a patent— believed to be the oldest to Kentucky lands—was granted by the British Crown to John Fry in 1772. The surveyor marked the survey, which is said to be a very accurate one, and on the beginning corner cut the initials "G.W." which circumstance obviously is the basis for the belief and statement that the survey was made by Washington in person or by some one acting under or for him.

Tradition relates that Washington personally surveyed for "John Savage and others" a tract of land on the Ohio above the Big Sandy River and that, in doing this, he carved with his own hand the words, "To the Living God, G.W." still to be seen on Chimney Rock, a freak stone formation back of Ceredo, West Virginia. According to tradition his camp was made at Washington's Spring on Hubbard's Branch, below the site of Huntington; and for the visitor was pointed out a comparatively young sycamore tree which allegedly grew from a hand spike stuck into the ground by Washington. Other corners of the Savage tract, one a stone in a great elm, receive a like mention. Washington named, it is also related, the streams Four Pole and Twelve Pole, which join the Ohio, although a map dated 1796, "according to the best authorities," while it enumerates several smaller local streams and the Guyandotte and the Big Sandy, makes no mention of them.

Many of the local claims revolve around the letters, "G.W." Highly prized in some families were pieces of furniture made from some tree bearing this mark; and firm in the belief that Washington carved the letters thereon, the owners refused to believe any evidence to the contrary. But what of the origin of these letters? It may be stated that the use of these letters was a common practice by such surveyors as Col. John Floyd, Alexander Spotswood Dandridge and Captain William Crawford, all of whom were deputy surveyors and surveyed military lands for the French and Indian War soldiers under the Dinwiddie Proclamation. Capt. Crawford, at the suggestion of Washington, was selected by these soldiers as the principal surveyor. The grant of John Savage and others (61 men of his company) is for 28,627 acres, "beginning at a small elm marked 'G.W.' standing on the bank of the Ohio River, etc." It is dated December 15, 1772. On December 1, 1773, 21,941 acres were granted to John Fry and others "beginning at a beech and hicory (sic) tree lettered 'G.W.' standing at the mouth of the Pocatallico on the lower side of where it falls into the Great Kanawha River." The name of Washington does not appear in connection with any of these lands in the records of the Virginia land office; and it is definitely known that he made only one tour of the Ohio Valley which covered the period from October 5, 1770 to December 1, 1770, and made no surveys whatever in person or by deputy in that region. Washington's diary covering the years 1769 and 1770, when he is reputed to have surveyed western lands, discloses his activities and whereabouts. He attended church at Pohick at least once a month during said period and visited Lord Fairfax at Belvoir as frequently.[5]

BOONE AND OTHERS IN THE BIG SANDY VALLEY (1767-68)

In the summer of 1767, Governor William Tryon of North Carolina laid out the boundary line of the Cherokee nation and issued a proclamation forbidding any purchase of land from the Indians and any issuance of grants for land within one mile of the boundary line. Notwithstanding this precaution, several North Carolina hunters during the following September ventured into the mountain region some sixty miles beyond the boundary and were fired upon and several of them killed by the resentful Cherokees.

Undismayed by these signs of impending danger, Daniel Boone never relinquished his long-cherished desire of exploring and hunting in the fair region of Kentucky. Communicating his purpose to one William Hill, that adventurous hunter readily consented to go with him; and in the autumn of 1767, Boone and Hill, accompanied, it is believed, by Squire Boone, Daniel's brother, set forth from Boone's home on the upper waters of Yadkin River in North Carolina, upon their hazardous expedition. Crossing the Blue Ridge and the Alleghanies and the Holston and Clinch Rivers near their sources, they finally reached the head waters of the west fork of the Big Sandy River. Surmising from its course that this stream must flow into the Ohio River, they pushed on about a hundred miles to the westward and finally by following a buffalo path, reached and went into camp at a salt lick about ten miles west of present Prestonsburg on Left Middle Creek. Here they beheld great herds of buffaloes that came to the salt lick to drink the water and/or to lick the brackish soil. After spending the winter of 1767-68 in exploring, hunting and trapping, the Boones and Hill, discouraged by the rough nature of the country which with its dense growth of laurel was exceedingly difficult to penetrate, abandoned all hope of reaching the Ohio and following it to the Falls by that route and made their way back to the Yadkin laden with the spoils of the winter's hunting.[6]

FOWLER AND OTHERS

It appears from depositions filed in 1796 in a court proceedings in Mason County, Kentucky, when that county embraced within its limits all the territory lying between the Licking and the Big Sandy Rivers, in Eastern Kentucky, that in December, 1775, William Thornton, James Fowler and William Pitman left Clinch River in Southwestern Virginia on an exploring and bear hunting expedition in what is now Eastern Kentucky. Passing through Little Paint Gap (Pound Gap?) and Shelby Gap they came onto the headwaters of Shelby Creek, in present Pike County, and continued down that stream some distance. Then turning northward they passed along an old Indian trail for some distance and leaving the trail camped on a stream called by Fowler, Beaver Creek, which name it has since borne. Continuing they came to the salt springs at the mouth of the Salt Lick fork of the Left Fork of Middle Creek about ten miles west of present Prestonsburg, Floyd County. Subsequently salt was made here and the place was known as Young's Salt Works. The party did not cross the Big Sandy River and probably had no knowledge of it. In March, 1796, one of the party, William Thornton, accompanied by one Philip Roberts, came to Fowler's lick for salt.[7]

FORTS AND STATIONS; FIRST SETTLERS

A minute study of history will show that the beginning of settlement of the mountain region of Kentucky was along the roads that led to the Bluegrass settlements. Taverns and hostelries for the accommodation of emigrants formed the nucleus from which the settlers expanded to the contiguous regions. Consequently, the Wilderness Road was the first region settled.

The first white settlers in the present Harlan County were the family of Samuel Howard (then spelled Hoard) who, in 1796, emigrated from a well developed community in Virginia and settled in the limits of the present city of Harlan. According to reputable authority Wix Howard, son of Samuel, was the first white child born in Harlan County—born under a cliff within the limits of the city of Harlan.[8]

Among the first settlers on the Cumberland River in present Harlan County, were the Howards, Turners and Middletons. Other early families were the Hensleys, Napiers, Smiths, Caywoods, Kellys, Sargents, Brittains, Cornetts, Creeches, Gilberts, Joneses, Wynns, Saylors, and Brookses. Among other pioneer settlers on the upper waters of the Cumberland River were the Logans, Mahans, Reddicks, Ballingers, McNeils, Goodwins, Campbells, Allsaps, Curnstalks, Shoemakers, DeWeeses, Barbours, Collinses, and Farises.

FIRST SETTLER OF CLAY COUNTY

The first settler or the first white man of whom there is any known record to have entered within the boundary of the present Clay County was James Collins, who, in 1798, built his cabin on the headwaters of Collins Fork. In 1800, at a salt spring which he had discovered while following a buffalo trail some months previously, he made the first salt made in the County.[9]

OLDEST VILLAGE IN KENTUCKY

The first village in Kentucky and the only one within the borders of the State prior to the settlement at Harrodstown in 1774 was in present Greenup County opposite the then mouth of the Scioto River where in 1805, stood the little village of Alexandria about a mile below the present city of Portsmouth, Ohio. The village was built by Shawnee Indians and French traders years before the French and Indian War (1754-63) and in 1773 consisted of nineteen or twenty log cabins with clapboard roofs, doors, windows and chimneys and some cleared ground. Every vestige of them disappeared, however, as early as 1790.[10]

MASSACRE OF EMIGRANTS BY INDIANS

In 1784 a small colony of pioneers from Pennsylvania, going westward on the Boone Trail, stopped for the night at a spot now in Levi Jackson Wilderness Road State Park, about three miles from present London, Laurel County, now called Defeated Camp, because twenty-eight of the thirty members of the party were massacred by the Indians. In the park are many family graveyards, in one of which is the grave of John Freeman, Revolutionary War soldier and first settler. Levi Jackson, also a Revolutionary War soldier, was granted most of the land for his military services. The Jackson homestead, originally the home of John Freeman, was built in 1792.

HARMAN'S STATION

Captain Mathias Harman, the founder of Harman's Station, a Virginian of German extraction, resident of Abbs Valley and one of the traditional "long hunters of Kentucky," established a number of settlements west of the New River and had a knowledge of the country west of the mountains. For thirty years he had intentions of making a settlement at the mouth of Johns Creek on the Big Sandy River. Finally in the early Fall of 1787, accompanied by a party of about twenty hunters, including his father, Henry Harman and his sons, Henry Skaggs, James Skaggs, Robert Hawes, some of the Damrons and one Draper, he crossed the mountains onto the headwaters of the Big Sandy. Here they constructed a rude hunting camp in a "rock house." Unfortunately the camp was located on an Indian trail, resulting shortly thereafter in bringing Harman and his party into an engagement with a mongrel band of warring

Shawnee, Cherokee and Delaware Indians in which some Indians were killed. As a reprisal, the savage leaders moved swiftly over the headwaters of the Big Sandy, as was their custom under such circumstances, and fell upon the outlying Virginia Settlements and perpetrated the Wylie massacre. Harman and his companions, anticipating such action, returned home in Virginia immediately, but too late to prevent the terrible atrocity. They soon organized a party and followed the savages and their captives, Mrs. Wylie and infant daughter, into the Big Sandy Valley. Harman intended to overtake the Indians and rescue the captives, if possible, and if not, to establish an outpost station in the Big Sandy Valley which would discourage further depredations by the marauding Shawnees and their allies in the Clinch and Holston River settlements. After following the Indians several days Harman and his companions lost the trail in the floodwaters of the Levisa Fork; and after prospecting the country carefully they selected a site in the Big Sandy bottoms about half a mile below the mouth of Johns Creek and about one hundred yards back from the east bank of the river in present Johnson County and erected, in the winter of 1787-88, a log fort which became known as Harman's Station. This was the first English outpost in the Big Sandy Valley of which there is any definite record. It was to this blockhouse that Mrs. Jennie Wylie fled after her escape from the Indians on Mud Lick Creek. Had it not been erected it is altogether likely that she would never have made her escape from the Indians or lived to relate the horrible story of her captivity. In the winter of 1789, Indian reprisals were continually directed against this station and Harman and his companions were forced to abandon it.[11]

The Shawnees looked with great disfavor on the attempts of Harman and similar attempts such as that of Vancouver at the forks of the Big Sandy to establish themselves in the region for the reason settlements would spoil one of the last large hunting-grounds of the Indians and would bar the only through and direct route available to the Shawnees leading to the growing settlements on the Holston and Clinch Rivers to the Southwest.

In 1790 Harman's Station was rebuilt at the mouth of Johns Creek, never again to be given up to the Indians. At the time of its establishment there was no settlement in either of the present counties of Pike, Floyd, Lawrence, Boyd, Greenup, Carter, Elliott, Morgan, Wolfe, Magoffin, Breathitt, Knott,

Letcher or Martin; nor were there any settlements on the Tug River or in the present counties of West Virginia touching that stream.

VANCOUVER'S FORT

Vancouver's Fort, in the forks of the Big Sandy River, near the site of the present city of Louisa, Lawrence County, was settled or established in 1789 by Charles Vancouver, a Londoner, and others, but was abandoned in 1790 and re-established about 1792 on the point of land at the confluence of the Levisa and Tug Rivers. A few years subsequently this settlement was known as "Balchlutha," and is so designated on the early maps of the State. In connection with this settlement, John Hanks, in an affidavit executed in 1838, when in his seventy-fifth year, deposed:

> I was employed by Charles Vancouver in the month of February, 1789, along with several other men, to got to the forks of the Big Sandy River for the purpose of settling, clearing and improving the Vancouver tract, situated on the point [of land] formed by the junction of the Tug and Levisa Forks and near where the town of Louisa now stands. In March, 1789, shortly after Vancouver and his men settled on the point, the Indians stole all their horses but one which they killed. We all, about ten in number, except three or four of Vancouver's men, remained there during the year and left the next March, except three or four men to hold possession. But they were driven off in April, 1790, by the Indians. Vancouver went East in May, 1789 for a stock of goods and returned in the Fall of the same year. We had to go to the mouth of the Kanawha River, a distance of eighty-seven miles, for corn; and no one was settled near us, probably the nearest was a fort [Harman's Station] about thirty or forty miles away; and this was built, maybe, early in 1790. The fort we built consisted of three cabins and some pens made of logs, like corn cribs and reaching from one cabin to the other.
>
> We raised some vegetables and deadened several acres of ground, say about eighteen, on the point, but the horses being (having been) stolen we were unable to raise a crop.[12]
>
> [Signed] John Hanks

On a tablet, erected in 1946 by the Louisa Chapter of the Daughters of the American Revolution at the approach of the bridge across the Big Sandy River at Louisa, is inscribed the following:

> On the point, 700 feet East of this spot, in the Spring of 1789, was established the first settlement in this section known as

VANCOUVER'S FORT

> Charles Vancouver was granted 15,000 acres on December 17, 1788, by Governor Beverly Randolph of Virginia. He and his men cleared land, built the fort and planted a crop. A year later they were driven out by the Indians.

LICKING STATION

Licking Station, known as Gardner's Hill, on the Licking River about a mile below the present Salyersville, Magoffin County, was settled in 1796 by Archibald Prather, Ebenezer Hanna and others from South Carolina.[13]

PRESTON'S STATION (PRESTONSBURG)

In 1787 a boundary of 100,000 acres of land on the headwaters of the Big Sandy River was entered for Colonel John Preston of Montgomery County, Virginia, as is evidenced by contract between John Preston and John Smith, Mathias Harman and Henry Skaggs of record in the Floyd County (Kentucky) Circuit Court. John Graham of Augusta County, Virginia, a young surveyor, was employed to do the surveying of this vast tract of land; and in 1797 he made his first survey covering the present Prestonsburg, Floyd County. Shortly thereafter he surveyed for his own homestead a 2,000 acre tract embracing all the bottom land on both sides of the Levisa fork of the Big Sandy River from present Cliff to the mouth of Beaver Creek.

In 1791 John Spurlock erected the first permanent house where Prestonsburg now stands and, although the temporary camps of John Graham and other Virginia surveyors had been built and occupied previously, to Spurlock belongs the credit of being the first to build his home in the vicinity. Spurlock's settlement being the first with respect to time, gives to Prestonsburg the distinction of being the oldest town on the Big Sandy River. The original cabin stood for many years as a landmark in the back-from-the-river part of Prestonsburg, near the residence of the late J. M. Davidson and around this cabin grew the settlement. Closely following Spurlock came a number of other families and within a year or so the place became known as Preston's Station. It was so called in honor of Colonel John Preston for whom the large tract of land had been entered as heretofore mentioned. Colonel Preston was descended from a long line of notable Scotch-Irish ancestors, his father being Colonel William Preston of Virginia, of border-warfare fame, and his grandfather, Colonel John Preston, the Scotch-Irish immigrant who settled in Augusta County, Virginia, about 1740, and who was the ancestor of many distinguished families in Virginia, Kentucky and the South. Colonel Preston was born in Virginia about 1760; married, first, Mary Radford of Richmond, and, second, Mrs. Mayo, formerly Miss Carrington.

He had been a member of the Virginia Legislature, general of the Virginia militia, surveyor of Montgomery County, Virginia, and for many years treasurer of that State. Neither he nor any member of his immediate family removed to Floyd County or to Eastern Kentucky. Obviously he cared very little for his wilderness domain. He made Harry Stratton his agent in the Big Sandy Valley and subsequently transferred his principal surveys to John Graham, the surveyor.

In 1799, when Floyd County was formed, Preston's Station became known as Prestonsburg which was made and has ever remained the county seat of the County.[14] In 1810 the town consisted of six families—those of James Cummings, Thomas Evans, Christian Jost, Benjamin Morris, Martin Simms and John Turman. It was incorporated as a town January 2, 1818.

PIONEER SETTLERS—FROM WHENCE AND HOW THEY CAME

As soon as the treaty of peace between England and America was signed (1783) there was a great inrush of newcomers into Kentucky. They came over the Wilderness Road; they came down the Ohio River; they tramped over the Cumberlands—population flowing in at a rate estimated at 8,000 to 10,000 a year. They were Anglo-Saxon stock; they were of English descent; descendants of Huguenots from France; from Germans from the Palatinate; of Scotch-Irish from Ulster, Northern Ireland; they were youths fresh from the Revolutionary War to whom land grants had been given; they came from Pennsylvania, Maryland, and the Carolinas; and an important quota came from Connecticut, New York and New Jersey.

The early settlers of the mountains of Kentucky were principally an overflow from the great stream of immigration westward bound from the seaboard towns of Pennsylvania, New York, New Jersey and Maryland and plantations of Virginia and the Carolinas. These people were for the most part home-seekers. Making their way up the great Valley of Virginia with the Blue Ridge to the East and the Alleghanies to the West, the most of these pioneers passed from the Shenandoah onto the headwaters of the New River, and thence to the Holston, the Clinch and Powell Rivers. From this point the principal trail led most of them through the Cumberland Gap into Kentucky over the Wilderness Road. Some keeping on, however, followed down the Clinch and the Holston and made their way overland into Central Tennessee, while others continued to push even further into the Southwest.

During the height of this great transmontane migration from 1785 to 1810 a few of the pioneers, annually, turned northward into the New River Valley and others left the trail for the North at Fort Chiswell (in present Wythe County, Virginia). These were principally Virginian and Carolinian, homeseekers, who were attracted by the reports of the rich bottom lands in the river valleys. They made their way over the heads of the Kentuck,, the Tug and the Levisa forks. Others, particularly those from New Jersey, New York and New England, continued westwardly to Pittsburgh and from thence they came down the Ohio River in flatboats.[15]

THE FIRST SETTLERS

There is no record of any white men having permanently settled in the mountain region of Kentucky prior to 1789. About this time emigrants began coming to the Big Sandy Valley from Virginia and the Carolinas and from parts of Pennsylvania and Maryland. In that year the Leslies attempted to form a settlement at the mouth of Pond Creek on the Tug River, but were driven out by the vigilance of the Indians. They returned however, in 1791; but instead of locating at the mouth of Pond Creek, they crossed over to Johns Creek and formed what was later known as the Leslie Settlement. About this time came the Damrons, Harmans, Auxiers, Grahams, Browns, Marcums, Johns, Hammonds, Weddingtons, Morgans, Harrises, Pinsons, Walkers, Williamsons, Marrs, Mayos, Lackeys, Laynes, Prestons, Borderses, and many others. Following these closely came the Clarks, Belchers, Brewers, Bevins, Dixons, Cecils, Goffs, Ganards, Hatchers, Meades, McGuires, McDowells, Millards, Fulkersons, Hatfields, Porters, Runyons, Friends, Ratcliffs, Osborns, Staffords, Strattons, Robinsons, Stumps.[16]

While these pioneer families were immigrating to the Big Sandy Valley the Adamses, Campbells, Mays, Finleys, Martins, Hayses, Blackburns, Andersons, Salyers, Days, Smiths, Taylors, Combses, Stallards, Lewises, Collinses, Webbs, Wrights, Kellys, Caudills, Crafts and Hammonds were settling on the headwaters of the Cumberland and Kentucky Rivers. Many of these families also came to the Big Sandy.

Peace having been restored along the frontier settlements by the terms of the Treaty of Greeneville (1795) after the defeat of the Indians by General "Mad Anthony" Wayne at the Fallen Timbers (1794) and no further dangers being apprehended from the Indians, there was a great rush to the most desirable parts of the New River Valley and westward by the people from eastern Virginia and western North Carolina. The middle New River settled rapidly. Coincident with this increase in immigration a vast throng of people from the New River Valley quickly penetrated the country between the New River settlements and the Ohio and settled on the Big Sandy, the Guyandotte and the Coal waters, even reaching the Ohio. Among these pioneer settlers were the McCommases, Chapmans, Lucases, Smiths, Coopers, Napiers, Hunters, Adkinses, Accords, Allens, Fryes, Dingesses, Lusks, Shannons, Baileys, Jarrells, Egglestons, Fergusons, Marcums, Hatfields, Bromfields, Haldeons, Lamberts, Pauleys, Lawsons, Workmans, Prices, Cookes, Clays, Godbeys, Huffs, McDonalds, Whites, Farleys, Keezees, Perdues, Ballards, Barretts, Toneys, Conleys, Stallings, Strattons, Buchanans, Deskins, Bryans, Van Hooses and many others who largely peopled the section and left honored descendants throughout it.[17] A great number of these families finally settled on the Kentucky side of the Tug Fork and Big Sandy River.

Near the forks of the Big Sandy, Samuel Short reared his cabin (near Cassville) about 1796 followed by others in 1798 and subsequent years. On the upper waters of Twelve Pole the first settlers arrived in 1799. The present territory of Cabell County was settled at a comparatively later date. The earliest settlements in the territory were on the Savage Grant, made in 1775, to Captain John Savage and his company of soldiers of the French and Indian War.

SETTLEMENTS ON THE LOWER BIG SANDY AND THE OHIO

While the early settlements of the upper Big Sandy progressed through migration from the New, the Holston and the Clinch Rivers, the continued hostilities of the Shawnees made it impossible for settlers to gain a foothold in the lower part of that stream. In 1793, travelers passing down the Ohio River to central Kentucky found no inhabitants at the mouth of the Big Sandy, the town site of Catlettsburg; and the site of Ashland was then a primeval wilderness and gave no indication of the large settlement that was taking place in the upper part of the Big Sandy Valley. As late as 1796 and 1797 the banks of the Ohio from Pittsburgh to Maysville were almost uninhabited. It is said that at this time there were scarcely thirty families settled along this great stretch of over four hundred miles. Following conclusion of peace with the Indians in 1795, however, immigration became rapid, and by 1802 log cabins of settlers dotted all along the Ohio and were frequently in sight of each other. Among the first settlers at or near the mouth of Big Sandy were Colonel Shortridge (1792), David White, the Hamptons, and the Catletts.[18]

Finally, though not until about 1807, the strategic position of Catlettsburg at the mouth of the Big Sandy was seen. About that time two large houses—one of logs and the other clapboarded with a signpost before the door—stood at this point and marked the location of the future city. One good brick house also stood at the mouth of Keys Creek on the Ohio, now known as Normal. A little farther down the Ohio on the Kentucky side opposite Hanging Rock a gentleman by the name of A. M. Colvin owned and lived in an excellent frame house.

SIMON KENTON AND OTHERS

Simon Kenton did not come to Kentucky as a surveyor or land hunter, but as a pure type of backwoodsman he was almost without peer. As huntsman, Indian fighter, scout or spy, he was never excelled. In July 1773 he, Michael Tyger and some others from Virginia made some surveys of land with "tomahawk" improvements along and near the Ohio River in present Boyd and Greenup Counties. The winter of 1773-74, Kenton, William, Grills, Jacob Greathouse, Samuel Cartwright, and Joseph Lock spent around the mouth of the Big Sandy in hunting and trapping. Kenton, however, sought refuge in Ft. Pitt (now Pittsburgh) on the breaking out of the Indian War (Dunmore's War). Volunteering in person, he performed active service as scout or spy for the armies of General Lewis and Lord Dunmore. After an honorable discharge, he returned to his former camp and hunting ground on the Big Sandy in the autumn of 1774 with one Thomas Williams. The old yearning for "cane land" overcame Kenton and, disposing of their furs, he and Williams embarked down the Ohio to the mouth of Cabin Creek, about six miles from present Maysville. The next day while hunting out from the river they came to the longed-for cane land. Here in May, 1775, they built their camp within a mile of present Washington, Mason County, the first seat of justice and oldest town in that county.

COLONEL DANIEL BOONE

According to the historian Collins, Colonel Daniel Boone, for a time just at the close of 1800, was a resident of Greenup County, living on the bank of the Ohio River at Riverton about one and one-fourth miles above the present Greenup. He relates that in March, 1857, a Mr. Warnock, then 79 years of age, made oath that he saw Daniel Boone, at a point about one and one-half miles up Little Sandy River, cut down a tree out of which he made a canoe; and that soon afterwards he saw Boone in the canoe when he started on his way to his new home in Missouri. The fact of Boone's residence in Greenup County for a short time is established beyond a doubt. (See the *Gilruth* manuscript).

NOTES
Chapter I

1. William E. Connelley and E. M. Coulter, *History of Kentucky*, Vol. I,
2. Connelley and Coulter, *History of Kentucky*, Vol. I, pp. 67-74.
3. Temple Bodley, *History of Kentucky*, Vol. I, pp. 87-88. Jillson, *The Big Sandy Valley*, pp. 41-45.
4. Judge Charles Kerr, editor, *History of Kentucky*, Vol. I, pp. 110-133. Jillson, *The Big Sandy Valley*, pp. 46-52.
5. Jillson, *The Big Sandy Valley*, pp. 52-53. Collins, *Historical Sketches of Kentucky*.
6. Jillson, *The Big Sandy Valley*, p. 53. Collins, *Historical Sketches of Kentucky*.
7. Jillson, *The Big Sandy Valley*, p. 55. Collins, *Historical Sketches of Kentucky*.
8. Elmond Middleton, *Harlan County, Kentucky*.
9. Collins, *Historical Sketches of Kentucky*.
10. Collins, *History of Kentucky*.
11. Temple Bodley, *History of Kentucky*, Vol. I, pp. 152-159.
12. Collins, *History of Kentucky*.
13. Collins, *History of Kentucky*.
14. Jillson, *The Big Sandy Valley*.
15. Jillson, *The Big Sandy Valley*.
16. Ely, *The Big Sandy Valley*.
17. *Semi-Centennial History of West Virginia*.
18. Ely, *The Big Sandy Valley*.

CHAPTER II

FLOYD COUNTY, KENTUCKY

BOUNDARY AND ESTABLISHMENT

FLOYD, the fortieth of the counties of Kentucky in order of formation, was established by an act of the General Assembly of Kentucky (2 *Littell's Laws of Kentucky*, 282), in 1799, out of parts of Fleming, Montgomery and Mason counties, which act is in part as follows:

Section 1. Be it enacted by the general assembly, That from and after the first day of June, 1800, all that part of the county of Fleming, Montgomery, and Mason, included in the following boundary, to-wit: Beginning at the mouth of Beaver creek near the narrows of Licking; thence north thirty degrees east to the Mason line; thence with said line to a point opposite the head of Little Sandy; thence a straight direction to the forks of Great Sandy; thence along the division line between this state and the state of Virginia to the headwaters of the main branch of Kentucky; thence down same to the mouth of Quicksand; thence a straight line to the fifty mile tree on the State road; thence along said road in a direction to Mount Sterling, to Blackwater; thence down the same to the mouth thereof; thence down Licking to the beginning, shall be one distinct county, and called and known by the name of Floyd. But the said county of Floyd shall not be entitled to a separate representation until the number of free male inhabitants therein contained, above the age of twenty-one years, shall entitle them to one representative, agreeable to the ratio that shall hereinafter be established by law.

Section 2. A court for the said county shall be held by the justices thereof, on the first Monday in every month, except the months in which the courts of quarter sessions are held, after the said division shall take place, in like manner as is provided by law in respect to other counties, and as shall be by their commissioners directed.

Section 3. The justices to be named in the commission of the peace for the said county of Floyd, shall meet at the house of James Brown, in the said county, on the first court day after the said division shall take place, and having taken the oaths prescribed by law, and a sheriff being legally qualified to act, the justices shall immediately proceed to appoint and qualify a clerk, and fix on a place for holding courts in said county. * * *

The boundary of the county as originally formed may be described as a line roughly drawn northeastwardly from the present town of Yale, Bath County, to the dividing ridge between the waters of Licking and Kentucky Rivers, formerly the line between Mason and Fleming Counties; thence southwardly with the said ridge and present Elliott County line to a point opposite the head of Little Sandy River; thence a straight line to the present city of Louisa, Lawrence County; thence up the Tug Fork of Big Sandy to the Virginia State line in the vicinity of the present town of Wharncliffe, West Virginia; thence southwestwardly along the top of the mountains and with the Virginia State line to the headwaters of the North Fork of the Kentucky River in the vicinity of present Jenkins, Letcher County; thence down Kentucky River to the mouth of Quicksand and present town of that name about four miles southeast of the present city of Jackson, Breathitt County; thence northwardly to the headwaters of Blackwater and down that stream to the mouth thereof; thence down Licking River to the beginning.

By section 7 of an act of the General Assembly, approved December 2, 1806 (3 *Littell's Laws of Kentucky*, 338), creating the county of Clay, additional territory was annexed to Floyd County, as follows: "All that part of Madison County and a tract of territory on the waters of the Kentucky River above the said county of Clay, shall be annexed to, and added to the county of Floyd."

The territory of Floyd County was so extensive that from it has since been formed the whole of Pike County, in 1821, and parts of Clay, in 1806; Harlan, in 1819; Perry, in 1820; Lawrence in 1821; Morgan, in 1822; Breathitt, in 1839; Letcher, in 1842; Johnson, in 1843; Rowan, in 1856; Boyd, Magoffin, and Wolfe, in 1860; Elliott, in 1869; and Lee, in 1870 — fifteen counties in all.

The county was named in honor of Col. John Floyd, surveyor legislator, famous Indian fighter, and distinguished Kentucky pioneer. He was born in the Piedmont section of Virginia in 1750 and was of Welsh and American Indian ancestry. His pateral grandfather and a brother emigrated from Wales to Accomac County, Virginia and from them sprang all the Floyds of Virginia, Kentucky and Georgia. His father, William Floyd, married, in Amherst County, Virginia, Abadiah Davis, whose mother was of Indian descent by the marriage of an English fur trader with an Indian squaw, a daughter of Chief Powhatan's brother. Thus Mr. Floyd was related, collaterally, to the Indian princess, Pocahontas, and likewise to the notable Virginia families of Randolph, Bolling, Cary, Fleming, Bland, Cabell, Page, Harrison, and many others.

When about eighteen years of age, Mr. Floyd married Miss Burfoot (or Burford) age fourteen, of Chesterfield County, Virginia, who died within the year leaving an infant daughter whom Mrs. Burfoot adopted and named Mourning.

Removing to Fincastle County, Virginia, about 1770, Mr. Floyd engaged in school teaching and surveying under the following circumstances as related many years later by Mrs. Letitia Floyd, his daughter-in-law, and a daughter of Col. William Preston:

> During Col. Preston's residence at Greenfield in 1770, a young gentleman by the name of John Floyd was introduced to him by Col. Joseph Cabell of Rockingham County, as very well qualified to fill the place of deputy in the surveyors office. It was always a rule with Col. Preston to require every young man who was employed in his office to teach school six months at least, thereby finding out his temper, diligence, and trustworthiness. Breckenridges, Smiths, and my sisters and brothers constituted Mr. Floyd's school.

At a county court held for Fincastle County on March 2, 1774, John Floyd presented a commission "under the Hands and Seals of the Masters of William and Mary College appointing him Deputy Surveyor of the said county"; he entered into and acknowledged bonds, and took "the usual oaths to his Majesties person and Government and subscribed the Abjuration Oath and Teste and also took the oath of Deputy Surveyor of said county." Also, he was appointed deputy sheriff of said county under the high sheriff, Col. William Preston.

Mr. Floyd was engaged in surveying under Col. Preston in the Ohio Valley in 1773 and 1774, and was, with other surveying parties, recalled by Governor Dunmore during the latter year by reason of the impending Indian War. Upon his return to Virginia, he joined the Point Pleasant Expedition, serving as a captain in Col. William Christian's regiment which reached the scene of conflict a few hours too late to engage. The following year he returned to Kentucky as surveyor for the Transylvania Company and remained until the summer of 1776. Returning to Virginia, he embarked on a privateering enterprise, cruised extensively and destroyed much British shipping, but was made a prisoner and with his partner, Col. Radford of Bedford County, Virginia, was taken to Dartsmouth, England, and imprisoned for nearly a year; was assisted to escape by his jailor's wife who had a brother in America and sympathized with the American cause, and was sent across the English Channel to France in a small vessel owned by a relative of the jailor's wife. Benjamin Franklin, then American agent in France, aided him to return to America and proceeding to the home of Col. William Preston, he married Miss Jane Buchanan, granddaughter of Col. James Patton, a Scotch-Irish pioneer settler of the Valley of Virginia who was killed by the Indians at Smithfield about 1738. Miss Buchanan was living at the time with her guardian and uncle, Col. Preston, and the marriage was consummated at his home.

In 1779, Col. Floyd and his wife set out for his final embarkation to Kentucky and settled and lived in Jefferson County. When, in March, 1783, the Virginia Legislature created a judicial district out of the then three counties of Kentucky, Col. Floyd and Samuel McDowell were made judges. About a month later—April 12, 1783—while riding through the woods near Floyd's Creek, Col. Floyd was fired upon by a body of Indians, in ambush, and mortally wounded. He was taken to the station, where he died a few hours after.

Col. Floyd's children who survived him were a daughter, Mourning, the wife of Gen. Charles Stuart of Georgia; a son, Col. George Rogers Clark Floyd, who had service in the War of 1812; and a son, John Floyd, of posthumous birth, who was born, April 24, 1783, near Louisville. For a time John Floyd attended Dickinson College, Carlisle, Pennsylvania, but in October, 1804, he entered the University of Pennsylvania as a student of medicine and upon graduation there in April, 1808, he settled in Washington County, Virginia, marrying his cousin, Letitia Preston, daughter of Col. William Preston. Subsequently, in 1807, he was a justice of the peace; a major of the Militia in 1808; served as a surgeon in the Virginia line in 1812 and in the same year was elected a member of the House of Delegates. Subsequently, he was a brigadier general in the Militia. In 1817, he was elected to the U. S. House of Representatives and by successive reelections served in that office until 1829, when he was elected Governor of Virginia which office he held until 1834. South Carolina cast her electoral vote for him for President in the Presidential election of 1832. He died August 15, 1837.

John Buchanan Floyd, son of Gov. John Floyd and Letitia (Preston) Floyd, was born in Blacksburg, Virginia, April 1, 1807, and married his cousin, Sally Buchanan Preston, daughter of Gen. Francis S. Preston, granddaughter of Col. William Preston and great niece of the statesman, Patrick Henry. He was graduated from the College of South Carolina in 1826; studied law and was admitted to practice. From 1836 to 1839, he resided in Arkansas, but settled in Washington County, Virginia, in the latter year and engaged in the practice of his profession and at the same time interesting himself in politics. He served in the Virginia Legislature from 1847 to 1849; was elected Governor of Virginia in 1850 and upon retiring from that office in 1853 he was again elected to the State Legislature. On March 4, 1857, he was appointed Secretary of War by President Buchanan and served as such until 1860, when he resigned to follow his state in the secession movement. He was commissioned a brigadier general in the Confederate Army; was in command at Fort Donelson and managed to withdraw his troops from the fort without serious loss leaving Gens. Pillow and Buckner to bear the brunt of General Grant's attack. He died near Abingdon, Virginia, August 26, 1863.

Governor John B. Floyd and his brothers of Tazewell County, Virginia, long operated salt wells on Beaver Creek, Floyd County, Kentucky. However, no member of the Floyd family ever resided permanently in Eastern or Southeastern Kentucky.

FIRST COURTS

December 27, 1799.

The Governor of Kentucky appointed James Harris, Neely McGuire, Henry Stratton, Goodwin Lycans, James Ewington and Barnet Wording as the first justices of the peace for Floyd County.

On December 27, 1799, the Governor of Kentucky appointed John McIntire, James Young, and Jesse Spurlock as the first judges of the Court of Quarter Sessions for Floyd County.

The Floyd County courthouse at Prestonsburg, the county seat—the first constructed—was destroyed by fire in the latter part of the year 1807 or in the Spring of 1808; and such of the public records as are usually kept on file in courthouses were likewise destroyed. Consequently the earliest available records of said county date from the Spring of 1808.

EARLIEST COURT ORDERS OF RECORD

At a circuit court held for the circuit and county of Floyd at the house of William James Mayo, in the town of Prestonsburg (the courthouse being (having been) lately destroyed by fire), on Monday the 18th day of April, 1808.

Present: the Honorable John Graham and Alexander Lackey, Esquires, Assistant Judges. David Brown, Gent., having made it appear to the satisfaction of the court that he had obtained a license to practice as an attorney at law; whereupon he qualified and took the oath prescribed by the act of the General Assembly in that case made and provided and hath leave to practice in this court.

* * *

Abraham Beavers, foreman, Jacob Slusher, Richard Priest, James Ratliff, Richard Ratliff, John Murphy, Richard Damron, Tandy Stratton, John Branham, John Hatcher, James P. Harris, Harris Wilson, Alex. Young, Thomas Brown, James Young and Robert Brown were sworn and empanneled as a grand jury of inquest for the body of this circuit, who, after having received a charge from William P. Fleming, Gent., retired to consult on their presentments and after some time returned into court and having made no presentments were discharged.

Ordered that this court adjourn until tomorrow morning 9 o'clock.

John Graham, (Judge.)

At a Circuit Court held for Floyd Circuit at the house of Joseph Janes and Battis Jerome in Prestonsburg on Monday the 26th day of June, 1808:

Present: The Honorable John Graham and Alexander Lackey, Esquires, Assistant Judges.

Abram Beavers, foreman, Michael Millions, John Hatcher, John S. Baisden, Hiram Stratton, John Damron, Moses Preston, R. Damron, Richard Priest, John Sellards, John Brown, James P. Harris, Edward Dorton, Tandy Stratton, Joseph Ford, M. Edwards, were sworn and empanneled a Grand Jury, and was charged by H. C. Bruce, Esq.; retired to consult on their presentments and after some time returned and presented * * *.

Court adjourned till tomorrow 9 o'clock.

At a court held for Floyd County at the house of Joseph Janes and Battis Jerome in Prestonsburg (the courthouse being (having been) destroyed by fire) on Monday the 16th day of May, 1808:

Present: James Patton, Thomas C. Brown, John Brown, Thomas Evans, and John Back, Esquires, Gentlemen Justices.

* * *

At a court held for Floyd County at the house of Joseph Janes and Battis Jerome in Prestonsburg on Monday the 24th day of October, 1808:

Present: The Worshipful James Patton. Thomas C. Brown, George Belsher, and John Hammonds, Esquires, Gentlemen Justices.

* * *

Daniel Peyton produced in court a commission from under the hand of Charles Scott, Esqr., Governor of Kentucky, with the seal of the Commonwealth thereto affixed, appointing him a Justice of the Peace in and for this county; whereupon he took, as well the oaths to support the constitution of the United States and of this State, as the oaths by the act of the Assembly in that case made and provided; whereupon he took his seat accordingly.

* * *

The court is adjourned till tomorrow, 8 o'clock.

(Signed) James Patton

At a court held for Floyd Circuit at the house of Joseph Janes and Battis Jerome in Prestonsburg on Tuesday the 27th of September, 1808:

Present: The Honorables John Graham and Alex. Lackey, Esquires, Assistant Judges.

* * *

Ward, et al. v. Spears. A jury sworn, to-wit: John Stratton, George Brown, Jesse Barnett, Samuel Pack, John Sullards, Edward Dorten, Thomas Auxier, John Pack (or Back), James Brown, James Allen, Nathan Preston, and Joseph Ford. Verdict returned for $100 * * *

25

PIONEER FAMILIES

According to tax lists and other official records there were approximately 550 families living in Floyd County in 1810. Jonathan Mayo, assistant to Joseph Crockett, United States Marshal for the District of Kentucky, enumerated the third decennial United States census of the county and on December 24, 1810, he certified and reported that he had enumerated a total of 3,485. Of this number 1,809 were white males, 1,561 white females, and 115 negro slaves. Below are given the names of the heads of families and/or taxpayers as of the year 1810, together with the number of slaves owned by each slaveholder.

A

Adams, John
(1 slave)
Adams, Benjamin
Adams, Spencer
(6 slaves)
Adams, Stephen
Adams, John D.
Adams, John
(3 slaves)
Adams, Stephen
Adams, Moses
Adams, William
Adams, John
(4 slaves)
Adkins, Bartlett
Adkins, Noton
Adkins, Joseph
Adkins, Thomas
Adkins, Spencer
Adkins, Jesse
Adkins, Isham
Adkins, Joel
Adkins, Moses
Akers, Valentine
Akers, Solomon
Allen, Sarah
Allen, William
Allen, George
Allen, Thomas
Auxier, Michael
Auxier, Thomas
Auxier, Simon
Auxier, Nathaniel
Auxier, John

B

Bivens, Thomas
Benee, Daniel
Brown, Samuel
Brown, Robert

Bivens, Coverton
Bence (or Bonce),
Lawrence
Brown, James
Brown, Thomas
Brown, James
Brown, Thomas
Brown, John
Brown, John, Jr.
Brown, Daniel
Burchett, Benjamin
Burgess, Henry
Burgess, Garland
Burgess, John
Bowers, John
Barnett, Jesse
Back (Bach), John
Branham, David
Branham, John
Branham, Edward
Branham, David
(1 slave)
Blair, James
Bailey, Benjamin
Burns, William
Banks, Christian
Blackburn, Thomas
Bentley, Daniel
Blankenship, Cody
Blankenship, William
Berry, Isaac
Burgess, William
Burgess, Edward
Burgess, Edward
Bowen, Adam
Bowers, Michael
Barnett, Gilbert
Baisden, John S.
(1 slave)
Bransham, William
Branham, Turner
Belcher, John
Belcher, George

Bailey, Joseph
Bailey, James
Booker, Odom
Bradley, George
Blackburn, William
Beavers, Abraham
(1 slave)
Blankenship, Obadiah

C

Chase, William
Casky, Thomas
Cameron, James
Combs, John
Conley, Thomas
Conley, John
Cordill, Sampson
Cordill, William
Casebolt, John
Collier, Richard
Crays, George
Childers, Abraham
Conway, Lewis
Chaffin, James
Carnutte, John
Caswell, Basil
Castile (Castle), J.
Joseph
Cathy, Samuel
Crum, Adam
Cook, Clayton
Cree, William
Cunningham, Jonathan
Coffee, William
Coburn, Samuel
Combs, Jeremiah
Conley, Henry
Conley, David
Cordill, James
Cordill, Matthew
Clark, Reuben
Craft, Archelaus
Click, John

Cooper, John
Chaffin, David
Cox, Flory
Chapman, William
Cains, Richard
Collins, Meredith
Crum, Henry
Crank, William
Cope, James
Craig, William

D

Damron, Joseph
Damron, Richard
(4 slaves)
Damron, Lazarus
(1 slave)
Dean, John
(1 slave)
Davis, Zachariah
Deal, John
Day, James
Dennison, John
Dennison, Jonathan
Davis, Robert
Dickson, John
Daniel, Isham
Day, Reuben
Dennison, Thomas
Davis, Jeremiah
Davis, James
Davis, Joseph
Dorton, Edward

E

Eastep, Cornelius
Eastep, Shadrack
Elswick, Edmund
England, Joseph
Ellington, David
Ellington, Jonathan
Elliott, James
Ellis, Benjamin
(1 slave)
Evans, John
Evans, Evan
Elkins, James
Eastep, Shadrack
Elswick, Bradley
Elswick, John
Ellidge, Elijah
(1 slave)
Ellington, Jacob
Ellis, Charles
Edwards, Meredith
Evans, Richard W.
Elkins, James

F

Frazier, William
Frazier, Sarah
Fitzpatrick, Thomas
Fitzpatrick, John
Fugit, Joseph
Fannin, David
Ferguson, Richard
Fitzgerald, William
Foster, Isaac
Fleetwood, Isaac
Frazier, Solomon
Ford, Joseph
Fitzpatrick, John
Fitzpatrick, John
Fugit, Randall
Ferguson, William
Ferguson, William
Franklin, John
Foster, Mark

G

Garrett, Elimelech
(3 slaves)
Graham, John
(2 slaves)
Garland, Ambrose
Giddens, Reuben
Ghost, John
Gibson, Archibald
Gibson, Ezekiel
George, Jennie

H

Hatfield, Martha
Hogg, Stephen
(2 slaves)
Haws, Robert
Hays, John
Hunt, John
Horn, Frederick
Hopkins, Gardner
Hanna, Samuel
Hale, Joseph
Hogg, James
Haws, Samuel
Haws, John
Haws, Azareel
Haws, Samuel
Hunt, John
Hopkins, William
Harman, John
Hanna, Ebenezer
Hale, Peter
Hoff (Huff), William
Harper, Stephen
Hackworth, John
Higgins, William

Hensley, David
Harris, James P.
Hilton, Jesse
Hilton, Rhoderick B.
Harrell, Enoch
Hazle, John
Holbrook, Randall
Hackworth, Jeremiah
Hatcher, John
Hensley, William
Hensley, James
Harris, John
Hilton, Benjamin
Hamilton, Benjamin
Harrell, William

I

Irient, James
Iliff, John

J

Jones, John
Jones, Lydia
Jones, William
James, Samuel
Johnson, Patrick
Johnson, Thomas
Johnson, Elias
Johnson, John
Johnson, William
(3 slaves)
Justice, William
(7 slaves)
Justice, John
Justice, Ezra
Justice, John
Jacobs, William
Jerome, Battis
Johns, Thomas
James, Mary
Jones, William
Jones, Ambrose
Jones, Nancy
Johnson, George
Johnson, Benjamin
Johnson, Andrew
Johnson, John
Johnson, Patrick
Johnson, Jacob
Justice, John
Justice, George
Justice, William
Justice, Simon
Justice, Simon
Justice, Simon
Janes, William
Josephs, William

27

K

King, Samuel
Kelly, John
Kelly, John
Kezee (Keesee), Richard
(2 slaves)
Kennedy, Charles
King, Elisha
Kelly, Thomas
Kelly, Sallic
Kezee, Benjamin
Keeton, William
(6 slaves)

L

Lester, James
Layne, Samuel
Layne, Samuel
Layne, James
(1 slave)
Leech, Asa
Little, Isaac
Lycan, Jeremiah
Lacy, John
Lawson, Travers
Lewis, Benjamin
Leslie, John
Lemasters, John
Lackey, Alexander
(7 slaves)
Lester, Abner
Layne, Abraham
Layne, James
Layne, John
Little, William
Lycan, David
Lycan, John
Lacy, James
Lewis, Thomas
Lewis, Charles
Leslie, Robert
Lucky, Jesse

M

Mainor, Moses
Mainor, James
Mainor, William
McCoy, John
McGuire, Cornelius
McGuire, John
McGuire, William
(2 slaves)
McClintock, William
McBrayer, Ichabod
Matthews, Matthew
Mann, William
Morgan, David
(11 slaves)
Mullins, Solomon

Mullins, Ambrose
Mankins, Peter
Moore, Christopher
May, Samuel
Mays, William
Miller, Robert
Miller, Philip
Murray, Samuel
Meeks, William
Mead, Samuel
Mead, Moses
Morris, Mary
Morris, John
Millirons, Michael
Mainor, Lewis
Mainor, Christopher
McCoy, William
McCoy, Samuel
McGuire, James
McGuire, Samuel
McDowell, William
McBridge, John
McIntosh, Rory
Macollee, Thomas
Matthews, James
Mann, Samuel
Morgan, John
Morgan, Nathan
Mullins, Joshua
Mullins, William
Mullins, John
Mullins, Booker
Mullins, Ambrose
Mullins, Booker
Mankins, Walter
Mayo, William J.
May, John
May, Caleb
Miller, William
Murray, Thomas
Meeks, James
Mead, Rhodes
Mead, Robert
(9 slaves)
Morris, Benjamin
Murphy, John
Montgomery, William
Martin, Richard
Martin, David
Menix, Charles
Maddox, George
Morris, Daniel
Martin, William
Martin, William
Mannin, Boaz
Mallett, Thomas
Mullett, Nathan

N

Nelson, Emanuel
Nickle, William

Newcomb, William
Nickle, Thomas
Nickle, Isaac
Newlin, William

O

Owens, Owen
Osborn, Solomon
Osborn, Edward
(3 slaves)
Oldfield, Elias
Owens, Thomas
Owens, David
Osborn, Elizabeth
Oakey, John
O'hare, Michael

P

Penley, John
Prater, William
Peyton, Daniel
(2 slaves)
Price, Richard
(2 slaves)
Patrick, James
Picklehymer (P'Simer),
Abraham
Patton, Henry
Patton, John
Pratt, Janus
Polley, Edward
Priggmore, Samuel
Potter, Edward
Pinson, Aaron
Pinson, William
Preston, Nathan
Preston, Isaac
Pack, Charles
Powers, Lewis
Prater, Archibald
Price, Thomas
Price, Thomas
Price, Jesse
Perry, John
Patrick, James
Patton, Christopher
Patton, James
Phillips, Elijah
Polley, David
(2 slaves)
Pinson, Thomas
Pinson, Allen
Pinson, Henry
Pearce, Benjamin
Preston, Moses, Sr.
(7 slaves)
Pelfrey, William
Pack, Samuel
Perkins, Stephen
Powell, Cader

Parsons, Jesse
Parsons, John
Parsons, Gabriel
Powell, David
Parsons, Sarah
Parsons, William
Priest, Ruel

R

Rose, Francis
Roberson, Thomas
Ramey, Jesse
Ramey, William
Rogers, William
Ratliff, William
(1 slave)
Ratliff, Jeremiah
Ratliff, Stephen
Runyon, Henry
Roberts, James
Ramey, William
Ramey, Daniel
Ramey, John
Reeves, John H.
Ratliff, Silas
Ratliff, Richard
Ratliff, James
Rutherford, Reuben
Russell, John

S

Scott, William
Stratton, Tandy
(1 slave)
Stratton, John
Stratton, Hiram
Stratton, Thomas
Stalcup, Swithin
Spurlock, David
Spurlock, Matthew
Stafford, Absalom
Stacy, Simon
Saunders, Jacob
Slone, James
(1 slave)
Salmons, Rowland
Sullivan, Peter
Scalf, John
Sowards, Fishie

Stratton, William
Stratton, Harry
(1 slave)
Stratton, Solomon
(1 slave)
Sullards, Samuel
Sullards, John
Spurlock, John
(6 slaves)
Speers, Thomas
Speers, Spencer
Sumner, John
Sykes, Drury
Slone, Mary
Slone, Shadrack
Stone, Ezekiel
Saulsberry (Salisbury).
William
Slusher, Jacob
Stevenson, James

T

Thompson, Andrew
Thompson, Samuel
Thompson, John
Tolar, Christopher
Tackett, George
Thompson, James
Thompson, Richard
Thompson, Lectius
Tolar, Robert
Toulson, Thomas

V

Venters, Arthur

W

West, Joseph
West, William
Ward, Solomon
Wallace, Timothy
Wells, William
(3 slaves)
Williams, Daniel
Williams, John
Williams, Mason
(2 slaves)
Webb, William

Webb, Benjamin
Winion, John
Walters, George
Wellman, Bennett
Wellman, Joseph
Waddle (Waddell),
William
Wooton, Silas P.
Wheeler, Stephen
Wilson, John
Williamson, John
Williamson, Benjamin
West, Frances
Whitehead, William
Ward, Sarah
Wells, John
Wells, Matthew
Williams, Joshua
Williams, John
(1 slave)
William, James
Webb, William
Webb, Samuel
Watts, George
Walters, William
Wellman, Elisha
Walker, Sarah
Wiley, Thomas
Wheeler, James
Wilson, Harris
Weddington, Henry
Williamson, Harman

Y

Young, John
Young, James
Young, Robert
Young, Alexander

TOWN OF
PRESTONSBURG

Cummins, James
Evans, Thomas
Jost, Christian
(1 slave)
Morris, Benjamin
Simms, Martin
(1 slave)
Turman, John

MARRIAGE LICENSES 1808-1844

Marriage Records of Floyd County, Kentucky, from the earliest available records to 1844, as shown by ministers' returns, marriage licenses and/or marriage bonds. In a few ·instances the records do not disclose the name of the bride.

Groom	Bride	Date of Marriage	By Whom

A

Groom	Bride	Date of Marriage	By Whom
Adams, Ben	Nancy Holbrook	June, 1817	Electius Thompson
Adams, Daniel	Jean Stone	Apr. 30, 1818	Simeon Justice
Adams, George	Henrietta Adams	Feb. 25, 1820	Daniel Duff
Adams, Irwin	Levisa Ellis	July 6, 1818	Simeon Justice
Adams, Jackson	Nancy Cooper	July 27, 1837	
Adams, Jesse	Rhoda Martin	June 9, 1816	Wm. Saulsberry
Adams, Matthew	Polly Patrick	Feb. 26, 1824	
Adams, Sylvester	Hannah Lacy	Aug. 1, 1819	William Coffee
Adams, William	Christine Crace	Feb. 24, 1818	Daniel Williams
Adams, William	Sarah Blair	June 27, 1841	
Adams, William	Mary Adams	Aug. 22, 1841	
Adams, William H.	Eunice Evans	Jan. 22, 1823	
Adkins, Caswell	Nancy Adkins	Mar. 22, 1821	James Honaker, J. P.
Adkins, Hezekiah	Susanna Adkins	Jan. 31, 1822	
Adkins, Hiram	Lorena Tackett	Feb. 14, 1841	
Adkins, Howard	Mary Coleman	July 19, 1818	Wm. J. Mayo, M. G.
Adkins, Jesse	Ann Morgan	Dec. 28, 1815	Wm. Saulsberry
Adkins, Lucas	Peggy Stotts	Mar. 20, 1818	Wm. Saulsberry
Adkins, Nathan	Mahaldy Drake	Feb. 4, 1817	Spencer Adkins, J. P.
Adkins, Nathan	Elizabeth Adkins	Dec. 29, 1808	Simeon Justice
Adkins, Spencer	Anna Posell	Nov. 13, 1808	George Belcher
Adkins, William	Charity Polley	Aug. 20, 1817	Spencer Adkins, J. P.
Akers, Blackburn	Keziah Meade	Apr. 24, 1823	
Akers, Blackburn	Elizabeth Baldridge	Oct. 24, 1843	
Akers, Daniel	Arty Justice	Oct. 11, 1843	
Akers, David	Elizabeth Collier	May 2, 1822	
Akers, Jonathan	Kitty Meade	May 19, 1812	Simeon Justice
Akers, Jonathan	Sally Howell	June 7, 1837	
Akers, Solomon	Matilda Meed	Feb. 27, 1812	Matthew Spurlock
Akers, William	Catherine Slusher	Dec. 18, 1817	Stephen Harper
Aldridge, David	Sally Hensley	Oct. 30, 1819	Reuben Giddins
Allen, David	Jane Martin	July 11, 1830	
Allen, Elijah	Catherine Williams	Nov. 13, 1821	William Coffee
Allen, Felix	Rhoda Martin	Oct. 2, 1840	
Allen, George, Jr.	Malinda Howard	Jan. 6, 1829	
Allen, George, Jr.	Susannah Gearhart	Feb. 20, 1843	
Allen, George W.	Rebecca Stephens	May 28, 1840	
Allen, John	Nancy Click	Mar. 21, 1831	
Allen, Richard	Edy Williams	Jan. 20, 1819	William Coffee
Allen, S.	Janie Patton	Apr. 4, 1815	Simeon Justice
Allen, Samuel	Sarah Ann Osborn	Oct. 6, 1842	
Allen, William	Catty (Katy) Gearhart	June 18, 1808	James Patton, J. P.
Alley, Turner	Rebecca Yates	June 24, 1841	
Alley, William	Sally Akers	May 22, 1816	R. Haws, J. P.
Alley, David	Urseda Branham	June 11, 1812	Simeon Justice
Alley, Paul	Rebecca Williamson	Mar. 26, 1820	Reuben Giddins
Anderson, William	Judy Slone	Sept. 19, 1816	Wm. Saulsberry
Arms, Aaron	Elizabeth Hitchcock	Aug. 16, 1832	
Arms, John	Mary Blanton	July 16, 1826	

Groom	Bride	Date of Marriage	By Whom
Arms, Moses	Emily Spradlin	Oct. 9, 1836	
Arms, Theophilis	Jane Loone	Apr. 22, 1826	
Arnett, Hiram	Serena Arnett	Jan. 19, 1840	
Arnett, Reuben	Sally Mann	July 1, 1827	
Arnett, Reuben	Lurany Jones	Jan. 21, 1844	
Arnett, Wiley	Elizabeth Sizemore	Jan. 21, 1844	
Arnold, John	Sally Travis	Dec. 17, 1826	
Auxier, Enoch	Polly Ann VanHoose	Dec. 28, 1833	
Auxier, George W.	Nancy Prater	Oct. 3, 1839	
Auxier, James	Susannah Bush	Jan. 1, 1815	Daniel Williams
Auxier, John	Jemima Ramey	Aug. 16, 1810	Thomas Brown
Auxier, John B.	Angeline Mayo	May 30, 1839	
Auxier, Nathaniel	Hesterann Mayo	Mar. 18, 1838	
Auxier, Samuel, Jr.	Rebecca Phillips	Oct. 1, 1812	Bazil Lewis

B

Groom	Bride	Date of Marriage	By Whom
Bailey, Alfred	Margaret Adams	Jan. 15, 1843	
Bailey, Benjamin	Fanny Steph (Stepp)	Aug. 20, 1820	Sam Hanna
Bailey, Benjamin	Nancy Adkins	Jan. 20, 1825	
Bailey, Benjamin	Anna Paugh	Oct. 11, 1837	
Bailey, Hugh H.	Margaret Helm	Oct. 1, 1833	
Bailey, John, Jr.	Dorcas Bradley	Aug. 5, 1833	
Bailey, Joseph	Susanna Clark	Aug. 18, 1831	
Bailey, Prier	Tally Dikes	Mar. 24, 1814	Sam Hanna
Bailey, Samuel	Ona Deiks	Oct. 14, 1813	Samuel Hanna, MG.
Bailey, Wallace	Polly Patrick	Oct. 7, 1814	
Baisden, Joseph S.	Lucinda Osborn	June 18, 1820	Reuben Giddens
Baldrige, Andrew	Martha Dawson	Jan. 8, 1835	
Ball, Moses	Betsy Mainor	Apr. 13, 1820	James Honaker, J. P.
Barnett, Elias	Nancy Blair	Mar. 29, 1826	
Barnett, Hiram	Peggy Click	May 28, 1825	
Barnett, James	Sally Pitts	July 23, 1834	
Barnett, John	Sally Pridemore	Aug. 26, 1826	
Blair, William	Sarah Spradlin	Mar. 26, 1835	
Blankenship, Hiram	Elizabeth Galloway	Aug. 26, 1841	
Blankin, William		Aug. 16, 1818	Simeon Justice
Blanton, James	Mary Davis	Sept. 24, 1840	
Blanton, William	Esther Cantrell	Jan 7, 1831	
Blevins, Elisha	Ailsey Tackett	Sept. 7, 1826	
Blevins, Nathan	Rebecca Wooten	Jan. 31, 1824	
Boggs, Hugh	Hannah Blevins	Aug. 9, 1821	Thomas C. Brown
Bond, John	Rebecca Hensley	Mar. 5, 1822	Harmon Williamson
Borders, Arch	Jenny Preston	Dec. 14, 1820	Sam Hanna
Borders, Hezekiah	Fanny Davis	Apr. 15, 1815	Hiram Stratton
Borders, John	Juny Nelson	June 13, 1814	Basil Lewis
Borders, Joseph	Julianna Brown	Sept. 5, 1839	
Borders, Michael	Christiany Pack	July 6, 1809	Henry Burgess
Bow, Thomas Hager	Sally Akers	Aug. 19, 1840	
Bowen, Daniel	Cynthis Mullett	Feb. 28, 1841	
Boyd, Cyrus	Mary Lane	Jan. 14, 1843	
Boyd, James	Nancy Daniel	Jan. 28, 1822	Thos. C. Brown, J. P.
Boyd, Thomas	Eliza Ann Crum	Feb. 20, 1840	
Boyd, William	Rebecca Pack	Mar. 23, 1822	Thos. C. Brown, J. P.
Bradley, Elias	Luanna Prater	June 30, 1839	
Bradley, James	Elizabeth Howard	Apr. 7, 1838	
Bradley, Jesse		Jan. 20, 1818	Stephen Harper
Bradley, Levi	Margaret Foster	Aug. 22, 1833	
Bradley, Micajah	Margaret Pridemore	Mar. 23, 1833	

Groom	Bride	Date of Marriage	By Whom
Bradley, Stephen	Polly Fillenger	Sept. 18, 1826	....
Braken (Bracken)			
John	Sally Phillips	Oct. 18, 1821	William Coffee
Brian (Bryan),			
Joseph	Elizabeth Blair	May 20, 1819	Daniel Williams
Briggs, Isaac	Elizabeth Morris	Mar. 23, 1823	....
Briggs, Jacob	Elizabeth Smith	Aug. 5, 1822	....
Barnett, John	Abby Ray	Aug. 18, 1837	....
Barnett, Natley	Leveny Fleetwood	Oct. 2, 1823	....
Barnett, Nelson	Sukey Bradley	Nov. 22, 1831	....
Barnett, Othy	Elizabeth Tackett	Mar. 30, 1824	....
Barnett, William	Sally Shepherd	Apr. 20, 1824	....
Barnett, William	Sarah Rule	Sept. 29, 1834	....
Barnett, Wilson	Mary Bradley	Nov. 15, 1827	....
Bays, Elijah	Margaret Rice	Feb. 14, 1833	....
Beatty, Andrew	Jane Maddix	Apr. 8, 1821	Mason Williams
Begley, Hiram	Synthia Allen	Jan. 12, 1832	....
Belcher, Bartlett	Rachael Ramey	Jan. 10, 1821	James Honaker, J. P.
Bentley, John	Peggy Hamilton	Feb. 18, 1819?	S. Justice
Bentley, Lewis	....................Mar. 4, 1819?		Simeon Justice
Bentley, Sol.	....................Mar. 11, 1819?		S. Justice
Berry, Isbell	Margaret Thompson	June 10, 1814	Bazil Lewis
Berry, John	Florence Allen	Nov. 1, 1831	....
Berry, Nathan	Elizabeth Redden	Nov. 20, 1818	Sam Hanna
Bickley, Benjamin	Permelia Hamilton	July 27, 1827	....
Bivins, David	Jenny Jones	Dec. 8, 1823	....
Bivens, William	Mary Jones (Janes)	Oct. 23, 1810	Thomas C. Brown
Blackburn, William	Jeney Maynor	Mar. 2, 1809	Simeon Justice
Blair, Brittain	Malinda Spradlin	Aug. 26, 1841	....
Blair, George W.	M. Spradlin	Nov. 8, 1840	....
Blair, John	Polly Barnett	July 27, 1815	Sam Hanna
Blair, John	Susanna Conley	Jan. 20, 1839	....
Blair, Levi	Rachael Cantrell	June 4, 1831	....
Blair, Noble	Mary M. Rule	Nov. 1, 1840	....
Blair, Noble	Tillithy (Talitha)		
	Stumbox		
	(Stambaugh)	July 10, 1846	....
Brown, ...	Celia James	Jan. 1, 1829	....
Brown, Aaron	Louisa Wadkins	Jan. 11, 1836	....
Brown, C.	Nancy Coburn	Mar. 24, 1841	....
Brown, Fleming H.	Debora L. Strother	Sept. 4, 1834	....
Brown, Francis A.	Edy Preston	June 1, 1811	....
Brown, J. Anderson	Sally Barnett	Sept. 14, 1826	....
Brown, James G.	....................May 23, 1818		Wm. Saulsberry
Brown, Jesse	Polly Porter	July 3, 1826	....
Brown, John	Elizabeth Cordill	June ...., 1817	....
Brown, John	Katy Borders	June 25, 1817	Sam Hanna
Brown, John	Bitha Ann Mainor	Apr. 4, 1834	....
Brown, John	Elisabeth Ritter	July 25, 1837	....
Brown, Robert	Nancy Herrell	July 29, 1822	....
Brown, Samuel	Rebecca McFarren	July 19, 1827	....
Brown, Thomas C.	Mary Brown	Dec. 15, 1823	....
Brown, Thomas S.	Emaline Damron	May 7, 1835	....
Brown, William	Lucinda Hardwick	Jan. 15, 1818	Daniel Williams
Brown, William	Levicy Barnett	Mar. 26, 1824	....
Bryant, Joseph	Betsy McGee	May 15, 1818	Wm. Saulsberry
Bunda Andrew J.	Betsy Watkins	Apr. 14, 1834	....
Burchett, Armstead	Elizabeth Butler	Dec. 14, 1820	Wm. J. Mayo
Burchett, Armistead	Rebecca Pigg	Mar. 11, 1841	....

Groom	Bride	Date of Marriage	By Whom
Burchett, Ben	Nancy Lewis	Aug. 30, 1821	Reuben Giddins
Burchett, Drury	Elizabeth McCowen	Jan. 31, 1816	Hiram Stratton
Burchett, John	Louis (Lois) Akers	Nov. 20, 1810	R. Hals Hays, J. P.
Burchett, Thomas	Milly Maynor	Feb. 29, 1816	Hiram Stratton
Burchett, William	Patsy Galloway	July 14, 1839	
Burchett, William	Frances E. Auxier	Jan. 9, 1840	
Burgess, Garland	Elizabeth Preston	Feb. 22, 1810	Benjamin Edge
Burns, William	Nancy Boteet	Nov. 1, 1808	Daniel Williams
Burton, John	Sally Benion	May 14, 1843	
Butler, George	Arte Herrell	Aug. 25, 1825	
Butler, Samuel	Anna Collins	Aug. 13, 1829	

C

Groom	Bride	Date of Marriage	By Whom
Campbell, Allen	Civilla Boyles	Apr. 11, 1822	William Coffee
Cantrell, Henry	Rachel Blanton	Sept. 29, 1825	
Cantrell, John	Peggy Smith	Jan. 25, 1820	Wm. J. Mayo, M. G.
Carpenter, Stephen	Nancy Walker	Apr. 5, 1822	John Morris
Carpenter, Wyatt	Mary Fraley	Jan. 2, 1834	
Carpenter, Wm.	Sally Howard	June 29, 1828	
Carruth, James	Sally Lyon	Jan. 24, 1822	
Carter, Jerry	Polly Williams	Oct. 14, 1827	
Carty, David I.	Letty Arnett	Mar. 27, 1844	
Casebolt, John	Sabra Estep	May 29, 1808	William McGuyer
Caskey, Gradner	Elisabeth Blair	Aug. 14, 1821	Edmond Wells, J. P.
Caskey, John	Hannah Lewis	Apr. 4, 1816	Daniel Williams
Cassell, Peterson	Letty West	July 18, 1839	
Castell, John J.	Caty (Katie) Broderick	Feb. 12, 1814	Simeon Justice
Castle, H.	Lucy Daniel	Sept. 24, 1840	
Castle, Jahite	Easter Ann Bowling	Oct. 29, 1840	
Castle, James	Betsey Cassel	Apr. 4, 1816	Stephen Harper
Castle, John	Elizabeth Francis	Dec. 28, 1815	Sam Hanna M. G.
Castle, William	Judith Lewis	Dec. 13, 1826	
Castle, Zachariah	Ruth Sellards	Jan. 9, 1840	
Caudill, Abijah	Elizabeth Slone	Apr. 29, 1835	
Caudill, John	Betsey Adams	Aug. 15, 1819	Simeon Justice
Caudill, Thomas	Jenny Caudill	May ...., 1847	Wm. Saulsberry
Cecil, William N.	Lucy Garrett	May 26, 1836	
Chapman, John		Oct. 11, 1810	Thomas C. Brown
Charles, John	Nancy Thompson	Oct. 22, 1820	James Honaker, J. P.
Childers, Jesse	Sally Belcher	Aug. 12, 1821	James Honaker
Childers, William	Sally Young	Oct. 28, 1819	Sam Hanna
Clark, John W.	Rebecca Mayo	July 20, 1841	
Clark, Lorenzo D.	Patience Williams	Apr. 29, 1835	
Clark, Morgan	Elizabeth Burchett	May 7, 1840	
Clark, Samuel	Nancy Gibson	May 6, 1824	
Clay, James	Lucinda Morrison	Jan. 26, 1837	
Clay, Matthew	Elizabeth Sullivan	June 29, 1834	
Clay, Peter	Patsy Clay	Oct. 19, 1828	
Clemmons, Benj.	Polly Harmon	Mar. 21, 1819	William Coffee
Clevenger, Joshua	Mary Mead	Dec. 24, 1820	Reuben Giddens
Click, David	Nancy Patton	Aug. 16, 1830	
Click, James	Jenny Salmon	May 12, 1822	
Click, John, Jr.	Polly Allen	July 25, 1830	
Cline, Henry	Nancy Murphy	July 13, 1821	Reuben Giddens
Cline, Peter	Mary Smith	Feb. 13, 1820	Reuben Giddens
Cline, Peter	Ray Trent	June 9, 1820	Reuben Giddens
Coburn, Jacob	Betsey Walker	Apr. 18, 1816	Stephen Harper

33

Groom	Bride	Date of Marriage	By Whom
Coburn, John C.	Phoebe Prater	Mar. 5, 1837	
Coburn, James		Feb. 8, 1810	Simeon Justice
Cockrell, Joseph		Jan. ...., 1818	Electious Thompson
Coffee, Ambrose	Lucinda Day	Nov. 8, 1812	Samuel Hanna, M G
Coffee, Elijah	Peggy Patrick	Jan. 20, 1819	William Coffee
Coffman, Henry	Sally Leek	Aug. 24, 1827	
Cogswell, Jesse	Danny Lewis	Oct. 15, 1818	Daniel Williams
Cole, John	Caty (Katie) Menix	Jan. 29, 1833	
Coleman, Alexander	Nancy Wooten	Jan. 2, 1818	Wm. J. Mayo, M G
Coleman, James	Elizabeth Williams	Dec. 28, 1820	Reuben Giddins
Collier, Jeremiah	Jenny Burks	Jan. 25, 1815	Simeon Justice
Collier, Levi	Nancy Hall	Nov. 30, 1820	Owen Owens
Collier, Patrick	Lida Estep	Mar. 28, 1823	Owen Owens
Collier, Stephen		July 21, 1819	Wm. Saulsberry
Collier, William	Lucy Layne	Mar. 19, ...	Wm. Saulsberry
Collins, Christopher	Cynthia Spears	May 18, 1832	
Collins, Edward	Polly Bryant	July 27, 1820	James Roberts, J. P.
Collins, Hiram	Eliza Ballard	Sept. 12, 1837	
Collins, Isaac	Nancy Black	June 14, 1841	
Collins, Thomas	Hannah Williams	July 13, 1810	David Williams
Collinsworth, David	Elizabeth Prater	Aug. 22, 1838	
Collinsworth, Mason	Margaret Evans	Apr. 9, 1835	
Collinsworth, Moses B.	Margaret Ratcliff	Feb. 26, 1829	
Collinsworth, Reuben	Morning Mathis	Mar. 7, 1816	Hiram Stratton
Collinsworth, William	Rachel Suthards	Sept. 10, 1825	
Colvin, Abner	Susanna Mahan	Sept. 8, 1833	
Colvin, Allen	Eveline Mahon	Aug. 24, 1840	
Combs, Nicholas	Elizabeth Combs	June ...., 1817	Electious Thompson
Conley, Abner	Elizabeth Rose	Aug. 8, 1811	Simeon Justice, M. G.
Conley, Carter	Polly Conley	Feb. 22, 1821	Thos. G. Brown, J. P.
Conley, Constantine	Celia Fairchild	June 26, 1828	
Conley, David	Peggy Phillips	Oct. 21, 1813	Electious Thompson
Conley, David	Phoebe Ratcliff	Dec. 25, 1826	
Conley, David	Mahala Robertson	Apr. 14, 1834	
Conley, Edmond	Nancy Tackett	Apr. 16, 1835	
Conley, Henry	Nancy Rice	Nov. 30, 1820	Mason Williams
Conley, Henry	Polly Thompson	May 30, 1821	Reuben Giddens
Conley, Henry	Rebecca Blair	Feb. 24, 1831	
Conley, Henry, Sr.	Tempy Hitchcock	Mar. 8, 1832	
Conley, John	Elizabeth Power	Apr. 14, 1836	
Conley, John	Mary Blair	Mar. 14, 1839	
Conley, Joseph	Susanna Jones	Mar. 22, 1827	
Conley, Sampson	Polly Smith	May 17, 1818	Wm. J. Mayo, M. G.
Conley, Thomas	Sally Fitzpatrick	Jan. 8, 1824	
Conley, Thomas	Mahala Davis	Sept. 12, 1833	
Conley, William	Catherine Arms	Nov. 26, 1829	
Conn, Ira	Eleanor Jarrell	Mar. 5, 1840	
Connelly, William	Anna McCarty	Mar. 31, 1831	
Cook, James	Ealiann Lacy	Apr. 28, 1826	
Cook, William	Sally Prater	Mar. 22, 1829	
Cooper, David	Cely (Celia) Prater	Apr. 17, 1823	
Cooper, John	Sally Smith	Jan. 13, 1820	John Brown
Cooper, Thomas	Elizabeth Neel	Apr. 13, 1815	Hiram Stratton
Copley, James	Rebecca Marcum	Feb. 20, 1817	Sam Hanna
Corder, James	Juda Murray	Feb. 9, 1826	
Corder, James	Leah Hilton	Aug. 26, 1832	

Groom	Bride	Date of Marriage	By Whom
Cordill, Isham	Nancy Phillips	Feb. 15, 1813	Simeon Justice
Cottle, Uriah	Smithanna Jones	Jan. 18, 1820	Daniel Williams
Craft, John	....	Aug. 2, 1818	Simeon Justice
Crafts, Peter	Mary Davis	Feb. 19, 1832	....
Craig, William	Sary Ellidge	July 7, 1809	Daniel Williams
Crank, Nathaniel	Susanna Fitzpatrick	Aug. 20, 1820	Thos. C. Brown
Crider, William	Elizabeth Vaughan	Sept. 2, 1841	....
Crisp, Ancel	....	July 20, 1820	Stephen Harper, J. P.
Crisp, David	Tabitha Robinson	May 19, 1831	....
Crisp, Carrell	....	Feb. 18, 1821	Stephen Harper, J. P.
Crisp, William	Milly Hale	Nov. 26, 1828	....
Crum, Adam	Elizabeth Bannister	Aug. 5, 1821	Wm. J. Mayo, M. G.
Crum, Frederick	....	Feb. 5, 1818	Stephen Harper, J. P.
Crum, Henry	Pricilla Wright	Apr. 7, 1822	Wm. J. Mayo, M. G.
Crum, Henry W.	Caty (Katie) Sullivan	Nov. 27, 1840	....
Crum, Jacob	....	Oct. 7, 1814	Simeon Justice
Crum, Jesse	Polly Mills	May 9, 1830	....
Crum, John J.	Hannah Lewis	Apr. 29, 1838	....
Crum, Jonathan	Peggy Mayo	Aug. 29, 1835	....
Crum, Michael	Vasti (Vashti) Garrell	July 21, 1814	....
Cunningham, Thomas	Patsy Matthews	Jan. 23, 1812	....
Cummings (Cumings), James	Elizabeth Jerome	May 16, 1812	Matthew Spurlock

D

Groom	Bride	Date of Marriage	By Whom
Daggs, Angress	Weimey McDaniel	Oct. 18, 1810	R. Haws
Damron, John	Nancy Branham	Jan. 25, 1821	James Roberts, J. P.
Damron, Joseph	Elizabeth Dykes	Dec. 3, 1815	R. Haws
Damron, Lazarus	Polly Mullins	Feb. 15, 1821	James Roberts, J. P.
Damron, Moses	Polly Preston	Mar. 28, 1811	R. Haws
Damron, Moses	Nancy Justice	July 26, 1838	....
Damron, Richard	Hannah Van Hoose	Aug. 26, 1821	Simeon Justice
Damron, Richard	Rhoda Fitzgerald	June 6, 1816	R. Haws
Damron, Samuel	Louisa Cobourne	Jan. 28, 1843	....
Daniel, George	Sally Dorton	Feb. 2, 1815	Sam Hanna
Daniel, Isham	Mary Borders	Aug. 15, 1809	Henry Burgess
Daniel, James	Elizabeth Wheeler	Feb. 11, 1830	....
Daniel, James B.	Lewrey Castle	Aug. 27, 1840	....
Daniel, Joseph	Nancy Ward	Aug. 17, 1832	....
Daniel, Thomas	....	Oct. 28, 1812	B. Lewis
Daniel Thomas	Winnie Ann O'Bryant	Aug. 12, 1835	....
Daster, Michael	Peggy Gearhart	Jan. 6, 1829	....
Davis, Alfred	Nancy Cantrell	Mar. 6, 1823	....
Davis, Edmond	Winny Sanders	Jan. 9, 1827	....
Davis, Elias	Elizabeth Curtis	Feb. 20, 1823	....
Davis, Henry	Polly Waters	Dec. 16, 1815	R. Haws
Davis, James	Martha Smothers?	Dec. 7, 1819	Daniel Williams
Davis, James	Hannah Strothers	July 1, 1832	....
Davis, Jeremiah	Jane Keeton	Feb. 22, 1831	....
Davis, John	Jemima Wheeler	Jan. 26, 1840	....
Davis, John, Jr.	Elizabeth Nipper (Napier)	June 18, 1834	....
Davis, Richard	Eleanora Reed	Aug. 31, 1835	....
Davis, Thomas	Clarinda Auxier	Sept. 27, 1819	Sam Hanna
Davis, Thomas	Elizabeth Sellards	July 13, 1823	....
Davis, William	Mary Taylor	Mar. 25, 1819	Reuben Giddins, J. P.
Day, Allen	Polly Allenton	Jan. 21, 1819	Daniel Williams

Groom	Bride	Date of Marriage	By Whom
Day, Hiram	Lyda Lyken	Jan. 1, 1821	Edmond Wells
Day, Jesse	Peggy Casky	Aug. 24, 1820	William Coffee
Day, John	Sarah Lyons	Jan. 9, 1814	Sam Hanna, M. G.
Day, John	Patsy Fraley	Aug. 17, 1820	William Coffee
Day, Joshua	Mary Casky	Nov. 19, 1813	Daniel Williams
Day, Peter	Franky Williams	Feb. 16, 1811	Daniel Williams
Day, Robert	Polly Davis	June 11, 1820	William Coffee
Day, Travis	Ann Lewis	July 6, 1811	Daniel Williams
Deal, David	Rebecca Painquin	Dec. 30, 1821	Harmon Williamson
Deal, Willoughby	Rebecca Lester	Mar. 21, 1820	John Kinney, M. G.
Dean, Davis	Polly Brown	Dec. 14, 1821	Thos. C. Brown, J. P.
Dean, Job	Peggy Gannon	June 18, 1816	R. Haws
Debord, Simpson	Nancy Davis	July 14, 1841	....
Deer, John	Polly Day	Mar. 30, 1822	....
Dennis, Jesse	Sidney Day	Feb. 7, 1822	Edmond Wells, J. P.
Dennis, Mathias	Patsy Day	July 27, 1820	William Coffee
Derossett, James	Milly Rose	Nov. 2, 1820	Wm. J. Mayo, M. G.
Derossett, Solomon	Clarinda Dunbar	Nov. 13, 1822	....
Derosset, Solomon	Nancy Rogison (Robinson)	Aug. 26, 1841	....
Deskins, John	Rebecca Holt	July 30, 1819	Reuben Giddins
Dillard, Robert	Elizabeth Pains (Payne)	Dec. 3, 1833	....
Dillian, ... (Dillon)	Nancy Carpenter	May 7, 1836	....
Dillian, John (Dillon)	Renasha Crum	Feb. 10, 1825	....
Dixon, Andrew F.	Abigail Kelly	Mar. 2, 1834	....
Dixon, James P.	Rachael Van Hoose	Oct. 20, 1838	....
Dixon, Thomas	....	Feb. 1, 1821	Daniel Duff
Dorton, William D.	Polly Stapleton	Mar. 17, 1821	Thos. C. Brown, J. P.
Drake, Michael	Lucy Hunt	Feb. 27, 1816	Spencer Adkins, J. P.
Dyer, Francis	Betsy Logan	May 24, 1821	Edmund Wells, J. P.
Dyer, Francis	Jemima Robens (Robbins)	May 22, 1820	William Coffee
Dyer, John	Polly Day	Mar. 30, 1822	Edmond Wells, J. P.
Dykes, Isham	Betsy McMillen	Apr. 24, 1825	....
Dykes, Isham	Celia Howard	Oct. 7, 1829	....

E

Groom	Bride	Date of Marriage	By Whom
Easterling, James	Elizabeth Morris	Sept. 18, 1828	....
Easterling, Henry	Frances Elem (Elam)	Aug. 13, 1820	William Coffee
Ellidge, Isaac	Sally Wells	Oct. 24, 1822	....
Ellidge, William	Peggy Perry	May 30, 1822	....
Ellington, John	Jenny Brown	Sept. 8, 1822	....
Elliott, James	Polly Melony (Maloney)	Oct. 22, 1821	Edmond Wells
Elswick, Bradley	Rebecca Bazwell (Bazzell)	Mar. 13, 1834	....
Elswick, William	Nancy Drake	Jan. 21, 1813	Simeon Justice
Estep, Corbin	Elizabeth Davis	Mar. 18, 1817	Stephen Harper
Estep, Samuel	Susanna Mullins	Feb. 11, 1830	....
Estep, Shadrack	Elizabeth Hunt	Mar. 2, 1809	Simeon Justice
Evans, Benjamin P.	Sally Arms	May 1, 1826	....
Evans, Edwin	Mary Ann Prater	Feb. 3, 1839	....
Evans, Jonathan	Polly Turner	Mar. 12, 1837	....
Evans, Jonathan	Alice Thornberry	June 4, 1843	....
Evans, Philip	Mary Jane Davis	Feb. 22, 1827	....

Groom	Bride	Date of Marriage	By Whom
Evans, Richard	....	June 27, 1820	Reuben Giddens
Evans, Samuel	Nancy Fitzpatrick	June 28, 1832	....
Evans, Thomas	Naomi Priest	Nov. 24, 1825	....

F

Groom	Bride	Date of Marriage	By Whom
Fairchild, Abina	Abigail Arms	Apr. 20, 1825	....
Fairchild, Asa	Nancy Conley	May 22, 1821	Thos. C. Brown, J. P.
Fairchild, Enoch	Frances Cantrell	Dec. 16, 1824	....
Fairchild, Leury	Sarah Lemaster	Sept. 5, 1833	....
Fanen (Fannin) David	Sally Day	Oct. 2, 1809	Daniel Peyton·
Farley, Thomas	Polly Phillips	Dec. 10, 1820	Reuben Giddens
Farrell, Enoch	Catherine Meade	July 29, 1825	....
Ferguson, James	Margaret Lykins	June 28, 1821	Mason Williams, J. P.
Ferguson, John	Elizabeth Williams	June ...., 1813	Daniel Williams
Field, Preston	Elizabeth Reatherford	Dec. 24, 1817	Simeon Justice
Fitzgerald, Thomas	Susannah Fitzgerald	Jan. 21, 1822	Wm. J. Mayo, J. P.
Fitzgerald, William	Catherine Gray	Mar. 4, 1821	Stephen Harper
Fitzpatrick, Jacob	Sally Hamilton	Aug. 21, 1813	Hiram Stratton
Fitzpatrick, Jacob	Rainey Haywood	Nov. 8, 1817	Joel Cook, M. G.
Fitzpatrick, James	Sarah Caudill	Feb. 11, 1836	....
Fitzpatrick, Jeremiah	Lucinda Blair	Oct. 2, 1829	....
Fitzpatrick, John	Fanny Rice	May 17, 1811	Thos. C. Brown, J. P.
Fitzpatrick, Jonathan	Agnes Haywood	Nov. 26, 1818	Wm. J. Mayo, M. G.
Fitzpatrick, Thomas	Nancy Kesterson	Feb. 7, 1837	....
Fitzpatrick, Wm.	Patsey Blair	May 8, 1813	Basil Lewis
Flannery, Isaac	Caroline Holbert	Nov. 20, 1836	....
Flannery, John	Arty Celam	June 16, 1835	....
Flannery, Singleton	Delilia Webb	Sept. 22, 1833	....
Fleetwood, Adam	Jany Prichett (Janie Pritchett)	Jan. 13, 1820	John Brown
Fleetwood, Isaac	Sally Brown	Aug. 26, 1819	Wm J. Mayo, M. G.
Fleetwood, James	Betsey Cantrell	May 18, 1822	Thos. C. Brown, J. P.
Fleetwood, Thomas	Katie Todd	June, 1817	Electious Thompson
Fletcher, Alexander	Mary Blair	Feb. 4, 1841	....
Fletcher, George	....	Sept. 1, 1815	Simeon Justice
Fletcher, George	Louisa Marshall	June 24, 1819	Wm. J. Mayo, M. G.
Fletcher, Isaac	Susan Gilbert	Jan. 4, 1844	....
Ford, Joseph	Rebecca Ratcliff	Nov. 11, 1816	R. Haws
Fortner, Jesse	Susannah Williams	May 20, 1822	Thos. C. Brown, J. P.
Fortune, James	Polly Buskett	Apr. 25, 1841	....
Foster, Charles	Lucinda Bradley	Apr. 12, 1832	....
Foster, John	Nancy Bailey	Jan. 17, 1834	....
Fraley, Benjamin	Margaret Harrell	Apr. 20, 1835	....
Fraley, James	Catherine Friend	Sept. 15, 1839	....
Fraley, James	Macy Cassidy	Mar. 4, 1839	....
Fraley, John	Louisa Thurman	Mar. 4, 1833	....
Francis, William	Betsey Roberts	July 12, 1809	Henry Burgess
Franklin, James	Charity Dickson	Nov. 24, 1833	....
Franklin, Joseph	Sally Spears	June 24, 1838	....
Franklin, Martin	Elizabeth May	Mar. 2, 1834	....
Frazier, Granville	Nancy Adams	Aug. 1, 1841	....
Frazier, Haston	Bethel Berry	Feb. 25, 1818	Sam Hanna
Frazier, James	....	Aug. 23, 1821	Stephen Harper, J. P.
Frazier, Lewis	Flizabeth Ratcliff	Aug. 9, 1809	Henry Burgess
Frazier, Robert	Jemima Thornberry	Aug. 27, 1837	....

Groom	Bride	Date of Marriage	By Whom
Frazier, Weeks	Anna Salmons	Feb. 23, 1815	Simeon Justice
Frazier, William	Polly Adkins	Mar. 21, 1816	Simeon Justice
Friend, Isaac B.	Caty (Katy) Dixon	July 14, 1835	....
Friend, Samuel K.	Patsy Vaughan	July 6, 1823	....
Friley, (Fraley) James	Patsey J. Lawhorn	Nov. 2, 1832	....
Frisley, John	Sally Day	May 19, 1813	Sam Hanna
Fryley, Daniel	Polly Hatfield	Jan. 3, 1811	Thos. C. Brown, J. P.
Fuget, James	Rebecca Cottel	Sept. 6, 1819	Daniel Williams
Fuget, Joseph	Jean Smithers	Apr. 9, 1809	Daniel Williams
Fuget, Randolph	Nancy Harris	Oct. 31, 1821	Sam Hanna
Fulks, John	Dicy Slone	July 15, 1816	Spencer Adkins, J. P.

G

Groom	Bride	Date of Marriage	By Whom
Gable, William	Martha A. Harris	Oct. 19, 1840	....
Gaines, Noble	Elizabeth Delong	July 20, 1826	....
Gallion, Thomas	Ruth Watson	July 1, 1820	Wm. J. Mayo, M. G.
Galloway, John G.	Catherine Hackney	Sept. 30, 1819	Reuben Giddens
Gannon, Daniel	Orpha Williams	Mar. 6, 1820	James Honaker, J. P.
Gannon, James	Polly Ratcliff	Sept. 27, 1815	Simeon Justice
Garrett, Hardin	Susanna Clark	Mar. 2, 1834	....
Gearhart, Adam	Rhoda Spurlock	July 9, 1808	Thos. Evans, J. P.
Gearheart, Adam	Esther Harris	Nov. 1, 1829	....
Gearheart, Allen	Eliza Justice	Mar. 31, 1839	....
Gearheart, John	Florence Patton	Nov. 5, 1825	....
Gearheart, Joseph	Sarah Martin	July 1, 1821	Stephen Harper, J. P.
Gearheart, Joseph	Caty (Katy) Pickle	Dec. 18, 1824	....
Gearheart, Valentine	Sally Justice	Apr. 28, 1833	....
Gearheart, William	....	Aug. 18, 1815	Simeon Justice
Gearheart, William	Malinda Moseley	Apr. 5, 1832	....
George, Alexander G.	Rachael Evans	Feb. 26, 1813	Bazwell, Lewis, M. G.
George, Alexander G.	Betsy May	July 1, 1819	Wm. J. Mayo, M. G.
George, John	Elizabeth Brown	Jan. 17, 1822	Thos. C. Brown, J. P.
George, Robert M.	Patsy Porter	Sept. 18, 1822	....
Gerrell, Thomas F.	Susannah F. Gerrell	Jan. 20, 1822	....
Ghost, John	Elizabeth Gillmore	Sept. 5, 1816	Daniel Williams
Gibbs, Milton	Jonah Pelfrey	Sept. 16, 1841	....
Gibson, Ezekiel	Jenny Johnson	May 30, 1819	John Brown, J. P.
Gibson, Isom	Cynthia Thornberry	July 30, 1834	....
Gibson, James	....	Nov. 18, 1819	Stephen Harper, J. P.
Gibson, Joel	Nancy Gilbert	Feb. 2, 1832	....
Gibson, John	Betsey Harper	June 2, 1818	John Brown, J. P.
Gibson, Squire	Francic Nicholas	June 29, 1843	....
Gibson, William	....	Jan. 14, 1819	Simeon Justice
Giddens, Rich F.	Jenny Walker	....	William Saulsberry
Gilliam, Chesley	Elizabeth Estep	Apr. 3, 1836	....
Gilmore, Enoch	Elizabeth G. Hart	Apr. 6, 1820	William Coffee
Gilmore, James	Anne Day	Feb. 5, 1818	Daniel Williams
Goodman, Andrew	Pennina Carver	Dec. 4, 1834	....
Goodman, Calvin	Elizabeth Moore	Mar. 5, 1839	....
Goodman, Enoch	Susanna Hale	Mar. 23, 1834	....
Goodman, Pleasant	Jane Patton	July 8, 1833	....
Grask, Nattgew	Ailsy Ausborn (Osborn)	Mar. 8, 1832	....
Graves, Hardy	Sally Childers	Apr. 5, 1821	Thos. C. Brown, J. P.
Gray, James H.	Charlotte Osborn	Nov. 17, 1836	....
Griffifth, David	Zina Cranes	Aug. 28, 1812	Matthew Spurlock
Griffith, Robert	Peggy Cains	Sept. 24, 1811	Thos. C. Brown, J. P.

Groom	Bride	Date of Marriage	By Whom
Grim, Chas. Jeff.	Elizabeth Helton (Hilton or Hylton)	May 6, 1824	
Gullett, Daniel	Jane Adams	Dec. 20, 1821	Mason Williams, J. P.
Gullett, Ezekiel	Eleanor Roberts	July 4, 1821	Mason Williams, J. P.

H

Groom	Bride	Date of Marriage	By Whom
Hackney, Thomas	Pricilla Drake	Apr. 16, 1817	Spencer Adkins, J. P.
Hackwith (Hackworth), George	Polly Hansburn	Oct. 15, 1833	
Hacksith, John		Nov. 7, 1817	William Saulsberry
Hacksith, Thomas	Jenny Preece	Nov. 5, 1816	R. Haws
Hackworth, Abner	Dorous (Doris) Patton	May 11, 1831	
Hackworth, George	Elizabeth Franklin	Jan. 17, 1830	
Hackworth, John	Betsy Allen	Feb. 2, 1829	
Hackworth, Thomas	Lucretia Spradlin	July 26, 1839	
Hagel, Abraham	Polly Williams	Nov. 12, 1815	Daniel Williams
Hager, Daniel	Vital (Violet Vertreese) Porter	Jan. 31, 1822	Sam Hanna
Hager, George	Polly Newland	Nov. 6, 1814	Hiram Stratton
Hager, George	Elizabeth Newman	Sept. 20, 1817	Hiram Stratton
Hager, James	Sally Porter	Nov. 26, 1818?	Wm. J. Mayo, M. G.
Hager, James	Susannah Porter	Sept. 2, 1819	Sam Hanna
Hagins, John		June 30, 1818	Simeon Justice
Hagins, Thomas	Rebecca Walters	Feb. 23, 1819	Wm. J. Mayo, M. G.
Hale, Benjamin	Anna Hall	July 29, 1821	John Morris
Hale, Benjamin	Milly Nunn	Dec. 6, 1826	
Hale, Brice		Sept. 26, 1815	Simeon Justice
Hale, Brice	Polly Vance	Mar. 23, 1826	
Hale, Franklin	Elizabeth Moore	Feb. 6, 1840	
Hale, Janus	Jane Sanders	Feb. 13, 1826	
Hale, John	Lovia Stone	May 7, 1838	
Hale, Smith	Elizabeth Moseley	July 13, 1835	
Hale, Zachariah	Rebecca Branham	June 4, 1812	Simeon Justice
Hall, Andrew	Letty Mullins	Jan. 17, 1839	
Hall, John		Sept. 27, 1821	Reuben Giddins
Hall, Wesley	B. Alexander	Feb. 3, 1833	
Hall, William		July 11, 1816	Wm. Saulsberry
Hall, William	Lucinda Justice	Aug. 16, 1829	
Hamilton, David	Sally Fitzpatrick	July 27, 1813	R. Haws
Hamilton, David	Drucilla Hill	Aug. 7, 1833	
Hamilton, John	Levena Brown	Dec. 14, 1840	
Hamilton, Stephen	Cynthis Spradlin	Feb. 13, 1822	Wm. J. Mayo, J. P.
Hamilton, Stephen, Jr.	Sally Hanshoe	Oct. 26, 1836	
Hamilton, Thomas	Sally Foster	Dec. 1, 1826	
Hamilton, Thomas	Jemima Hall	Apr. 16, 1839	
Hammon, Jilson P	Polly Franklin	Oct. 11, 1828	
Hampton, Reuben	Mahala Wells	Apr. 7, 1840	
Haney, William	Elizabeth Auxier	July 4, 1835	
Hanna, James	Polly Hamilton	Feb. 11, 1819	Samuel Hanna
Hanna, John	Anna Curtis	Nov. 29, 1821	Sam Hanna
Hanna, Joseph	Nancy Hamilton	Jan. 22, 1818	William Coffee
Hanna, Sam	Janey Chandler	Apr. 28, 1825	
Hanna, Samuel	Frances Amelia Auxier	Apr. 27, 1820	Sam Hanna
Hansburn, Harrison	Edy Prater	June 6, 1836	
Harkins, Hugh	Maranda James	Sept. 26, 1835	

Groom	Bride	Date of Marriage	By Whom
Harmon, Lorenzo D.	Polly Hobbs	Aug. 3, 1836	
Harmon, William	Catherine Waller	May 25, 1826	
Harper, David	Cynthis Salmons	May 15, 1823	
Harper, Harrison	Sally Charles	May 25, 1818	Wm. J. Mayo, M. G.
Harrell, James	Elizabeth Woods	Mar. 21, 1831	
Harrell, James	Sally Young	May 19, 1831	
Harrell, Nathan, Jr.	Lydia Ogdon	Sept. 29, 1833	
Harrell, Wilson	Sally Dillian (Dillon)	Nov. 11, 1826	
Harris, Benjamin	Susanna Slone	Aug. 25, 1830	
Harris, David K.	Polly Hamilton	July 15, 1813	Hiram Stratton
Harris, David K.	Margaret Horn	Dec. 1, 1839	
Harris, David K.	Ann Spurlock	Mar. 23, 1816	R. Haws
Harris, John B.	Tabitha Graham	June 25, 1835	
Harris, John M.	Elizabeth Gearheart	Feb. 6, 1839	
Harris, Simon	Mary Taylor	Aug. 11, 1811	John Johnson
Harris, William	Alsy Nickell	Apr. 12, 1836	
Harris, William, Jr.	Elizabeth Reynolds	Mar. 17, 1836	
Hart, Jacob Aaron	Elizabeth McKinster	Sept. 17, 1823	
Hase (Hays), William	Elizabeth J. Martin	July 8, 1839	
Hatcher, George F.	Amanda J. Burns	Aug. 4, 1831	
Hatcher, John G.	Thursa Stratton	Mar. 1, 1832	
Hatfield, James	Dicy Herrell	May 3, 1821	Wm J. Mayo, M. G.
Hatfield, Jeremiah	Sally Waller	Aug. 17, 1816	R. Haws
Hatfield, Robert	Winny Vaughan	Feb. 19, 1830	
Hatfield, Samuel	Mary Franklin	Apr. 28, 1815	Hiram Stratton
Havens, William	Elizabeth Shriner	Apr. 13, 1815	Hiram Stratton
Haws, Azreal	Sarah Matthews	June 28, 1810	Robert Haws, J. P.
Haws, Elk	Esther O'Brien	Apr. 25, 1820	
Haws, Elkijah	Nancy Brafford	Jan. 10, 1822	
Haws, John	Polly Preston	Nov. 7, 1809	William McGuyer
Haws, Sampson	Polly Mathis	May 21, 1811	R. Haws
Haws, Samuel	Catherine Evans	June 25, 1821	Thos. C. Brown, J. P.
Hays, John	Elizabeth Anderson	Mar. 10, 1815	R. Haws, J. P.
Haywood, Lewis	Betsy Fitzpatrick	Sept. 24, 1816	Sam Hanna
Haywood, Lewis	Elizabeth Higgins	July 4, 1824	
Henshaw, Andrew	Patsy Wilson		R. Haws
Hensley, Daniel	Jemima Davis	July 25, 1809	R. W. Evans
Hensley, Elijah	Polly Giddins	Oct. 25, 1818	Wm. J. Mayo, M. G.
Hensley, George		Aug. 24, 1817	Electius Howes
Hensley, Isaac	Rebecca	Dec. 11, 1817	John Brown, J. P.
Hensley, Robert	Judy Thompson	July 27, 1817	Spencer Adkins, J. P.
Henson, William	Levisa Osborn	Apr. 7, 1824	
Herald, Robert	Lucinda Turman	Aug. 2, 1815	Sam Hanna
Herald, William	Peggy Droddy?	May 8, 1817	Wm. J. Mayo, M. G.
Herrell, John	Rebecca Matthews	Mar. 8, 1827	
Herrell, William	Patsy Bazil (Bazzell)	Apr. 6, 1824	
Herrell, Wm., Jr.	Malinda Brown	Feb. 16, 1830	
Hicks, George W.	Elizabeth Setser	Feb. 23, 1837	
Hicks, Henry	Sarah Nolin	Mar. 28, 1839	
Hicks, Hiram	Fanny Brown	Mar. 24, 1831	
Hicks, James	Oney Salmon	Oct. 1, 1840	
Hicks, Wm. J.	Polly Nolin	Apr. 2, 1839	
Hill, Burton	Sally Brown	June 10, 1841	
Hill, Edward	Sally Hamilton	July 27, 1815	Sam Hanna
Hill, Edward P.	Irany Wireman	May 28, 1843	
Hill, Ephriam E.	Elizabeth May	May 6, 1830	

Groom	Bride	Date of Marriage	By Whom
Hill, James W.	Mahala George	Sept. 21, 1843	
Hill, Spencer	Lucy Ramey	Jan. 7, 1819	Sam Hanna
Hilton, Roberson H.	Alsey Castle	Aug. 3, 1834	
Hitchcock, John	Maly (Mallie) Fitzpatrick	Nov. 21, 1822	
Hobbs, Arthur W.	Mary Ann Fraley	Feb. 12, 1839	
Hoff, John	Didam Rogers	July 26, 1832	
Hoff, William	Nancy Slone	Jan. 10, 1839	
Hogg, Hiram		Dec. 14, 1821	Daniel Duff
Holbrook, Ben		Mar. 2, 1820	Simeon Justice
Holbrook, John		Jan. 6, 1820?	Simeon Justice
Holton, John	Charity Maine	May 21, 1820	Daniel Williams
Honaker, James	Levisa Owens	Apr. 25, 1816	Hiram Stratton
Honaker, Thomas D.	Nancy Layne	Feb. 15, 1843	
Horn, George	Rosanna Dillion	Feb. 18, 1832	
Horn, John	Polly Ann Riddle	Aug. 14, 1839	
Horn, Michael	Susanna Crum	Aug. 4, 1833	
Horn, Thomas	Nancy Barnett	Jan. 30, 1842	
House (Howes), John	Jane Young	Oct. 13, 1835	
Howard, Benjamin	Nancy Arnett	Dec. 31, 1825	
Howard, Benjamin	Nancy Adams	Apr. 1, 1834	
Howard, James	Polly Seph	Mar. 30, 1820	Samuel Hanna
Howard, John	Nancy Camron	Oct. 5, 1817	Simeon Justice
Howard, Moses	Ann Patrick	Oct. 29, 1817	Joel Cook, M. G.
Howard, Samuel	Delianna Jones	Feb. 3, 1838	
Howard, William	Anna Arnett	May 8, 1823	
Howard, William	Nancy Fraley	Feb. 13, 1828	
Howell, David, Jr.	Polly Ally	Aug. 18, 1836	
Howell, Granville H.	Elizabeth McKenny	Mar. 26, 1839	
Howell, Jesse	Fanny Collett	Oct. 12, 1826	
Howell, Joel	Charlotte Branhan	Dec. 18, 1825	
Howell, John	Jane Sturgeon	Jan. 6, 1841	
Howell, William	Phoebe Profil	Nov. 4, 1814	Electius Howes
Howerton, James	Susanna Fuget	Feb. 20, 1817	William Coffee
Howerton, John	Barbara Jones	June 26, 1817	Daniel Williams
Hubbard, James	Sarah Reynolds	Apr. 24, 1832	
Huey, Robert S.	Minerva A. E. Friend	Dec. 7, 1834	
Huff, German W.	Dicy Prater	May 26, 1838	
Huff, T. W.	Polly Ann Hamilton	Mar. 12, 1834	
Hunt, Thomas	Judy Mainor	Jan. 4, 1832	Harmon Williamson
Hutton, James G.	Elizabeth Harris	June 23, 1836	
Hyden, William	Margaret Hanna	May 20, 1841	

I

Indicutt, Joseph	Patsy Spaulding	Jan. 23, 1820	Sam Hanna
Ingle, Joseph	Cadance Osborn	Aug. 3, 1809	Simeon Justice
Isaac, Isaac	Vicy Triplett	Feb. 23, 1834	

J

Jackson, Isaac	Sally Patrick	Dec. 31, 1817	Joel Cook, M. G.
Jacobs, Carter		..........., 1819	Wm. Saulsberry
Jacobs, Carter	Polly Ares (Ayers)	Feb. 1, 1829	
Jacobs, Claud		July 22, 1820	John Morris, P. S.
Jacobs, William	Rachael Prewitt	May 19, 1827	
James, Isaac	Margaret Giddens	Aug. 10, 1820	Reuben Giddens
James, John	Millie Vaughan	Apr. 6, 1817	Stephen Harper

41

Groom	Bride	Date of Marriage	By Whom
James, Samuel	Viney Dean	July 30, 1811	R. Haws
Jameson, James	Elizabeth Perry	June 26, 1820	James Honaker, J. P.
Jarrell, Carrell	Polly Roberson	Jan. 16, 1812	R. Haws, J. P.
Jarrell, Hiram	Cynthia Meade	June 9, 1834	
Jarrell, Park	Jenny Roberson	Nov. 15, 1827	
Jarrell, Ruel	Nancy Conn	Apr. 30, 1838	
Jenkins, Gilbert	Hannah Brown	Feb. 27, 1834	
Jenkins, Robert, Jr.	Rebecca Hill	Mar. 23, 1836	
Jerome, Batis	Elieth Young	Apr. 6, 1809	Thomas Evans, J. P.
Jewell, Solomon	Nancy Davis	Mar. 16, 1812	Marcus Lindsey, M.G.
Johns, Thomas P.	Elizabeth Graham	Mar. 8, 1838	
Johnson, Ben B.			Wm. Saulsberry
Johnson, Elester	Polly Tackett	Feb. 7, 1822	
Johnson, Eli		Dec. 11, 1811	Simeon Justice
Johnson, Elisha	Patsy Tackett	Feb. 7, 1822	Owen Owens
Johnson, Herance	Belsy Isaach (Isaacs)	Nov. 24, 1820	John Morris
Johnson, Joseph	Eleanor Francis	Apr. 2, 1833	
Johnson, Love	Ansy Hall	Nov. 20, 1828	
Johnson, Patrick	Anna Martin	June 13, 1813	Simeon Justice
Johnson, Thomas		May......., 1817	Wm. Saulsberry
Jones, Adis		June 3, 1817	Simeon Justice
Jones, Charles	Jemima Spradlin	June 30, 1822	James Lacy, J. P.
Jones, Claybourn	Milly Martin	Apr. 9, 1829	
Jones, Isham	Nancy Sadler	Oct. 23, 1831	
Jones, John	Anna Day	Nov. 20, 1817	William Coffee
Jones, John	Virginia Hamilton	May 7, 1833	
Jones, Lindsay	Polly Milam	Oct. 12, 1829	
Jones, Richard	Freelove Williams	Sept. 14, 1815	Daniel Williams
Jost, Christine (Christian)	Savy Ann Wiley	Jan. 9, 1814	R. Haws
Justice, Allenson	Ivy Hubbard	Jan. 5, 1835	
Justice, Amos	Sally Branham	Nov. 25, 1822	
Justice, Arch		Nov. 3, ...	S. Justice
Justice, Caleb	Elizabeth Branham	Sept. 29, 1831	
Justice, Ed		Feb. 17, ...	S. Justice
Justice, Ezra		Mar. 3, 1818	Wm. Saulsberry
Justice, Ezra	Hannah Johnson	Sept. 13, 1835	
Justice, James	Thisklah Mead	Jan. 22, 1843	
Justice, Jonathan	Nancy Meade	Mar. 3, 1843	
Justice, Peyton	Polly May	July 10, 1814	Spencer Adkins, J. P
Justice, Peyton	Polly Slone	Dec. 25, 1818	James Honaker, J. P.
Justice, Thomas	Elizabeth Blackburn	Oct. 2, 1812	Matt Spurlock
Justice, Tubal	Polly Morgan	July 27, 1820	James Roberts, J. P.
Justice, Wade		Feb. 15, 1810	Simeon Justice
Justice, William		Oct. 30, 1821	Simeon Justice

K

Kash, Caleb	Catherine Wilson	Nov. 26, 1818	Daniel Williams
Kash, Caleb	Polly Wilson	Nov. 2, 1820	William Coffee
Kash, John R.	Hannah Meade	July 1, 1818	Wm. J. Mayo, M. G.
Keaton, Elijah	Anna Johnston	Jan. 16, 1815	Sam Hanna
Keaton, Nelson	Sarah Lewis	Feb. 11, 1819	William Coffee
Keaton, Thomas	Jane Bank	Jan. 12, 1823	
Keaton, William	M. Luie Childers	Apr. 3, 1819	Samuel Hanna
Kehoot, Robert	Rhoda Mollett	Mar. 5, 1812	Matthew Spurlock
Kelly, John	Elizabeth Stratton	Feb. 15, 1825	
Kelly, Joseph	Nancy Preston	Oct. 28, 1830	

FLOYD COUNTY, KENTUCKY

Groom	Bride	Date of Marriage	By Whom
Kelly, Thomas	Nancy Mullins	Apr. 28, 1808	John Brown
Kelly, William	Eliza Evans	Aug. 2, 1819	William Coffee
Kesner, William	Nancy Kendrick	Oct. 31, 1834	
Keezee, Jesse	Elizabeth Kitchen	Aug. 8, 1821	
Kezee (Keesee), Elias	Polly Curnutte	Oct. 29, 1818	Sam Hanna, M. G.
Kezee (Keesee), Avery	Betsy Fitzpatrick	Aug. 10, 1820	Sam Hanna
King, Franklin	Elander Williamson	Jan. 27, 1821	Harmon Williamson
King, John	Peggy Charles	Feb. 13, 1820?	Reuben Giddens
King, William	Sally Lester	Apr. 1, 1819	James Honaker, J. P.
Kinnard, Samuel	Joanna Cook	Dec. 10, 1820	William Coffee
Kirk, John	Clara Marcum	Sept. 26, 1821	Reuben Giddens
Kirtby, David	Polly Brown	Jan. 25, 1827	

L

Groom	Bride	Date of Marriage	By Whom
Lacy, John C.	Martha Ecton	Sept. 11, 1823	
Lauhorn, John B.	Elizabeth Evans	Mar. 13, 1823	
Lawson, John	Nancy Banks	Mar. 10, 1819	William Coffee
Lawson, Joseph	Mary Ann Belcher	Oct. 31, 1816	William Coffee
Layne, James	Nancy Solomons	Oct. 22, 1809	Simeon Justice
Layne, James	Polly Waller	Feb. 20, 1817	Wm. J. Mayo, M. G.
Layne, James H.	Sarah M. May	Apr. 29, 1836	
Layne, John L.	Elizabeth Priest	May 12, 1829	
Layne, John N.	Polly M. Stratton	Oct. 22, 1836	
Layne, Lindsey	Edy Meade	Aug. 5, 1834	
Layne, Samuel	Judith Elkins	Feb. 28, 1825	
Layne, Tandy M.	Elizabeth Johns	Apr. 21, 1831	
Layne, William	Sopha Graham	Dec. 28, 1832	
Leak, Shelton	Sally Williams	July 8, 1825	
Leak, Thompson	Polly Patton	Jan. 8, 1832	
Lemaster, Benjamin	Elizabeth Wireman	Oct. 10, 1839	
Lemaster, Francis	Eleanor Janes (Jaynes)	Feb. 4, 1813	Bazil Lewis, M. G.
Lemaster, Isaac	Sally Pelfrey	June 12, 1834	
Lemaster, James	Mary Williams	Dec. 23, 1824	
Lemaster, James	Elizabeth Blanton	May 22, 1822	Thos. C. Brown, J. P.
Lemaster, James	Frances Auxier	Sept. 7, 1832	
Lemaster, John	Rachel Davis	Aug. 25, 1818	Samuel Hanna
Lemaster, John, Jr.	Polly Colvin	Dec. 26, 1833	
Lemaster, Joseph	Eleanor Wheeler	Apr. 19, 1832	
Lemaster, Lancaster	Rachael Phillips	Mar. 30, 1824	
Lemaster, Lewis	Sarah Tackett	Mar. 21, 1843	
Lensford, Isaac	Elizabeth Fuget	Dec. 24, 1815	Daniel Williams
Leslef (Leslie) James Harvey	Mary Jane Stratton	Mar. 2, 1843	
Lester, John	Nancy Helton (Hilton or Hylton)	Jan. 24, 1820	John Kenny, M. G.
Lewis, Bracken	Matilda Preston	Dec. 23, 1819	Sam Hanna
Lewis, Frances	Eleanor Perry	Aug. 1, 1811	Daniel Williams
Lewis, George	Mary Mankins	Mar. 22, 1813	B. Lewis
Lewis, John	Martha Lewis	Sept. 12, 1823	
Lewis, Squire	Katherine Sullivan	Apr. 9, 1839	
Lewis, Thomas, Jr.	Sopha Burchett	Feb. 11, 1830	
Lewis, William	Jean Perry	Jan. 16, 1812	Daniel Williams
Litteral, Daniel	Sarah Conley	Dec. ?, 1829	
Litteral, George	Mahala Mankin	Aug. 21, 1834	
Litteral, John	Polly Kenard	Mar. 12, 1837	

43

Groom	Bride	Date of Marriage	By Whom
Little, James	Elizabeth May	June 10, 1813	R. Haws
Little, William	Betsy Terrell	Jan. 10, 1817	Spencer Adkins, J. P.
Locker, John	Polly Evans	June 3, 1819	Wm. J. Mayo, M. G.
Lovelady, Thomas	Nancy Briggs	Aug. 20, 1821	John Morris
Lykin, David	Nancy Williams	Mar. 19, 1809	Daniel Williams
Lykin, Marcus	Nancy Burton	Sept. 11, 1821	William Coffee
Lykin, Marcus M.	Sally Neal	July 7, 1823	
Lykin, Peter	Vina Williams	Sept. 20, 1821	William Coffee
Lykin, William	Nancy Keaton	May 22, 1814	Sam Hanna

M

Groom	Bride	Date of Marriage	By Whom
Maggard, John		Aug. 13, 1818	Simeon Justice
Mainor, Charles	Lucy Mainard	Feb. 24, 1821	Reuben Giddens
Mainor, Edward	Catherine Mainor	Dec. 7, 1820	Reuben Giddens
Mainor, William	Sarah Campbell	Apr. 22, 1821	Reuben Giddens
Mankin, John	Polly Slone	Nov. 9, 1820	Thos. C. Brown, J. P.
Mankin, Walter	Polly Lowe	Mar. 28, 1826	
Mann, Sam	Preshi Dikes	Feb. 25, 1815	Sam Hanna
Mann, William	Rhoda Howard	June 19, 1832	
Marcum, Jacob	Rhoda Saddler	Feb. 20, 1817	Sam Hanna
Marcum, James	Dicy Chapman	Feb. 19, 1817	Sam Hanna
Marcum, Joshua	Frances Stephens	Mar. 16, 1821	Sam Hanna
Marcum, Moses	Edy Bryant	June 11, 1819	Reuben Giddens
Marshall, George	Elizabeth Howard	Oct. 17, 1833	
Marshall, James	Matilda Adams	Feb. 9, 1836	
Marshall, Johnson	Barshaba Adams	Feb. 4, 1830	
Marshall, Mason	Polly Barnett	May 30, 1840	
Marshall, Reuben, Jr.	Delila Spradlin	Mar. 22, 1832	
Marshall, William	Matilda Patrick	Mar. 30, 1823	
Martin, Alexander	Malinda Martin	May 5, 1839	
Martin, Anthony H.	Milly Stratton	July 7, 1839	
Martin, George	Levina McGuire	Mar. 27, 1816	Hiram Stratton
Martin, James	Milly Martin	Feb. 18, 1811	Simeon Justice
Martin, James	Judy Meek	Aug. 16, 1821	Thos. C. Brown, J. P.
Martin, Job	Jemima Saulsberry	May 21, 1835	
Martin, Joel	Rebecca Fletcher	Mar. 15, 1812	Simeon Justice
Martin, Joel	Judith Turner	Mar. 11, 1843	
Martin, John	Anna Gearhart	Nov. 1, 1831	
Martin, John P.	Elizabeth Lackey	Mar. 24, 1835	
Martin, Simpson	Elizabeth Turner	Oct. 14, 1841	
Mathews, John	Polly Mainor	June 27, 1816	Hiram Stratton, J. P.
Mathews, Thomas	Cynthia Collingsworth	June 22, 1813	Hiram Stratton
May, Blair	Sally Adams	May 17, 1829	
May, Daniel	Peggy Allen	Dec. 8, 1824	
May, James	Mary Adams	Mar. 30, 1820	William Coffee
May, James	Matilda Whitaker	Nov. 26, 1830	
May, John	Elizabeth Adams	Mar. 3, 1821	Mason Williams
May, Reuben	Sally Allen	Nov. 27, 1825	
May, Samuel	Catherine Evans	May 3, 1808	Thos. C. Brown, J. P.
May, Samuel	Polly Ann George	June 14, 1827	
May, Thomas	Dorcas Patton	Aug. 19, 1813	Simeon Justice
Maynor, Christopher	Isabel Williams	Oct. 5, 1815	R. Haws
Maynor, James	Laura Welch	Feb. 19, 1814?	Spencer Adkins, J. P.
Mayo, G. W.	Sarah B. Auxier	June 15, 1839	
Mayo, George W.	Martha Ann Smith	Mar. 8, 1838	
Mayo, Henry B.	Peggy McGuyer	Jan. 14, 1812	Simeon Justice, M. G.
Mayo, Jacob	Rebecca Graham	Dec. 14, 1826	

Groom	Bride	Date of Marriage	By Whom
Mayo, James J.	Rebecca McComas	Sept. 21, 1837	
Mayo, Jonathan	Polly Morgan	Nov. 6, 1817	Joel Cook, M. G.
Mayo, Mial	Susanna Mathews	Oct. 10, 1816	Hiram Stratton
Mayo, Wilson	Jenny Stratton	Sept. 24, 1818	James Honaker, J. P.
Mayo, Winston	Cynthia S. Friend	June 24, 1834	
Mays, James	Elizabeth Rowe	Apr. 6, 1820	James Honaker, J. P.
McBrayer, James R.	Anna Sanders	July 7, 1823	
McBrayer, William J.	Elizabeth Fisher	Oct. 29, 1832	
McBroom, David	Mahala Sowards	Dec. 15, 1815	Hiram Stratton
McBroom, Joseph	Phoebe Young	July 28, 1814	R. Haws
McClintick, ...	Sally Case	Oct. 23, 1818	Daniel Williams
McClure, William	Lucretia Chapman	Mar. 14, 1816	Sam Hanna
McCowan, John	Polly Blankenship	July 14, 1841	
McCoy, Benjamin	Melia Mainor	Apr. 17, 1821	James Honaker, J. P.
McCoy, Daniel	Peggy Taylor	Feb. 12, 1819?	Spencer Adkins, J. P.
McCoy, James	Nancy Nolin	Mar. 8, 1827	
McCoy, Joseph	Mary Mainor	July 7, 1816	Spencer Adkins, J. P.
McCoy, Richard		Aug. 27, 1815	Simeon Justice
McDole (McDowell), William	Jenny Cains	June 27, 1809	Thomas Evans, J. P.
McDonald, Jacob	Levina May	Oct. 29, 1840	
McDowell, John	Jenny Ramey	Aug. 3, 1820	Thos. C. Brown, J. P.
McFerren, Robert	Rebecca Lacy	Sept. 1, 1825	
McGinnis, Hiram	Nancy Stone	Oct. 24, 1833	
McGinnis, Hiram	Sally Delong	Feb. 27, 1837	
McGlone, James	Elizabeth Stone	Nov. 14, 1833	
McGuinn, Alexander	Levisa McHenry	Jan. 27, 1818	William J. Mayo
McGuire, Harry S.	Diana K. Friend	Aug. 24, 1837	
McGuire, Jesse	Elizabeth Garrett	June 17, 1821	Wm. J. Mayo, M. G.
McGuire, Samuel	Jeneth Ferguson	June 1, 1809	Daniel Williams
McGuire, Samuel	Emily Sullivan	Nov. 2, 1837	
McGuire, William	Polly Stratton	July 25, 1827	
McGuyer, James	Hannah Casky	Oct. 14, 1813	Daniel Williams
McGuyer, Solomon	Susanna Garrett	Jan. 14, 1812	Simeon Justice, M. G.
McKee, John	Elizabeth Hager	Aug. 22, 1811	Cornelius McGuyer
McKenney, Daniel	Elizabeth Hale	Mar. 5, 1837	
McKenney, John	Lydia Hicks	Sept. 26, 1840	
McKenzie, John	Esther Hamilton	Jan. 31, 1822	James Lacy, J. P.
McKenzie, Newton J.	Margaret Picklesimer	Feb. 9, 1843	
McKinster, Ambrose	Betsy Spencer	Sept. 28, 1819	Sam Hanna
McKnight, James		July 26, 1810	Thos. C. Brown
McQuary, John	Miranda Dean	Dec. 12, 1818	Wm. J. Mayo, M. G.
McReynolds, John W.	Anna Morgan	Sept. 2, 1821	Wm. J. Mayo, M. G.
Meade, Eli	Siller Akers	Nov. 7, 1811	Simeon Justice
Meade, Moses	Polly Hackworth	Oct. 4, 1810	Simeon Justice
Meade, Rhodes	Polly Branham	Apr. 24, 1825	
Meade, Robert	Susanna Clark	July 6, 1823	
Meade, Robert	Lydia Van Hoose	May 16, 1837	
Meade, S.		Aug. 5, 1813	Simeon Justice
Meade, William	Elizabeth Johnston	Aug. 8, 1841	
Meek, Isaac	Sally Ward	June 19, 1828	
Meek, James	Malinda Price	Sept. 7, 1815	Sam Hanna
Meek, William	Peggy McCord	Jan. 24, 1820	Thos. C. Brown, J. P.
Menix, Charles, Jr.	Margaret Patrick	Mar. 19, 1833	
Menix, James	Sally Stone	Jan. 29, 1829	
Miller, Abraham	Katy Hensley	July 21, 1814	Samuel Hellums
Miller, Benjamin	Dosha Bradley	Oct. 11, 1821	Wm. J. Mayo, M. G.
Miller, Edward B.	Levisa Stratton	Apr. 21, 1819	Thomas Evans, M. P.

Groom	Bride	Date of Marriage	By Whom
Mills, George	Molly Crum	May 9, 1830	....
Mimnes, (Mimms),			
John D.	Arminta D. Friend	Nov. 22, 1838	....
Montgomery, Joseph	Matilda Howard	Oct. 29, 1817	Joel Cook, M. G.
Montgomery, Phillip	Marjory McClintick	Nov. 25, 1814	Daniel Williams
Moore, C.	....	Mar. 18, 1818	Simeon Justice
Moore, Christopher	Mary Auxier	Oct. 5, 1808	Thos. C. Brown
Moore, James	Nancy Barnett	Dec. 26, 1816	R. Haws
Moore, John	Peggy Porter	Dec. 14, 1826	....
Moore, Samuel	Polly Brown	Mar. 9, 1822	Thos. C. Brown, J. P.
Moore, William	Wilmouth Teators	June 25, 1843	....
Morgan, David	Eleanor Graham		
Morgan, Jared	Sally Polly	Mar. 22, 1817	Spencer Adkins, J. P.
Morgan, Morgan	Artius Spurlock	Apr. 11, 1836	....
Morgan, Wells	Betsy Lewis	Mar. 9, 1813	Daniel Williams
Morgan, William C.	Sorilda Ann Thurman	May 4, 1824	....
Morris, Benjamin	Elizabeth Jacobs	Mar. 27, 1808	James Patton, J. P.
Morris, Ezekiel	Mary Rose	June 17, 1809	Daniel Williams
Morris, Isaac	Peggy Oney	July 30, 1826	....
Morris, John	Mary Carehart		
	(Gearhart)	May 9, 1811	John Johnson
Mosley, William, Jr.	Susanna Smith	Jan. 23, 1840	....
Mullins, Booker	Polly Johnson	Apr. 19, 1821	James Roberts, J. P.
Mullins, David	Janny (Janie)		
	Short	Feb. 10, 1820	James Roberts, J. P.
Mullins, Isaac	Polly Wireman	Apr. 18, 1835	....
Mullins, James	Agnes Little	Mar. 12, 1812	Simeon Justice
Mullins, John	Polly Hamilton	..........., 1817	Wm. Saulsberry
Mullins, Marshall	Sarah Littell	Sept. 19, 1811	Simeon Justice, M. G.
Mullins, Owen	Lyda Hall	May 27, 1841	....
Mullins, Sherwood	....	Apr. 8, 1813	Simeon Justice
Mullins, William	....	Sept. 1,............	Wm. Saulsberry
Murray, Thomas	Susanna Johnson	Feb. 22, 1821	Thos. C. Brown, J. P.

N

Napier, Ashford	Eleanor Wells	Mar. 19, 1818	Daniel Williams
Nelson, William	Sally Strand	Mar. 1, 1822	Thos. C. Brown
Newsom, Henry	Nicy Hall	Aug. 18, 1841	....
Nickel, David	Kitty Reed	Feb. 29, 1816	Sam Hanna
Nickel, John	Nancy Kesh (Kash)	Nov. 25, 1813	Daniel Williams
Nickel, John	Civillar Jones		
	(Jaynes)	May 1, 1822	William Coffee
Nickel, Joseph	Rachael Kesh		
	(Kash)	Dec. 18, 1813	Daniel Williams
Nipp, Samuel	Elizabeth Vaughan	June 26, 1817	R. Haws
Nix, John	Peggy Young	Aug. 20, 1816	Sam Hanna
Nolin, Isaac	Peggy Music	June 14, 1818	John Brown, J. P.
Nolin, Stephen	....	July 22, 1820	John Morris, P. S.
Norman, John	Ricy (Reecie)		
	Meadows	Apr. 5, 1821	James Honaker, J. P.
Nott, Samuel P.	Mary Ramey	Sept. 15, 1841	....
Nott, William H. H.	Phoebe Ramey	Jan. 14, 1840	....
Nunn, Henry	Rebecca Herrell	Nov. 30, 1823	....
Nunn, Thomas	Ruthie Brown	Feb. 6, 1834	....

O

Oakley, John	Peggy Lewis	Feb. 28, 1810	Daniel Williams
O'Bryant, Herrell	Peggy Pack	Mar. 24, 1820	Thos. C. Brown, J. P.

Groom	Bride	Date of Marriage	By Whom
O'Bryant, Stephen	Peggy Hawes	Aug. 6, 1840	....
O'Bryan, William	Mary Chandler	Aug. 6, 1837	....
Ogden, Abraham	Rebecca Lacy	May 16, 1813	Daniel Williams
Ohair (O'hara), Michael	Lucretia Bails (Bales)	Nov. 16, 1820	William Coffee
Ohair (O'hara), Thomas	Rachael Jones (Janes)	Oct. 24, 1810	Richard Stephens
Oldfield, Jesse	Elizabeth Hamilton	Feb. 19, 1814	B. Lewis
Osborn, Albert	Mary Burchett	Oct. 18, 1840	....
Osborn, Ben	Susanna Baker	Feb. 28, 1813	Simeon Justice
Osborn, Edward L.	Rhoda Spurlock	Mar. 10, 1829	....
Osborn, Hiram	Nancy Mullins	Sept. 16, 1819	James Honaker
Osborn, S.	....	Apr. 28, 181....	Simeon Justice
Osborn, Stephen	Maranda Wireman	Jan. 6, 1840	....
Osborn, William	Jemima Friend	Dec. 16, 1835	....
Owens, Greenberry	Susanna Clark	Dec. 8, 1839	....
Owens, Hiram	Abigail Akers	Apr. 18, 1838	....
Owens, James	Elan Collier	Mar. 4, 1817?	Simeon Justice
Owens, John	Deborah Meade	Dec. 27, 1821	James Honaker, J. P.
Owens, John K.	Amanda L. Friend	June 16, 1839	....
Owens, Robert	Ruth Howard	Mar. 8, 1826	....
Owens, Tom	....	Mar. 13, 1810	Simeon Justice
Owens, William	Lydia Ratcliff	May 19, 1816	R. Haws
Owney (Oney), William	Susanna Coburn	Aug. 24, 1831	....

P

Pack, Charles	Anna Sellards	....	....
Pack, Charles	Betsy Crum	Nov. 17, 1808	Thomas Evans, J. P.
Pack, George	Sally Layne	Sept. 27, 1819	Sam Hanna
Parsons, George	Susanna Campbell	May 17, 1821	Reuben Giddens
Parsons, Simeon	Elizabeth Campbell	June 14, 1818	Wm. J. Mayo, M. G.
Patrick, Brice	Rebecca Prater	Mar. 20, 1834	....
Patrick, Brice	Fanny Menix	Mar. 8, 1838	....
Patrick, Hiram	Polly Haywood	Jan. 20, 1833	....
Patrick, Hugh	Barbara Bailey	May 11, 1809	Mathew Spurlock M. G.
Patrick, Hugh	Mary Prater	June 3, 1826	....
Patrick, James	Mary Hatfield	Feb. 9, 1813	Samuel Hanna, M. G.
Patrick, Jeremiah	Nancy Marshall	July 12, 1823	....
Patrick, Jeremiah	Sarah Salyers	Sept. 25, 1837	....
Patrick, John	Patsy Kennard	Apr. 9, 1818	William Coffee
Patrick, John	Charlotte Patrick	Aug. 11, 1836	....
Patrick, Munday	Rebecca Williams	Dec. 26, 1822	....
Patrick, Richard	Eleanor Kennard	Jan. 8, 1824	....
Patrick, William	Nancy Prater	Dec. 28, 1824	....
Patton, Christopher	Susanna Akers	Dec. 28, 1824	....
Patton, David	Polly Gilbert	Apr. 29, 1832	....
Patton, David	Rebecca Prater	July 21, 1833	....
Patton, Frazier	Esther Conley	June 21, 1833	....
Patton, Granville	Patty Jones	Dec. 16, 1840	....
Patton, Henry J.	Lydia Goodman	Nov. 3, 1836	....
Patton, Sam	....	Apr. 12, 1810	Simeon Justice
Patton, Washington	Polly Cooper	Nov. 9, 1825	....
Patton, William	Jenny M. Brown	Feb. 12, 1812	R. Haws
Paugh, Joseph	Jane Bailey	Aug. 16, 1838	....
Pelfrey, Alexander	Alsey Lemaster	Oct. 28, 1813	B. Lewis
Pelfrey, Daniel	Lydia Williams	June 24, 1819	Sam Hanna

Groom	Bride	Date of Marriage	By Whom
Pelfrey, Eleasor	Temperance Ramey	July 1, 1838	
Pelfrey, James	Polly Dean	Sept. 5, 1833	
Pelfrey, Stephen	Sarah Lemaster	Dec. 31, 1840	
Pelfrey, William	Nancy Hannah	Sept. 29, 1814	Bazil Lewis
Pelfrey, William	Mary Lemaster	May 23, 1841	
Pendleton, James	Frances Gearhart	July 7, 1833	
Penix, Henry	Rachael Jenkins	June 18, 1834	
Pennington, James		Dec. 19, 1819	Simeon Justice
Pennington, John		Sept. 16, 1819	Simeon Justice
Pennington, William	Martha Blanton	Dec. 8, 1836	
Perry, Arnold	Polly Ratcliff	Aug. 8, 1816	Spencer Adkins, J. P.
Perry, Daniel	Nancy Dyer	Aug. 10, 1820	William Coffee
Perry, Lou B.	Geary Collins	Mar. 25, 1836	
Perry, Thomas	Martha Wells	Oct. 8, 1819	Daniel Williams
Petry, John	Polly May	June 16, 1817	Samuel Hanna
Peyton, Daniel	Nancy Perry	Oct. 22, 1818	Daniel Williams
Peyton, Phillip	Elizabeth Hanks	Mar. 10, 1814	Daniel Williams
Phillips, John	Sally Kelly	Jan. 16, 1815	Sam Hanna
Phillips, Samuel	Mary Cordill (Caudill)	Feb. 15, 1813	Simeon Justice
Phlerty, Francis	Betsy Indicut	Jan. 1, 1813	R. Haws
Picklesimer, David	Sally Prater	Apr. 15, 1817	Sam Hanna
Picklesimer, John	Polly Tackett	Oct. 19, 1826	
Picklesimer, Nathan	Susanna Williams	Feb. 20, 1821	Thos. C. Brown
Picklesimer, Samuel	Rachael Tackett	Feb. 16, 1831	
Picklesimer, Thomas	Milby Stephens	Feb. 27, 1823	
Pinson, Allen	Peggy Belshi	Mar. 24, 1808	William McGuyer
Pinson, Jarred	Polly Walters	Mar. 19, 1820	James Honaker, J. P.
Pinson, John	Polly Honaker	Sept. 1, 1811	R. Haws
Pinson, John	Cynthia Meade	June 13, 1839	
Pinson, T.	E. Milam	Sept. 11, 1814	Simeon Justice
Pinson, Thomas	Rachael Leslie	Sept. 29, 1814	Simeon Justice
Pinson, William	Anne Law	July 12, 1810	William McGuyer
Pitts, Mexico	Dicy Shepherd	July 3, 1833	
Pitts. Thomas	Rachael Sturgeon	Dec. 27, 1840	
Pitts. Washington	Sarah Ann Morrison	Feb. 1, 1843	
Poe, Edmund	Agnes Marshall	Dec. 1, 1832	
Poe. James	Tabitha Thacker	Apr. 7. 1841	
Polley, Henry	Patsy Hall	Apr. 15, 1819	John Brown, J. P.
Poor, Benjamin	Charlotte Williams	May 2, 1812	M. Lindsey, M. G.
Porter, Benjamin	Abijah Blevins	Jan. 23, 1827	
Porter, John	Polly Webb	June 4, 1824	
Porter, Joseph	Mary Williamson	Dec. 28, 1817	Wm. J. Mayo, M. G.
Porter, Patrick, Jr.	Sally Blevins	July 19, 1827	
Porter, William G.	Jane Layne	Nov. 26, 1840	
Powell, Henry	Pricy Vermillion	Jan. 15, 1810	Spencer Adkins, J. P.
Powell, John W.	Thursa Hatcher	Sept. 22, 1843	
Power, Holloway	Clarinda Prater	Jan. 12, 1837	
Prater, Elijah, Jr.	Jemima Patrick	Sept. 15, 1832	
Prater, James	Nancy Patrick	Mar. 20, 1823	
Prater, John	Jemima Auxier	Nov. 29, 1838	
Prater, Jonathan, Jr.	Peggy Bailey	Dec. 6, 1835	
Prater, Joseph	Elizabeth Reffit	June 10, 1834	
Prater, Lorenzo D.	Sarah Bradley	Apr. 1, 1843	
Prater, Robert	Cynthia Rice	July 30, 1840	
Prater, Samuel	Rebecca Pitts	Feb. 1. 1843	
Prater, Thomas	Rebecca Cope	Jan. 15, 1813	Samuel Hanna, M. G.
Prater, Thomas	Elizabeth Saulsberry	June 14, 1818	John Brown, J. P.

Groom	Bride	Date of Marriage	By Whom
Prater, William	Nancy Case	Nov. 6, 1808	Daniel Williams
Prater, William	Obedience Prater	Aug. 8, 1811	Simeon Justice, M. G.
Prater, William	Levisa Kennard	Aug. 5, 1832	
Pratt, Henry	Sally Gibson	Sept. 20, 1828	
Pratt, James	Rebecca Wright	July 1, 1827	
Preece, Alexander B.	Looince Stratton	Oct. 24, 1822	
Preece, Richard	Caty (Katy) Newland	Feb. 14, 1811	Simeon Justice
Pregman, Daniel	Rebecca Gilbert	Mar. 30, 1839	
Presley, John	Lucy M. Conley	Dec. 23, 1819	Daniel Williams
Preston, Elijah	Jean Conley	Jan. 22, 1815	Sam Hanna
Preston, Eliphus	Anna Pelfrey	Dec. 10, 1815	Sam Hanna, M. G.
Preston, Isaac	Polly Slone	Feb. 1, 1812	Simeon Justice
Preston, James	Anna Wheeler	May 3, 1835	
Preston, Shadrack	Polly Pelfrey	Feb. 2, 1823	
Preston, Thomas	Polly Murray	Aug. 16, 1830	
Prewitt, Henry	Fanny Briggs	Apr. 15, 1819	Wm. J. Mayo, M. G
Prewitt, Hiram	Rebecca Bradley	Apr. 4, 1822	
Prewitt, William		July 11, 1820	John Morris, P. S.
Price, Jesse	Lynchie Preston	Dec. 29, 1808	William McGuyer
Price, John	Nancy Johnson	June 13, 1814	Daniel Williams
Price, Jonathan	Sally Lungins	July 23, 1817	R. Haws
Price, William	Polly Preston	Aug. 9. 1838	
Pridemore, John	Rachael Gibson	Nov. 25, 1828	
Pridemore, Washington	Mahala Wallen	Nov. 6, 1843	
Profit, Joseph	Rebecca Fairchild	Jan. 15, 1815	Electius Thompson
Profit, Joseph	Elizabeth Teaders	May 16, 1818	John Brown
Pruitt, Henry	Elizabeth Bradley	Apr. 4, 1822	John Morris
Puckett, Cobb	Polly Craft	June 29, 1843	
Puckett, Morgan	Susanna Whitaker	Jan. 24, 1822	James Lacy, J. P.
Puckett, Thomas	Polly Ramey	June 29, 1818	Samuel Hanna

Q

Quillen, Teague			Wm. Saulsberry

R

Ramey, Alexander	Tabitha Horn	Sept. 22, 1837	
Ramey, Charles	Mary Picklesimer	July 29, 1830	
Ramey, Ephriam	Polly Kelly	Apr. 5, 1836	
Ramey, James	Mary Wheeler	Dec. 24, 1818	Sam Hanna
Ramey, John	Sarah Keeth (Kieth)	Feb. 9, 1843	
Ramey, John	Peggy Hitchcock	Sept. 15, 1816	Sam Hanna
Ramey, Thomas	Luxey Brown	Feb. 8, 1829	
Ramey, William	Caty (Katy) Stafford	Dec. 20, 1830	
Ramey, William H.	Sally Turner	Apr. 11, 1841	
Ramey, William J.	Elizabeth Jane Turner	Sept. 29, 1839	
Randell, Dr. Percy	Mahala May	July 30, 1839	
Ratcliff, Harrison	Peggy Hatcher	Feb. 27, 1840	
Ratcliff, Joseph	Lucinda Clark	Jan. 26, 1837	
Ratcliff, Lewis	Sarah Spradlin	Mar. 30, 1821	Thos. C. Brown
Ratcliff, Richard	Sally Childers	Jan. 6, 1820	James Honaker, J. P.
Ratcliff, Silas	Anne Spradlin	May 17, 1827	

Groom	Bride	Date of Marriage	By Whom
Ratcliff, Silas	Margaret Dawson	Jan. 30, 1840	
Ratcliff, William		June 27, 1813	Simeon Justice
Ratcliff, William	Susanna Sanders	May 28, 1829	
Ratcliff, William	Rachael James	Sept. 6, 1840	
Ray, Elijah	Celia Brown	Oct. 19, 1828	
Reckey, Jeffrey	Elizabeth Auxier	Mar. 12, 1822	Thos. C. Brown, J. P.
Redefort, John	Anne Phillips	Dec. 25, 1814	Simeon Justice
Reed, Asa	Dorcas Ramey	Nov. 9, 1833	
Reed, James	Alcy Ferguson	Mar. 28, 1822	William Coffee
Reed, John	Eleanor Auxier	June 14, 1832	
Reed, John M.	Nancy Deering	Oct. 9, 1837	
Reterford,Reuben,Jr.	Nancy Kezee (Keesee)	Jan. 28, 1821	Reuben Giddens.
Reynolds, Hamilton	Malinda Justice	Feb. 20, 1834	
Rice, Isaac	Celia Conley	Mar. 29, 1839	
Rice, John	Nancy Mullett	Aug. 30, 1840	
Rice, Martin	Malinda Davis	Apr. 21, 1831	
Rice, Martin	Sarah Menix	Sept. 6, 1832	
Rice, Samuel	Phoebe Hitchcock	Dec. 24, 1815	Sam Hanna, M. G.
Rice, Samuel	Jane Patrick	Nov. 11, 1841	
Rice, Washington	Elizabeth Auxier	Sept. 26, 1839	
Rice, William	Dicy Prater	Aug. 27, 1835	
Richardson, Daniel	Polly Stone	Oct. 19, 1825	
Richardson, Daniel	Polly Prater	Dec. 6, 1840	
Riddle, Andrew	Susannah Vaughan	Oct. 8, 1837	
Riddle, George		Nov. 8, 1818	Stephen Harper, J. P.
Rite, (Wright) Isaac	Delila Moore	Feb. 2, 1836	
Rite, Lewis	Edy Flannery	Sept. 12, 1832	
Rite, Solomon	Betsy Yates	July 3, 1826	
Risnor, Archibald	Nancy Howard	Mar. 14, 1840	
Risnor, Elias	Polly Fletcher	Oct. 3, 1830	
Risnor, Jacob	Mary Ann Marshall	Mar. 17, 1836	
Risnor, John	Elizabeth Howard	May 25, 1840	
Risnor, William	Abigail Salyer	Feb. 27, 1840	
Ritchey, (Ritchie) Jeptha	Elizabeth Auxier	Mar. 12, 1822	
Roark, John		June ...., 1817	Electius Thompson
Roberson, George	Peggy Ratcliff	Feb. 27, 1822	James Honaker, J. P.
Roberson, James H.	Sarah Lawson	Aug. 6, 1837	
Roberson, Jesse	Susanna Jarrell	Feb. 26, 1832	
Roberson, John	Elizabeth Conley	Mar. 21, 1829	
Roberson, Richard P.	Polly Ratcliff	May 7, 1821	Reuben Giddens
Roberson, Samuel	Patsy Spradlin	Jan. 28, 1836	
Roberson, William	Evaline Auxier	Sept. 7, 1826	
Roberts, Cornelius	Nancy Stanley	Apr. 16, 1820	James Honaker, J. P.
Roberts, Sinclar (St. Clair)	Anna Stobangh (Stambaugh)	Jan. 29, 1822	
Rogers, Jonathan	Margaret Hoff	Jan. 19, 1832	
Roop, John	Malinda James	Sept. 14, 1843	
Rose, Francis	Polly Hale	Nov. 17, 1808	James Patton, J. P.
Rose, William	Nancy Osborn	Jan. 26, 1837	
Rowland, Daniel R.	Emily Lemaster	Dec. 5, 1841	
Rowland, Samuel H.	Isabel Evans	Apr. 25, 1822	Wm. J. Mayo, M. G.
Rule, Anderson	Eleanor Friend	Dec. 26, 1826	
Rule, Andrew	Sally Young	Oct. 10, 1809	Daniel Williams
Rule, Harrison B.	Margaret B. Kelly	Sept. 3, 1837	
Rule, James Milton	Sarah Fitzpatrick	Nov. 4, 1839	

Groom	Bride	Date of Marriage	By Whom

S

Groom	Bride	Date of Marriage	By Whom
Sadler, George		Mar. 13, 1818	Simeon Justice
Sagraves, Samuel	Sarah Osborn	Dec. 13, 1825	
Salmons, Benjamin	Sally Harper	Feb. 27, 1823	
Salmon, Carter B.	Cynthis Webb	Dec. 23, 1837	
Salmons, Randall	Ona Frazier	Sept. 5, 1813	Simeon Justice
Salmons, Lewlance		June 7, 1821	Stephen Harper, J. P.
Salmons, Thomas	Artemenia Frazier	Apr. 28, 1823	
Salisberry (Saulsberry), Milton	Levisa Johnson	July 21, 1831	
Saulsberry, William	Elizabeth Walker	Mar. 17, 1812	Simeon Justice
Salyer, Abner	Nancy Hale	July 17, 1821	John Morris
Salyer, Benjamin	Franky Conley	Feb. 15, 1821	Thos. C. Brown, J. P.
Salyer, David	Susanna Miles	Apr. 6, 1837	
Salyer, Fielden	Peggy Hale	Sept. 2, 1825	
Salyer, Isiah	Phoebe Arnett	Aug. 12, 1837	
Salyer, Jacob	N. Rowland	Sept. 9, 1823	
Salyer, John	Margaret Jayne	Nov. 25, 1828	
Salyer, Thomas	Violet Montgomery	Nov. 16, 1843	
Salyer, William	Dorcas Patton	Dec. 26, 1843	
Sanders, Jacob, Jr.	Prose Osborn	Apr. 15, 1830	
Sanders, Thomas		Apr. 13, 1820	Wm. Saulsberry
Sellards, Cornelius	Anna Sullivan	May 1, 1825	
Sellards, Thomas	Mary Clark	Jan. 16, 1834	
Sheets, George	Ruth Fitzpatrick	Aug. 7, 1821	Wm. J. Mayo, M. G.
Shepherd, Jesse	Sally Howard	Apr. 30, 1822	
Shepherd, John	Sally Hale	Mar. 10, 1844	
Sherman, Henry	Matilda Preston	Dec. 1, 1831	
Short, Charles			Wm. Saulsberry
Short, Thomas	Jemima Chapman	July 12, 1809	Henry Burgess
Sizemore, Lewis	Katy Gearhart	April 2, 1821	John Morris
Spradlin, Abraham	Sally Evans	May 3, 1820	Wm. J. Mayo
Spradlin, Benjamin	Martha Evans	Aug. 24, 1820	Thos. C. Brown
Spradlin, Jesse	Sally Slone	Sept. 13, 1820	Wm. J. Mayo
Spradlin, John	Margaret Fitzpatrick	May 4, 1820	Wm J. Mayo
Spradlin, Robert	Levisa Fitzpatrick	Sept. 5, 1816	Samuel Hanna
Spradlin, John	Dorcas Prater	July 5, 1825	
Spradlin, Nehemiah	Anna Evans	July 19, 1824	
Spriggs, Hiram	Miranda Ward	Sept. 30, 1840	
Spriggs, John	Sally Burchett	Jan. 12, 1825	
Spry, William	Nancy Howard	Dec. 14, 1834	
Spurlock, Charles	Clara Akers	Dec. 15, 1820	Owen Owens
Spurlock, Hiram	Martha G. Osborn	Apr. 4, 1816	Stephen Harper
Stacy, William	Rebecca Proffitt	June 24, 1819	John Brown, J. P.
Stafford, John	Calista Nott	Apr. 8, 1825	
Stambaugh, Lawrence	Betsy Reynolds	Mar. 26, 1821	John Morris
Stambaugh, Philip	Dicy Johnson	May 2, 1833	
Stamper, James		Nov. 16, 1817	Electius Thompson
Stamper, James	Sarah Stamper	June 8, 1820	John Kenny
Stapleton, Andrew	Peggy Stapleton	Mar. 17, 1830	
Stapleton, Charles	Mary Evans	May 1, 1826	
Stapleton, Inman	Nancy Davis	June 6, 1821	Thos. C. Brown
Stapleton, Israel	Mahany Murray	July 3, 1826	
Stare, James		Oct. 25, 1821	Reuben Giddens
Staton, Charles	Nancy Kezee (Keesee)	Aug. 13, 1820	Reuben Giddens

51

Groom	Bride	Date of Marriage	By Whom
Stephens, Andrew	Susanna Williams	Dec. 11, 1821	Thos. C. Brown
Stephens, Samuel	....	July 26, 1821	Stephen Harper
Stephenson, Zachariah	Jincy Brown	Jan. 1, 1810	Benjamin Edge
Steward, Thomas	Sally Mathis	Oct. 7, 1819	Reuben Giddens
Stone, Cudbeth (Cuthbert)	Polly Hill	May 19, 1836	....
Sizemore, Russell	Anna Prewitt	May 11, 1823	....
Skaggs, John	Polly Woods	Oct. 1, 1818	Samuel Hanna, M. G.
Skaggs, Lewis	Nancy McDowell	Aug. 21, 1812	Marcus Lindsay, M. G.
Skaggs, Solomon	Slyvemes Caesus	Oct. 14, 1817	Wm. J. Mayo
Slater, John	Polly Alexander	Feb. 8, 1833	....
Slone, A.	Milly Sanford	Sept. 24, 1812	Simeon Justice
Slone, Alexander	Matilda Martin	Jan. 13, 1838	....
Slone, C.	....	Aug. 2, 1810	Simeon Justice
Slone, Hiram	....	Sept. 24, 1818	Stephen Harper
Slone, Isham	Polly Reynolds	Oct. 26, 1815	Simeon Justice
Slone, William	Sally Casebolt	Apr. 27, 1826	....
Slusher, Phillip	Polly Howard	Dec. 31, 1825	....
Smith, James	Polly Briggs	Mar. 29, 1812	Mathew Spurlock
Smith, John	Rachael Murphy	May 24, 1821	Reuben Giddens
Smith, John	Elizabeth Wather	Oct. 7, 1832	....
Smith, Wiley	Nancy Saulsberry	Jan. 27, 1831	....
Smith, William	Elizabeth Lester	July 27, 1816	Spencer Adkins, J.P.
Smith, William	....	June ...., 1817	Electius Howes
Smith, William	Agnes Slone	Feb. 6, 1819	Wm. J. Mayo, M. G.
Smith, William	Elizabeth Childers	Feb. 21, 1820	John Brown
Snips, William R.	Susanna Hanshaw	Nov. 23, 1839	....
Sowards, George	Anne Chapman	Aug. 15, 1816	Sam Hanna
Sparks, Allen	Elizabeth Keezie (Keesee)	June 27, 1822	....
Sparkman, William	Drucilla Harris	Aug. 19, 1819	Wm. J. Mayo
Spears, Enoch	Jane Porter	Aug. 21, 1831	....
Spears, Robert	Elizabeth Waller	Jan. 5, 1814	R. Haws
Spears, Spencer	Talitha Young	June 24, 1816	R. Haws
Spears, Spencer	Rosanna Wells	Nov. 13, 1828	....
Spears, Wm. G.	Rhoda Gerrell	Oct. 22, 1840	....
Stone, Iraley	Jenny Talley	Feb. 6, 1838	....
Stone, James	Nancy Dawson	Sept. 16, 1835	....
Stone, James	Elizabeth Bryant	Aug. 25, 1836	....
Stone, John	Polly Hanna	Apr. 7, 1833	....
Stone, Thomas	Betsy Stafford	May 15, 1823	....
Stone, William	Tacy Music	May 23, 1822	....
Stout, Eben	Levina Hanna	Apr. 28, 1825	....
Stout, Jonathan	Margaret Hanna	Apr. 28, 1825	....
Stratton, Charles	Hanna Lester	Feb. 25, 1808	William McGuyer
Stratton, James	Cassander Garrett	Oct. 29, 1820	Wm. J. Mayo
Stratton, Solomon	Sarah Walker	Sept. 17, 1812	Simeon Justice
Stratton, Solomon	Jenny Layne	Nov. 30, 1820	Wm. J. Mayo
Stratton, Solomon C.	Elizabeth Stratton	Dec. ...., 1834	....
Stratton, Tandy	Polly Preece	May 25, 1813	Matthew Spurlock
Stratton, Tandy	Mahala Lewis	July 24, 1823	....
Sturgill, Jesse	Malinda Williams	May 11, 1843	....
Sturgeon (Sturgill), Eli	Pricilla Meade	May 4, 1826	....
Sturgeon, John W.	Elizabeth Herrell	Sept. 20, 1832	....
Sullivan, James	Elizabeth Burks	May 11, 1840	....
Sullivan, Wilson	Fanny Young	Apr. 18, 1815	Hiram Stratton
Sutton, John	Seatta Hays	Jan. 18, 1832	....

Groom	Bride	Date of Marriage	By Whom
Swetnam, Zepheniah	Charlotte Burgess	Apr. 14, 1836	
Swetnam, John J.	Rebecca Osborn	Nov. 22, 1840	
Sword, John		Sept. 20, 1818	Stephen Harper

T

Tackett, Francis		July 30, 1817	Wm. Saulsberry
Tackett, John	Sally Pelphry	Aug. 22, 1821	Thos. C. Brown
Tackett, Phillip	Sarah Arms	Feb. 20, 1834	
Tackett, Robert	Elizabeth Tackett (Alias Barnett)	Mar. 20, 1837	
Tackett, William	Sally Lemaster	Jan. 16, 1822	Thos. C. Brown, J. P.
Talyard, John	Polly Wadkins	Nov. 2, 1820	John Morris, P. S.
Taylor, John	Mary Jarrell	Dec. 30, 1837	
Templeton, James	Phoebe Hubbard	Nov. 17, 1829	
Terry, Benjamin	Elizabeth Broderick	Mar. 28, 1822	
Terry, Daniel	Sally Slone	Nov. 11, 1830	
Terry, Leonard			Wm. Saulsberry
Terry, Thomas	Patsy	Jan. 1, 1817	John Brown
Terry, William	Sabra Casebolt	Apr. 30, 1816	Stephen Harper
Thacker, Nathan		Oct. 20, 1820?	Simeon Justice
Thompkins, Garsham	Mary Harris	Nov. 17, 1818	James Honaker, J. P.
Thompson, Abner	Polly Powell	Sept. 21, 1820	James Honaker, J. P.
Thompson, Samuel	Hannah Kearby	July 12, 1809	Henry Burgess
Thornsberry, Edward	Nancy Moseley	Nov. 30, 1835	
Tirey, (Tyree) Benjamin	Elizabeth Broderick	Mar. 28, 1822	John Morris
Todd, Lewis	Nancy House (Howes)	May 23, 1837	
Toulson, Warren		June ...., 1817	Electius Howes
Travis, John	Ibby Howard	Feb. 18, 1827	
Trimble, Edwin	Dorothea Graham	July 22, 1827	
Triplett, Lec.	Rachael Thornsberry	Aug. 19, 1835	
Turner, Adam	Margaret Patton	July 15, 1840	
Turner, James	Anna Waller	Jan. 2, 1820	Reuben Giddins
Turner, John P.	Matilda Hatfield	Jan. 24, 1841	
Turner, Sudith D.	Sally Franklin		

V

Vance, John	Mary Wilson	Mar. 4, 1813	Mathew Spurlock
Vance, Richard	Mary Seins	Mar. 25, 1818	Mathew Spurlock
Vanderpool, John M.	Nancy Hoskins	Aug. 20, 1841	
Van Hoose, Bracken	Polly Pelfrey	July 29, 1841	
Van Hoose, James	Betty Preston	Sept. 25, 1811	Thos. C. Brown
Van Hoose, Jesse	Mary Brown	Nov. 16, 1826	
Van Hoose, John	Lydia Lewis	Mar. 24, 1813	B. Lewis
Van Hoose, Thomas	Elizabeth Damron	Jan. 4, 1832	
Van Hoose, Valentine	Leasy Price	June 11, 1840	
Varney, Alexander	Susanna Runyan	Oct. 17, 1819	R. Giddins
Varney, Andrew	Sally Stafford	May 9, 1820	
Vaughan, Burwell	Susannah Hendricks	June 29, 1823	
Vaughan, Leroy	Amanda Riddle Mills	Dec. 26, 1829	

Groom	Bride	Date of Marriage	By Whom
Vaughan, Patrick	Susannah Hatfield	Aug. 22, 1819	R. Giddens
Venters, Jesse	Laura Baker	July 26, 1813	Spencer Adkins

W

Groom	Bride	Date of Marriage	By Whom
Waddle, (Wadell) Wm.	Lydia Collier	Mar. 9, 1809	Simeon Justice
Wadkins, Benedict, Jr.	Elizabeth Pew (Pugh)	Feb. 27, 1841	....
Wadkins, James	Peggy Fraley	May 9, 1831	....
Wadkins, Joseph	Sally Cameron	June 18, 1827	....
Wadkins, Thomas, Jr.	Lucinda Howard	May 12, 1834	....
Wadkins, William	Elizabeth Wadkins	Mar. 5, 1827	....
Wadkins, William	Margaret Brown	Aug. 1, 1835	....
Waldeck, John	Clarinda Dorset	Nov. 10, 1832	....
Waldeck, John	Mary Ann Bolton	Dec. 6, 1839	....
Waldeck, Nicholas C.	Marie Dunlap	Dec. 30, 1841	....
Waldeck, Nicholas C.	Pamelia W. Vest	July 3, 1836	....
Walker, Delaware	Ann House (Howes)	Apr. 25, 1833	....
Walker, John W.	Elizabeth Hackworth	Jan. 29, 1835	....
Walker, Robert	Elizabeth Douglas	Apr. 25, 1820	Wm. J. Mayo
Wallace, James H.	Marie E. Given	June 10, 1818	Wm. J. Mayo
Waller, Jacob	Catherine Porter	Dec. 25, 1823	....
Waller, Jesse	Polly Priest	Feb. 1, 1818	Wm. J. Mayo
Waller, Nathan	Nancy George	Sept. 1, 1814	R. Haws
Walters, Calvin	Judith Ward	May 13, 1830	....
Walters, William	Elizabeth Woods	June 13, 1830	Joseph Farrow
Ward, Hezekiah	Elizabeth Bowen	Nov. 13, 1822	....
Ward, Hiram	Polly Johnson	Dec. 3, 1830	....
Ward, James	Lucinda Meek	Apr. 13, 1820	Sam Hanna
Ward, James	Jane Wheeler	Jan. 31, 1839	....
Ward, Jesse	Mary Wheeler	July 30, 1837	....
Ward, Jonathan	Malinda Meek	Sept. 28, 1823	....
Ward, Solomon	Nancy Ann Kidd	June 22, 1828	....
Ward, William	Elizabeth Meek	Jan. 11, 1816	Sam Hanna
Ward, William	Elizabeth Hilton	Sept. 5, 1818	Samuel Hanna, M. G.
Ward, William	Lottie Howard	Nov. 14, 1822	....
Watkins, Ben	....	Aug. 10, 1818	Electius Thompson
Watson, Jonathan	Anna Clark	Mar. 4, 1824	....
Watson, Jonathan	Elizabeth Jarrell	May 26, 1842	....
Webb, Jackson	Mary Ann Picklesimer	Feb. 9, 1843	....
Webb, Jonathan	Elizabeth Porter	Oct. 3, 1826	....
Webb, William	Nancy Wells	Mar. 1, 1826	....
Webb, William	Frances Dixon	May 17, 1840	....
Wellman, Elisha	Patsy Chaffin	Oct. 28, 1808	Thomas Evans, J. P.
Wellman, Joseph	Nancy Chapman	Mar. 20, 1809	Thomas Evans
Wells, Benjamin	Elizabeth Perry	Jan. 24, 1822	William Coffee
Wells, David	Nancy Howerton	Oct. 24, 1822	....
Wells, George	Elizabeth Gaines	Sept. 29, 1831	....
Wells, Peter	Polly Porter	Apr. 4, 1833	....
Wells, William	Sally Prater	Oct. 24, 1827	....
Wheeler, Daniel	Elizabeth Hager	Nov. 22, 1840	....
Wheeler, James	Elizabeth Ramey	Mar. 13, 1817	Sam Hanna
Wheeler, Jesse	Susanna Nott	Jan. 13, 1840	....
Wheeler, John	Anna Ramey	Apr. 12, 1831	....
Wheeler, John	Mary Davis	Mar. 18, 1838	....

Groom	Bride	Date of Marriage	By Whom
Whitaker, James	L. Fletcher	Jan. 8, 1829	
Whitaker, Johnston	Susanna Howard	Feb. 27, 1824	
Whitt, John B.	Sally Oney	Oct. 2, 1833	
Whitt, Richard	Vicy Adkins	Oct. 23, 1812	Spencer Adkins, J. P.
Wilcox, James	Caroline Auxier	June 25, 1837	
Wiley, A. B.	Sally Stapleton	July 26, 1821	Thos. C. Brown
Wiley, Hezekiah	Lucretia Nelson	Aug. 13, 1815	Sam Hanna
Wiley, William	Nellie Dillion (Dillon)	Oct. 29, 1823	
Wiley, William	Sarah O'Bryan	July 18, 1830	
Wiley, William	Mary Dorton	May 4, 1835	
Williams, David	Cynthia Hanna	Nov. 4, 1819	William Coffee
Williams, Elijah	Elizabeth Prater	Mar. 12, 1829	
Williams, George	Polly Hall	July 26, 1832	
Williams, Hardin	Elizabeth Picklesimer	July 8, 1838	
Williams, Isaac	Betsy Lykins	Apr. 25, 1820	Daniel Williams
Williams, Isaac	Polly Meade	Aug. 2, 1842	
Williams, John	Phoebe Ferguson	Sept. 21, 1809	Daniel Williams
Williams, John	Martha Addington	June 4, 1812	Samuel Hanna
Williams, John	Nancy Maynor	Oct. 5, 1815	R. Haws
Williams, John	Eveline Yates	Aug. 10, 1836	
Williams, John	Christina Salyers	Oct. 28, 1841	
Williams, Lucas P.	Elizabeth Picklesimer		
Williams, Thornton	Jean Jones	Mar. 19, 1812	Daniel Williams
Williamson, Alden		Oct. 29, 1812	Basil Lewis
Williamson, R.		Oct. 11, 1810	Thos. C. Brown
Wilson, Andrew	Esther Husk	Feb. 12, 1819	Daniel Williams
Wilson, Andrew	Crecy Shepherd	Oct. 2, 1831	
Wilson, John	Nancy Mead	Apr. 28, 1824	
Wilson, Joseph	Polly Kash	Dec. 27, 1821	Charles Harper
Wilson, William	Rachael Hale	Apr. 2, 1822	John Morris
Wireman, Abraham	Sally Dean	Jan. 23, 1819	John Evans
Wireman, Jacob		Apr. 23, 1820	Stephen Harper, J. P.
Wireman, John		May 31, 1818	Stephen Harper
Witley, William	Sally Stratton	Mar. 27, 1811	Cornelius McGuyer
Witson, Samuel	D. Wilson	Feb. 7, 1830	
Witten, Jacob	Elizabeth Lester	Apr. 18, 1820	John Kenney, M. G.
Witten, Thomas	Polly Lackey	Oct. 1, 1820	Simeon Justice
Witten, William	Lockey Hackworth	Oct. 24, 1819	James Honaker
Wolf, Daniel	Joanna Bence	Nov. 18, 1808	Thomas Evans
Woolen, (Wooten) Silas G.	Sarah Adams	July 4, 1821	Lewis Wellman
Wooten, George W.	Polly Bannister	Mar. 21, 1820	Sam Hanna
Wooten, Levi	Alpha Taylor	Aug. 14, 1820	Reuben Giddens
Wooten, W. S.		July 27, 1817	Samuel Demeset
Wright, George	Pricilla McGuyer	Sept. 26, 1811	Cornelius McGuyer
Wright, Isaac	Delila Moore	Feb. 2, 1836	
Wright, James	Anna Hilton	Feb. 13, 1840	
Wright, Lewis	Edy Flannery	Sept. 12, 1832	
Wright, Solomon	Betsy Yates	July 3, 1826	

Y

Groom	Bride	Date of Marriage	By Whom
Young, Charles	Peggy McBrown	Nov. 14, 1813	Hiram Stratton
Young, Chas. W., Jr.	Levina Hilton	May 11, 1834	
Young, David	Eliza Davis	June 18, 1834	
Young, Hiram		Feb. 1, 1821	Daniel Duff

Groom	Bride	Date of Marriage	By Whom
Young, Jesse	Nancy McCoun	June 21, 1838	....
Young, John	Polly Castle	Jan. 8, 1824	....
Young, William	Sally Nex	Apr. 27, 1816	Sam Hanna
Young, William	Nuhanny Stapleton	Dec. 25, 1832	....
Young, William	Cynthia Brown	Feb. 9, 1836	....

CHAPTER III

KNOX COUNTY, KENTUCKY

BOUNDARY AND ESTABLISHMENT

KNOX COUNTY, the 41st formed in the State, was carved out of Lincoln County, pursuant to an act of the General Assembly, approved December 19, 1799 (2 *Littell's Laws of Kentucky*, 298-9) which act is in part as follows:

Section 1. That from and after the first Monday in June, next, all that part of the County of Lincoln, included in the following bounds, to-wit: Beginning where the Pulaski line strikes the Tennessee line, and with said Tennessee line east to the top of the Cumberland mountain: thence along the said mountain to the line of Madison County, and with the same to a point due east of the mouth of the branch of the Kentucky River that the wilderness road goes down; thence up the said branch to the said road; thence with the said road to the aforesaid Madison line, and with the same to the head of Rockcastle River, and down the said river to the Pulaski line, and with the Pulaski line to the beginning, shall be one distinct county, and called and known by the name of Knox. A court for the said county shall be held by the justices thereof on the fourth Monday in each month in which the court of quarter sessions are not hereafter directed to be held.

Section 2. The justices to be named in the commission of the peace for the said county of Knox shall meet at the house of John Logan, in the said county, on the first court day after the said division shall take place; and having taken the oaths prescribed by law, and a sheriff being legally qualified to act, the justices shall proceed to appoint and qualify a clerk, and fix on a place for holding courts in the said county, at or near the centre thereof as the situation and convenience will admit; and thenceforth the said courts shall proceed to erect the necessary public buildings at such place; and until such buildings be completed to appoint such place for holding courts as they shall think proper***** Each court shall appoint its own clerk, a majority of such court concurring therein; but a majority of those present on any court day may appoint a clerk pro tempore.

Section 3. And be it further enacted, That a court of quarter sessions for the said county of Knox shall be held, annually, in the months of March, May, August and November.

Parts of the territory as originally formed have been taken in forming each of the counties of Clay in 1806, Rockcastle in 1810, Whitley in 1818, Harlan in 1819, Laurel in 1825 and Josh Bell in 1867.

The county was named in honor of General Henry Knox, born in Boston, July 25, 1750, who early in life was a bookseller. At the age of 18 he was chosen one of the officers of a company of grenadiers and evinced a fondness for the military profession. He was a veteran at Bunker Hill and afterwards was entrusted with command of the artillery department with rank of brigadier general. In the battles of Trenton, Princeton, Germantown and Monmouth he displayed peculiar skill and bravery and subsequently contributed greatly to the surrender of Cornwallis. He was promoted to major general and was one of the commission to adjust terms of peace.

General Knox was commander at West Point; and served as Secretary of War, 1785-1794. He died at his seat in Thomason, Maine, October 25, 1806, at the age of 56.

EARLIEST COURT ORDERS OF RECORD

County Court Order Book "A"

At the house of John Logan, Junr., on the 23rd day of June one thousand eight hundred and inst., the ninth year of this Commonwealth, it being the place appointed by an act of the General Assembly of Kentucky for holding the first court for Knox County.

A commission of the peace from his Excellency James Garrard, Esqr., Governor of Kentucky, directed to James Mahan, George Brittain, John Reddick, John Ballinger, and Jonathan McNeil, Gentlemen, Esquires, was produced, read and thereupon pursuant to the said commissions James Mahan, Gentleman, administered the oaths of office and of fidelity to George Brittain, John Reddick, John Ballinger and Jonathan McNeil, Esquires, and then John Ballinger, Esquire, administered the oaths of office and of fidelity to James Mahan, Esquire.

Alexander Goodwin produced a commission from his Excellency James Garrard, Esquire, Governor of Kentucky, bearing date December the 21st., 1799, appointing him sheriff of Knox County, which said commission was read and thereupon the said Alexander Goodwin took the oaths of office as the law directs.

Alexander Goodwin, sheriff, * * * together (with) John Ballinger and James Mahan as his sureties entered into and acknowledged their bonds payable to the Governor in the penalty as the law directs. The sheriff then opened the first court for Knox County in the name of the Commonwealth.

The court being thus constituted they proceeded to elect a clerk and Richard Ballinger was appointed clerk, protem; whereupon he took the oaths of office prescribed by law and he together with George Brittain and John Ballinger, Esquires, his securities (sureties) acknowledged their bonds unto the Governor in the penalty as the law directs.

John Campbell produced a license from Caleb Wallace and George Muter, Judges of the Court of Appeals, permitting him to practice as an attorney-at-law in any court of this Commonwealth which (license) was read and thereupon the said John Campbell, Gentleman, took the oath of office as the law directs.

Ordered that the county be laid off in four constable districts, Viz: All that part of the county above Brownings Creek shall be considered as one district and known by the name of Number One. All that part below Brownings Creek and above Richland Creek shall be called Number Two. Between Richland (and) Laurel, Number Three, (and) the balance of said county, Number Four.

Ordered that John Allsap be appointed constable in the second district, John Allsap having taken the oaths of office agreeable to law, as constable, and he together with John and Richard Ballinger his securities (sureties) acknowledged their bonds to the Governor in the penalty of two hundred dollars as the law directs.

Ordered that Isaac Curnstalk be appointed constable in the third district. Isaac Curnstalk having taken the oath of office agreeable to law, as constable, and he together with Leonard C. Shoemaker and David Duese (De Weese), his secureties (sureties), acknowledged their bonds to the Governor in the penalty of two hundred dollars as the law directs.

Ordered that court doth adjourn till tomorrow 9 o'clock at this place.

(Signed) James Mahan.

* * *

At a court continued and held for Knox County at the house of John Logan, Junr., on the 21st day of June 1800:

James Mahan, George Brittain, John Reddick, John Ballinger and Jonathan McNeil, Gentlemen, Esquires, present.

John Ballinger produced a commission from his Excellency James Garrard, Esquire, Governor of this Commonwealth, appointing him surveyor of said county, it being read in court; whereupon the said John Ballinger took the oaths of office prescribed by law and he together with Richard Ballinger, Senr., and James Barbour, Senr., his securities (sureties), acknowledged their bonds to the Governor in the penalty as the law directs.

Ordered that James Mahan, George Brittain and Jonathan McNeil be appointed and licensed by this court to solemnize the rights (sic) of matrimony in the county. James Mahan took the oaths of office and together with Joel Collins, his surety (surety) acknowledged their bonds to the Governor in the penalty as the law directs. George Brittain took the oath of office and he together with John Ballinger, his security (surety), acknowledged their bonds to the Governor in the penalty as the law directs. Jonathan McNeil took the oaths of office and he together with Nimrod Farris, his security (surety) acknowledged their bonds to the Governor in the penalty as the law directs.

Ordered that Joel Collins, Alexander Goodwin and Nimrod Farris be appointed processioners in and for this county. Joel Collins, Alexander Goodwin and Nimrod Farris took the oaths of office proscribed (prescribed) by law.

Ordered that no man in this county be allowed to mark their (his) stock with a half crop in the right ear and a swallow fork in the left except Jonathan McNeil, Esquire.

Ordered that no man in this county be allowed to mark their (his) stock with a swallow fork in the right ear and a half crop in the left except John Reddick, Esquire.

Ordered that fixing the seat of justice be postponed till next court.

Ordered that court doth adjourn till court in course at this place.

(Signed) James Mahan.

PIONEER FAMILIES

There were approximately 912 families living in Knox County in 1810, as shown by original tax lists and other public records. Peter Engle, assistant to Joseph Crockett, United States Marshal for the District of Kentucky, enumerated the third decennial census and on December 23, 1810, he certified and reported an enumeration aggregating 5,875. Of this number 2,867 were white males, 2,661 white females, 307 negro slaves and 40 free colored. Below are given the heads of families and/or taxpayers as of the year 1810 together with the number of negro slaves owned by each slaveholder.

A

Alsop, John
Allen, Nisbat
(Nesbit)
Adams, Daniel
Anderson, Daniel
Arnett, David
Arnett, Reuben
Anderson, William
(2 slaves)
Allison, Hugh
(1 slave)
Adams, John
Adams, Randolph
(6 slaves)
Alexander, Thomas
Adkins, Joshua
Alsop, James
Adams, Sincks ?
Arthur, Elias
Arthur, John
Arthur, John
Allen, John
Allen, John
Arnett, Elijah
Arthur, Joseph
Arnett, Stephen
Ackman, John

Arthur, Samuel
Adams, John
Arthur, Thomas
(1 slave)
Arthur, Thomas
(4 slaves)
Adkins, Thomas

B

Bishop, Malin
Bodkin, Richard
Bowtau, Margaret
Borden, Christopher
Brock, James
Brock, Jesse
Ballow, Richard
Baker, Brice
Barton, William
Bledsoe, Elizabeth
Ballenger, Richard
(12 slaves)
Bain ? , Robert
Box, Samuel
Blevins, Daniel
Bray, Peter
Bailey, Mary
(14 slaves)
Beard, William

Brische, William
Berry, John
Burkheart, George
Beams, James
Bailey, Ezekiel
Benge, David
Bennett, John
Burns, James
Baker, Joseph
(2 slaves)
Bruster, James
Blakely, Charles
Brummet, William
Butler, James
Booker, Abraham
Brittain, George
(10 slaves)
Brown, John
Burns, Isaac
Bennett, Solomon
Bracket, John
Boyd, Robert
Blake, Rebecca
Black, John
Bryant, Peter
Belcher, James
Bunch, James
Brock, George
Brock, Aaron

Burk, John
Brittain, Lucy ?
Bryant, William
Brown, Lewis
Brumment, James
Barber, John
Brown, George
Bryant, John
Bull, Isaiah
  (2 slaves)
Baswell, Harrison
Blanton, William
Blakely, Curtis
Barton, Susan
Brische, John
Burk, Elihue
Ballow, Mary
Blake, Archiblad
Bunch, Solomon
Breadlove, John
Bunch, George
Blakely, Robert
Begley, Thomas
Baker, William
  (1 slave)
Bryant, James
Ballenger, Edward
Blair, Charles
Black, David ?
Bailey, Lewis
Brummett, Reese
Brown, John
Brown, Joshua
Brewster, Zadoc
Baughman, John
Burnett, Nicholas
Bishop, William
Bryant, William
Bull, John, Sr.
Bull, James
Bryant, Allen
Brummett, James
Bull, John
Blanton, John
Bailey, James

C

Chestnut, John
Callums (M'Collum), John
Culton, John
Cain, Peter, Jr.
Cox, John
Carson, James
Cooper, Sherod
Cox, Jesse
Cathers, Edward
  (6 slaves)
Cautrill, James
Cox, William

Coddell (Caudill), James
Cumstalk, Joseph
Cox, Stephen
Cantrill, Joseph
Collins, David, Sr.
Campbell, David
Cumstalk, William
Craig, Andrew
Curtis, Samuel
Cox, Thomas
Cox, Christopher
Chick, James
Coulson, James
  (1 slave)
Cox, Frederick
Cox, Nathan, Jr.
Cope, Andrew
Chestnut, Abraham
Coffee, John
Coulson, John
  (4 slaves)
Cox, Nathan
Cummings, William
Conn, Benjamin
Cox, David
Craig, George W.
  (2 slaves)
Cole, John
Craig, William
Chestnut, Benjamin
Cox, Amos
Cox, Nathan
Cantrell, Charles
Creekmore, Ballentine
Cockerham, William
Culton, Joseph
Comer, Mary
Carter, Isaac
Chumley, John
Cumstalk, Elizabeth
Campbell, William, Jr.
Catchen, Benjamin
Collins, David
Chandler, Shadrack
Cantrill, William
Colby, Daniel
Chester, William
Campbell, James
Cox, William
Curtis, Nathan
Cumstalk, Isaac
Campbell, William
Craig, David
Campbell, William, Sr.
Catcher ? , John
Coldiron, Conrad
Cain, Peter
Cobbs, Ambrose
Cantrell, John
Cox, Samuel

Cox, Amos
Collins, Isiah
Cook, William ——
Cain, Daniel
Cox, John, Sr.
Cox, John
Cottrell, John
Chestnut, Samuel
Campbell, John
Cutberth, Benjamin
Cummings, Hugh
Cox, Joseph
Callums, Daniel
Collins, Aaron
Cox, Solomon
Campbell, James
Craig, Robert, Jr.
  (6 slaves)
Cummings, John
Campbell, Arthur

D

Dangherty, Joseph
Davenport, Zachariah
Daniel, Robert
Daniel, Spencer
Davis, William
Dunlap, Morning
Davis, Abner
Dudley, James
Davis, Richard
  (2 slaves)
Duncan, Lawrence ——
Davidson, Alexander
Drace, Daniel
Davis, William
Dean, John
Davis, James, Sr.
Duncan, John ——
Daniel, John
Dorton, Moses
  (11 slaves)
Dugger, James
Dancy ? , John
Duncan, John ——
  (2 slaves)
Daniel, James
Davis, John
Davis, John
Davis, Jonathan
De priest, Robert
Durbin, Christopher
Dickens, Thomas
Dobson, Elinor
Davis, James
Davis, William, Jr.
Dickson, ...
Dunahoe, Michael
Dean, Isaac

Davis, Zachariah
Dickson, John
Davis, Isaac
Durham, John
Dowes (Dawes), Jesse
De Weese, David
Dugger, William
Day, John
Davis, Jesse

E

Ely, Anthony
Ely, William, Jr.
England, Thomas
Engle, John
Elliott, Sally
Engle, George
Evans, William
Evans, Andrew
  (1 slave)
Ely, William, Sr.
Early, Joseph
Early, Thomas
Elliott, Elizabeth
Ellison, Asa
Engle, Peter
Eaton, John
Elliott, Aschel
Evans, John
Edwards, William
Evans, Archibald
Eubanks, James
Evans, William, Sr.
Early, William
  (1 slave)

F

Forrister, John
Foley, Thomas
Fulks, Elizabeth
Farris, George
Fowler, Jesse
Fletcher, John
Foley, Spencer
Franklin, Samuel
Fletcher, John
Farris, Isom
Flecher, Ambrose
Fields, Lansford
Farmer, Stephen
Fields, Patsy
Finley, James
  (3 slaves)
Freeman, John
  (4 slaves)
Ferguson, Thomas
Fulks, Gabriel
Ferguson, Andrew

Falkner, Francis
  (1 slave)
Foley, Elijah
Fox, Benjamin
Falkner, James
Farris, John
Fletcher, William
Fowler, Isaac
Farris, Paul
Ford, Rebecca
Farris, John, Sr.
Freeman, Aaron
Fletcher, Verdiman

G

Gillis, Joseph, Sr.
Gibson, Garret
Gatliff, Moses
Goin, Isiah
  (2 slaves)
Gatliff, Aaron
Graham, Thomas
  (3 slaves)
Green, Elijah
Gaston, Hugh
Gibson, Valentine
Gibson, John
Garner, Thomas
Goldin, Stephen
Gibson, William
Goodin, Alexander
Goodin, Thomas
Grindstaff, Michael
Gerton, Elijah
Grimes, Robert
Githens, Edward
  (1 slave)
Goodin, John
Gatliff, James
Gerton, Elijah
Gillis, Joseph
Goodin, Joseph
Gregory, William
Griffin, Zachariah
Gatliff, Charles
  (10 slaves)
Gregory, Thomas
Green ? , George
Gibson, Isaac
Grubb, Christopher
Gardener, David
Green, Lewis
Goodin, Alexander
Gregory, Beverly
Goodin, Hezekiah
Goodin, Thomas
Gibson, Barnabas
Golden, Edmond
Gibson, James
Gibson, James

H

Hart, John
Hall, Kinchan
Hyden, Richard
Harmon, Jacob
Heatherley, John
Hendrickson, John
Hunter, Robert
Helms, John
Hall, James
Harrison, John
Hopper, William
Holcomb, Solomon
Hammons, Isaac
Horn, Edward
Helton (Hilton),
  John
Huffs, Joseph
Howard, John
Howard, James
Harris, Benjamin
Hackler, Rose
Hancock, Thomas
Hatfield, Stanley
Hamlin, Dant
Henderson, Edward
Howard, James
Harris, Thomas
Hill, John
Hays, Willis
Harris, John
Hoskins, Thomas
Hammer, George
Holmes, William
Howard, Andrew
Herndon, Henry
  (3 slaves)
Helton, Arthur
Hamlin, John
Hogan, Texriah ?
Helems, James
Hannah, Frederick
Hurd, James
Hamlin, George
Hays, Jonathan
Hoskins, John
Hambleton, Samuel
Hogan, William
Helms, Jonathan
Harp, Tobias
Hays, Jane
Hendricks, Margaret
Hunter, Francis
Hodges, James
Helton, Shadruck
Helton, James
Helton, Peter
Howard, Julius
Howard, Benjamin
Hibbard, Samuel

Hatfield, Reuben
Holt, Dozwell
Holt, Drury
(1 slave)
Herndon, John
Horn, Christopher
Hoskins, George
(1 slave)
Hall, Anthony
Hammons, Obidah
Holman, John
Holder, Alston
Henderickson, Joshua
Howard, Adrian
Herndon, Richardson
(5 slaves)
Hart, James
Hogan, David
(2 slaves)
Hibbard, Lemuel
Hoskins, Reuben
Heaton, John
Hind, John
Hall, William
Howard, William
Heaton, James
Hines, Joseph
Hays, Joshua
Hodgson, David
Hogan, William
(17 slaves)
Hales, James
Howard, Thomas
Hoskins, Ninian
Hurd, William
Hays, Joshua

I

Inman, Elisha, Sr.
Ingram, Ebenezer
Inman, Thomas
Inman, Elisha, Jr.
Ingram, William

J

Johnson, John
Johnson, Joseph
Johnson, Thomas
(18 slaves)
Jimerson, Samuel
Jones, William
Jackson, Garnet
Johnson, James
Johnson, Aaron
Jones, James
Jones, Robert
Jones, Edmund
Jones, William
Jones, Elijah

Jones, John
Jackson, Gabirel
Johnson, David
Johnson, William
Jarvis, Peter
Jacoway, Archibald
Johnson, Thomas
(1 slave)
Jackson, John
(7 slaves)
Johnson, Thomas
Johnson, Michael
Jones, Stephen
Jones, John
Johnson, William
Johnson, Daniel
Jones, James
Jackson, James
Jones, Thomas
Johnson, Robert
Johnson, David

K

Keewood, Berry
Kidd, Milly
Kelly, Matthias
Kelly, Jonathan
Kitchen, John
King, Hillman
(1 slave)
King, John
King, Ezekiel
(3 slaves)
King, Isaac
King, Zachariah
Kunce (Kountz), George
Kirk, Garret
King, Wilsmon
King, Polly
(1 slave)
King, Thomas
King, Spencer
(1 slave)
Kidd, Elias
(1 slave)

L

Lay (Leigh), Jesse
Lawson, David
Lackey, Joel
Long, William
Logan, William
Laws, John
Lytton, Solomon
Leebow, Daniel
Leebow, Isaac
Layne, Samuel
Ledington, Ephraim
Laughlin, John

Lay, Jesse
Love, James
Laws, Thomas
Lewis, Abner
Layne, William
(4 slaves)
Lambert, Hugh
Lytton, Burton
Laughlin, Thomas
(1 slave)
Lock, Abraham
Logan, John
(1 slave)
Law ? , Holman
Laughlin, John
Lawson, Nathan
Logan, James
Lay, Joel
Lewis, John
Litterrell, Thomas
Logan, William, Jr.
Lovitt, Edward
Lee, Andrew

M

McFarland, George
McCormack, Thomas
McFadden, Jesse
McKey, Matthias W.
McKey, Elias
Mitchell, Alexander
Moore, Samuel
Mitchell, Mordacei
Meadows, Thomas
Mayfield, John
Miller, Robert
McBride, John
McKey, William
McHargue, William
(2 slaves)
Messer, John
Moses, Joshua
Meadows, Thomas, Jr.
Myers, John
Morris, George
McFarland, Duncan
McMahan, Abraham
McHargue, Agnes
McKee, John
McQuown, John
Morgan, James
Mason, Robert
Morgan, William
Meadows, Ison
Moore, John
(1 slave)
McKey, Benjamin
McHolland, David
McKee, Matthew
McWhorter, Robert

McNeill, Jonathan
Mahan, James
Mason, James
Meadows, Isaiah
Martin, William C.
Miller, Martin
Massie, Joseph
Miller, George
(1 slave)
Muncy, Joshua
Massie, Thomas
Moore, Ephraim
(1 slave)
Messer, Jacob
Miller, Joshua
Moore, James
Moses, John
Matthews, James
Mead, Absolom
Marshall, Thomas
Moody, James
Maggard, Samuel
Moore, Jesse
(3 slaves)
Marlow, Thomas
Muncy, John, Sr.
Mulkey, Philip
Mills, Sally
Murphy, John
Matthews, William
Minton, Isaac
Martin, Jesse
Meadows, Edward
Muncy, John
Martin, Isaac
Moore, Jesse
Miller, William
Moran, John
Mullens, William
Mahan, Thomas
Miller, David
Murphy, Sally
Mays, William
(11 slaves)
Mullins, John
Moore, Levi
Moore, Moses
Miller, Jane
Moore, Thomas
Martin, Zadock
Miller, Daniel
(3 slaves)

N

Neill, John
Nicholson, Thomas
Newland, John
Newton, Isaac
North, John
Noe, John

Neill, Arthur
(2 slaves)
Newton, William
Newton, William

O

Osborn, Jesse
Onstatt ? , John
Oliver, Wilson
Owens, Matthew
Osborn, Ephraim
O'Bear, Constan
Oliver, John
Osborn, Peggy
Owens, Moses
Osborn, Solomon
Osborn, Nathan

P

Parsons, Jesse
Parrot, Armstead
Prewitt, David
Patterson, William
(5 slaves)
Pennington, James
Prewitt, Samuel
Prewitt, Stephen
Payne, Elisha
Piercifield, Joseph
Payne, Joseph
(1 slave)
Parsons, Robert
Phillips, John
Prewitt, David
Prewitt, John
Pierce, John
Potter, Thomas, Jr.
Potter, Thomas
Pennington, Abel
Pitman, Richard
(5 slaves)
Piercefield, Jeremiah
Patebridge, Richard
Parton, Shelton
Payne, William
Potter, John
Prewitt, William
Potter, Thomas
Permin, Giles
Potter, Richard
Parker, Charlotta
(1 slave)
Porter, William
Pitman, Thomas
(1 slave)
Potter, Uriah
Piercifield, John
Pemberton, William
Prewitt, Elijah
Perrigim, Jacob

Parton, Winston
Prichard, Thomas
(1 slave)
Pace, Jesse
Parton, Vincent
Peace, Joseph
(3 slaves)
Parsons, James
Potter, William

R

Ross, Thomas
Reynolds, Tarleton
Rains, Allen
Riley, Joseph
(2 slaves)
Reed, John
Riggs, Charles
Rains, Thomas
Rose, Samuel
Rains, John
(1 slave)
Reynolds, Daniel
Ross, Angus
Reed, Solomon
Reynolds, Thomas
Reese, John
Reed, Robert
Reed, Matthias
Ryan, Joseph
Rains, Henry
(4 slaves)
Reed, William
Ripley, Pleasant
Ruddick, Elisha
Ross, Samuel
Richmond, John
Rockhold, Charles
Robertson, Thomas
Rice, James
Reed, Samuel
Ross, Zachariah
Reynolds, John
Robertson, Thomas
Rice ? , William
Robertson, Nathaniel
(5 slaves)
Rainbolt, Michael
Rogers, James
Rodes, William
Rains, Jonathan
Rizener, Michael
Root, Daniel
(2 slaves)

S

Sheldis (Childress),
Jackson
Smith, Abraham

KNOX COUNTY, KENTUCKY

Steel, Samuel
Sears, John
(3 slaves)
Southerland, Philip
Slaughter, Elizabeth
Sto, Joel
Stewart, Joseph
Smith, Jonathan, Jr.
Smith, James
Segraves, Joseph
Stotts, James
Smith, Foster
Saylor, Joseph
Sims, Starling
Segraves, William
Stone, John
Salyers, Benjamin
Sneed, Charles
Smith, Brooks
Smith, John
Stephens, Joshua
Shull, John
Sexton, Jacob
Shackleford, Henry
Spencer, Jesse
Seego, James
Snyder, Simon
Saunders, Joseph
Stewart, Isaac
Shoemaker, Leonard C
Smith, James T.
Smith, Henry
Smith, James
(5 slaves)
Sears, William
Selby, Joseph
Stephenson, William
Stotts, Isaac
Sumpter, George
Smith, Josiah
Stewart, John
Stephens, Solomon
Sears, James
Shull, Frederick
Skidmore, John
Snyder, Peter
Sears, Jesse
Saunders, Henry, Jr.
Saunders, Henry, Sr.
Shull, Joseph
Stapleton, Joseph
Saylor, Solomon
Smith, Jonathan, Sr.
Steel, William
Spurlock, William
Smith, William
Stapleton, William
Shull, Philip
Stapleton, Thomas
Slone, Thomas
Stapleton, Edward

Stanfield, Sampson
Smith, Isaac
Shelly, Jane
(1 slave)
Shelton, John
Stephens, Gilbert
Sto, Robertson
Snyder, Frederick
Snyder, Jacob
Stephens, Lewis
Sutherland, George
Stewart, Alexander
Sullivan, James
Shoemaker, James
Sexton, Isaac
Stewart, James
Sibly, Thomas
Scott, Thomas
Smith, John
Shotwell, Daniel
Smith, John
Solomon, William
Slusher, Philip
Smith, Jeremiah
Siler, Joseph
Sutton, John
Stinson, Robert
Stephens, Moses
Smith, Nathaniel

T

Tye, George
Terrell, Solomon
Taylor, William
Trosper, James
Turner, William
(7 slaves)
Teague, David
Thomas, John
Tinsley, Thomas
Turner, Berry
Turner, George
Trosper, Elijah
Trosper, Nicholas
Tye, John
Turner, John
Teague, Nathaniel
Trosper, Nicholas
Thomas, Joseph
Turner, John, Sr.
Turpin, Obediah
Tudis, Sally
Tackett, Philip
Tye, Elizabeth
Tackett, William
Taylor, Stephen
Tuggle, Thomas
(6 slaves)
Trosper, Robert
Templeton, James

Turtle, John
Taylor, David
Tye, Joshua
Tinsley, William
Tipton, James
Teague, Joshua
Tackett, Lewis

V

Vannoy, Jonathan
Vannoy, William
(10 slaves)
Veach, Amos
Veach, Isaac

W

Woodson, Wade
Wilson, William
Wyatt, Thomas
Worley, Wiley
White, Hendrick
White, Richard
Wallen, Elisha
Wells, John
(2 slaves)
Walters, John
Whoten (Wooten),
William
Wees ? , Samuel
Walker, Evan
West, Joseph
Wyatt, Samuel
(7 slaves)
Wilson, Michael
Williams, Charles
Williams, Jacob
Wilder, William
Waters, Enoch
Wilhite, Matthew
Wells, Benjamin
Walker, John
Wilkerson, Thomas
Wilson, James
Woodson, Henry
Watson, Pearson
Wright, James
Whitaker, Joseph
Walters, Robert
Wilson, Richard
Whoten, Reuben
Watkins, Chapman
Walker, Renelder
White, John
Watson, Thomas
Waters, Ezekiel
Williams, Luke
Williams, Bat
Williams, Thomas
Wilson, Samuel

65

Wilder, Joseph
Wright, Richard
Wilhite, Ezekiel
Wilburn, Edward
Warfield, Rezin
(1 slave)
White, William
(3 slaves)
Wilder, Sampson
Warner, Moses
Wilson, Charles

Wazes ? , Benjamin
Williams, Richard
Williford, John
Watkins, Joel
(1 slave)
Wood, John
Whitson, Isaac
Wilson, David
Wollum, Andrew
Watkins, Luke
Williams, Alier ?

Wright, Rosanna
Wilder, Joab
Waters, John
Wilson, Joseph
Wells, Levi

Y

Yeager, Joseph
(1 slave)
Young, John
Young, John

MARRIAGES 1800—1819

Marriage Records of Knox County from its organization, June 1800, to 1819.

Groom	Bride	Date of Marriage	By Whom
A			
Arnett, Stephen	Elizabeth Howard	Jan. 13, 1803	Geo. Brittain, J. P.
Arthur, Joseph	Susannah Arthur	Dec. 9, 1803	Alex. Stewart
Arthur, Samuel	Hannah Jones	Mar. 8, 1804	Alex. Stewart
Alsop, John	Nancy Shoemaker	July 24, 1806	Elijah Foley
Alsop, James	Ann Stewart	Mar. 20, 1805	Alex. Stewart
Allen, Nesbit	Bellanna Maupin	Feb. 6, 1806	Alex. Stewart
Adams, Lujmord (?)	Rebecca Davis	Mar. 22, 1808	John McClure
Arthur, Ambrose	Jane Fletcher	Jan. 22, 1811	E. Foley
Arthur, John	Katy Dudley	Aug. 31, 1815	M. Foley
Arthur, Grace	Nancy Bailey	Sept. 14, 1815	R. Hopper
Anderson, Daniel	Rebecca Blakely	June 10, 1806	Jas. Sullivan
Adams, Lewis	Nancy Chestnut	June 4, 1807	Alex. Stewart
Anderson, John	Betsey Rogers	Nov. 28, 1811	Jas. Sullivan
Allison, Thomas	Rosanna Linder	Sept. 12, 1816	M. Foley
B			
Ball, Joseph	Phoebe Slaughter	Jan. 6, 1803	Alex. Stewart
Ballew, Joseph	Mary Davis	May 26, 1803	Alex. Stewart
Baker, William	Elizabeth Dean	Oct. 6, 1803	Alex. Stewart
Blakely, Curtis	Marian Wilson	Mar. 7, 1805	E. Foley
Barton, John	Elizabeth Engle	Feb. 20, 1806	E. Foley
Beaty, Martin	Betty Hogan	Dec. 24, 1815	Alex. Stewart
Bodkin, John	Emma Hale	Apr. 4, 1805	Alex. Stewart
Ballew, Richard	Sally Adams	Dec. 25, 1804	Alex. Stewart
Baker, Brice	Mary Arthur	Jan. 26, 1804	Alex. Stewart
Borden, George	Polly King	Apr. 9, 1807	James Sullivan
Brummet, Reese	Keziah Murphy	Mar. 17, 1808	E. Foley
Barton, William	Polly Roach	May 5, 1808	E. Foley
Ballew, Peter	Nancy Moody	July 21, 1808	E. Foley
Baugh, George	Anna White	Sept, 8, 1808	E. Foley
Brummett, Nicholas	Polly White	Aug. 21, 1808	John McClure
Bailey, Nimrod	Katy Moore	Sept. 29, 1809	E. Foley
Ballenger, Edward	Nancy Parker	Dec. 21, 1809	E. Foley

Groom	Bride	Date of Marriage	By Whom
Barnes, Abraham	Abagail Davis	Nov. 3, 1809	E. Foley
Bennett, Levi	Nancy Harrison	Dec. 1, 1809	E. Foley
Ballinger, Richard	Millie Herndon	June 21, 1810	E. Foley
Begley, John	Rebecca Stewart	Feb. 13, 1810	E. Foley
Bailey, Robert	Alcey Hendrickson	Nov. 27, 1810	Jas. McNeill, J. P.
Brummett, Banam	Eve Stephens	Feb. 7, 1811	E. Foley
Baugh, Drury	Betsey Lawson	Aug. 15, 1811	E. Foley
Brittain, Hezekiah	Peggy Helton	Feb. 20, 1811	Jas. Sullivan
Bryant, John	Elizabeth DeMoss	May 9, 1811	Jas. Sullivan
Brummett, Ezekiel	Sally Tip	Jan. 9, 1812	Thomas Wilson
Blanton, William	Susannah Brock	Aug. 18, 1811	Geo. Brittain
Brock, Amon	Molly Osborn	Sept. 26, 1811	Geo. Brittain
Bowers, Samuel	Isabel Bodkin	Feb. 15, 1816	Jas. Sullivan
Bingen, William	Sarah Green	Nov. 16, 1815	Danl. Duff
Beake, William	Sally Garland	Sept. 8, 1816	Jas. Sullivan
Bingham, William	Sally Green	Nov. 21, 1815	D. Duff
Burton, David	Jane Pitman	Feb. 7, 1818	Thos. Robinson
Black, Samuel	Betsey Mushon	Apr. 12, 1818	T. Robinson
Barton, Henry	Sally Barton	Sept. 30, 1819	M. Foley
Barnett, James	Betsey Benjey	July 21, 1819	
Bailey, Thomas	Fanny Wyatt	Oct. 2, 1814	B. Hopper
Barnett, James	Betsy Benjey	July 21, 18....	bond

C

Groom	Bride	Date of Marriage	By Whom
Cooper, John	Susannah Cumstock	May 7, 1801	Jas. Mahand, J. P.
Cummins, Hugh	Kezia Davis	Dec. 30, 1801	Jas. Mahan
Cumstoak, William	Mary Hampton	Sept. 24, 1805	Elijah Foley
Carter, Samuel	Rachel Wilkerson	Sept. 2, 1805	Elijah Foley
Cumstalk, Joseph	Mary Cullonan ?	Mar. 20, 1805	E. Foley
Craig, Andrew	Sophia Laughlin	Mar. 19, 1807	E. Foley
Cornelius, Elihu	Mary Heson	June 10, 1804	Alex. Stewart
Coursey, Lewis	Elizabeth Owens	Nov. 3, 1805	Alex. Stewart
Cox, John	Tobitha Contrell	June 25, 1807	Jas. Sullivan
Cain, Daniel	Tempy Cannery	Mar. 24, 1808	E. Foley
Cooper, Sherod	Lulu Wilkerson	Dec. 13, 1809	E. Foley
Cox, Nathan	Polly Cox	Feb. 11, 1809	E. Foley
Culton, John	Euphemie Stewart	Feb. 23, 1809	E. Foley
Cantrell, William	Lucretia Hays	Apr. 16, 1809	E. Foley
Cooley, Daniel	Agnes Chandler	Apr. 22, 1810	E. Foley
Cantrell, Joseph	Elizabeth Murphy	Feb. 8, 1810	E. Foley
Cox, Joseph	Rebecca Lancaster	July 23, 1812	E. Foley
Cox, Nathan	Lucy Perkins	July 21, 1812	Jas. Sullivan
Campbell, Alexander	Betsey Wilson	Sept. 3, 1812	Angus Ross
Carter, Solomon	Franky Johns	Aug. 20, 1811	E. Foley
Cox, William	Alsey St. John	Dec. 8, 1813	Angus Ross
Cutbirth, David	Mary Wilson	Feb. 14, 1813	Jas. Sullivan
Cathers, William	Susannah Sinney	Oct. ...., 1913	T. Robinson
Carr, William	Rebecca Johnson	July 14, 1814	Jas. Sullivan
Cottonwing ?, William	Farmetta Ashley	Feb. 23, 1814	M. Foley
Con, Jacob	Jane Gatliff	Sept. 28, 1814	M. Foley
Clark, William	Polly Arthur	Feb. 14, 1815	Jas. Sullivan
Cox, Joseph	Polly Rains	July 27, 1815	Jas. Sullivan
Carr, Samuel	Esther Johnson	Feb. 29, 1816	Jas. Sullivan
Cravens, Jesse	Louvena Slaughter	May 1, 1816	Jas. Sullivan
Cross, James	Prudence Messer	Mar. 10, 1816	R. Hopper
Cox, John	Rachel Cox	Nov. 24, 1809	E. Foley

Groom	Bride	Date of Marriage	By Whom

D

Groom	Bride	Date of Marriage	By Whom
Dugger, James	Peggy Rosson	June 1, 1809	E. Foley
Dowes, William	Rebecca Johns	May 3, 1809	E. Foley
Dean, John	Elizabeth Hunter	Sept. 17, 1810	E. Foley
Dobson, John	Priscilla Arthur	Jan. 3, 1811	Jas. McNeill, J. P.
Dugger, Mark	Jinsey Ross	Feb. 17, 1811	E. Foley
De Moss, John	Patsy Mayfield	Apr. 16, 1812	Jas. Sullivan
Dugger, Julius	Ann McHargue	Aug. 12, 1813	M. Foley
DeWeese, Jesse	Jane Wood	...., 1813	T. Robinson
Dean, John, Jr.	Betsy Gregory	...., 1811	....
Dean, Abraham	Charity Gregory	Dec. 2, 1813	B. Hopper
Davis, Joseph	Polly Hall	Sept. 2, 1814	B. Hopper
DeMoss, John	Nancy Cravens	Mar. 7, 1809	Jas. Sullivan
Davis, James	Anna Dover	May 26, 1814	M. Foley
Davis, John	Polly Curtis	Sept. 28, 1814	M. Foley
Daniel, Abraham	Jennie Sneed	Nov. 30, 1815	M. Foley
Duncan, John L.	Jemima Sullivan	July 1, 1817	R. Browning
Dizney, Elijah	Sarah Miller	Oct. 21, 1819	M. Foley
Doan, Stephen S.	Eliza Jane Hurst	Apr. 5, 1835?	W. S. Doak
Daimony, John	Delilah Johnson	Dec. 20, 1802	Alex. Stewart
Daniel, Robert	Rebecca Cox	June 20, 1808	E. Foley
Doan, Stephen S.	Eliza Jane Hurst	Apr. 5, ...	Wm. Hopper

E

Groom	Bride	Date of Marriage	By Whom
Ellison, Thomas	Olive Cox	July 27, 1806	Elijah Foley
Engle, John	Polly Campbell	Oct. 30, 1806	E. Foley
Elliott, Thomas	Elizabeth Reese	July 26, 1807	E. Foley
Ertis, Smith	Katy Cunningham	Jan. 8, 1807	Jas. Sullivan
Edwards ?, William	Elizabeth Stinson	Mar. 23, 1808	John McCleese
Ely, William	Rebecca Saylor	Aug. 18, 1809	Geo. Brittain
Ellison, Jesse	Mariam Foley	Mar. 29, 1810	E. Foley
Elliott, Henry	Letitia Reese	...., 1810	Jas. Sullivan
Engle, George	Ibby Hodgson	July 25, 1811	E. Foley
Evans, Ambrose	Betsy Golden	Dec. 23, 1810	Jas. Sullivan
Early, William	Priscella Stinson	Dec. 30, 1813	M. Foley
Engle, Jacob	Rachel Vale	Mar. 18, 1814	M. Foley
Edwards, Wight	Patsy Martin	Jan. 12, 1815	Jas. Sullivan
Elliott, Michael	Peggy Reese	Sept. 5, 1815	Jas. Sullivan
Elliott, Francis	Sarah Gray	Aug. 25, 1815	M. Foley
Eaton, Benjamin	Sally Grubb	Feb. 25, 1816	Jas. Sullivan
Engle, Peter	Mildred Click	June 22, 1823	B. Hopper

F

Groom	Bride	Date of Marriage	By Whom
Farris, George	Martha McNeal	Jan. 27, 1903	Alex. Stewart
Farris, Hezekiah	Eliza Smith	Dec. 10, 1805	E. Foley
Farris, Paul	Patsey Howard	Mar. 7, 1805	Alex. Stewart
Farris, Isom	Elizabeth Yancy	Jan. 9, 1806	Alex. Stewart
Faulkner, Joncer	Letitia Ham	Oct. 23, 1811	E. Foley
Farris, Joseph J.	Betsy Parker	Oct. 25, 1811	James Sullivan
Farris, Joseph	Sarah McWhorter	Mar. 24, 1812	M. Foley
Flannigan, John B.	Charlotte Smith	Oct. 9, 1811	Jas. H. Campbell J.P.
Farris, James	Sally McFarland	Oct. 12, ...	....
Fowler, Thomas	Polly Fowler	Nov. 9, 1815	M. Foley
Farris, Isom	Monah Cottrell	Nov. 30, 1815	M. Foley
Ferguson, Andrew	Betsy Green	Nov. 4, 1815	T. Robinson
Faulkner, John	Kizzie Richards	Oct. 17, 1816	B. Hopper
Ferguson, Andrew	Margaret Craig	Oct. 28, 1803	A. Stewart

Groom	Bride	Date of Marriage	By Whom

G

Goodwin, John	Sally Arthur	Nov. 29, 1801	Alex. Stewart
Gatliff, Moses	Mary Walker	Sept. 5, 1803	Alex. Stewart
Gatliff, Aaron	Betsy Cravens	Mar. 8, 1805	E. Foley
Grimes, Robert	Nancy Chessler	Jan. 15, 1807	E. Foley
Gourley, John	Jemima Carter	Jan. 12, 1806	Alex. Stewart
Grindstaff, Henry	Nancy Goodin	May 5, 1807	Alex. Stewart
Goodin, Thomas, Sr.	Mary Ingram	Sept. 4, 1804	A. Stewart
Gilbert, John	Mary Bowlin	Sept. 11, 1804	A. Stewart
Golden, Edmund	Polly Charles	Jan. 8, 1810	E. Foley
Goodin, Joseph	Ellender Cox ✓	Apr. 6, 1809	E. Foley
Graham, William	Susanna Begley	Jan. 25, 1810	E. Foley
Gillis, Joseph	Elizabeth Craig	May 24, 1810	J. Sullivan
Gherton, James	Betsy Lows	Feb. 13, 1812	J. Sullivan
Gray, James	Sarah Davis	Aug. 11, 1813	J. Sullivan
Green, Elisha	Nancy Bingham	June ...., 1813	G. Brittain
Gilreath, Benjamin	Nancy Moore	Mar. 27, 1810	A. Ross
Gregory, Robert	Millie Arthur	June 2, 1814	B. Hopper
Gherton, Elijah	Sally Duncan ✓	Dec. 15, 1808	J. Sullivan
Gatliff, Charles	Rachel Cummins	June 19, 1809	J. Sullivan
Gibson, Lewis	Priscilla Wilson ✓	Feb. 10, 1814	M. Foley
Gamstutter, Peter	Nancy Hudgins	May 7, 1816	B. Hopper
Green, Thomas	Susan Pitman	Feb. 7, 1818	Thos. Robinson
Gheeton, Robert	Betsy Swift	Nov. 21, 1815	R. Browning
Grinstoff, Drury	Hannah Cooke	Oct. 10, 1819	James Sear
Garrard, James	Betsy Williford	Aug. 24, 1816	D. Duff

H

Herndon, Richardson	Nancy Hogan	May 5, 1801	Alex. Stewart
Hensley, Lewis	Nancy Hoard	Sept. 1, 1803	Geo. Brittain, J. P.
Hignite, Moses	Phoebe Hammond	Nov. 11, 1802	A. Stewart
Hight, Joseph	Sally Pratt	Aug. 30, 1805	J. Sullivan
Hatfield, Reuben	Mary Cumstalk	Mar. 27, 1806	E. Foley
Holman, John	Polly Farris	Jan. 21, 1808	E. Foley
Hodge, James	Mary Fugman	Dec. 14, 1806	A. Stewart
Hogan, David	Betsy Dortan	Apr. 15, 1806	A. Stewart
Hay, Aaron	Sarah Kinkead	Apr. 20, 1806	A. Stewart
Huddleston, David	Effie Green	Jan. 8, 1806	A. Stewart
Hebbert, Samuel	Nancy Barber	Mar. 9, 1806	A. Stewart
Hammer, Frederick	Abagail Sellars	Oct. 28, 1807	E. Foley
Hatfield Stanley	Anna Crumstalk	Aug. 16, 1808	E. Foley
Hammonds, Peter	Patsy Hale	Sept. 10, 1809	E. Foley
Hilton, Shadrack	Polly Brock	May 24, 1809	G. Brittain
Helms, William	Susannah Blakely	Sept. 30, 1810	E. Foley
Harp, Benjamin	Jane Moody	July 12, 1810	E. Foley
Hilton, Arthur	Susannah Lawson	Feb. 20, 1810	E. Foley
Hays, Joshua	Lydia Shull	July 15, 1810	J. Sullivan
Howard, Elbert	Phoebe McNeil	Oct. 24, 1811	J. Sullivan
Huff, William	Sarah Joseph	Nov. 20, 1808	G. Brittain
Hales, Hugh	Peggy Higgins	Dec. 10, 1812	M. Foley
Hammer, John	Hannah Deevers	Mar. 5, 1812	E. Foley
Holder, James	Susannah Helton	June 10, 1813	B. Hopper
Hogan, William	Hannah J. Ballinger	July 1, 1813	E. Foley
Hammer, Jacob	Polly Onstatt	Oct. 13, 1811	Jas. McNeil, J. P.
Henderson, Robert	Polly Woods	Jan. ...., 1812	....
Hudson, John	Peggy Stephens	Mar. 10, 1813	R. Browning

Groom	Bride	Date of Marriage	By Whom
Hammons, Obediah	Susannah Garland	July 18, 1814	....
Hales, James	Patsy Athey	Mar. 24, 1814	M. Foley
Herndon, John	Creecie Dorton	Sept. 20, 1815	B. Hopper
Haynes, Nathan	Judy Shoemaker	July 13, 1815	G. Britain
Hoskins, Thomas	Betsy Brewster	Aug. 10, 1814	D. Duff
Hoskins, Josiah	Sally Lytton	Oct. 29, 1814	D. Duff
Hoskins, Levi	Sally Merrix	June 20, 1816	D. Duff
Hilton, James	Hannah Early	July 14, 1816	J. Sullivan
Hammond, John	Patsy Garland	June 27, 1816	B. Hopper
Horn, Chappell	Rhoda Wyatt	Dec. 24, 1816	B. Hopper
Hargis, John	Sabre Morgan	Nov. 5, 1815	Elijah Barnes
Hilton, Peter	Polly Barton	Feb. 6, 1817	E. Foley
Hemphill, Joseph	Katie Tate	Mar. 31, 1817	D. Duff
Harrison, John	Rachel Busby	July 18, 1819	M. Foley
Hubbs, Stephen	Betsy Terrill	July 11, 1819	M. Foley
Hays, Robert	Nancy Parrott	Nov. 17, 1825	Wm. Hopper

I

Inman, Thomas	Priscilla Sanders	Sept. 4, 1806	J. Sullivan
Irvin, John	Sally Cutbirth	Feb. 10, 1814	J. Sullivan
Ingram, Isaac L.	Betsy Walters	Dec. 14, 1815	B. Hopper

J

Johnson, Dannie	Nancy Arthur	Oct. 4, 1810	E. Foley
Johnson, Moses	Nellie McHolland	Aug. 18, 1811	G. Brittain
Johnson, Benjamin	Sarah Messer	July 28, 1811	Jas. McNeil
Johnson, Richard	Nannie McPherson	Aug. 22, 1813	M. Foley
Johnson, George	Polly Walters	Aug. 26, 1813	B. Hopper
Jones, William	Elizabeth Prewitt	Mar. 30, 1815	M. Foley
Johnson, William	Nancy Breedlove	Jan. 14, 1819	M. Foley

K

King, Isaac	Jane Laughlin	Sept. 1, 1808	E. Foley

L

Lytton, Burton	Jane Smith	Aug. 12, 1801	Alex. Stewart, J. P.
Livingston, Robert	Dianah Alsop	Jan. 27, 1807	E. Foley
Lewis, Jesse	Peggy Cox	Mar. 5, 1807	Jas. Sullivan
Litteral, Thomas	Rachel Waters	May 13, 1806	J. Sullivan
Lay (Leigh), Jesse	Jennie Ellison	Oct. 25, 1807	E. Foley
Laughlin, John D.	Sally Gillis	Nov. 19, 1807	E. Foley
Lyons, James	Patsy Neill	Sept. 18, 1808	E. Foley
Lund, William	Sarah Dugger	July 12, 1808	J. McCleese
Logan, William	Sally Shoemaker	May 9, 1809	E. Foley
Lewis, Stephen	Martha McWhorter	May 7, 1811	E. Foley
Loe (?), Joseph	Betsy Withers Ballenger	Nov. 11, 1811	E. Foley
Lytton, Hiram	Patsy Cox	Oct. 26, 1812	J. Sullivan
Lear, James B.	Jane D. Walker	Dec. 3, 1812	J. Sullivan
Logan, Samuel	Polly Cox	Feb. 18, 1813	E. Foley
Lamme, Claybourn	Nancy Civilly	July 29, 1813	B. Hopper
Lambert, Hugh	Sally Jones	June 24, 1809	Jas. Sullivan
Long, Robert	Peggy Sexton	Jan. 21, 1806	J. Sullivan
Lynch, John	Mary Ann Coffett	Oct. 17, 1816	B. Hopper
Love, James	Lucy L. Ballinger	June 14, 1816	M. Foley

Groom	Bride	Date of Marriage	By Whom

M

Mahan, Thomas	Anna Cox	Sept. 8, 1800	James Mahan, J. P.
McCoun, James	Lidda Cox	Sept. 23, 1802	Alex. Stewart
Mahan, Hezekiah	Sarah Hickey	Feb. 13, 1803	Alex. Stewart
Martin, William C.	Betsy Gatliff	Jan. 10, 1805	E. Foley
Miller, David	Elizabeth Mahan	May 15, 1806	E. Foley
McNutt, William B.	Eliza DeWitt	Feb. 19, 1807	E. Foley
Martin, Zadock	Sukey Brown	Aug. 13, 1807	E. Foley
McCoun, Malcomb	Polly Cox	Sept. 18, 1806	J. Sullivan
Mercer, Jacob	Polly Morgan	Feb. 5, 1807	Alex. Stewart
Mahan, Hezekiah	Betsy Arthur	Feb. 2, 1805	E. Foley
McMahan, Abraham	Betsy Y. Criswell	Oct. 18, 1807	E. Foley
McGadgen, Jesse	Sally Chestnut	Nov. ...., 1808	....
Miller, Martin	Susannah Stewart	Nov. 30, 1809	E. Foley
McHolland, David	Joanna Bailey	Nov. 12, 1809	E. Foley
Mahan, James	Rebecca Trosper	...., 1810	E. Foley
Meadows, Edward	Abagail Thomas	Apr. 19, 1810	J. S.
Moore, Isaac	Sarah Ingram	Feb. 28, 1811	E. Foley
McKee, Alexander	Sally Golden	Feb. 14, 1811	E. Foley
Mangum, Henry	Elizabeth Slaughter	Feb. 4, 1812	M. Foley
Messer, Moses	Winnie Golden	Apr. 9, 1812	M. Foley
Miller, William	Esther Kobb	July 9, 1812	E. Foley
McHargue, William	Barbara Stoun	May 12, 1812	E. Foley
Mercer, Stephen	Sally Gregory	Oct. 5, 1812	B. Hopper
McFadden, Edward	Nancy Williams	June 8, 1813	B. Hopper
McNeill, James	Drusella Hoard	Aug. 10, 1813	T. Robinson
McKenny, Francis	Winniford Foley	June 6, 1813	E. Foley
Moore, Abraham	Polly Boyd	Oct. 21, 1813	M. Foley
Massie, William	Polly Fletcher	Oct. 6, 1814	B. Hopper
Moses, John	Polly Richmond	Apr. 13, 1809	J. Sullivan
Mays, John	Leemah Blair	Feb. 25, 1814	M. Foley
Myers, Isaac M.	Sally H. Ballinger	Feb. 10, 1814	M. Foley
Mays, Solomon	Peggy Doons	Feb. 14, 1814	M. Foley
Mayfield, Robert	Elizabeth Mayfield	Feb. ...., 1815	J. Sullivan
Miller, Benjamin	Rachel Mayfield	June 22, 1815	J. S.
Mason, Jacob	Patsy Dozier	Aug. 3, 1815	....
Melcan ? , John	Elizabeth Gregory	Sept. 12, 1811	M. Foley
Morris, John	Lydda Wyatt	Aug. 22, 1815	B. Hopper
Muncy, Reuben	Sally Owens	Apr. 17, 1816	B. Hopper
Morris, Henry	Jennie Mack	Dec. 19, 1816	Benjamin Edge
McNeill, John	Mahala Tuggle	Nov. 19, 1818	Thos. Robinson
McKee, Matthew	Polly Clarke	Feb. 6, 1819	M. Foley
McKee, Mathias Wall	Betty Potter	May 14, 1807	E. Foley

N

Nicholson, Joseph	Elizabeth Burris	Dec. 31, 1806	Alex. Stewart
North, John	Jinsey Fulks	Jan. 12, 1807	Alexander Stewart
Nicholson, Thomas	Susanna Barbour	Oct. 26, 1809	Geo. Brittain
Nichols, Rodes	Betsy Skeen	Sept. 13, 1812	Richard Browning
Newman, George	Jane Johnson	Sept. 22, 1815	M. Foley
Nicholson, Jacob	Franky Stanfield	Jan. 30, 1817	R. Browning

O

Oliver, Wilson	Anna Loveton	Aug. 17, 1809	E. Foley
Osborn, Jesse	Elizabeth Lancaster	Feb. 18, 1809	Geo. Brittain
Oldham, Goodman	Kitty Jackson	Apr. 7, 1812	M. Foley
Oufield, William	Jane Laughlin	Oct. 13, 1815	J. Sullivan

Groom	Bride	Date of Marriage	By Whom

P

Payne, Joseph	Polly Stewart	Apr. 1, 1801	George Brittain, J.P.
Payne, William	Abagail Stewart	Apr. 1, 1801	Geo. Brittain
Parker, John	Letitia Ruddick	Jan. 27, 1807	E. Foley
Prichard, William	Fanny Smith	Sept. 11, 1806	Jas. Sullivan
Potter, Richard	Jean Sneed	Mar. 23, 1804	Alex. Stewart
Payne, Elisha	Polly Miller	Dec. 28, 1809	E. Foley
Pearce, James	Lucinda Ellison	May 12, 1810	E. Foley
Partring, Vincent	Elizabeth Ingram	July 26, 1810	E. Foley
Prichard, Joseph	Polly Tye	Sept. 6, 1810	E. Foley
Patton, John	Patsy Dorton	Jan. 12, 1813	E. Foley
Piercefield, Jeremiah	Hannah Durham	Apr. 4, 1812	J. H. Campbell
Parsons, James	Charity Begley	Apr. 16, 1812	M. Foley
Payne, Elijah	Rachel Miller	----, 1811	....
Perman, Joseph	Nancy Vantrick	June 3, 1813	E. Foley
Phelps, William M.	Betsy Johnson	Aug. 14, 1814	Thos. Robinson
Popejoy, William	Katy Allen	Sept. 15, 1814	B. Hopper
Powers, Jesse	Rebecca Bennett	May 24, 1814	M. Foley
Parker, James	Polly Mays	Apr. 20, 1814	M. Foley
Perkins, Solomon	Nancy Fueman	May 12, 1814	M. Foley
Popejoy, Fanents ?	Drusilla McKee	Oct. 19, 1814	M. Foley
Peanan, Charles	Elizabeth Soper	Mar. 25, 1819	M. Foley
Prewitt, John	Judith DeMoss	Aug. 10, 1805	Jas. Sullivan
Pierce, Richard	Matilda Tinsley	Mar. 11, 1806	A. Stewart
Pope, William	Susan Tuggle	Dec. 31, 1835	Wm. S. Hickey

R

Reid, Matthews	Betsy Cox	Oct. 1, 1804	Alex. Stewart
Reynolds, William	Abagail Heenys	Sept. 16, 1807	E. Foley
Ruddick, William	Betsy Wilson	Feb. 25, 1808	E. Foley
Reynolds, Taulton	Polly Sneed	Sept. 8, 1808	Jas. McNeill
Rochester, Nathaniel	Millie Johnson	Mar. 31, 1810	R. Browning
Reynolds, George	Dorcas Millsaps	Aug. 3, 1813	E. Foley
Richmond, James	Sarah Leago	Aug. 17, 1809	A. Ross
Rapier, Jesse	Polly Brown	Feb. 17, 1814	J. Sullivan
Richard, John	Katy Walker	Oct. 15, 1815	B. Hopper
Rogers, John	Jennie Eaton	Jan. 11, 1806	J. Sullivan
Robinson, Thomas	Polly McNeill	Nov. 27, 1806	Alex. Stewart
Ross, Lamech	Peggy Gray	Jan. 6, 1814	A. Ross

S

Stewart, Charles	Susannah Arthur	Sept. 21, 1801	A. Stewart
Smith, Abraham	Margaret Frazier	Aug. 19, 1802	A. Stewart
Seveton ?, Moses	Agnes Hobbs	Mar. 7, 1805	Joel Matthews
Stewart, James	Sally Baker	May 10, 1807	E. Foley
Stoe (Stowe), Robert	Katy Cox	Feb. 12, 1807	Jas. Sullivan
Shotwell, Daniel	Edy Farris	July 6, 1806	Alex. Stewart
Stewart, Isaac	Elizabeth Wyatt	Sept. 9, 1807	A. Stewart
Salyers, John	Rebecca Blake	Oct. 6, 1807	Alex. Stewart
Saylor, Joseph	Nancy Banion	Jan. 21, 1808	E. Foley
Seals, Anthony	Polly Bishop	Jan. 31, 1808	E. Foley
Sanders, Joseph	Nancy Cox	Aug. 22, 1808	J. McCleese
Stephens, Elisha	Sally Wilson	Aug. 12, 1808	E. Foley

Groom	Bride	Date of Marriage	By Whom
Stephens, Moses	Betsy Brummett	Aug. 11, 1809	E. Foley
Shoemaker, James	Anna Logan	Jan. 31, 1809	E. Foley
Stanfield, Joel	Elizabeth Ripley	Dec. 3, 1809	E. Foley
Sneed, Charles	Betsy Findley	Nov. 11, 1809	E. Foley
Stewart, John	Betsy Begley	Feb. 15, 1810	E. Foley
Sawyers, Isaac	Margaret Campbell	May 31, 1810	E. Foley
Shull, Joseph	Polly Cutbeith	Mar. 22, 1810	J. Sullivan
Sanders, Henry	Susannah Inman	July 19, 1810	J. Sullivan
Swift, John	Katy Reid	June 23, 1812	J. Sullivan
Sullivan, Joseph	Narcissa Duncan	Aug. 2, 1812	T. Nelson
Stewart, Thomas	Jane Baker	Dec. 26, 1812	B. Hopper
Shelly, Nathan	Mary Meadows	June 29, 1813	A. Ross
Stewart, Joseph	Margaret McWhorter	Nov. 23, 1813	M. Foley
Spencer, William	Sally Dana	Dec. 19, 1813	M. Foley
Smith, John	Hannah Lay (Leigh)	Apr. 26, 1810	A. Ross
Stone, Marvil	Nancy Reese	Oct. 20, 1813	J. Sullivan
Simmerman, John	Sally Smith	Nov. 11, 1813	E. Foley
Sheull, Eli	Nancy Phin ?	Jan. 13, 1814	M. Foley
Smith, Drury	Polly Murphy	Apr. 14, 1814	M. Foley
Sexton, William	Nancy Hickson	Sept. 21, 1815	J. Sullivan
Sexton, Lemuel	Patty Davis	Oct. 6, 1816	J. Sullivan
Sebent, Daniel	Sally Cottingame	Mar. 27, 1816	M. Foley
Sexton, Frederick	Polly Morgan	Dec. 26, 1816	E. Barnes
Skeen, Henry	Lucy Piercefield	May 29, 1817	R. Browning
Stickley, F. P.	Susan H. Tuggle	Oct. 28, 1857	W. S. Doak
Sampson, Joseph	Emaline Kellans	Mar. 11, 1851	H. Goodin, M. G.

T

Turner, George	Polly Johnson	Aug. 27, 1801	G. Brittain
Truman, Peter	Polly Todd	Dec. 21, 1806	J. Sullivan
Tye, Joshua	Elizabeth Cummins	Mar. 12, 1805	A. Stewart
Tye, George	Mary Mays	Apr. 18, 1808	E. Foley
Trosper, James	Nellie Mahan	Aug. 11, 1808	E. Foley
Tuttle, James	Ann Dixon	...., 1811	....
Thomas, Samuel	Susannah Bradford	Jan. 20, 1811	J. Sullivan
Tye, John	Betsy Powers	Mar. 5, 1812	J. Sullivan
Tackett, Lewis	Lucy Smith	Mar. 31, 1811	G. Brittain
Taylor, Cornelius	Sally Walker	Mar. 1, 1814	B. Hopper
Tackett, James	Jemima Worley	Aug. 18, 1814	S. Ross
Trosper, John	Anne Woolsey	Sept. 8, 1814	S. Ross
Tuggle, William	Martha Tuggle	May 22, 1830	Wm. Hopper
Tuggle, Richardson	Mary Pogue	Sept. 8, 1835	Wm. Hopper

V

Vannoy, Samuel	Sally Dapper	June 9, 1811	Jas. Sullivan
Vautreace, John	Julia Ham	Dec. 18, 1810	J. Sullivan

W

Whitecotton, George	Susannah DeMoss	Sept. 13, 1802	A. Stewart
Wilburn, Edward	Sarah Bingham	Jan. 1, 1803	G. Brittain
Watkins, Jonathan	Aggie Daniel	Oct. 2, 1805	E. Foley
Wilkerson, Brannock	Polly Slaughter	Jan. 15, 1807	E. Foley
Williams, Charles	Judith Brummett	Mar. 26, 1807	E. Foley

Groom	Bride	Date of Marriage	By Whom
White, Hendrick	Peggy Newton	Nov. 20, 1806	J. Sullivan
Wilson, William	Sally Hamlin	Jan. 8, 1807	J. Sullivan
Wilson, Richard	Mary Green	Dec. 15, 1806	A. Stewart
Warfield, Reason	Mary W. Woodson	Nov. 6, 1805	A. Stewart
Watkins, Chapman	Sally Chestnut	Nov. 11, 1807	A. Stewart
Wilder, William	Jane Stephens	Apr. 16, 1809	E. Foley
Wyatt, John	Mary Stewart	Feb. 28, 1810	E. Foley
Wilder, Joab	Elizabeth Bincoe	Mar. 31, 1810	R. Browning
Woodson, Wade N.	Alsey Cheek	Nov. 11, 1813	M. Foley
Wright, James	Polly Smith	Sept. 7, 1809	A. Ross
Walker, Christopher	Elizabeth Stewart	Dec. 2, 1813	B. Hopper
Wilson, Solomon	Sally Caldwell	Aug. 10, 1808	J. Sullivan
Wilson, David	Polly Whitt	Mar. 18, 1815	J. Sullivan
Wilson, Carleton	Lucy Wyatt	Aug. 15, 1815	M. Foley
Wambler, Joshua	Rebecca Wager	Oct. 17, 1815	B. Hopper
White, Harrison	Anna Perkins	Nov. 30, 1815	A. Ross
Wilson, John	Fannie Wilson	Aug. 29, 1816	J. Sullivan
Wicker, Asa	Mary Ann Beaty	Jan. 3, 1817	D. Duff
White, John	Lydda Matthias	Sept. 19, 1816	R. Browning
Williams, Hiram	Nancy Barton	Sept. 30, 1819	James Sear
Wyatt, James	Sally Hibbard	Feb. 23, 1809	E. Foley
Walker, Nathaniel	Peggy Goodin	Oct. 31, 1811	J. Sullivan

CHAPTER IV

GREENUP COUNTY, KENTUCKY

BOUNDARY AND ESTABLISHMENT

GREENUP, the forty-fifth of the counties of Kentucky in order of formation, was established by an act of the General Assembly of Kentucky, approved December 12, 1803 (3 *Littell's Laws of Kentucky*, 117) out of part of Mason County, which act is in part as follows:

Section 1. Be it enacted by the General Assembly, That from and and after the first day February, next, all that part of the county of Mason that is included in the following boundary, to-wit: beginning on the Ohio, opposite to the mouth of Big Scioto River; thence a course so as to include all the branches of Tygarts Creek, until it intersects the Fleming line; thence with the line of Fleming County to the line of Floyd County; thence with the line of Floyd County to Big Sandy River, and down Big Sandy to the Ohio; and thence with the Ohio to the beginning, shall be one distinct county, and called and known by the name of Greenup.

* * *

Sec. 3. The justices named in the commissions of the peace for the said county of Greenup shall meet at the house of Andrew Hood, on the first court day after the said division shall take place; and having taken the oaths prescribed by law, and the sheriff being duly qualified, the court shall proceed to appoint and qualify 'their' clerk.

Sec. 4. *And be it further enacted*, That Duval Payne, Joseph Donophan, Philemon Thomas, Abraham Drake, and Thomas Sloo, or any three of them, shall, and they are hereby appointed commissioners to meet at the mouth of Little Sandy, on the first Monday in March, next, or as soon thereafter as may be, who, being first duly sworn by some justice of the peace for said county, shall proceed to view and fix upon the proper place for the permanent seat of justice in and for the said county, as near central as the situation and the nature of the case will permit; ***.

The boundary of the County as thus formed may be described as a line roughly drawn from Fullerton, Greenup County, southwestwardly to Yale, Bath County; thence eastwardly to the head of the Little Sandy River and thence a straight line to the present Louisa, Lawrence County; thence down the Big Sandy to the mouth and down the Ohio River to the beginning. Parts of its original territory have been taken in the formation of Lawrence County in 1821; Carter, in 1838; and Boyd, in 1860.

The County was named in honor of Governor Christopher Greenup. Governor Greenup was of Scotch-Irish and English ancestry, and was born in the colony of Virginia—probably in Loudoun County—about 1750. His father was John Greenup and his mother was Elizabeth Witten, eldest daughter of Captain Thomas Witten. (See Witten and Cecil Families). The Wittens and Cecils migrated from Cecil County, Maryland, to the territory then known as Southwestern Virginia about 1767. The Wittens were of Teutonic origin, but left Saxony and emigrated to England about the ninth century where they became identified with the Anglo-Saxons. The Cecils were of pure Celtic blood and natives of the British Isles. Tradition and documentary evidence reveal that the progenitors of both families in America came from England with the Calverts and settled in Maryland, then Lord Baltimore's colony.

Governor Greenup's mother was a direct descendant of the Honorable William Cecil, Lord Burghley (or Burleigh), prime minister of England for forty years during the reign of Queen Elizabeth.

Governor Greenup had service in the Revolutionary War. He was commissioned a first lieutenant in Colonel Grayson's Regiment, February 2, 1777; resigned April 1, 1778; and subsequently was a colonel in the Virginia militia. He also had service in the Indian wars on the Western frontiers.

Colonel Greenup came to Kentucky with his parents in 1783; and on the 4th of March, that year, he was admitted to the bar in the old court for the District of Kentucky, established by an act of the Virginia Legislature; and on March 18, 1785, he was appointed clerk of that court and served as such until the dissolution of the court. When Kentucky was organized as a state in 1792, he was elected a Representative in Congress and was reelected and served until 1797 after which he was clerk of the Kentucky Senate until his election as Governor in August, 1804. Subsequent to his service as Governor, he was elected to the Kentucky Legislature from Franklin County, and in 1812 was a justice of the peace for that county. For years he was a director of the Bank of Kentucky.

Governor Greenup married, in 1787, Mary Catherine Pope, daughter of Nathaniel Pope of Virginia. He died April 27, 1818, at Blue Lick Springs.

Organization of First Courts—Earliest Court Orders

February 1, 1804, John Nichols, Reuben Rucker, John Davis Poage, Charles N. Lewis, Moses Fuqua, Jr., John Chadwick, George Hardwick, and Jacob Lockwood produced commissions from His Excellency, the Governor of Kentucky, constituting and appointing them justices of the peace for the said County of Greenup. Whereupon the said Reuben Rucker administered the oath of fidelity to the Constitution of Kentucky, the pledge to support the Constitution of the United States and the oath of office as justice of the peace to the said John Nichols who then administered the said oaths to the said Reuben Rucker, John Davis Poage, Charles N. Lewis, Moses Fuqua, Jr., John Chadwick, George Hardwick and Jacob Lockwood. Thereupon a court was held for the County of Greenup. Josiah Davidson produced a commission from the Governor of Kentucky appointing him sheriff of Greenup County. Whereupon he took the necessary oaths and entered into bond with Jesse B. Boone and Reuben Rucker, his securities, as the law directs.

The court then appointed Isaac Hockaday as clerk pro tem. Whereupon he took the necessary oath and entered into bond with John Nichols and Jesse Boone, his securities.

James Howe was appointed Commissioner of Revenue Tax for the present year. Whereupon he took the necessary oath with Robert Poage as his security.

On motion of Isaac Hockaday, Clerk of the Court, John Hockaday was permitted to take the necessary oath [as deputy clerk?] with John Nichols, Moses Fuqua and William Lowery [as sureties on his] bond to Governor Garrard in the sum of 1,000 pounds.

James Clark and Thomas Daugherty qualified as attorneys-at-law. James Clark was appointed as Commonwealth's Attorney.

COURT OF QUARTER SESSIONS

A Court of Quarter Sessions was organized February 20, 1804, at the home of Andrew Hood with Thomas Waring, Jesse B. Boone and Seriah Stratton as judges.

CIRCUIT COURT

The first Circuit Court was organized May 6, 1806, with Honorable John Colvin, Judge; Thomas Waring and Jesse B. Boone, Assistant Judges; John Hockaday, Clerk; and Thomas Grayson, Commonwealth's Attorney.

Thomas Daugherty, David Trimble, Robert Grayson, James Clark and William Roper qualified as attorneys-at-law.

FIRST GRAND JURY

The first grand jury empaneled for the county consisted of Robert Poage, Robert Davidson, John Davis Poage, William Lowery, David Ellington, Benjamin Uling (Ulen), Thomas Hood, Absolem Burton, James Lowery, James Norton, Jesse Griffith, James McGinness, James Warnick, John How, John Terrill, Andrew Hood, and William Dupuy.

FIRST LAW SUIT

The first case tried in court was styled *Christopher Stump,* plaintiff, V. *Aaron Littlejohn,* defendant.

FIRST PUBLIC ROAD ESTABLISHED

On motion of Jesse Boone it is ordered that John Mackoy, Andrew Hood, Josiah Davidson and Andrew Wolf be appointed to review the necessary and best way for a road to be opened from the county line opposite the mouth of the Scioto River to the mouth of Big Sandy and make report of same to the court.

PIONEER FAMILIES

It appears from tax lists and other public records that there were approximately 325 families living in Greenup County in 1810. Clement H. Waring, assistant to Joseph Crockett, United States Marshal for the District of Kentucky, enumerated the third decennial census of the County and reported and certified a total enumeration of 2,369. Of this number 1,039 were white males, 835 white females, 484 negro slaves and 11 free negroes. Below are given the names of the taxpayers and/or heads of families as of the year 1810, together with the number of slaves owned by each slaveholder.

A

Adams, William
Alexander, Alcey
Alexander, John
Anderson, John
Ashley, Holt

B

Banfield, Thomas
Barkello, Edward

Barkello, Ruth
Ballach ? , Harris
Baker, Humphrey
Bartley, Joshua
Bassett, Amos
Bell, Thomas
Benough, George
(7 Slaves)
Biggs, Douglas
Blake, Kenneth
Blackburn, William

Blankenship, Daniel
Blankenship, John
Boone, Jesse B.
(12 Slaves)
Branham, John
Brown, John
Brown, Nelson
Brown, John
Bruce, William
Bradshaw, George
Bradshaw, William

Brumley, William
Brumfield, Shinar
Bryant, John
Bryant, Zehaniah
Burbridge, Robert
Buckhannon, William
Burton, Abednego

C

Cain, Jacob
Cain, John
Cain, Job
Cain, Thomas
Cameron, John
Campbell, Jesse
Campbell, Johnson
Canterberry, Benjamin
Canterberry, John
Canterberry, Nimrod
Canterberry, Reuben
Catlett, Alexander
(5 Slaves)
Catlett, Alexander, Jr.
Catlett, Horatio
(2 Slaves)
Carter, Hebe
(12 Slaves)
Chaffin, Jordan
Chapman, James
Chapman, Reuben
Chinn, Benjamin
(2 Slaves)
Clark, John
Cobb, John
Colgin, William
Cogzel, John
Colvin, John
Colegrove, Jeremiah
Cooper, Charles
Creacraft, Charles
Creacraft, John
Creekpaun, Michell
Craig, William
Crook, Joseph
Crow, David
Culp, Cornelius
Culp, Tilman
Cummings, Melkier
Curry, Henry S.
(5 Slaves)

D

Dail, Charles
Davidson, Josiah
Darral?, Levi
Davis, Lamech
(7 Slaves)
Davis, Rezin
(5 Slaves)
Deering, Antonio

Deering, Richard
(5 Slaves)
Dew?, Peter
(5 Slaves)
Dupuy, William
(4 Slaves)
Duncan, Joseph
Durbin, Amos
(1 Slave)

E

Eason, Edward
(2 Slaves)
Ellington, David
(1 Slave)
Ellington, Pleasant
(2 Slaves)
Ellison, John
Evans, William
Everman, Jacob
Everman, John

F

Farmer, Jeremiah
Farmer, Joshua
Flaugher, Christopher
Flynn, Arthur
Foster, Job
Frazier, Micajah
Friend, Andrew
(1 Slave)
Friend, Jacob
(6 Slaves)
Fuller, Michael
Fulsom, James
Fuqua, Mary
Fuqua, Moses
(16 Slaves)
Fuqua, Moses, Jr.
(2 Slaves)
Fuqua, William
(5 Slaves)

G

Gains, Francis H.
(15 Slaves)
Gammon, Richard D.
Gardner, Joseph
(8 Slaves)
Garrett, Ignatius
Gholson, William S.
Gill, John
Gilkey, Edward
Goble, Abraham
Goble, Ephraim
(2 Slaves)
Gorman, William
Grayson, George W.
(5 Slaves)

Grayson, Robert H.
(49 Slaves)
Greenslate, John

H

Ham, Jacob M.
Hainton, Antonio
Hannah, Robert
(2 Slaves)
Hardwick, George
(1 Slave)
Harrison?, Garrett
Harrison, George
(1 Slave)
Hatcher, Edward
(2 Slaves)
Hatton, William
Hedges, Solomon
Henderson, Robert
Higgins, John
Hockiday, John
(2 Slaves)
Holland, Wright
Hood, Andrew
Hood, Massah
Hood, Robert
Hord, Thomas
Horsley, James
Horsley, Matthew
Horsley, Taylos
Howe, James
Howe, John W.
(7 Slaves)
Huffman, Jacob
Huson, James

J

Jeffries, James
Johnson, John
Johnson, Priscilla
Jordan, William

K

Keith, Anderson
(2 Slaves)
Kelly, Alexander
Kibbey, Amos
(12 Slaves)
Kibbey, Moses
(9 Slaves)
Kisson, Jacob
Kite, James
Knapp, Joseph
Knox, George
Kouns, Jacob
(7 Slaves)
Kouns, John
(10 Slaves)
Kouns, John

79

L

Lawless, Theophilus
Lawson, Thomas
Littlejohn, John
Lemison, James S.
Lester, John
Lewis, Charles N.
  (20 Slaves)
Lowery, James
Lowery, John
Lytton, John

M

Madden, Dennis
Madden, Nathan
Mayhew, Elisha
Mayhew, Ezra
McAllister, Jane
McAllister, Michael
McCleese, David
McCloud, William
McConnell, John
McCoy, John
  (10 Slaves)
McDowell, John
McFarland, David
McGlone, Owen
McGuire, James
  (2 Slaves)
McGuire, John
McIntyre, James
McKinney, Lambkin
McMahan, John
  (1 Slave)
Meeks, James
Middaugh, James
Miller, John
Moore, Jeremiah
Morrison, William
Morton, John
  (3 Slaves)
Morton, Josiah
  (22 Slaves)

N

Nailor, Paul
Nichols, Cassander
  (13 Slaves)
Norman, Joseph
Norton, James

O

Osborn, William

P

Pancake, Abraham
Parks, Robert
Payne, Adam

Payne, Charles
Pettit, Stot?
Phillips, Edmund
Poage, Allen
  (5 Slaves)
Poage, James
  (1 Slave)
Poage, John
  (4 Slaves)
Poage, Mary
  (9 Slaves)
Poole, Andrew
Porter, Micajiah
Powers, Jacob
Powell, Joseph
Price, Edmund
Price, Sampson

R

Ratliff, Daniel
Retherford, William
Rice, James
Richards, James
Richards, Thomas
Rucker, Elzaphan
  (1 Slave)
Rucker, Reuben
  (3 Slaves)
Rucker, Wick

S

Saladay, Samuel
  (1 Slave)
Sammons, Thomas
Savage, John
Shadwick (Chadwick),
Sharp, Richard
Scott, David
Scott, Thomas
Shepard, John
Shortridge, Margaret
  (8 Slaves)
Short, Aaron
Skidmore, Joseph
Skidmore, Joseph
Skidmore, Samuel
Sperry, James
Smith, Moses
Smith, Jacob
Smith, Randall
Smith, Richard
Smith, Robert
  (2 Slaves)
Smith, Woodson
  (8 Slaves)
Smith, Thomas
Stewart, Charles
Stewart, Matthew

Stevenson, Richard
  (4 Slaves)
Story, John
Stratton, Seriah
Sykes, Sarah

T

Terry, Hannah
Thompson, Woody
  (1 Slave)
Timerlake, Oba
  (2 Slaves)
Timerlake, Oba, agent
  for A. Grayson
  (24 Slaves)
Tinsley, Joseph
Tolbert, Thomas
Tyree, William

U

Ulan, Benjamin
Ullett, John
Ulett, Thomas

V

Vanbibber, James
  (2 Slaves)
Van Meter, Henry
Vice, Enoch
Vice, Manning
Virgin, Kenzie
Virgin, Rezin
  (1 Slave)
Virgin, Thomas

W

Wade, John
Ward, James
  (15 Slaves)
Ward, Thompson
  (2 Slaves)
Waring, Clement H.
Waring, Francis
  (3 Slaves)
Walker, John
Waring, James H.
Waring, Thomas
Waring, Thomas T. G
Warnock, James
Warnock, James
  (5 Slaves)
Warnock, Samuel
  (1 Slave)
Warnock, William
White, Solomon
White, David
  (4 Slaves)

White, William
Wells, John E.
Williams, Eli
Williams, Mordecai
Wilson, Alexander

Wilson, James
Wilson, Lloyd
Wingo, James
Witherow, John
Woods, Andrew

Wooton, Charles

Y

Young, John
(8 Slaves)

HEADS OF FAMILIES AND/OR TAXPAYERS OF GREENUP COUNTY AS OF THE YEAR 1811, NOT ENUMERATED IN THE U. S. CENSUS FOR 1810:

A

Allison, John
Anglin, Gabriel
Anglin, John

B

Bacon, Benedick
Ball, James
Ball, Robert
Barr, Henry
Bailey, Wyatt
Barnes, Robert
Bartley, John
Bean, Stephen
Boone, Nathan
Bragg, Armistead
Brown, Davis
Brubaker, Abraham
Bruce, John
Bryson, William
Buckles, Robert

C

Carter, George
Cartwright, Thomas
Cartwell, Robert
Catlett, Elisha
Chaffin, Christopher
Chaffin, Nancy
Chitwood, John R.
Cohlin, Gideon
Colvin, Samuel
Cornelius, Austin
Crank, John
Crank, Jacob
Crank, Joseph
Curren, Joseph
Cummings, Henry

D

Davis, George N.
Davis, Samuel
Demit, Samuel

Downs, John
Duncan, Alexander
Duncan, Charles
Drury, Salson (Lawsor
Dummit, William

E

Edwards, John
Ellington, John

F

Friend, Jonas
Fuqua, David
Fuqua, Samuel

G

Gibson, James
Goble, Daniel
Grayson, Alfred W.
Greene, Robert H.

H

Hannah, Gabriel
Hatton, Elijah
Hargus, John
Henderson, Robert, Jr.
Hensley, George
Hitchcock, Caleb
Howe, Joseph

J

Jackson, Charles
Johnson, Levi
Jones, Peter

K

Kilgour, David
Kiser, Jacob

L

Lacy, John
Littlejohn, Valentine
Lockwood, Jacob
Lowery, Melvin
Lowery, William
Lyons, Hezekiah

M

McAlester, James
McCallester, James
McCallister, Luke
McGlone, Andrew
McLaughlin, William
Meek, Samuel
Miller, William
Morton, Jonathan

N

Nicholls, John

O

Oscar, James

P

Parker, David
Parker, Elias
Parker, Robert
Perry, Daniel
Pettitt, Matthew
Pettitt, Samuel
Pickett, Younger
Porter, Jacob

R

Reason, Lewis
Riddle, John
Roberts, Jesse
Robertson, Winslow
Rucker, Ambrose

FIRST SETTLERS OF GREENUP COUNTY

Early settlers, probably the first, of Greenup County and settlement of Greenupsburg (Greenup) as shown by the following excerpts from a manuscript prepared by Rev. James Gilruth, a resident of the locale in his youth, and published in an Ironton, Ohio, newspaper about 1879:

I now think it proper to cross the river (Ohio) and begin below Little Sandy River and come up on the Kentucky side.

Between the narrows and the mouth of Little Sandy about 1803 settled John Nichol(s) (or Nicholson). His wife's name was Cassandra Wilcox. Their children's names were John, Patty, Nicholas, James, Nancy, Cassandra and Alfred. I never knew who John and Nicholas married. Patty₁ married Benjamin Chinn, and Cassandra₂ married James Bartley. Nicholas had several slaves which rapidly increased. He had a blacksmith shop and in a way worked at that, but lived by farming. After clearing up a large farm, for the time, he died. The widow and family moved up and settled in the bottoms out back of Ferguson's sand bar (now Union Landing).

When the Nichols family moved to this county they left their son John in Maryland. Some years after his father's death, he moved here and settled on the river bank a little above Hanging Rock (Kentucky side). He was considered the swiftest runner in Greenup County, Lawrence County, Ohio, or Scioto County (Ohio), except John Martial (Marshall?) of Scioto, between whom, as far as was publicly known, it remained an unsettled question.

About the time (1803) that Nicholas settled below the mouth of Sandy, Lewis Wilcox (or Wilcoxon) settled in the upper point; he was an uncle of Mrs. Nichols. They had no children. He had four able-bodied negroes—men. He built a hewed (sic) log house with clap-board roof, chinked it with wood, daubed it with common clay, with outside chimney, which in fact, was about the universal position of chimneys in those days. I have been thus particular in describing this house because it was the first house ever built in what is now known as Greenupsburg (now Greenup). When Wilcox settled here, the land was covered with a heavy growth of beech, poplar, oak, etc. But his slaves soon cleared up a field of several acres where Greenup now stands.

About one-half mile above Sandy settled Andrew Hood, commonly called Major Hood. Their children were Sarchet, Thomas, Elizabeth, Patty, Andrew, Rachael, Henry and Catherine. Thomas married Sarah Pickney. Sarchet married Jesse Griffith. Andrew married Miss Crain (?). Rachael married Joseph Howe. Major Hood was the first settler in that part of Greenup County, if not the first in the County. Hood's Run forked some two or three hundred yards from the mouth. The left hand fork lay parallel with the river and cut the channel down below the old bed, so that it no more passed down the former channel, and is now known as Howe's Run. This, in time of high water in the river, puts the whole bank down to Hood's Run in the condition of an island. When the owners of the Little Sandy Salt Works began to export salt by wagon down to the Ohio River, Hood, to facilitate this—his yard being their depot—also for the convenience of his own farm, built a high frame bridge over this branch of the Run. This bridge was the first frame bridge on either side of the river between Big Sandy and Big Scioto Rivers that had any connection with public utility. After Hood's death the salt depot was moved up to Boone's and this bridge fell into decay. After Greenup County became organized, court was held for some years in a rough plank shed attached to the north end of his (Hood's) house. The judges' seats were on a rough plank scaffold, raised sufficiently to overlook bar, jury and audience.

In those days such a thing as a bolt for flour was never heard connected with any mill in these parts. Hood bought a fine brass wire sieve 18 inches in diameter for which he paid $2.00 and fixed up a little room adjoining the courtroom with all the conveniences necessary for sifting, and gave all the neighbors free privilege to fetch their grists there to sift their flour. The opportunity was readily embraced by all who had any wheat ground, though it cost them hours of weary labor to get a little coarse flour.

In a shed attached to the end of his (Hood's) house was kept the first dry goods store on either side of the river between the Big Sandy and the Big Scioto. It was kept by Benjamin Chinn. Hood owned no slaves, but owned the largest breed of hogs in the County; kept a large flock of geese, the first kept in these parts; was an industrious farmer; cleared up a big farm and set out the first apple orchard in Greenup County. He was a respected and good citizen.

Next above his father (Major Hood) settled Thomas Hood. His wife's name was Sarah Pickett. Their first child was named Libni T. Hood, and was the first man in all these parts who raised a nursery of apple trees, all seedlings, on R. Hood's land.

Near the hill on the bank of Hood's Run, in a rough log cabin built for the purpose, was kept the first school between Big Sandy and Tygarts Creek; and I am certain it was the first in Greenup County. The school was made up of scholars from both sides of the river and was kept by Silas Wooten. His wife's name was Theba. They had two children, Rhoda and William. Wooten was a teacher of the true backwoods type as to literary qualification. Some years later he moved back on the waters of East Fork of Little Sandy; became a Methodist and sustained a good character as a citizen. After he (Wooten) left the house was occupied some time by a man named Robinson. He was a tailor. His price for making a neat body coat for a man was $2.50. I would not have mentioned this man, but that you might know who was our first tailor and what it then cost to get a coat made.

DANIEL BOONE

The next above settled the celebrated Colonel Daniel Boone. But before detailing my recollections of the Boone family, I wish to preface them with a few remarks of a general nature:

Before Kentucky became organized into a state, she was under the laws of Virginia whose land policy authorized individuals, under authority of a land warrant issued by her, to take up land for his own private use. The individual then got a surveyor to run around the land which he wished to take up, had the corners, distances and courses all noted and then got his survey, with his warrant, recorded in the office where the law required them to be recorded. The first survey recorded held the land. In such a way of doing business it was next to impossible but that individuals in laying their warrants would lap over on each others surveys. Had states concocted a system to produce litigation and trouble in this country, it is difficult to conceive how they could have produced one more effectual for the purpose than the land policy of Virginia.

Col. Boone, in a conversation with my father, gave the following account of his Kentucky land failure: He got his warrant and laid it on a tract of 4,000 acres of choice land lying on the waters of a stream called Elkhorn. Apprehending no danger he omitted for some time to get his warrant and survey recorded. In the meantime, Robert Johnston (Johnson), the father of Richard M. Johnston, afterwards Vice President of the United States, laid his warrant on the land covered by Boone's, and being a prompt man to attend to his own interests in these matters, got his warrant and survey recorded. Suit was entered to decide who should hold the land, and after litigating the matter for some time, one day they met in the street. Said Johnston, "Boone, I will keep you out of that land as long as I live, but to settle the matter and end our lawing, I will give you for your claim, 400 acres on the Ohio River one mile about the mouth of Little Sandy for which I will give you a warrantee (sic) deed." Boone rejected Johnston's proposition and went and told his lawyer what Johnston had proposed. His lawyer advised him by all means to accept Johnston's offer, which he ultimately did. Boone then left Kentucky with his family and moved to Big Kanawha, lived there sometime, then moved back down here about 1800. Their children's names were Daniel, Jr., Jesse, Nathan. Previous to coming here Daniel (junior) had gone to Missouri. Who he married I never knew. Jesse married Chloe Van Bibber. They had two children when they came here, viz: Harriet and Alphonso, and, as I stated in a former letter, after they came here Nathan married Olive Van Bibber. They built a rough log cabin in which they lived until the Colonel moved away. In the meantime, Jesse built a "hewed" log house about 20 by 30 (feet), two stories high, with a shingle roof. This was the first shingle-roofed dwelling house built in the county.

At this time the Colonel's eyes had begun to fail. I remember being there one day with my father. Their attention was attracted by an object on the other side of the river and Colonel Boone got his spectacles to ascertain what that object was; then he said he "used these glasses in shooting." While he lived here he did not hunt much, though game of all kinds was plentiful. What he did was for pastime. Jesse and Nathan were both good hunters but took no special interest in it further than their convenience.

Mrs. Boone, as I remember her, was a little taller than the common size, rather spare, slightly aquiline nose, fine forehead, good countenance and of genteel manner. The Colonel said she was a better horseman than he, "for she had set her horse and jumped him up and down benches of rocks in crossing the mountains that he could not." The Colonel was a little over common size, of well proportioned figure, neither spare nor compulent; features formed on the Grecian countenance; in manner what we might call one of nature's gentlemen.

While the Colonel lived here he and my father spent much of their time together, recounting the adventures of past life. He expressed great dissatisfaction with the land policy and his treatment. He said that after he had risked his life and the lives of his family and done what he had to promote the settlement of that fine country, to be stripped of what he believed to be justly his in equity, through the technicalities of the law, rasped his feelings and led him to determine to quit the country. Accordingly, he formed the resolution of going to Missouri, which at that time belonged to Spain. So, after this, accompanied by his wife, he left for Missouri.

I heard by one who ought to know that the Spanish Governor, in view of the value which he set upon the Colonel as an acquisition to the country, made a grant of ten miles square, but that when the country came to be deeded to the United States, in consequence of some failure of the United States to establish this grant, he lost it [words omitted] but that the United States, in lieu of it, gave him these grants. I cannot vouch.

Jesse Boone remained on the place, lived by farming, owned several slaves, became judge of the court (Greenup County), was active in promoting schools and in every way proved to be a first class citizen. While living here there were added to his children Minerva, Panthea and Mattison. Minerva married Winecup Warner.

The Colonel's last Kentucky cabin was converted into a school house in which a Mr. Johnston taught a common English school for three months. This was the last of my schooling in Kentucky. The cabin at last went the way of all backwoods cabins.

In 1819 Jesse Boone and his family moved to Missouri. When they were aboard their keel boat about to shove off, I stepped on board to bid them farewell. This is the last time I ever saw one of this much respected family.

The last time I saw Nathan Boone was some years after the Colonel moved to Missouri. He was back on business. Court was being held at Major Hood's. The yard was full of men. A man by the name of Wooten, a slab built six-footer, for some cause struck Jesse Boone, who at the time was nearly bed-ridden with fever and ague, on the head with a stick like an Irish shillalah. The blood gushed, which Nathan, seeing, sprang at Wooten. Wooten took to his heels with Nathan after him. About every other jump Nathan's fist would light on Wooten like a mallet. Wooten redoubled his efforts and fled as for dear life, but no locomotive ever could save him from Nathaniel's fist until he had given him what he thought he deserved which was done much to the gratification of the spectators.

Some years ago when I was at the French Grant, I visited Major John C. Kountz who was then living at Greenupsburg. In speaking of the Boone family he said "he wondered that none of the writers of Col. Boone's life had ever mentioned the fact of his having lived in this country; that the Historical Society of Cincinnati had written to him to furnish them what he knew of Boone's life with that of any other prominent first settlers but that he had neglected it." I mentioned, doubtingly, the report of his having once lived at Big Kanawha. Kountz replied: "There is no mistake of his once having lived there. I know that he certainly did."

Next above Daniel Boone settled Josiah Davidson, commonly called "Short Si" to distinguish him from any other Davidson. I only remember their two sons, Reuben and Jesse. Reuben married a daughter of William Guthrie, a Baptist Minister. One of the daughters married John Thomas and another married William McCartney.³ Davidson was a farmer but not a slave holder. After living here a few years, this family moved on the waters of the East Fork of Little Sandy.

Next above him (Short Si Davidson), settled Stephen Colvin. His son John married Margaret Davidson. Mr. Colvin was a farmer and owned slaves. He, in connection with a gentleman by the name of Barkley who lived at Rumley (Romney, Hampshire County), Virginia, bought of Congress all that fine bottom in the lower end of Lawrence County, Ohio, between Luke Kelly's section and the French Grant. He kept the best blooded horses of any man in all this region of country. From his house and that of "Short Si" Davidson was obtained the best view of the Hanging Rock.

Next above Stephen Colvin settled Josiah Davidson. To distinguish him from the first Josiah, he was called "Long Si." He was a farmer. Their children were: Lizzie, Malply and Samuel. This family did not live here many years. After they left, the place was occupied by a William Roby. This family stayed but a few years and moved into Ohio, down in Miami County.

Next above settled Joseph Powell, an illustrious farmer and a member of the Baptist Church. Their children's names were Vincent, Catherine and Benjamin. Vincent married Polly Kelly. Benjamin married Rev. John Young's daughter. What became of Catherine I have forgotten.

Having now arrived at a point nearly opposite where I commenced, I shall go no further but return and give you some of the early settlement of Greenupsburg.

In a former letter I told you that Lewis Wilcox first settled there and cleared up a part of the ground where Greenupsburg now stands. The land, as I understood, belonged to Robert Johnston of Kentucky (Col. Boone's land antagonist). To give aid to the formation of the contemplated town he (Johnston) came up and built a little tub mill at the Falls of Little Sandy. This was the first attempt at improving the water power. Johnston was a heavy set man, and at this time a little inclined to corpulency. His son Richard (he that afterwards was Vice President of the United States) was also here for a short time. I do not remember that Johnston or his son was ever here but one summer. James McGuire put up the first carpenter shop. O. S. Timberlake put up and kept the first tavern. Reason (Rezin?) Davis put up the first hat shop. He lived in the Wilcox house and kept the first ferry. Robert Daugherty established the first dry goods store. Jones and Noble put up a small cotton spinning factory, ran it for a time, then moved it to Portsmouth where it fell through. Mr. Seaton established the first school in the shape of an academy, run it a little while; it fell through and he turned lawyer. The first resident lawyer was a man named Fishback. The first resident doctor was a man by the name of Green. I think that the first sermon in Greenupsburg was preached by R. Lindsey, an itinerant Methodist minister, about 1812, who came then to establish circuit preaching in town, but not meeting with any encouragement, on the invitation of Thomas Gilruth of the French Grant, he made his house a preaching place. I think the second sermon there was preached by the celebrated Lorenzo Dow. His description of sinful conduct made considerable talk among the town people, in as much as the description so closely fitted some cases that it puzzled some of them to account for it. Up to 1818 I haven't the most distance knowledge of there having lived in the place so much as one man, woman or child that made any profession of or gave any evidence of being religiously inclined. Benjamin Locke of the French Grant built the first court house. A frame building composed of white pine lumber, for which he received $900. I have forgotten who built the jail. It was a double walled building composed of logs, "hewed," about 10 inches square with a log ceiling above. The first man put in it as a criminal was a hatter by the name of Bryman who, in a quarrel with William Webb, struck him a fatal blow with his fist in the stomach which killed him outright.

Next above Boone settled John Hockaday. He came to these parts a single man, not far from 1804 or 1805. He was said to possess $3,000 in cash. He kept school for one term in an old cabin between Thomas Hood's and Jesse Boone's. He bought a tract of unimproved land (I think that it was a part of the Boone tract), built a "hewed" log double house with an open entry between nearly as wide as either end was long, shingle roof and brick chimneys. I mention these things because brick chimneys and shingle roofs were not yet common in these parts and the plan of the house was rather novel. Hockaday obtained the Clerkship of the Court of Greenup County, kept his office in his own house a few miles above Greenupsburg. After living here some years he married Margaret Donathan, a young lady of good family and of respectable character. On settling here Hockaday commenced improving his land in which he succeeded to a considerable extent. He was considered a good shot with the rifle and enjoyed as a gentleman the chase and the fishing rod, but did not let them interfere with business. He owned some slaves and was never known to use his tongue or his talents to the injury of others. Few men sustained a more amiable and worthy character than John Hockaday.

Not far from 1802 or 1803, next above settled John How (Howe). Their children's names were Joseph, Rebecca, Ellenore, Sarah, William, Daniel and John. Joseph married Rachael Hood; Rebecca married James Warnock; Ellenore married Roland Cornelius. Whom the younger members of the family married, I never knew. William How owned several slaves. After liying here a few years he moved back a few miles among the hills and opened a new farm which they called Willow Cave?. How was strongly attached to the British form of government and while living here he took a trip to Canada on foot to see the country and what were the prospects of settling there. After Howe moved back from the river, the place (vacated) was occupied by Reuben Dawson. Their children's names were Gabriel, Fanny, Arthur, Henry, Joseph. None of them married while they lived here. Fanny was considered to be very handsome young lady. Dawson lived by farming, was a slave owner. About 1807 he built the first keel boat on either side of the Ohio River between Portsmouth and Gallipolis. She was about 9 tons burden.

Next above was a 1,000-A. tract. This was bought and settled by L. Wilcox (a brother of Mrs. Nicholson). Their children's names were—I have forgotten, except two oldest sons, Levin and Lloyd Wilcox. Failing to make payment for this tract of land he left and the last time I knew anything of the family they were living on the Scioto some miles above Portsmouth.

After he (L. Wilcox) left the place was bought by Martin Smith. Their children's names were Robert, William,4 Woodson, Nancy, Elizbeth and John. Elizabeth married John C. Kountz; Nancy married William Ward. Martin Smith owned more slaves than any other man in the country. He was a farmer and employed his force in the improvement of his land.

The next above and just below Tailor's Run settled Benjamin Ulin. Their elder children's names were: Benjamin, John, Nancy and Samuel. Ulin was a farmer. He owned one man-slave. Ulins lived here several years; then moved back several miles among the hills [Ulin's Branch]. Benjamin married the widow of Roland Cornelius (she was Ellenore Howe). John became an itinerant Methodist preacher and after traveling several years as an acceptable minister, he died of cholera down in the Miami country.

Next above settled Reuben Rucker.5 Their children's names were: Nancy, Ambrose and Edwin. What became of this family has escaped my memory. Rucker was a man of respectable character and I think for some time acted as sheriff of the county. He was commonly known by the title of Major Rucker.

Next, but back in the bottom, settled Mr. Terrell. They had one daughter named Margaret; she was a pious member of the Baptist Church. Mr. Terrell was a farmer, owned slaves and was considered a first class citizen.

MARRIAGES 1804—1838

Marriage Records, Greenup County, from organization of the county, February 1, 1804, to December 21, 1838, as shown by the records now available. The records covering this period are fragmentary.

Groom	Bride	Date of Marriage
A		
Adams, Robert	Anne Duncan	Feb. 14, 1823
Andrews, Shepherd	Sally Jones	Apr. 5, 1825
Arthur, Coleman	Mary Rice	May 1, 1833
Arnold, Jackson	Rhoda Boyd	Sept. 28, 1833
Akin, John	Sarah Hood	May 10, 1836
Anderson, Jacob	Eliza Hurt	Feb. 9, 1836
Artrup, John	Elizabeth Farmer	Feb. 20, 1836
Amos, Charles	Matilda Toler	Feb. 21, 1838
Arthur, Isaac	Jemima Arthur	Apr. 26, 1838
Abrims, Gabriel	Mariah Mills	Apr. 12, 1838
Alexander, Lewis	Elizabeth Gorman	Nov. 29, 1825
Apps, James	Susan Shelton	March 1, 1825
Applegate, Jeremiah	Mary Ann Sullivan	Aug. 25, 1832
Allen, Thomas J.	Catharine Duvey	Oct. 24, 1832
Arthur, Caleb	Rebecca Arthur	Mar. 27, 1835
Andrews, Herman T.	.... Remmeck	Apr. 1, 1833
Artrup, Jesse	Elizabeth Lasey	Sept. 14, 1836
Alexander, John	Catharine Long	Feb. 22, 1838
B		
Botts, Rowland	Lucy M. Terrill	Feb. 21, 1808
Bryant, Zephemiah	Rachel Roman	July 11, 1807

Groom	Bride	Date of Marriage
Bryant, John	Catherine Shope	Apr. 1, 1805
Botts, John	Judith Cornelius	Jan. 8, 1806
Brandom, John	Pedasam (?) Pankake	Nov. 13, 1809
Bruce, William	Peggy Ferguson	July 9, 1808
Bryant, John	Sally Leakins	Jan. 31, 1805
Barr, Thomas A.	Marinda Kouns	July 2, 1823
Bellomy, George W.	Margaret Stewart	Apr. 3, 1828
Bush, John	Margaret Migard	Apr. 1, 1829
Boyd, James	Ruthy Clarke	July 20, 1829
Blankenship, Richard	Susannah Miller	Sept. 5, 1829
Brown, William	Mary Warnock	Dec. 23, 1829
Bostick, Mortimer	Amanda M. Kouns	Mar. 4, 1828
Bush, Aaron	Catharine Johnson	Sept. 19, 1832
Bennett, William	Nancy Harris (?)	Sept. 28, 1832
Butler, William	Franky Wood	March 13, 1832
Braford, John	Elizabeth Alexander	Jan. 16, 1832
Banfield, Esquire	Sidney Martin	April 23, 1832
Burton, Joshua	Mary Ann Patton	Oct. 2, 1832
Brown, C. C.	Rebecca Brewbaker	Dec. 9, 1832
Bryson, William	Elizabeth Lawson	Sept. 23, 1833
Biggs, William	Lucy Davis	Oct. 15, 1827
Blake, Henry	Martha Ann Hockaday	Dec. 1, 1830
Bradshaw, Alexander	Nancy Rayburn	June 1, 1833
Bradshaw, Robert	Jane Warnock	Feb. 11, 1833
Blankenship, Richard	Rebecca Lanton	Dec. 1, 1836
Bradford, William	Martha Sturgeon	May 12, 1836
Boley, William B.	Nancy Ann Elizabeth Hackworth	Oct. 29, 1836
Bradshaw, George	Georgiann Grove	June 21, 1838
Bush, Daniel	Ruth Bailey	Aug. 24, 1838
Blankenship, Greenville	Mary Ann Ellison	Feb. 13, 1838
Bechtol, Nathan	Nancy Griffith	May 30, 1838
Bowling, Enoch	Precilla Leymans	Sept. 4, 1838
Bagby, John	Sarah Thompson	Apr. 5, 1838
Belford, George	Cassandra Nichols	Dec. 21, 1838
Boyce, John William	Elizabeth M. Paul	Dec. 5, 1836
Bryson, William P.	Hannah Sloane	Aug. 6, 1836

C

Cornelius, Rowland	Eleanor Howe	Oct. 6, 1804
Colgin, William	Nancy Hatton	Mar. 10, 1808
Chinn, Benjamin	Patsey, Nichols	Feb. 28, 1808
Cornelius, Austin	Jane Cobb	Mar. 1, 1808
Cain, John	Lucinda Wells	June 2, 1807
Cummins, Malke	Ann Everman	Dec. 22, 1806
	Moses Kibbe or Kibbey, surety. Jesse B. Boone, witness, to father's consent.	
Canterbury, Benjamin	Susannah Huzor (?)	Jan. 1, 1806
Canterbury, Reubin	Elizabeth Lycan	Sept. 29, 1908
Crank, William	Susannah Biggs	Mar. 4. 1805
Clark, Isaac	Mary Horsley	Apr. 8, 1823
Clark, William	Elizabeth Warnock	Sept. 5, 1825
Cravens, Nehemiah A.	Martha McCoy	July 22, 1828
Craycraft, William	Sarah Littlejohn	Jan. 19, 1828
Craycraft, Capt. Charles	Elizabeth Dillon	Feb. 1, 1828
Cooper, Robert	Elizabeth Patton	Apr. 21, 1829
Colegrove, Dyer	Elizabeth Long	July 27, 1833

Groom	Bride	Date of Marriage
Collins, John	Maria Hood	Apr. 27, 1833
Curtis, Andrew	Nancy Stewart	Apr. 5, 1836
Crawford, Sanders	Lavina Warnock	Dec. 21, 1836
Canterbury, Jeremiah L.	Catharine Waugh	Dec. 23, 1836
Campbell, Thomas J.	Eliza (?) Zornes	Jan. 1, 1836
Callahan, Thomas	Nancy Hannah	Nov. 6, 1836
Connor, William	Sidney Davis	June 16, 1824
Cooper, Eli	Rachel Dugan	Aug. 17, 1824
Callahan, Daniel	Nancy McAllister	Nov. 20, 1836
Craycraft, Charles C.	Maria Hunt	Sept. 24, 1838
Crosby, Obed	Mary Hubball	July 25, 1838
Cazill, John	Almyra Neamsley	Aug. 28, 1838
Craycraft, Rierson	Emma Hyde	Dec. 14, 1833
Callahan, Charles	Nancy Douglass	Nov. 9, 1833
Cummings, Johnson F.	Nancy E. Anglin	July 8, 1836
Cumington, James	Nancy Keesee	June 13, 1832
Christman, Charles H.	Elizabeth Glover	Jan. 28, 1836
Corum, William	Edith Passmore	Dec. 3, 1834

D

Deering, Richard	Sally Stratton	July 5, 1809
Deatly, John	Nancy McKenny ?	Oct. 16, 1804
Dixon, John	Mahala Rowland	May 29, 1824
Dugan, Ezekiel W.	Rebecca Cornelius	Aug. 4, 1824
Davis, Moses	Mildred T. Gibbs	Sept. 26, 1829
DeBord, James	Elizabeth Davis	Oct. 5, 1829
DeVore, David	Sarah Gee	Jan. 26, 1828

Robert Gee, father, gave his consent to marriage, Jan. 24, 1828.

Davis, Hezekiah	Elizabeth Friend	Jan. 7, 1833
Deaver, George	Jeanette Thomas	Nov. 14, 1833
DeWitt, William	Angeline Howe	Dec. 11, 1833
Day, Lewis B.	Cynthia Genat	Feb. 29, 1836
Deegins, William	Amanda McIntyre	Feb. 16, 1836
Dixon, John	Narotha Hackworth	May 26, 1838
Davis, Henry	Elizabeth Hall	Oct. 24, 1838
DeHart, John	Nancy Hill	Apr. 20, 1838
Dupuy, A. G.	Kissiah Metz	May 3, 1832

E

Everman, Samuel	Phoebe Skidmore	Dec. 12, 1825
Everman, William	Elizabeth Toler	Sept. 29, 1829
Ewing, Joseph	Sally M. Chadwick	Apr. 6, 1829

F

Friend, Jacob	Ann Stratton	Apr. 23, 1808
Frame, George	Anna Tate	Jan. 5, 1808
Frame, David	Katy Everman	July 15, 1808
Ford, James	Elizabeth Fisher	May 17, 1805
Foster, John	Sarah Culp	Oct. 30, 1824
Friend, Jonathan	Jane Ruggles	Apr. 16, 1823
Fisher, Gustavus	Judith Morton	Feb. 3, 1829
Francis, John	Minewa Evans	May 23, 1832
Francis, Elijah	Jane Hasty	Feb. 20, 1833
Finn, Willis	Christine Kizer	Dec. 17, 1833
Foster, William	Kezziah Richards	Sept. 9, 1836
Fitzmorris, David	Sally Ann Hardwick	May 9, 1836

Groom	Bride	Date of Marriage
Farmer, George	Mary Ross	June 28, 1836
Fitzpatrick, Nathan	Mary Ann Pully	Nov. 10, 1838
Ferguson, Elijah	Alcey Lewis	Nov. 14, 1838
Fisher, Frederick	Sally Wilson	June 2, 1838
Frizzell, Alfred H.	Eliza Scott	Jan. 3, 1838
Ferguson, William	Aramatha Lewis	May 13, 1833
Fuqua, William	Lydia Waring	Apr. 21, 1823
Frazier, Lewis	Elizabeth Ratliff	May 18, 1805

G

Groom	Bride	Date of Marriage
Goble, Ephraim	Hannah Virgin	Nov. 2, 1808
Gilkerson, James	Malinda Mayhew	Sept. 16, 1805
Gandy, John	Nancy Campbell	Sept. 3, 1824
Galligher, John	Polly Gray	Mar. 24, 1824
Garrett, Clifton A.	Sarah M. King	Nov. 8, 1824
Gorman, William	Ann Miller	May 20, 1823
Goble, Daniel	Polly Fain	May 6, 1823
Gilkerson, John	Jane Keesee	Aug. 4, 1823
Goodrich, Justus	Jane Hillman	Mar. 3, 1828
Garvin, Johnson	Elizabeth Garrett	Mar. 6, 1828
Gilkey, John	Margaret Gee	Aug. 10, 1829
Gilkey, Edward	Emily Ginat	Jan. 14, 1833
Gustin, Alfred	Abigail Ferguson	Sept. 23, 1833
Gastin, Robert	Sophia Crump	July 7, 1833
Gammon, Joshua S.	Harriet Stewart	Jan. 28, 1833
Griffith, Jesse	Eunice Mayhew	Feb. 28, 1833
Goodwin, Theophlius	Sofanna Meade	Jan. 8, 1833
Gollihue, John	Polly Rice	July 29, 1833
Gray, Joseph	Delila Frailor	....
Gitthens ? , John	Rebecca Cooper	Sept. 8, 1836
Gee, Robert Anderson	Theresa Williams	Nov. 15, 1836
Gaunce, Joseph	Emmaline Clark	Feb. 1, 1836
Giles, James	Nancy Myers	Jan. 7, 1825
Gustin, Alfred	Judith Eastham	Mar. 28, 1836
Gollihue, Henry W.	Ruth Rice	Sept. 8, 1838
Garrett, Clifton A.	Mary Ann Culbertson	Nov. 12, 1832

H

Groom	Bride	Date of Marriage
Holland, Wright	Drusilla Crone	June 7, 1808
Hood, Andrew	Polly Cain	Oct. 19, 1807
Ham, Jacob M.	Sally Stephenson	Nov. 27, 1805
Hedges, Salomon	Susannah Russell	June 29, 1802
Hitchcock, Caleb	Susannah Ferguson	Mar. 7, 1808
Hord, Robert C.	Julianna Pickett	Nov. 24, 1824

Order of the Jefferson County Court, November, 1824: "On motion of Sarah Mayfield (the mother), the court appoints Robert C. Hord guardian to "Julian" Pickett, infant orphan of John Pickett, deceased; whereupon he gave bond in the penalty of four thousand dollars with Thomas Parker, William Sale, and Hancock Taylor, his sureties, according to law. A copy Teste: Worden Pope, C.J.C.

By Robert Tyler D.C.J.C.C."

Groom	Bride	Date of Marriage
Head, Simeon C.	Malinda Poage	Feb. 7, 1824
Hord, Thomas T.	Clarinda Kibby	Mar. 13, 1823
	Moses Kibby gave his consent for	
	daughter to marry,	Mar. 12, 1823.
Hill, Joseph	Isle ? Lawson	Aug. 27, 1825
Hannah, William	Judith Woodcocke	Mar. 29, 1825
Hardin, Henry	Anna Cain	Apr. 11, 1825
Hood, Jacob	Joanna Lewis	Nov. 20, 1829
Huffman, Allen	Sally Warnock	Nov. 6, 1829
Howe, Daniel L.	Angeline Ellison	Mar. 12, 1828
Hiser, Edwin	Rebecca Corum	Oct. 24, 1826
Hastings, Hiram	Saray Bush	Sept. 3, 1828
Huffman, Solomon	Betsy Warnock	Jan. 20, 1829
Harlow, Nicholas	Nancy Kidd	July 6, 1829
Hord, Philip B.	Katharine England	July 18, 1829
Henry, John	Patsy Ann Harris	Oct. 10, 1832
Hardwick, Henry	Matilda Downs	Jan. 31, 1832
Hatton, Wiley	Eliza Ann Dixon	Sept. 3, 1832
Hull, Moses	Rachel Kizer	Jan. 21, 1833
Hoobler, George	Mary Jones	Mar. 11, 1833
Hornbuckle, William	Charlotte Patton	Jan. 23, 1833
Higgins, Daniel	Sophia Raison	Apr. 25, 1833
Holderness, Skiffington	Mary Ann Poage	Apr. 6, 1833
Hunt, Carlisle	Rebecca Craycraft	Feb. 11, 1833
Harvey, James J.	Ann B. Chinn	July 25, 1836
Howard, James W.	Catharine Sparks	Dec. 12, 1836
Harr, Torman	Thomasins ? Richards	Oct. 17, 1836
Howell, Charles	Vashti Davidson	Aug. 24, 1836
Howell, John A.	Mary Crumb	...., 1838
Hensley, Robert	Rutha Miller	July 5, 1838
Hoobler, Jacob	Melvina Jackson	Mar. 21, 1838
Hannah, Perry	Jane Powell	Nov. 1, 1838
House (Howes)	Susannah Petitt	Feb. 19, 1838
Hollingsworth, John	Elizabeth Ann Kouns	Dec. 1, 1845

J

Johnson, Levi	Almira Middaugh	Sept. 1, 1823
Johnson, Andrew	Patsy Yeley	July 28, 1828
Jackson, Henry	Mary Hannah	May 29, 1832
Jones, Isaac	Mary Corum	July 4, 1833
Jones, Samuel	Eleanor Dotson	Sept. 28, 1833
Jones, Thompkins	Sobrina White	Aug. 3, 1833
James, George	Sally Smith	Oct. 18, 1836
James, William	Elizabeth Ross	Oct. 18, 1836
Jones, Benjamin F.	Elizabeth Jane Bradford	Aug. 24, 1836
Jones, David	Ann Oliver	Feb. 12, 1838
Jones, John	Scitha Barney	Dec. 18, 1838
Jamison, James	Jane Willis	Jan. 17, 1838
James, Ephraim	Leanna Biggs	Feb. 13, 1824

K

Kite, James	Peggy Rucker	Sept. 14, 1809
Knox, George	Nancy Franklin	Mar. 7, 1808
Kibby, Jacob	Malinda Everman	June 9, 1824
	John Everman, father, gave his consent, June 8, 1824.	

Groom	Bride	Date of Marriage
Kouns, John C.	Elizabeth Smith	Nov. 21, 1818
Kelly, Balis	Polly Amos	Mar. 29, 1823
Kelly, Stephen	Esther Binges ?	Sept. 10, 1825
Keesee, Robert	Melvina Chitwood	Apr. 4, 1829
Kidd, Jesse	Phoebe Goble	Dec. 25, 1828
Kibby, David	Eliza Womack	Sept. 1, 1828
Kissic, James	Sally Freeland	Sept. 21, 1829
King, Benjamin	Nancy Mackoy	Nov. 26, 1832
Kouns, Christian	Amanda Triplett	June 29, 1836
Kibby, Marcus L.	Elizabeth C. Clarke	Dec. 10, 1836
Kouns, Henry	Maria Triplett	Oct. 8, 1836
Kouns, William	Nancy Womack	Nov. 3, 1836
Kouns, William Smith	Caroline Van Bibber	Oct. 21, 1841

L

Littlejohn, John	Lucy Chapman	Nov. 17, 1806
Lacy, John	Betsy Mayhew	June 23, 1806
Ladley, John	Rachel Petitt	Aug. 1, 1808
Litton, Thomas	Nancy Trotter	Mar. 25, 1807
Leaton, John	Elizabeth Everman	Oct. 29, 1807
Landreth, John	Elizabeth Hammonds	Dec. 8, 1806
Lynch, Jeremiah	Naomi Hull	Oct. 28, 1823
Lambart, Elias	Elizabeth S. Powell	Aug. 7, 1828
Lore?, William	Elizabeth Hampton	Nov. 2, 1829
Lester, Samuel	Sidney Flaugher	Dec. 8, 1829
Lawson, Jacob	Fanny Walker	Nov. 10, 1829
Loving, George	Lucinda Arthur	May 30, 1829
Littleton, George	Mary Choat	Feb. 3, 1829
Loving, John	Nancy Burwell	July 5, 1832
Lampton, John B.	Martha Smith	Apr. 30, 1833
Littrill, Stephen	Dulcena Sparks	Oct. 12, 1833
Laughlin, Thomas	Mary Kirkpatrick	Oct. 12, 1836
Lawhorn, Daniel	Malissa Ferguson	Dec. 28, 1836
Lawson, Milton	Sophia Glover	June 21, 1836
Lavender, Lewis	Mary Douglass	June 6, 1836
Lionbarger, John	Mary Susanna Lyon	Aug. 6, 1836

M

McGlothin, William	Mary Everman	Sept. 28, 1807
Mayhew, Myra	Rebecca Currant	Jan. 13, 1806
McCrum, John	Dorcas Flynn	July 28, 1832
McMains, John	Margaret Hatton	Sept. 18, 1806
McCool, James	Rebecca Nolan	June 18, 1824
McCartney, William	Betsy Davidson	Aug. 13, 1823
McCutchon, William	Rebecca Scott	June 18, 1825
McGlone, John	Lucretia Friend	Mar. 7, 1825
McIntosh, Thomas	Catharine Fightmaster	July 22, 1828
McCoy, Obadiah F.	Melvina Powell	Oct. 18, 1838
Munyan, William	Elizabeth Parker	Jan. 2, 1828
Martin, Henry	Sarah Martin	Jan. 5, 1829
Mayhew, William	Matilda Keesee	Dec. 1, 1829
McLaughlin, David	Catharine Fightmaster	Jan. 10, 1829
Mills, John	Nancy Richards	Apr. 24, 1832
McCarty, Scott	Mary Stewart	Oct. 26, 1832
Martin, Jefferson	Nacky Goble	May 5, 1832
Mills, Isaac	Jane Norton	Sept. 20, 1832
McCarty, James	Malinda Lowe	June 30, 1832

Groom	Bride	Date of Marriage
Mitchell, John	Elizabeth Hensley	Oct. 12, 1833
McCarroll, John	Martha Ann Gladden	Nov. 29, 1833
McGlosson (McGlothan), John	Eliza L. England	Oct. 21, 1833
Murphy, John	Eyrinia? Owens	Apr. 9, 1833
McCoy, John	Judith Morton	Nov. 20, 1820
Majors, Jesse W.	Mary Ann Eastham	Dec. 2, 1833
McCole, William	Ruth McGuire	Feb. 6, 1824
Markin, Charles	Eunice Gilkerson	Feb. 22, 1825
Metz, Benjamin	Jane Lawson	Apr. 19, 1833
McAllister, John Jr.	Elizabeth Lewis	May 5, 1836
Mocobee, David	Anne Brinegar	Sept. 26, 1836
Miller, E. Rastus	Mary Gibbs	Mar. 7, 1836
McAllister, George W.	Mary Ann Hardin	Oct. 8, 1836
Morton, David	Fernada Trailor	Jan. 25, 1836
Marns, John	Letitia Ratcliff	June 27, 1836
Middaugh, John	Mary Stepter	May 5, 1838
Miller, William H.	Melvina Ratcliff	Feb. 26, 1838
McGlone, Alfred	Mary Henderson	May ...., 1838
McWhorter, Harvey	America Winn	Mar. 28, 1838
McMahon, Joseph	Ally (Olly) Hannah	Oct. 17, 1809
Mills, Aaron	Betsy Lowry	Apr. 5, 1823
Mills, Abram H.	Evaline Amos	Nov. 27, 1828

N

Groom	Bride	Date of Marriage
Newcomb, James	Clarinda Alington	Nov. 4, 1806
Neal, Jacob	Sally Kouns	Sept. 6, 1804
Noel, Daniel	Nancy Brown	Dec. 4, 1823
Norton, James	Elizabeth West	Apr. 28, 1823
Norris, Charles	Levisa Jamison	Apr. 27, 1832
Nelson, John A.	Eliza Roberts	Feb. 16, 1833
Nunnelley, David	Ruth Miller	Feb. 8, 1836
Nunnelley, Daniel	America Skaggs	Feb. 23, 1836

O

Groom	Bride	Date of Marriage
Offill, Allen	Louisa Hargett	Apr. 25, 1825
Oliver, George	Anna Howland	Sept. 1, 1828
Oaton, Randolph	Lydia Pierce	Mar. 19, 1829
Offill, Elzaphan	Martha Everman	Sept. 26, 1829
O'Brian, John	Rachel Halphinstine	Aug. 10, 1825

P

Groom	Bride	Date of Marriage
Poage, James	Jane Poage	Oct. 20, 1806
Poage, Allen	Peggy Terrill	June 2, 1806
Pogue, William L.	Ann McCormick	Nov. 8, 1824
Pool, John	Celia McGinnis	Mar. 12, 1823
Pollard, Broxton C.	Sally Powers	Sept. 3, 1825
Powell, Andrew M.	Elizabeth Powell	Sept. 25, 1828
Pratt, Lott	Polly Lewis	July 1, 1829
Pope, Lewis	Polly Bumgardner	Nov. 20, 1829
Patton, James	Kizzah Meed	Aug. 25, 1829
Pugh, James Y.	Cinderilla D. Pugh	Sept. 25, 1832
Plunkett, Jesse	Narcissa Cummings	Mar. 12, 1832
Poynter, David E.	Judith B. Moseley	Dec. 22, 1833
Pollard, Henry B.	Sophia Y. Poage	Feb. 18, 1833
Pepper, Nothy D.	Ann Glover	Apr. 15, 1836
Porter, Zehaniah	Martha H. Mathews	Apr. 14, 1836

GREENUP COUNTY, KENTUCKY

Groom	Bride	Date of Marriage
— Powell, Abel	Frances Turman	Dec. 5, 1836
Pray, John	Clarinda Applegate	Feb. 4, 1824
Pearce, William	Mary D. Vallance	Jan. 13, 1836
Pully, David	Louanna Hale	Nov. 3, 1838
Palmer, Samuel	Martha Stewart	May 23, 1829
Puthuff, Joseph B.	Melcena Howe	May 23, 1838
Pollock, Joseph	Sarah Kouns	Oct. 20, 1850

R

Retherford, Thomas	Mary Collins	Mar. 17, 1806
Rigg, Joseph	Elizabeth Gholson	Aug. 20, 1810
Rigg, Garrett P.	Mary Deering	Nov. 9, 1829
Rigg, George W.	Delila Kibbey	July 6, 1832
Rigg, Ewell	Rhoda Brown	Feb. 18, 1833
Rigg, James S.	Polly Rice	Nov. 22, 1833
Rucker, Reubin	Mary I. Love	Oct. 10, 1808
Rucker, Elzaphan	Polly Deatty	Aug. 4, 1808
Ratcliff, Daniel	Stacy Frazier	May 12, 1805
Rice, Jeremiah	Sally Hiatt	Mar. 24, 1824
Rankins, Alexander	Elizabeth Sanders	Feb. 2, 1825
Robertson, William	Sarah Rigg	Feb. 1, 1825
Rice, David	Susanna Hedges	Sept. 6, 1828
Roberts, Alexander	Rachel Mayhew	Mar. 19, 1828
Rice, James	Tabitha Stevens	May 11, 1832
Roberts, James	Colba Culp	Apr. 7, 1832
Richardson, Amos	Mary Shane	Apr. 25, 1832
Ruffner, James	Martha Morton	Nov. 12, 1832
Rucker, Bazil	America McGuyre (McGuire)	Sept. 10, 1832
Robinson, Samuel	Elizabeth Hughes	June 4, 1832
Richards, Grant	Margaret Hasty	Dec. 18, 1833
Roberts, George W.	Elizabeth T. Hord	June 3, 1833
Roberts, John H.	Jane Gilkerson	Nov. 7, 1836
Rawlings, Franklin	Mary Hornbuckle	Sept. 24, 1836
Ratcliff, Samuel	Mary Bryson	Mar. 16, 1836
Raybourn, Patrick N.	Jane Bradshaw	Oct. 3, 1836
Riley, William	Patsy Farris	Mar. 6, 1838
Runyon, William	Elizabeth Adams	Oct. 5, 1838
Robinett, Hiram	Anna Colley	Apr. 14, 1838
Reid, Charles	Chloe Roby	Jan. 13, 1808
Rankins, Alexander	Elizabeth Saunders	Feb. 2, 1825

S

Snegedar (Snedegar), John	Rosanna Shoup	Oct. 13, 1804
Scott, John	Hannah Applegate	July 19, 1808
Stambaugh, David	Rhoda Gillilan	Nov. 3, 1807
Strahan, William	Elizabeth Rigg	Feb. 7, 1824
Stewart, James	Nancy Bartley	Oct. 5, 1824
Stewart, James	Elizabeth Stewart	July 26, 1823
Sartin, Wilson	Ebby James	Mar. 22, 1825
Stratton, Tollman	Sally Richards	Aug. 27, 1825
Scott, John	Margaret Gray	Jan. 23, 1828
Smith, Samuel	Cynthia McDowell	Aug. 1, 1828
Shortridge, George	Judith Terrill	Nov. 24, 1828
Salmon, Jacob	Abigail Gilkerson	Jan. 28, 1828
Spencer, James C.	Evaline G. Kouns	Jan. 26, 1828
Stevenson, Edward	Mahala Crump	Feb. 4, 1828
Sparks, William	Emaline Hyde	Jan. 1, 1828

Groom	Bride	Date of Marriage
Scott, Henry	Jane Bradford	Dec. 19, 1829
Smith, Benjamin	Sally Patton	July 8, 1829
Shelton, Hardin	Polly M. McAllister	Dec. 2, 1829
Simms, Gabriel	Patsy Rosel ?	Jan. 18, 1832
Scott, Robert	Catharine Garrett	Nov. 15, 1832
Squires, Samuel	Mary Frost	June 20, 1832
Stewart, James	Edy Skidmore	Feb. 2, 1832
Smith, Rezin	Cynthia Greenslate	Jan. 9, 1833
Sparks, Isaac	Lucinda Thomas	Mar. 15, 1833
Smith, Clabourn	Chloe Lusk	Nov. 26, 1833
Smith, William	Elizabeth Waugh	Nov. 20, 1833
Scott, James	Leah Rouse	Apr. 20, 1833
Sanders, Jonathan	Louisa Thompson	Jan. 8, 1833
Sperry, Alfred	Elizabeth Ann S. Gitthens	Jan. 18, 1833
Stewart, John	Nancy Farmer	Dec. 16, 1833
Shelton, Peter	Frances Kizer	Dec. 4, 1836
Scatch, John	Ann Thomason	May 28, 1836
Smith, Caswell	Sarah Smith	Mar. 25, 1836
Stewart, Thomas J.	Eliza T. Waring	Aug. 1, 1836
Stewart, Charles	Rebecca Philips	June 6, 1836
Sanders, James	Anna Drody	Aug. 2, 1836
Swearingin, John	Polly Williams	Jan. 1, 1838
Stepter, James	Rebecca Morrison	May 24, 1838
Seaton, John	Mary Elizabeth Rice	Nov. 19, 1845

T

Tanner, George	Elizabeth Corum	July 17, 1824
Townsend, Jackson	Jane Dixon	Mar. 31, 1829
Terrill, William	Ann Colvin	Feb. 2, 1829
Tate, David	Nancy Wilson	Jan. 28, 1828
Toler, Stephen	Adelphia Zorns	Nov. 15, 1828
Tyree, Zachariah	Eliza H. Flaugher	Aug. 17, 1832
Thomas, William	Harriet Jones	Aug. 31, 1833
Thomason, Jackson	Winney Alexander	June 11, 1836
Turley, Thomas	Susan Dodd	Jan. 26, 1836
Thornsbury, Martin	Nancy Gipson	Jan. 4, 1836
Toler, Caleb	Nancy Johnson	Jan. 22, 1838
Tannahill, Francis	Eliza Loper	Sept. 5, 1829

U

Underwood, Willis	Margaret Underwood	Nov. 29, 1823

V

Van Bibber, Cyrus	Mary Timberlake	Dec. 26, 1821
Vansky, Nicholas	Sarah Sutton	Mar. 29, 1832
Van Bibber, Ezekiel	Susan Rice	Dec. 20, 1833
Vallance, Harvey	Sally Barney	July 31, 1838
Van Bibber, Jacob	Margaret Bryson	Feb. 11, 1829
VanHoose, John	Almira Keesee (Benjamin Keesee's daughter	Oct. 27, 1836

W

Wade, John	Prudence Elington	....
Webb, Samuel	Polly Frasher (Frazier)	May 29, 1829
Waring, James	Lydia W. Waring	Feb. 3, 1808

Groom	Bride	Date of Marriage
Willis, George	Anna Rucker	Sept. 14, 1808
Wells, John E.	Rebecca Virgin	July 25, 1806
Walker, John	Rachel McCool	Feb. 20, 1804
Webb, William	Elizabeth Reid	Nov. 14, 1823
Winn, Benjamin	Nancy Young	Aug. 14, 1824
Womack, Archer	Miriam Kouns	July 4, 1823
Wornock, Matthew	Lydia Wornock	Apr. 5, 1828
Walker, Robert	Margaret Deering	July 10, 1828
Walker, Thomas	Dulcena Sparks	Nov. 19, 1828
Westlake, Josiah	Kerilla Lyon	Feb. 16, 1828
Westlake, Thomas	Polly Huffman	Dec. 6, 1828
Waring, Bazil	Jane R. McCall	Dec. 28, 1829
Womack, William	Jacintha Kibbey	Dec. 29, 1829
	Moses Kibbey, father, gave his consent.	
Wilson, Givan	Rebecca Lewis	July 14, 1832
Womack, Richard D.	Harriet D. Ward	Feb. 28, 1833
Waring, Thomas	Catharine Laughlin	Jan. 14, 1833
Womack, James A.	Ann Lampton	Oct. 29, 1833
Warnock, John	Grace Guilkey	Apr. 1, 1833
Wemsley, Avington	Elizabeth Smith	Mar. 19, 1836
Wamsley, Avington	Elizabeth Turner	Aug. 13, 1836
Welsh, William	Elizabeth DeWitt	Dec. 5, 1836
Wallace, George	Cynthia McDaniel	Aug. 17, 1836
Webb, Joseph	Sally Riffe	Aug. 7, 1838
Woodson, William G.	Theresa Green	June 21, 1838
Woodrow, William H.	Sarah Ann Collins	July 7, 1838
Welsh, Walter	Jane Higgins	Feb. 15, 1838
Woodrow, William	Theresa Sophie Green (?)	June 26, 1836

NOTES

Chapter IV

1. Patsey Nichols married Benjamin Chinn in Greenup County, February 28, 1808.

2. One Cassandra Nichols married George Belford in Greenup County, December 21, 1838.

3. William McCartney married Betsy Davidson in Greenup County, August 13, 1823.

4. One William Smith married Elizabeth Waugh in Greenup County, November 20, 1833.

5. Reuben Rucker was commissioned by Governor Garrard as one of the first justices of the peace of Greenup County; was surety, jointly with Jesse B. Boone, on the official bond of Josiah Davidson, the first sheriff of Greenup County, 1806-1809; and was the ancestor in the maternal line of Governor William Jason Fields of Kentucky.

CHAPTER V

CLAY COUNTY, KENTUCKY

BOUNDARY AND ESTABLISHMENT

CLAY COUNTY, the 47th formed in the State, was carved out of Madison, Knox and Floyd Counties pursuant to an act of the General Assembly, approved December 2, 1806 (3 *Littell's Laws of Kentucky* 338) which act is in part as follows:

November Sessions
Chapter CCCXLV

Section 1. Be it enacted by the General Assembly, That from and after the first day of April, next, all that part of the counties of Madison, Knox, and Floyd, that is included in the following bounds, to-wit: Beginning on the Kentucky River midway between the mouth of Ross's and Sturgeon Creeks; thence along the ridge that divides the waters of Sturgeon from those of Ross's and Station Camp creeks to the dividing ridge between the waters of Kentucky and Rockcastle water; thence along said ridge to the head of Horse Lick creek; thence down the said creek to Rockcastle; thence down Rockcastle to the state road leading from Madison Court House to Cumberland Gap; thence along the said road to Langford's road leading to Goose creek salt-works; thence with the same to Rockcastle; thence up Rockcastle to the head; thence along the dividing ridge between the waters of Cumberland and Kentucky to a point from which by running due East will pass by Collins' fork of Goose creek, midway between Outlaws salt-works and Peter Hammond's; thence a course to strike the ridge between Cumberland and Kentucky at the War Gap; thence with said ridge to a point at which running north-west will strike the mouth of Lott's creek; thence up Lott's creek to head; thence with the ridge dividing the waters of Kentucky from Licking, to the head of Quicksand; thence down Quicksand to the Kentucky River; thence down the Kentucky River to the beginning, shall be one distinct County, to be called and known by the name of Clay.

* * *

Section 3. The Justices of the peace for the said county of Clay shall meet at the house of Robert Baker on a court day, after the said division shall take place, and having taken the oaths required by the constitution of the United States and of this state, and the sheriff being also qualified according to law, shall proceed to appoint and qualify a clerk.

* * *

Section 7. All that part of Madison County and a tract of territory on the waters of the Kentucky river above the said County of Clay shall be annexed to and added to the County of Floyd.

Parts of the territory as originally formed have been taken in forming each of the counties of Perry in 1820; Laurel in 1825; Breathitt in 1839; Owsley in 1843; and Jackson in 1858.

The County was named in honor of General Green Clay, a resident of Madison County, probably of Welsh extraction. General Clay was born in Powhatan County, Virginia, August 14, 1757. He was a son of Charles Clay and descended from John Clay, a British grenadier, who came to Virginia during Bacon's Rebellion and declined to return to England when the King's troops were sent back. It is not definitely known whether this ancestor was from England or Wales, but the prevailing belief is that he was born in Wales.

General Clay came to Kentucky in early youth and the first few years after his arrival were spent in examining the county and aiding in expelling the Indians. He then entered the office of James Thompson, a commissioned surveyor where he more thoroughly studied the principles and acquired the art of surveying. Soon he was made a deputy surveyor and became minutely acquainted with the lands in the upper portion of the then County of Kentucky. He became a very large landowner not only in Kentucky but in other states, particularly in Louisiana.

Notwithstanding his great responsibilities in connection with his land business, General Clay devoted several years of his life to politics. Before Kentucky was a State he was elected a delegate to the general assembly of Virginia; was a member of the convention that formed the second constitution of Kentucky. After the State was admitted into the Union, he represented Madison County many years in each branch of the legislature. He was a major general of the militia and took an active part in the War of 1812. He died October 31, 1826.

ORGANIZATION—EARLIEST COURT ORDERS

April the 13th 1807.

In pursuance to an act of the General Assembly of Kentucky, approved the 2nd day of December, 1806, erecting a new county out of the counties of Madison, Knox, and Floyd—called and known by the name of Clay—the justices named in the commission of the peace from his Excellency Christopher Greenup, Esquire, Governor of the Commonwealth of Kentucky, met at the house of Robert Baker, Esquire, and there the said commission was produced and read, appointing Ezekiel Smith, John Haddocks, John Gilbert, John Bates, Robert Baker, Elijah Bowman, and William Strong, Justices of the Peace for the said county of Clay; whereupon Ezekiel Smith, Esquire, administered to John Gilbert, Esquire, the several oaths in support of the constitution of the United States and of this state as well the oath of office; and the said John Gilbert, Esquire, administered the said several oaths to Ezekiel Smith, John Bates, Robert Baker, Elijah Bowman, and William Strong, Esquires.

Benjamin Strawn, Gentleman, produced a commission from his Excellency Christopher Greenup, Esquire, Governor of the Commonwealth of Kentucky, appointing him sheriff of this county; whereupon he took the oath in support of the constitution of the United States and of this state as well the oath of office, and together with John White and John Crook entered into and acknowledged bond in the penalty of $3,000, conditioned as the law directs; and thus a court was held at the house of Robert Baker, Esquire, on the 13th day of April 1807. Present: Ezekiel Smith, John Gilbert, John Bates, Robert Baker, Elijah Bowman, (and) William Strong, Esquires.

Abner Baker (was) appointed clerk, protem, of this court; whereupon the said Baker took the several oaths in support of the constitution of the United States and of this state as well the oath of office, and together with Sam McKee, George Walker, Henry Buford, Andrew Bradley, and John Baker, entered into and acknowledged bond in the penalty of 1000 pounds (?) conditioned as the law directs.

A surveyor being wanting in this county, a majority of the justices being present and concurring, (ordered) that Andrew Bradley and John Hebbard be recommended to his Excellency Christopher (Greenup), Esquire, as a fit person to be appointed in this county.

Ordered that Court be adjourned till court in course

(Signed) Ezekiel Smith

* * *

April Term—1807.

In pursuance of an act of the General Assembly of Kentucky, approved December the 2nd 1806, at the house of Robert Baker, Esquire, a Circuit Court was held for the Circuit of Clay on the 13th day of April 1807.

* * *

Present: the Honorable Samuel McDowell.

Hugh White (and) Adrem Hay, Esquires, produced a commission from his Excellency Christopher Greenup, Esquire, Governor of the Commonwealth of Kentucky, appointing them assistant judges for the county and circuit of Clay and a certificate of their qualification as the law directs and ordered to be recorded***.

Abner Baker was appointed clerk protem to this court and together with Samuel McKee, George Walker, Henry Buford, Andrew Bradley, and Jo. Baker, entered into and acknowledged bond in the penalty of 1,000 pounds (?), conditioned as the law directs.

A grand jury, sworn for the body of the county, John Hebbard, foreman, William Hudson, Philip Singleton, Stephen McCollum, David McCollum, Richard Singleton, Samuel Smith, David Gentry, Henry Clark, Samuel Percifield, William Morris, Jesse Pace, Adoneram Allen, Daniel McCollum, Andrew Hambleton, John Baker, Bowling Baker, Absolem Sweeten, Morris Baker, William Allen, and Dile Asher, having received their charge returned to consult of their presentments.***

Samuel McKee, Jeremiah Swopsher, George Morrison, George Walker, Joseph Eve, Rodes Gath, produced their license to the court as counsel and attorney at law (and) took the oath in support of the constitution of the United States and of this state as well the oath of office and are allowed to practice in this court as such.

* * *

Ordered that Rodes Gath, Esquire, be, and is, appointed attorney for the county and circuit of Clay.

* * *

Ordered that court adjourn until court in course and then to meet at the house of Richard Singleton at the lower Lick.

(Signed) Sam'l McDowell.

PIONEER FAMILIES

There were approximately 330 families living in Clay County in the year 1810, as shown by original tax lists and other public records. John Hibbard, assistant to Joseph Crockett, United States Marshal for the District of Kentucky, enumerated the third decennial census and, on December 19, 1810, he certified and reported a total enumeration of 2,398. Of this number 1202 were white males, 1055 white females, and 141 negro slaves. Below are given the names of the heads of families and/or taxpayers as of the year 1810, together with the number of slaves owned by each slaveholder.

A

Amis (Amos),
  Catherine
Abner, Elisha
Alldridge, Elijah
Allen, John
Allen, William
Allen, James
Abner, Elisha, Jr.
Alexander, John
Abrams, Gabriel
Allen, Adoruam ?
Anglin, James
Allcorn, George
Austin, Nathan
Amis, Lincoln
Allen, John
Abbett, James
Allcorn, Robert
Asher, Dillon
Anderson, John
  (1 slave)

B

Blythe, Daniel
Bagley, John
Boling, Ely
Boze, Will
Burris, Isiah
Bagley, Henry
Bowman, Thomas
Baker, Robert
Baker, John, Jr.
Broaddus, Beverly
  (6 slaves)
Burkham, Charles
Bunton, Isaac
Boling, James
Broughton, James
Bryant, William
  (4 slaves)
Broaddus, Jlos ?
  (3 slaves)
Barret, David
Bullock, David

Bowman, Sarah
Bowman, Jacob
Baker, Abner
  (8 slaves)
Bunton, John
Baker, Boling
Barton, John
Broaddus, Elijah
Blythe, John
Bates, John
  (15 slaves)
Barger, John
Bagley, Will
Boling, William
Benge, David
Bryant, William Jr.
Bowman, Elisha
Blankinship, Asa
Baker, John, Sr.
Blair, John
Boles, James
Bowman, Will

101

Birgin, John
Burns, Brice
Boling, Joseph
Barnett, Mary
Boling, Jesse
Barger ?, Abraham
Boling, Christopher
Bishop, Samuel
Boling, John
Burris, Thomas
Bowman, Elijah
(1 slave)
Bales, John
Baker, George
Boling, Isham
Brinnegar, Thomas
Bunton, James
Bradley, Andrew
Broughton, William
Boling, Justus

C

Cundiff, John
Cornett, Samuel
Cornett, Roger
Clark, Henry
Carnague (Carnegie), James
Clark, Thomas
Casteel, John
Combs, John
Cornett, Will
Cornett, Robert
Cornelius, Elihu
Cope, Wileigh ?
Clark, Randolph
Combs, Elijah
(3 slaves)
Combs, Shade
Cornett, Nathaniel
Cope, Andrew
Clark, David
(1 slave)
Combs, Mason
(2 slaves)
Cornett, Lydia
Croocks, Hezekiah
Clark, William
(1 slave)
Combs, Nicholas
(1 slave)
Campbell, William
Combs, Jeremiah
Combs, Jeremiah
Collum, (McCollum)
Sam'l W.
Cutright, John
Cunningham, James
Cody, John
Cloth, Jae Fair ?

Carr, John
Callahan, Isaac
Chestnut, Samuel
Cockrell, Simon
(1 slave)
Combs, Will
Cottell, Will
Callahan, Edward
(10 slaves)
Cane, Jacob
Campbell, John
Campbell, John
Combs, George
(3 slaves)
Cockrell, Duncan
Cox, Joseph
Clemmons, Will

D

Dwiggins, John
Davidson, John
Davidson, Thomas
Daniel, Nancy
Darnell, Barton
Duecase ?, Peter
Dickson, Henry
Dickerson, Arch
(9 slaves)
Daniel, Thomas W.
Dulin, Jacob
Dayton, James
Davidson, Daniel
(1 slave)
Dirham (Durham),
William
Davidson, Samuel
Davidson, James
Deakins, John

E

Ellison, Arch
Eversole, John
Ervine, Jameson
Evans, Edward
Eversoul (Eversole),
Peter
Eversole, Jacob
Eldridge, Rachel
Eldridge, John
Estes, John
Eliame ? (Elam),
William
Elkins, Joshua
Ellett, Thomas
Eldridge, James

F

Field, Will. W.
Fuget. Jonathan

Frasier, Elec
Freeman, George
Fox, Jonathan
Fuget, Martin
Frasier, John
Fryer, Daniel
Fuget, Zachariah
Felkner, John
Flowars, Micajah
Fields, John
Fuget, Ben
Ford, Egbert
Fortner, Jesse
Facket (Tacket?),
Thomas

G

Gilbert, John
(1 slave)
Gunn, Will
Grigsby, John
Gentry, Elisha
Graves, Williamson
Guye, Henry
Gray, Mark
Gambill, James
Gentry, David
Garrard, Joel ?
Gassase ?, Mary
Gambill, Thomas
Grigsby, Thomas
Gibson, William
Garrard, Daniel
(21 slaves)

H

Hibbard, Jediah
Hubbard, Moses
Howard, James
Hamilton, Patrick,
Sr.
Henson, Paul
Huff, Leonard
Harris, Elisha
Hall, Hezekiah
Hide (Hyde), Jesse
Hibbard, James
Hollinsworth,
Beasley
Henson, James
Hicks, Henry
Hollinsworth, Will
Haddox, Colby
Hamilton, Patrick,
Jr.
Hornback, John
Hodges, Drewry
Hibbard, John
(1 slave)

Harris, James
Henson, John
Hollinsworth, James
Hicks, Robert
Hollinsworth, John
Haddox, William
Henson, Richard
Hitchcock, John
Harriss, William
Hudson, William
Hart, Hardy
Henson, Paul
Houck, John
Hitchcock, Isaac
Hodges, Shadrock
Hollinsworth, Isaac
Haddox, Samuel
   (3 slaves)
Halsey, Elizabeth
Hall, Jacob
Hodges, James
Hosley, Joseph
Harrison, James
   (2 slaves)

I

Igue ?, Joshua
Isham, Arch.
Isham, George
Isaacs, Godfire
   (Godfrey)

J

Jones, Moses
Jilton, Thomas M.
   (1 slave)
James, James
Johnson, John
Jones, John
Johnson, Thomas
   (3 slaves)
Jones, William
Johns, Jacob
Jones, Ruth
Jackman, John
Johnson, John
Jones, Isaac
Joseph, Reason
Jorgison ?, William
Johnson, Pleasant

K

King, Charles
Keeney, Joseph
Kennedy, John

L

Lyon, James
   (2 slaves)

Lewis, James
Lucas, Richard
Lewis, James
Logan, Nathan
Lewis, Thomas
Lewis, Nathan
Lewis, William
Lewis, James
Lewis, James
Lewis, John
Lusk, Samuel
Lindon, Ben
Lewis, Messenger
Lush, John

M

Martin, Moses
Moore, Samuel
M'Guire, James
   (3 slaves)
McRoberts, Thomas
   (4 slaves)
Maloney, John
Maupin, John
M'Collum, Daniel
Miller, William
Murphy, John
   (1 slave)
M'Intosh, Peter
M'Camron, John
M'Collum, Daniel
McGill, Samuel P.
McCray, John
Mitder, John
Maupin, Dabney
McWhorter, James
   (6 slaves)
Morriss, James
M'Guire, Arch
M'Intosh, William
M'Intosh, Nimrod
M'Camron, William
Miller, Samuel
Maupin, Perry
M'Collum, David
M'Guire, Elizabeth
Moore, William
Mattel ?, William
Moore, Wilson
McFarland, Ben
M'Guire, William
M'Grady, Edward
Moore, James
McMiller, Francis
May, Jacob
McCullough, William
McCollum, Stephen
Miller, Stephen
M'Collum, William
McDaniel, George

N

Noble, William
Noble, A. J.
Nicholson, John
Noble, Nathan
Nicholson, Richard
Neil, William
Nelson, James

O

Oakley, Fielding
Oldham, Newport
Ogdon, Stephen
Osborn, Squire

P

Phillips, John
Perl, William
Plummer, Samuel
Pigg, William
Powell, Thomas
Paul, George
Parker, David
Parker, James
Parker, Pleasant
Percifield, Valentine
Pogue, John
   (5 slaves)

R

Ridsel, John
Riley, Patrick, Jr.
Roney, George
Roberts, Moses
Richey (Ritchie)
   Croctrel ?
Riley, James
Robbins, Elender
Rees, John
Robbins, Daniel
Rose, John
Riley, Patrick, Sr.
Roberts, Jesse
Roberts, James

S

Smith, Jabel
Stacy, Peter
Smith, William
Small, George
Singleton, Richard
Shirley, Charles
Smith, John
Sizemore, George
Smith, Randlee
Sebourn ?, Jacob
   (4 slaves)
Siglar, John

Schoolcraft, John
Sweeten, Lane
Smith, Thomas
Strong, William
Sizemore, John
Stewart, William
Smith, John
Smith, Richard
  (1 slave)
Sizemore, Rhoda
Singleton, Ann
Stepp, James
Shackleford, John
Sweeten, William
Swafford ?, Isaac
Stewart, Daniel
Smith, Robert
Stewart, John
Smith, Samuel
Spurlock, Jesse
Stone, John
Smallwood, Elijah
Smith, William
Shackleford,
  Edward
  (2 slaves)
Skidmore, James
Smith, Charles
  (1 slave)
Smith, John

Smith, John
  (3 slaves)
Spurlock, John
Singleton, Philip
Smith, Jeremiah
Smith, Richard
Sybert, Daniel
Sizemore, Edward
Stansberry, Solomon
Sanders, John
Stots, John
Sweeten, Absalom
Sneathen, William

T

Todd, James
  (1 slave)
Thomas, Marchant
Tincher, George
Tuttle, Peter
Todd, Samuel
  (2 slaves)
Turner, Edward
Tincher, J. ?
Talby, Samuel
Taylor, Francis
Trammell, Sampson
Tolby, Isaac
Teyman ?, Boward
Taylor, Absolom

Templeton, James
Turner, John
Turpin, Champin ?
Tucker, Henry

W

Williams, John
Waters, Robert
Wilson, Jonathan
Winn, John
Wooton, Sarah
Wilson, Philip
  (1 slave)
Williams, Philip
Woods, Samuel
Williams, Jalin
White, Hugh
  (3 slaves)
Whitesides, William
White, Thomas
Watts, George
Willis, Thomas
Wooton, Frederick
White, John
Whiteker, Isaac
Williams, James
Webb, David

Y

York, Jeremiah

MARRIAGES 1807—1830

Marriage Records of Clay County from date of organization, April 1, 1807, to 1830:

Groom	Bride	Date of Marriage or License
A		
Amis (Amos), Lincoln	Anna Nicholson	June 2, 1810
Alcorn, William	Debby Phillips	August 28, 1810
Alcorn, Robert	Nancy Shirley	January 31, 1812
Allen, John	Esther Baker	August 25, 1812
Abner, Monroe	Aggy Bowlin	March 23, 1813
Alcorn, James	Anna Duck	Nov. 30, 1813
Alcorn, John	Polly King	Dec. 26, 1813
Asher, Dillon	Hermitta Bowlin	April 20, 1816
Allen, William	Keturah Givens	July 16, 1817
Akeman, John	Sally Murshan (?)	Feb. 28, 1820
Allen, Adoniram	Nancy Hunt	July 3, 1820
Allison, Archibald	Tabitha Nicholson	Aug. 20, 1820
Abner, Enoch	Anna Price	Jan. 18, 1822

CLAY COUNTY, KENTUCKY

Groom	Bride	Date of Marriage or License
Allen, Morris	Rachel Bishop	April 8, 1822
Applegate, Ed	Polly Hollingsworth	Sept. 4, 1822
Asher, Robert	Susannah Norris	Dec. 30, 1822
Ashcraft, James	Betsy McCollum	Aug. 5, 1824
Akers, William	Delin Pitman	Sept. 24, 1824
Amos, Thomas	Mary Asher	Mar. 13, 1826
Angel, James	Elizabeth Cummingham	Sept. 2, 1825
Asher, Robert	Polly Sizemore	March 26, 1827
Abner, Elisha	Jennie Baker	June 2, 1827
Asher, Robert	Rachel Piercefield	Jan. 7, 1820
Ayres, Henry	Katherine Gill	Apr. 28, 1828
Ambrose, Meredith	Ann Clark	May 9, 1828
Asher, John	Elizabeth Murphy	Oct. 27, 1829
Abner, Minion	Lucinda Benge	Oct. 7, 1829
Abner, John	Millie Noble	Oct. 7, 1829

B

Groom	Bride	Date
Bowlin, Joseph	Nancy Bowlin	May 7, 1807
Bowman, William	Malinda Walters	Aug. 21, 1807
Bowling, Christopher	Nancy Baker	March 6, 1808
Bowlin, James	Kize Lockard	May 25, 1808
Bowman, Elisha	Anna Evans	Jan. 7, 1810
Bullock, David	Mary Abbott	Feb. 12, 1810
Baker, John	Mary Campbell	Feb. 22, 1810
Bates, Isaac	Patsy Henson	Apr. 3, 1810
Bradley, Andrew	Betsy Nicholson	Jan. 14, 1811
Baker, James	Phoebe Allen	June 18, 1811
Bales, Edward	Abby Bales	Feb. 18, 1815
Baker, John	Mary Campbell	Feb. 18, 1815
Bates, Isaac	Betsy Henson	Apr. 3, 1816
Bowlin, John	Polly Lewis	Apr. 15, 1816
Benge, John	Philadelphia Hunt	Jan. 8, 1817
Bales, William	Susannah Morris	Feb. 4, 1817
Barrett, Murrel	Betsy Price	Mar. 1, 1817
Bishop, William	Sarah Burns	Apr. 10, 1817
Bowling, Eli	Nancy Wilson	July 23, 1817
Bales, Hawkins	Nancy Johnston	Sept. 8, 1817
Bowman, Cornelius	Elizabeth Gabbard	Aug. 10, 1816
Bowman, Nicholas	Isabella Moore	Oct. 5, 1818
Bunch, Samuel	Phoebe Parker	Nov. 30, 1813
Bales, Hawkins	Eady Gunn	May 13, 1816
Baker, William	Polly Bales	Apr. 7, 1817
Brashears, Robert S.	Mary Cornett	Jan. 8, 1818
Bunch, George	Nancy Maupin	Mar. 11, 1818
Benge, William	Catherine Wilson	Mar. 30, 1818
Baker, James	Betsy Colly	Mar. 16, 1818
Bowling, John	Sarah Henson	Apr. 11, 1818
Boulin, Elijah	Susannah Roberts	Mar. 18, 1819
Bowling, Jesse	Nancy DeWeese	Mar. 2, 1819
Bowman, Edward	Margaret Gabbard	Dec. 20, 1820
Baker, John, Jr.	Keziah Burns	Mar. 17, 1821
Baker, Robert, Jr.	Sarah Rogers	July 25, 1820
Burns, Wiley	Polly Baker	Aug. 30, 1821
Bowlin, Russell	Nancy Reams	Oct. 9, 1821
Burns, Andrew	Nancy Baker	Dec. 10, 1822
Blevins, Ryal	Ibby Neil	Dec. 16, 1823
Baker, John C.	Patsy Anderson	Jan. 14, 1824

105

Groom	Bride	Date of Marriage or License
Bailey, John	Sally Jones	Sept. 4, 1811
Bishop, Samuel	Polly Abner	Nov. 11, 1811
Bunchs, William	Ann Benge	Jan. 28, 1812
Bunch, George	Martha Morris	May 23, 1812
Bishop, Stephen	Rebecca Miller	Apr. 20, 1813
Bishop, Stephen	Sarah Noble	July 23, 1813
Begley, Henry	Betsy Roberts	Sept. 23, 1813
Best, Humphrey	Ebby Skidmore	Nov. 4, 1813
Bryant, Hiram	Sally Evans	Apr. 12, 1814
Barrett, Jesse	Sally Edwards	July 15, 1814
Barton, Thomas	Polly Carr	Aug. 30, 1814
Bowman, Elijah	Hannah Gabbard	Jan. 8, 1814
Bates, Daniel	Mary Baker	Aug. 21, 1824
Begley, William	Jennie McCollum	Oct. 27, 1823
Burns, William	Rachel Asher	.... 16, 1824
Bowlin, Robert	Katy	Feb. 24, 1825
Baker, John H.	Lucinda Amos	...., 1825
Baker, William	Jane Baker	Sept. 15, 1825
Black, Sam H.	Ollie Jones	Feb. 10, 1826
Black, John C.	Clarissa Jones	Feb. 10, 1826
Burns, Charles	Aggy Robertson	Aug. 16, 1826
Baker, Samuel	Rachel Davidson	June 24, 1827
Bowling, Esam	Edith Lane	July 6, 1827
Brown, Thomas	Fanny Herrold	Aug. 27, 1827
Burton, John	Berella Cundiff	....
Bowman, John W.	Elizabeth McCollum	Jan. 19, 1828
Brown, Benjamin	Patsy Cornelius	Feb. 14, 1828
Braingbury, Joseph	Rhoda Hamilton	May 7, 1828
Burns, James	Polly Piercefield	July 8, 1826
Burns, William	Annie Hacker	Jan. 5, 1829
Bowlin, James	Hala Wilson —	Jan. 3, 1829
Brittain, William	Mary Lewis	April 3, 1830
Bramlet, Hawkins	Elizabeth Rader	Sept. 24, 1830
Bowman, Elisha	Mary Mahala Philips	Dec. 12, 1830
Bowlin, Stokley	Elizabeth Wilson	Dec. 27, 1830

C

Cockrell, Jeremiah	Sarah Sowards	Aug. 18, 1807
Cunningham, William	Patsy McDaniel	Aug. 8, 1808
Codey, John	Elizabeth Summers	Mar. 14, 1809
Cain, Jacob	Anna McCommon	Apr. 2, 1810
Combs, Jeremiah	Betsy Combs	May 29, 1810
Combs, Matthew	Fanny Bround	May 28, 1810
Clark, William	Sarah Higgins	Mar. 14, 1808
Callahan, Isaac	Mahala Wilson —	July 5, 1810
Cunningham, James	Nancy Roberts	Aug. 23, 1810
Clark, William	Rebecca Bales	Nov. 12, 1810
Cornett, Archer	Juda McDaniel	June 8, 1812
Campbell, John	Cassa Joseph	Nov. 22, 1812
Campbell, James	Polly Campbell	Mar. 24, 1813
Cornett, William	Polly Peppee	Oct. 18, 1813
Combs, John, Jr.	Rebecca Combs	Dec. 13, 1813
Combs, Hardin	Hacy Combs	Aug. 25, 1814
Campbell, William	Elizabeth Cornett	Sept. 11, 1815
Clark, David	Polly Fox	Nov. 13, 1815
Combs, Henry	Nancy Brown	Mar. 11, 1816
Campbell, John	Patsy Smith	Nov. 10, 1816

Groom	Bride	Date of Marriage or License
Carpenter, Samuel	Betsy McCollum	Jan. 6, 1816
Combs, Benjamin	Jane Brown	Apr. 8, 1816
Cornett, Jesse	Nancy Kelly	May 12, 1816
Crook, Hezekiah	Mary Burns	Oct. 4, 1816
Combs, William	Sarah Combs	Dec. 13, 1817
Cornett, John	Phoebe Kelly	Jan. 8, 1818
Collett, Samuel	Mary Stuart	June 14, 1819
Clark, Hiram	Esther Martin	June 5, 1819
Combs, Samuel	Nancy Cornett	Dec. 13, 1819
Cates, John	Talitha Cummins	Feb. 28, 1820
Cain, Mathias	Peggy Roberts	May 24, 1820
Combs, William	.... Wilmuth	June 15, 1820
Campbell, Lewis	Matilda Fugate	Dec. 22, 1820
Cope, Andrew	Betsy Asher	Jan. 22, 1821
Cornett, Isaac	Warwing (?) Bowling	Aug. 6, 1821
Cornett, Isaac	Margaret Rogers	Feb. 9, 1821
Cornelius, William	Decy Parris	May 25, 1822
Carren, David	Elizabeth Sellers	Mar. 22, 1823
Cornett, Samuel	Lucretia Pigg	Aug. 8, 1823
Cornett, William	Nancy Benge	Jan. 8, 1825
Cornett, Henry	Rosanna McWhorter	Jan. 8, 1825
Clark, Hiram	Susannah McDaniel	Nov. 7, 1825
Cook, Joseph	Eliza Yeager	Feb. 9, 1827
Collins, Jesse	Mary Reid	Nov. 24, 1827
Collins, Hiram	Elizabeth Reid	Nov. 24, 1827
Collins, Abraham	Christena Poulston (?)	....
Cottingham, Pierce	Lucinda Lucas	June 24, 1829
Crawford, Gideon	Nancy Hatton	Sept. 9, 1829
Cottingham, Belian	Elizabeth Philphot	Apr. 14, 1830

D

Davidson, Thomas	Sally Sweeten	July 13, 1807
Dickerson, Samuel	Susannah Cain	Jan. 11, 1811
Davidson, David	Polly Miller	Aug. 6, 1812
Davidson, Silas	Phoebe Lewis	Nov. 25, 1812
Davidson, Tyre	Sarrah Morris	Aug. 20, 1817
Dane, Joseph	Polly Tedders	Sept. 30, 1817
Deaton, Brantly	Rachel Spencer	Nov. 4, 1817
Davidson, White	Polly Spencer	July 13, 1818
DeWeese, Louis	Sarah Eversole	Dec. 26, 1817
Davis, Syra	Polly Parsons	July 30, 1820
Deaton, William	Polly Ayres	Nov. 29, 1820
Davis, James	Phoda Morris	Oct. 14, 1822
Dane, Henry	Winny Tuders	Feb. 11, 1824
Davidson, Samuel	Polly Wilson —	Nov. 18, 1822
Deas, John	Rachel Metcalf	July 23, 1824
Davidson, Martin	Susannah Spurlock	July 16, 1824
Davis, Joll	Melly Cornelius	June 20, 1826
Davidson, Daniel	Jane Thomas	Feb. 8, 1826
Davis, James	Polly Piercefield	Feb. 8, 1826
Davidson, John	Polly Campbell	Jan. 13, 1827
Davidson, James	Rachel Allen	Apr. 27, 1827
Davis, James	Anna Baker	Aug. 30, 1828
Dorton, James	Sarah McRoberts	Apr. 6, 1829
Dotson, John	Peggy Parker	Aug. 4, 1829
Davidson, Samuel	Susannah Dent	Oct. 7, 1824
Davis, Benjamin	Patsy Cornelius	Feb. 14, 1828
Davidson, Daniel	Isabella McCollum	Feb. 9, 1829

Groom	Bride	Date of Marriage or License

E

Elliott, Thomas	Polly Swindler	Sept. 29, 1810
Eversole, Peter	Peggy May	Dec. 3, 1810
Eversole, Abraham	Sarah Williams	Feb. 26, 1811
Elliott, Jesse	Nancy Tugman	May 19, 1812
Elliott, Daniel	Atelsy (?) Tugman	Feb. 17, 1813
Eversole, Woolridge	Lucy Cornett	June 17, 1813
Evans, John	Nancy Phemer	June 9, 1814
Eversole, Joel	Sylva Gregsby	Dec. 11, 1817
Evans, Jesse	Edee Smith	Jan. 9, 1822
Eatherton, John	Catherine Rogers	Feb. 3, 1823
Evans, Henry	Rachel Plummer	Oct. 11, 1823
Evans, Edward	Sarah Reynolds	Oct. 3, 1825
Easter, David	Sally Lady	Feb. 21, 1828

F

Forbish, William	Sarah McCommon	Dec. 2, 1808
Freeman, George	Sarah Benge	Nov. 18, 1810
Fleetwood, John	Sylva Gregsby	June 8, 1812
Fulford, Abraham W.	Elizabeth Bales	July 24, 1812 ?
Fugate, Eli	Sarah Noble	Feb. 10, 1815
Falkner, Henry	Jane Baker	May 13, 1816
Frazier, Alexander	Clarky Russell	Oct. 22, 1816
Foster, Joshua	Sally Lewis	June 29, 1819
Forbis, John	Polly Hines	Feb. 18, 1820
Frammel (?), William	Peggy Riley	Apr. 14, 1821
Filpot (Philphot), John	Millie Bennett	Nov. 9, 1822
Frost, John	Rachel Turman	Mar. 16, 1823
Foster, James	Sarah Martin	Dec. 20, 1823
Farmer, James	Margaret Asher	Mar. 17, 1830
Foster, John	Elizabeth Hutson	May 21, 1809

G

Goosey, John	Susan Alford	May 24, 1808
Grisby, John	Patsy Campbell	Oct. 9, 1809
Green, Abraham	Susan Philpot	Nov. 11, 1811
Garrard, Joel	Sarah Jones	May 20, 1813
Gibson, Archiles	Polly Begley	July 2, 1814
Geaslin, William	Anne Hubbard	June 20, 1818
Gabbard, Jacob	Susan Bowman	July 4, 1818
Gabbard, Edward	Sarah Bowman	Mar. 8, 1817
Gregory, John	Keziah Jones	Apr. 16, 1818
Gray, John	Martha Damron	Feb. 12, 1820
Gunn, William	Patsy Walters	Oct. 3, 1820
Gabbard, Wathens	Sally VanHoose	Apr. 30, 1822
Gilbert, Wallace W.	Susan Jones	Oct. 22, 1823
Gray, Gudi	Kezziah Carroll	June 1, 1822
Gunn, Stephen	Elizabeth Cornelius	Dec. 14, 1822
Gibson, Jacob	Nancy Bowman	Jan. 17, 1824
Gilbert, William	Martha Douglass	Feb. 21, 1825
Gibson, William D.	Rebecca Johnston	July 28, 1825
Gambrill, James	Rachel Hubbard	July 3, 1826
Gabbard, Isaac	Jane Isaac	May 20, 1827
Gamble, William	Nancy Anderson	July 31, 1827
Gentry, Belitha	Martha Sandlen	Dec. 18, 1827
Guy, Russell	Mary Rice	Feb. 25, 1828

Groom	Bride	Date of Marriage or License
Gilbert, Felix	Isabella Benson	Mar. 19, 1827
Gray, Stephen	Lucinda Bowlin	Oct. 2, 1830
Gamble, William	Ann May	Oct. 28, 1830

H

Henson, John	Darkie May	Dec. 12, 1807
Henson, Paul	Peggy Smith	Aug. 20, 1808.
Harris, Sherod	Sarah Harper	July 23, 1809
Hollingsworth, James	Polly Smith	Nov. 16, 1809
Henson, Paul, Jr.	Rebecca Price	Jan. 4, 1810
Hodge, Drew	Sarah Frazier	Jan. 23, 1810
Halcey, Joseph	Martha Henson	June 10, 1810
Harris, Thomas	Peggy Hinds	Aug. 9, 1811
Hodge, Shadrack	Rebecca Ferguson	Dec. 10, 1811
Henson, James	Polly Lewis	Aug. 1, 1812
Hyde, Isaac	Ann Singleton	Oct. 9, 1812
House (Howes), John	Polly Lucas	Jan. 27, 1814
Hyde, Jesse	Betsy Piercefield	Jan. 28, 1815
Hughes, Young	Mary Turner	Mar. 20, 1815
Hart, Harman	Franky Haddix	Aug. 14, 1815
Herd, William	Rebecca Hudson	Aug. 30, 1815
Henson, John	Mary Hubbard	Aug. 8, 1817
Hicks, Wess	Betsy Everheart	Mar. 7, 1816
Henson, Richard	Polly Bates	July 15, 1816
Hoskins, Moses	Peggy Helton	Jan. 8, 1819
Hollingsworth, Jonathan	Mary Powell ——	Dec. 2, 1819
Hubbard, Solomon	Polly Jackson	Mar. 17, 1820
Harris, Tye	Lucy Cormons	July 3, 1820
Hay, John	Lusly Hadden	Nov. 15, 1820
Hadden, John	Sarah Hadden	Dec. 28, 1819
Hacker, Daniel	Nancy Burns	Feb. 22, 1821
Hillard, William	Betsy Grimes	July 17, 1821
Hubbard, Joseph	Teddy Hubbard	Nov. 21, 1821
Haddie, John	Rebecca Miller	July 23, 1821
Hilford, William	Betsy Grimes	July 17, 1821
Hughes, Lyttle	Mahala Bowman	Sept. 1, 1821
Hacker, Youles	Peggy Herd	Oct. 14, 1821
Hollingsworth, James	Patsy Reid	Feb. 13, 1822
Holeman, Thomas	Kezziah Tugman	June 16, 1821
Hays, John	Jane Callahan	Aug. 11, 1822
Hubbard, Isaac	Ann	Oct. 18, 1822
Hodge, Robey	Kezziah Frazier	Feb. 21, 1823
Haddie, Henly	Elizabeth Reynolds	Apr. 5, 1823
Hacker, Samuel	Chaney Roberts	Apr. 5, 1823
Hubbard, Joseph	Relly Hollingsworth	Mar. 27, 1823
Herd, Elijah	Betsy Shootman	Mar. 27, 1823
Haddie, John	Rebecca Miller	July 23, 1821
Herd, James	Elizabeth Lewis	Dec. 23, 1823
Hubbard, Benjamin	Sally May	Apr. 15, 1824
Hubbard, Richard	Mary Bowers	Aug. 2, 1824
Hacker, Clabourn	Action Roberts	Sept. 25, 1824
Hodge, Andrew	Cena Frazier	Nov. 28, 1824
Hubbard, Thomas	Polly Hall	Feb. 3, 1825
Hibbard, Samuel	Elizabeth Woodson	Mar. 18, 1826
Hunt, Lewis	Nancy Morris	May 11, 1826
Hibbard, Hiram	Ann Johnston	Aug. 22, 1826
Hacker, John	Polly Piercefield	Nov. 6, 1827
Hays, Alexander	Jane Lucas	Jan. 3, 1827

Groom	Bride	Date of Marriage or License
Henson, James	Charlie Hollingsworth	May 12, 1828
Henderson, John	Elizabeth Lyon	Nov. 17, 1828
Hunt, Lee Caswell	Susan Turner	Aug. 27, 1829
Hubbard, James	Lucinda Hubbard	Oct. 1 , 1829
Hutson, Joseph	Peggy Bowlin	May 25, 1829
Hendricks, William	Tempa Cooper	Feb. 1, 1830
Henson, Thomas	Salina Jones	Jan. 27, 1830
Hacker, Hogan	Vina Gibson	Feb. 7, 1830
Hays, Creed	Lyzena Cunduff	Apr. 26, 1830
Henson, Henry	Sarah Hendricks	Apr. 29, 1830
Hammond, Peter	Nancy Begley	May 16, 1830
Hubbard, Eli	Elizabeth Silcore	May 8, 1830
Hutson, Franklin	Elizabeth Asher	Feb. 4, 1832

I

Isaac, Godfrey	Betsy Howard	Feb. 2, 1810
Ingram, George	Mary Hicks	Aug. 28, 1811
Isaac, Frielen	Susan Bowman	June 9, 1830
Isaac, Elijah	Sally Bowman	Apr. 15, 1830
Isaac, Jacob	Rebecca Bowman	Oct. 5, 1832

J

Jones, John	Eunice Smith	Jan. 8, 1810
Jones, Moses	Kezziah Smith	June 10, 1810
Johnston, John	Mary McCoy	Sept. 25, 1810
Jones, Vincent	Susannah Williams	Dec. 23, 1811
Jones, John	Nancy Martin	July 2, 1811
Jones, Joseph	Sally Smith	Apr. 20, 1816
Jones, William	Cynthia Williams	Mar. 6, 1818
Jeffreys, William	Louvina Cope	Mar. 17, 1816
Jackson, Lewis	Susan Hubbard	Mar. 17, 1820
Johnston, James	Judy Riley	May 8, 1820
Jones, Gabriel	Sally Cirtright	Aug. 25, 1820
Jones, Isaac	Sarah Busham	July ...., 1821
Jackson, Josiah	Lydia Hubbard	Nov. 21, 1821
Johnson, John	Nancy Haddie	Nov. 4, 1822
Jones, William	Mary Jones	Mar. 16, 1823
Johnston, John S.	Catharine Thomas	July 22, 1824
Jones, David	Nancy Sizemore	Oct. 28, 1824
Jackson, Moses	Polly Stuart	June 25, 1825
Johnston, Shadrack	Betsy Muncy	Feb. 16, 1826
Jackson, Daniel	Lucy Hubbard	Nov. 16, 1826
Jones, Gabriel	Kezziah Bishop	Jan. 21, 1827
Jett, Stephen	Nancy Gibson	Mar. 26, 1827
Johnston, Jesse	Eleanor Bowman	Sept. 20, 1828
Jones, John	Lucinda Piercefield	Sept. 10, 1828
Johnston, William	Polly Bales	Jan. 9, 1826
Jones, Milton B.	Elizabeth Jones	Dec. 23, 1828
Jones, John	Esly Clifton	Sept. 24, 1829
Jones, James	Lucinda Hubbard	Oct. 16, 1829
Jackson, Mason	Anna Hubbard	Apr. 16, 1831

K

King, Jeremiah	Tabitha Alcorn	Aug. 2, 1814
Kenningham, Lyne S.	Margaret J. White	Mar. 14, 1817
Kelsey, Edgar	Nancy Walker	Jan. 28, 1832

Groom	Bride	Date of Marriage or License

L

Groom	Bride	Date
Lowder, Mathias	Mary Smith	July 16, 1807
Lewis, Joseph	Sarah Weaver	July 8, 1811
Lewis, William	Hannah Sneathen	May 30, 1815
Lockard, Thomas	Sally Asher	Jan. 25, 1816
Lewis, Thomas	Polly Barker	July 25, 1816
Lewis, David	Chaney Cope	Oct. 25, 1819
Lewis, James	Mary Herd	Jan. 5, 1820
Lewis, Absalom	S. Williams	July 26, 1820
Luicks, Frederick	Nancy Hays	Nov. 14, 1820
Lunsford, John	Polly Peantham	July 28, 1821
Lucas, John	Lucy Cundiff	July 8, 1821
Lynks, Frederick	Polly Cornett	Nov. 25, 1822
Lincher, William	Matilda Bowman	Dec. 6, 1823
Letcher, William	Ann White	Dec. 21, 1824
Langford, James	Nancy Griffin	Feb. 15, 1825
Lunsford, Stephen	Elizabeth Lunsford	Feb. 2, 1826
Lais (Lewis), William	Rachel Bowles	Apr. 12, 1826
Lunsford, William	Nancy Lunsford	Sept. 21, 1827
Lucas, John B.	Fanny McLucas	Sept. 27, 1827
Lunce, Silas	Nancy Hollingsworth	Nov. 27, 1828
Lunsford, Hiram	Ledy Hollingsworth	Feb. 11, 1828
Lewis, David	Lucy Rogers	July 29, 1828
Lewis, Daniel	Ledia Baker	Apr. 26, 1830
Lunsford, Jacob	Decey Taylor	Aug. 4, 1830
Lunsford, Stephen	Rhoda Hubbard	Dec. 25, 1830

M

Groom	Bride	Date
Maupin, Perry	Rachel	Feb. 15, 1809
Maupin, Dobney	Sally Dennis	Mar. 12, 1809
Martin, Moses	Sarah Wakefield	Mar. 12, 1810
Maupin, Howard	Lucy Gossett	Apr. 16, 1816
Magill, Samuel	Nancy Shackleford	Sept. 29, 1810
Morris, James	Lyda Asher	Dec. 24, 1814
Morrow, John	Mollie Haddix	Jan. 13, 1815
Mitchell, John	Harriet Love	Sept. 25, 1815
Morris, William	Margaret Sandlin	Jan. 30, 1817
McClure, William	Nancy Morris	May 20, 1817
Morris, Robert	Minta Johnson	July 14, 1817
Meads, Jesse	Rhoda Holland	Apr. 8, 1819
Moore, Elias	Sally Reynolds	Oct. 20, 1818
Mullins, Morgan	Lucy Vency ?	Oct. 12, 1818
Morris, Abraham	Jane Wilson ———	Oct. 12, 1818
Meeks, Jesse	Rhoda Holland	Apr. 22, 1819
Murphy, William	Betsy Clarke	June 25, 1819
Morris, George	Elizabeth Johnston	Dec. 30, 1819
Morrow, Jesse S.	Retta Williams	Oct. 12, 1820
Moore, Allen	Margaret Lewis	Feb. 2, 1821
Miller, Andrew	Peggy Miller	Aug. 6, 1821
Markham, Wilson	Edy Baker	Nov. 4, 1822
Mershan, William	Cynthia Parker	May 15, 1824
May, Andrew	Ann Smith	Oct. 25, 1824
Morris, Mack	Ann Mullins	Sept. 16, 1825
Madden, Samuel	Harmot Bowman	Jan. 8, 1827
Moore, James	Isabella McQueen	Mar. 2, 1827
Morris, John	Elizabeth Murphy	Oct. 31, 1827
Moore, James W.	Lucinda Evans	Jan. 22, 1828

Groom	Bride	Date of Marriage or License
Martin, Milton	Rebecca Roberts	May 8, 1828
McGee, James	Delitha Peters	June 4, 1828
Muncy, James	Sally Stivers	Aug. 6, 1828
McColly, Joseph	Malinda Lucas	May 28, 1828
McKindley, Benjamin	Polly Bowman	Aug. 5, 1828?
Melton, William	Vina Peters	Oct. 5, 1828
Marcum, Squire	Susan Herd	Oct. 15, 1829
Marcum, Berry	Sarah Foster	Jan. 25, 1831
McIntosh, William	Franky Fugate	Mar. 1, 1809
McDaniel, Thomas	Sarah Evans	Dec. 7, 1810
McWhorter, Elijah	Polly Pigg	Jan. 13, 1811
McIntosh, James	Katy Fugate	Sept. 10, 1813
McCourtney, Abner	Ibby Stacy	Sept. 16, 1813
McIntosh, Samuel	Polly Demere	Oct. 28, 1813
Martin, Elijah	Betsy Skidmore	Mar. 15, 1815
McGuin, Charles	Lucy McDaniel	Jan. 10, 1815
McClure, William	Nancy Morrison	Mar. 17, 1817
McCollum, Isaac	Nancy Baker	Oct. 3, 1819
McCollum, David	Jane ? Sandlin	Oct. 12, 1819
McDaniel, George	Sarah Hadden	Dec. 28, 1819
McCollum, Isaac	Mariam Gilbert	Apr. 2, 1821
McCowman, James	Mahala Simpson	Oct. 23, 1821
McQuinn, Thomas	Nancy Tinchis ?	Apr. 6, 1824
McRobert, Andrew	Sally Gilbert	Jan. 15, 1825
McGee, James	Delila Peters	June 4, 1828
McGuire, James	Nancy Anglue	May 11, 1826
McKinney, Benjamin	Patty Bowman	Aug. 11, 1827
McCollum, Daniel	Lydia Johnston	Jan. 3, 1828
McDaniel, Randolph	Lockey Oxeford	July 22, 1828
McCollum, Samuel	Easter Davidson	Oct. 29, 1830

N

Norris, Robert	Minta Johnston	Apr. 4, 1817
Noble, Adam J.	Lucy P. Shackleford	Aug. 30, 1810
Noble, William	Rachel Allen	Sept. 2, 1818
Neil, Daniel	Ibby Cornett	Oct. 18, 1817
Nelson, James	Lethia Bush	Feb. 11, 1820
Night (Knight), Nathan	Anna Benton	Aug. 30, 1821
Norris, John	Ann Elkins	Jan. 18, 1826
Norris, Joseph	Nancy McWhorter	Oct. 30, 1834

O

Outon (Wooton), William	Polly Cornett	Mar. 22, 1815
Oxford, William	Nancy McCollum	Apr. 16, 1829
Oxford, Jonathan	Chaney Spurlock	Mar. 4, 1830

P

Park, John	Mary Elizabeth Hutson	May 25, 1809
Parker, William	Sarah Halso	July 21, 1809
Parker, James	Phoebe Fry	May 23, 1811
Pennington, Abel	Elizabeth Bowlin	Apr. 15, 1815
Pace, Jonathan	Rachel Joseph	Dec. 4, 1815
Parrest, Ezekiel	Polly Brumit (?)	Oct. 12, 1818
Phillips, Thomas	Edy Guinn	Oct. 23, 1817
Purnfite, Sampson	Sally Jones	July 15, 1820

Groom	Bride	Date of Marriage or License
Philphot, Joseph	Polly Chandler	Aug. 20, 1820
Pierce, Thomas	Sally Smith	May 17, 1821
Pennington, Micajah	Cynthia Jones	Dec. 8, 1822
Pluman, Samuel	Elizabeth Evans	Sept. 16, 1822
Piercefield, William	Edy Cope	....
Parker, Joseph	Peggy Metcalf	Aug. 2, 1824
Peters, Edward	Amelia Martin	Mar. 18, 1823
Piercefield, William	Jennie Cain	Oct. 24, 1824
Price, Gabriel	Elizabeth Garrard	Nov. 11, 1824
Parker, John	....	Dec. 23, 1825
Piercefield, William	Rebecca Hollingsworth	Jan. 18, 1826
Potter, Abraham	Patsy Hollingsworth	Feb. 16, 1827
Parker, Alfred ?	Zilpha Cornett	Feb. 24, 1828
Piercefield, John	Rachel Powell	Oct. 16, 1828
Powell, John	Susannah Cooper	Mar. 28, 1830
Price, Charles	Jane Becknell	Aug. 17, 1831

Q

Groom	Bride	Date of Marriage or License
Quinn, Charles W.	Lucy McDaniel	June 30, 1816
Queen, Stephen	Elizabeth Cornelius	Dec. 14, 1822
Queen, Samuel	Isabella Tincher	July 21, 1828

R

Groom	Bride	Date of Marriage or License
Reese, Henry	Isabella Roberts	Jan. 24, 1808
Rose, Robert	Esther Moore	Nov. 19, 1810
Robbins, David	Sabra Robbins	Dec. 8, 1810
Riley, Zachariah	Mary Gibson	Mar. 6, 1812
Ramey, Isaac	Sarah Minian	June 15, 1812
Roark, James	Phobe Cornett	May 20, 1814
Ruford, Abraham H.	Elizabeth Bales	July 28, 1814
Roberts, Farris	Ora Asher	June 1, 1815
Richy (Ritchie), Gabriel	Nancy Falkner	Sept. 13, 1815
Rogers, George	Katy Wild	Feb. 12, 1818
Riley, James	Delila Gibson	May 23, 1816
Riley, John	Elizabeth Williams	Aug. 22, 1816
Ripple, Joshua	Sarah Hicks	Nov. 3, 1818
Rice, David	Nancy Swethen	Mar. 11, 1819
Reid, John	Nancy Hollingsworth	Mar. 9, 1819
Riley, William	Susannah Smith	May 12, 1819
Roberts, Swinthfield	Peggy Lewis	Jan. 5, 1819
Riley, John	Jane Johnston	May 8, 1820
Rogers, Julins	Anna Willisford ?	Sept. 23, 1820
Richardson, Rodford	Betsy Cobb	Aug. 12, 1822
Reader, George	Polly Ambrose	Sept. 15, 1822
Riley, Zachariah	Sally Sweeten	Oct. 20, 1822
Roberts, Jesse	Rebecca Bolin	Nov. 28, 1822
Reid, Richard	Polly Halbert	Mar. 27, 1823
Rogers, Julius	Katy Alcorn	Sept. 4, 1823
Rogers, David	Franky Alcorn	Feb. 26, 1824
Rogers, Robert	Cynthia Alcorn	Feb. 26, 1824
Reid, Randolph	Rhoda Hollingsworth	Feb. 17, 1825
Roberts, James	Ann Bowman	Oct. 4, 1825
Roberts, John	Sacky H. Smith	Feb. 27, 1826
Riley, Patrick	Margaret McIntosh	June 17, 1826
Roberts, Thomas	Nancy Bowlin	July 1, 1826

Groom	Bride	Date of Marriage or License
Reed, Stephen	Nancy Powell	Dec. 13, 1827
Reed, Richard	Kepsy Collins	Jan. 6, 1827
Reed, William	Ledia Laughlin	Dec. 13, 1820

S

Smith, Andrew	Nancy Smith	June 8, 1807
Smith, Zobell	Rhoda Jones	Dec. 12, 1807
Smallwood, John	Jemima Smith	Jan. 25, 1808
Sadler, John	Rachel Hibbard	Mar. 3, 1808
Smallwood, Elijah	Sarah Clark	Aug. 19, 1808
Smith, Thomas, Jr.	Polly Eversole	June 10, 1810
Smith, Randolph	Anna Henson	Nov. 13, 1810
Sevier, Joseph	Sarah Wooton	July 7, 1811
Sams, James	Charlotte Ware	Sept. 10, 1811
Stivers, George	Lethia Tunders	Mar. 30, 1812
Stacy, George	Mary Summers	Nov. 27, 1812
Strong, Edward	Elizabeth Spencer	Dec. 29, 1812
Strong, John	Susannah Davidson	Apr. 10, 1813
Smith, Jeremiah	Betsy Jones	Sept. 11, 1813
Smith, William	Nicy Singleton	June 17, 1814
Smith, Henry	Harriet Gilbert	Dec. 10, 1814
Stewart, William	Sally Bowlin	May 15, 1815
Sizemore, Henry	Rachel Jones	Dec. 25, 1815
Smallwood, William	Polly Clark	Feb. 15, 1816
Strong, William	Patsy Pennington	July 11, 1816
Smith, John	Elizabeth Taylor	Sept. 8, 1817
Smith, Benjamin	Nancy Clemmens	Jan. 8, 1818
Spencer, Elijah	Elizabeth Duere	Mar. 20, 1818
Stephens, John	Mary West	July 16, 1818
Spencer, John	Sarah Stacy	Feb. 9, 1816
Sebastain, John	Sally Turner	Mar. 24, 1818
Stivers, Basel	Nancy Barger	Mar. 8, 1819
Strong, Moses	Sarah Plainer	Nov. 29, 1819
Smith, Isham	Laken Abner	Nov. 15, 1819
Strong, Thomas	Mahala Callahan	July 8, 1820
Sherman, John	Sally Mershan	Feb. 10, 1820
Smith, Thomas	Nancy Stewart	Aug. 20, 1820
Sundlin, James	Zeepha Baker	Mar. 16, 1821
Seabourn, Robert	Polly McClure	Aug. 10, 1821
Sanders, Allen	Anna Sanders	Nov. 17, 1821
Smith, Paul	Betsy Stewart	Mar. 14, 1822
Siaburn, Robert	Polly McClure	Mar. 13, 1822
Smith, Henry	Susannah Smith	June 22, 1822
Smith, Samuel	Cretia Mitchell	July 18, 1822
Step, Reuben	Sabra Chappell	Feb. 19, 1823
Sellers, Edward	Amelia Martin	Mar. 20, 1823
Stewart, Isham	Peggy Smith	Apr. 20, 1823
Smith, Alexander	Susan Tuttle	May 16, 1823
St. John, Samuel	Frances Burton	Sept. 21, 1823
Sanders, William	Anna Riley	May 20, 1824
Smith, John	Matilda Sanders	May 24, 1824
Stewart, Robert	Rachel Jackson	Feb. 4, 1825
Smith, Eli	Nancy Smith	Aug. 6, 1825
Smith, Malikiah	Anise Smith	Aug. 6, 1825
Smith, Zobel	Rhoda Swafford	Sept. 28, 1826
Smith, Robert	Rhoda Smith	Apr. 12, 1827
Sandlin, Lewis	Patsy Anglin	Aug. ...., 1828

CLAY COUNTY, KENTUCKY

Groom	Bride	Date of Marriage or License
Stewart, Ben amin	Rhoda Smith	Jan. 9, 1828
Spurlock, William	Martha Gilbert	June 10, 1829
Smith, Nimrod	Selah Goun	July 9, 1828
Stewart, Benjamin	Rhoda Smith	Mar. 9, 1829
Stephens, Richard	Sarah Ambrose	June 3, 1829
Spurlock, William	Martha Gilbert	June 7, 1829
Strong, Thomas	Mahala Callahan	July 8, 1820
Smallwood, Wesley	Sallie Eversole	June 23, 1831
Smallwood, Elijah	Anna Smith	Sept. 6, 1831
Smith, Milton	Sallie Smith	Sept. 6, 1831

T

Thompson, Drury	Margaret Sweenten	May 25, 1807
Turner, Andrew	Peggy Woods	July 11, 1811
Turner, Jesse	Cynthia Roberts	Oct. 8, 1811
Turner, James	Polly Baker	May 1, 1812
Turner, Marhack	Jennie Pennington	Feb. 10, 1817
Turner, Thomas	Nancy Butre	Aug. 9, 1817
Taylor, Isaac	Rhoda Smith	Aug. 17, 1817
Tuttle, Thomas	Peggy Jones	Sept. 25, 1817
Turner, William	Matilda Roark	Oct. 19, 1817
Thrush, David	Jemima Prewitt	June 12, 1821
Tuttle, John	Nancy Jones	Oct. 9, 1823
Treadway, William W.	Margaret Bowman	Dec. 11, 1823
Treadway, Peter	Margaret Evans	Nov. 10, 1823
Turner, John	Tempy Reynolds	Jan. 22, 1824
Thomas, Isaac	Elizabeth Smith	Jan. 15, 1827
Turner, Thomas	Alexelen Kassold	Aug. 5, 1829
Tuttle, James	Elizabeth Yager	Feb. 22, 1830
Turner, James	Margaret Asher	March 17, 1830
Turner, David	Nancy Rogers	May 20, 1830
Turner, Thomas	Mary Johnston	Sept. 24, 1833

V

Valentine, William	Polly McCreary	July 8, 1833

W

Woods, James I.	Martha J. Clark	Jan. 15, 1807
West, John	Mary Miller	Sept. 9, 1807
Wooten, James	Sarah Miller	Nov. 10, 1807
Wood, John	Darky Abny	Dec. 12, 1808
Williams, John	Rebecca Combs	July 17, 1809
Wilson, William	Nancy Herde	March 12, 1812
Waters, Elijah	Betsy Skidmore	March 9, 1812
Wilson, John	Rachel Roberts	March 25, 1812
Waters, Joel	Nancy Sweeten	March 31, 1813
Wood, Samuel	Becky Wilson	May 16, 1813
Williams, Hardin	Sarah Campbell	Sept. 14, 1814
Wilson, Pleasant	Leah York	June 22, 1815
Wages, John	Polly Mays	Sept. 16, 1815
Williams, Lewis	Betsy Hunt	Feb. 22, 1818
Williams, Edward	Sarah Gibson	Dec. 19, 1817
Waters, James	Elsa Wade	Nov. 16, 1818
Woodson, George W.	Sarah Bunton	Mar. 17, 1818
Wells, John	Elizabeth Lewis	Dec. 11, 1817

Groom	Bride	Date of Marriage or License
Walker, John	Polly DeWees	March 8, 1818
Woodson, Henry	Hannah Debbard	April 24, 1818
Williams, John	Jane Gay	Dec. 14, 1819
Wells, Sepe ?	Rhoda Holland	April 22, 1819
Wilson, Philip	Patsy Allen	Nov. 29, 1820
White, C. W.	Susan C. White	Nov. 8, 1820
Wright, Nathan	Anna Benton	Aug. 30, 1821
Woods, Joseph	Elizabeth Martin	July 19, 1822
Williams, Samuel	Peggy	April 14, 1821
Wilson, Davis	Rebecca Moore	Dec. 19, 1822
Wilson, Lemuel	Ella Moore	March 18, 1825
Williams, James	Betsy Cash	July 12, 1825
White, James	Sallie Ann Taylor	Dec. 30, 1825
Wiles, Philip	Sarah Gandlin	Dec. 25, 1825
Wild, Felin	Betsey Chesnut	April 24, 1826
Work, James	Malinda Bowlin	July 6, 1826
Weaver, Joseph	Fanny B. Bledsae	May 29, 1828
Woodson, Thomas I.	Martha Ann Gilbert	Aug. 6, 1829
Williams, Riley	Ibbe Campbell	Feb. 3, 1826
White, Hugh	Mara T. Browner	Aug. 9, 1828
Williford, John	Susannah Smallwood	Aug. 9, 1829
Wilson, John	Mary Thomas	Aug. 12, 1830
Waram (?), John	Seia Smith	Nov. 20, 1830
Williams, Amos	Lucinda Burns	Oct. 11, 1831
Wather, William	Sarah Bates	Oct. 3, 1833
Wilson, Philip	Polly Moore	March 6, 1834
Williams, Sidney M.	Margaret Garrard	Jan. 16, 1834

Y

Yarbish, William	Sarah McCommon ?	Dec. 7, 1808
York, Joseph	Rhoda Davidson	Feb. 4, 1828
Young, James	Elizabeth Cennagin ?	Aug. 31, 1825

CHAPTER VI

LAWRENCE COUNTY, KENTUCKY

ORGANIZATION—EARLY COURT ORDERS

March Court, 1822

Be it remembered that at the house of Andrew Johnson on Monday the twenty fifth day of March (it being the fourth Monday in said month of March) Edward Burgess, Nimrod Canterberry, Lewis Wellman, James Wheelor, John Haws, Thomas Thompson, John Stafford and Isaac Bolt produced commissions from under the hand of John Adair, Governor of the Commonwealth of Kentucky, for the time being with the seal of the Commonwealth thereto affixed appointing them * * * Justices of the Peace in and for the county of Lawrence; and thereupon the said Edward Burgess, the first numbered in the said commissions, before the said Nimrod Canterberry (the second numbered in the said commissions) did, on the Holy Evangelist of Almighty God, took (take) as well the oath to support the Constitution of the United States and of this State as the oath of a justice of the peace together with the oath prescribed by the act of assembly entitled "an act more efficiently to suppress the practice of duelling"; and then the said Edward Burgess administered, on the Holy Evangelist of Almighty God, to the said Nimrod Canterberry, Lewis Wellman, James Wheelor, John Haws, Thomas Thompson, John Stafford and Isaac Bolt, the persons named in the said commissions, as well to support the constitution of the United States and of this state as the oath of justice of the peace together with the oath prescribed by the act of assembly entitled "An act more effectively to suppress the practice of duelling." And thereupon a court was formed for the county of Lawrence and now here at a court held agreeable to the act of assembly establishing the county of Lawrence approved the sixth day of December one thousand eight hundred and twenty-one, at the house of Andrew Johnson as aforesaid on Monday, the twenty fifth day of March (being the fourth Monday therein) anno domini one thousand eight hundred and twenty-two and in the * * * year of the Commonwealth of Kentucky.

Present: Edward Burgess, Nimrod Canterberry, Lewis Wellman, James Wheelor, John Haws, Thomas Thompson, John Stafford and Isaac Bolt, Esquires, Gentlemen Justices.

* * *

William Graves produced a commission from under the hand of John Adair, Governor of the Commonwealth of Kentucky, with the seal of the said commonwealth thereto affixed appointing him sheriff of this county. Whereupon the said Edward Burgess, the presiding justice of the peace of this county, administered to the said William Graves, on the Holy Evangelist of Almighty God, as well the oath to support the constitution of the United States and of this state as the oath of a sheriff together with the oath prescribed by the late act of assembly more effectually to suppress the practice of duelling; and thereupon the said William Graves together with Henry Burgess, Edward Burgess, Henry B. Mavo, Samuel May, and Joseph R. Ward, his securities (sureties) entered into and acknowledged their bond in the penalty of three thousand dollars conditioned agreeable to law.

* * *

Joseph R. Ward is appointed clerk *pro tempore* of this court who accordingly qualified as the law directs and gave bond with Alexander

Lackey, Robert Walker, Zeke Rice, William Graves, his securities, entered into and acknowledged their bond in the penal sum of one thousand pounds * * * .

* * *

Thompson Ward, Robert Walker, William Triplett and Samuel Seaton, made satisfactory proof of their being licence (licensed) as attorneys-at-law in this state (and they) took the necessary oaths prescribed by law and are admitted to practice as attorneys-at-law in this court.

* * *

John Haws and Reuben Canterberry, Jr., are recommended to the Executive as proper and fit persons to fill the office of surveyor in this county, a majority of the justices of the peace in said county being present and concurring in this recommendation.

* * *

Benjamin Canterberry and Andrew J. Chapman are recommended to the Executive as proper and fit persons to fill the office of coroner in this county in the place of Hiram Chadwick who was commissioned by the Governor as coroner of this county (and) who refused to qualify, a majority of all the justices of the peace in this county being present and concurring in this nomination.

* * *

Ordered that the court be adjourned till tomorrow 9 o'clock, anti meridian.

(Signed)   Edward Burgess

MARRIAGES 1822-1859

Marriage Records of Lawrence County, Kentucky, from organization of county, in 1822, to 1859, inclusive:

Groom	Bride	Date of Marriage
A		
Adair, James	Catherine Hensley	Oct. 14, 1836
Adair, John	Swendy Kirk	Mar. 19, 1839
Adair, Samuel	Nancy Hensley	July 7, 1836
Adams, Alley	Ann Bannister	Dec. 23, 1826
Adams, Constantine	Alavr (Alifair) Scott	Dec. 8, 1850
Adams, Elias	Elizabeth Lewis	Sept. 22, 1834
Adams, H. F.	Elizabeth Griffith	May 22, 1856
Adams, John	Kitty Large	Oct. 21, 1838
Adams, Martin	Fanny Derrifield	Feb. 4, 1850
Adams, Nathan	Precitta Wilson	July 25, 1823
Adams, Perry	Rebecca Berry	July 17, 1855
Adams, William	Elizabeth Carter	Dec. 4, 1845
Adams, William	Nancy Berry	Oct. 20, 1855
Adkins, A. J.	Catherine Plumley	Dec. 1, 1859
Adkins, Berry	Sally Defoe	Mar. 14, 1830
Adkins, Enoch	Sally Burchett	Nov. 16, 1833

Groom	Bride	Date of Marriage
Adkins, Hardin	Nancy Young	Feb. 1, 1855
Adkins, John	Nancy Evans	Dec. 25, 1825
Adkins, William	Lucinda Wiley	Sept. 1, 1850
Adkins, William	Nancy Foster	Nov. 3, 1857
Akers, Burwell	Rachael Sperry	June 13, 1849
Aldridge, Francis	Nancy Muncy	Dec. 7, 1832
Aldridge, James	Dila Polly	July 12, 1855
Allender, Preston	Mrs. .... Gilkerson	Feb. 27, 1856
Allison, Isaac	Catherine Burns	Nov. 5, 1843
Anderson, James W.	Elizabeth Fulkerson	Feb. 2, 1837
Andrews, George W.	Octavia M. Burgess	Feb. 1, 1857
Arthur, Eli	Margaret Shockey	Mar. 26, 1840
Artrip, Alexander	Arzette Fraley	June 22, 1853
Artrip, William	Polly Skaggs	................, 1837
Asberry, (Asbury) Thomas	Horten Patina Swan	Jan. 2, 1853
Ashington, ? Andrew	Jemima Burton	Feb. 18, 1857
Attison, Miller	Nancy Ann Salyer	Nov. 4, 1844
Austin, John	Rosani Mead	Mar. 14, 1859
Austin, Thomas	Virginia Miller	Mar. 21, 1850
Auxier, Christopher	Peggy Collins	Aug. 23, 1827
Auxier, John	Sarah Hensley	Aug. 24, 1850
Auxier, Simon	Elizabeth Fugate	July 30, 1824
Auxier, Thomas	Nancy Large	May 23, 1822

B

Baisden, Elias	Louanna Branham	Oct. 17, 1857
Bailey, James	Sarah Davis	Sept. 29, 1836
Bailey, Stephen	Cynthia McDowell	Mar. 6, 1852
Bainard, V.	Catherine Hicks	Aug. 25, 1859
Baisden, Sol	Mary A. Chaffin	Sept. 1, 1831
Baker, Alfred	Caroline Dean	Jan. 28, 1857
Ball, Calvin	Barbara Diamond	May 5, 1857
Ball, Elihu	Pricie Thompson	Oct. 10, 1843
Ball, Hardin	Polly Caldwell	Mar. 4, 1835
Ball, John	Mattie Large	About 1835
Ball, John	Nancy Berry	Sept. ...., 1835
Ball, John C.	Lulina W. Clay	Aug. 16, 1832
Ball, R.	Nancy Moore	About 1838
Ball, Solomon	Rachael Lewis	Dec. 25, 1850
Berry, Alfred	Hannah Miller	Jan. 28, 1850
Berry, A. P.	Nancy Ball	Aug. 8, 1852
Berry, James	Jency Adams	Sept. 17, 1835
Berry, John	Kezziah Lambert	Jan. 15, 1837
Berry, John	Elizabeth Thompson	Jan. 26, 1826
Berry, Thompson	Dorisa Curnutte	Mar. 27, 1835
Berry, William	Pricie Ball	Dec. 23, 1841
Berry, Wiley	Martha Miller	July 8, 1838
Berry, William	Polly Thompson	Mar. 1, 1859
Berry, William	Elizabeth Burton	Apr. ...., 1835
Bevens, Joseph	Rebecca Borders	Nov. 28, 1858
Bevens, Joseph	Elizabeth Owsley	June 13, 1852
Biggs, Hiram	Nancy Skidmore	July 21, 1822
Biggs, J.	Nancy Lesley	May 31, 1845
Biggs, Reuben	Katherine Grubb	July 6, 1826
Biggs, Robert P.	Sally Musgrove	Oct. 25, 1829
Billups, J. S.	Nancy McClure	Jan. 9, 1859
Binard, Washington	Elizabeth Mills	July 18, 1852
Bishop, Gartha	Elizabeth Swan	Apr. 5, 1853

119

Groom	Bride	Date of Marriage
Bishop, Thomas	Sarah Castle	Mar. 16, 1851
Blankenship, Henry	Elizabeth White	Aug. 22, 1837
Blankenship, John W.	Eleanor Campbell	Aug. 7, 1834
Blankenship, Johnson	Elizabeth Hoover	Jan. 19, 1838
Blankenship, S.	Matilda Spurlock	Dec. 9, 1830
Blankenship, Shorten ?	Manared ? Martin	Mar. 27, 1837
Blankenship, William R.	Elizabeth Rice	Feb. 15, 1858
Blevins, Ephraim	Letitia Davidson	........, 1823
Blevins, James	Catherine Tackett	Dec. 30, 1828
Blevins, James	Elizabeth Mullett	........, 1838
Blevins, Riley	Sally Barker	Aug. 12, 1835
Banfield, Chrisley	Martha Prichard	Aug. 16, 1849
Bannister, Pleasant	Polly Crum	Apr. 12, 1835
Barber, Charles	Pacific Davis	Mar. 9, 1835
Barber, John	Mossa Wilson	Sept. 13, 1835
Barber, Reuben	T. Ross	Apr. 25, 1857
Barker, Harvey	Lucinda Wilson	Apr. 11, 1833
Barker, Isaac	Hannah Blevins	Dec. 23, 1857
Barker, John	Frances Fields	Oct. 3, 1843
Barker, William	Phoebe Holbrook	Apr. 20, 1828
Barnard, David	Rhoda Grant	Dec. 22, 1858
Barnett, Auld	Nancy Justice	July 7, 1854
Barnett, Oliver	Polly Hardwick	Aug. 23, 1849
Barr, Lewis	Sarah Sperry	Aug. 19, 1852
Bartram, ...	.... Fannin	Mar. 21, 1852
Bartram, David	Lucy Sperry	Mar. 27, 1825
Bartram, James	Jane Frasher	Oct. 2, 1833
Bartram, William	Elizabeth Law? (Loar)	Oct. 3, 1833
Bartram, William	Lorana Wellman	Aug. 23, 1836
Baugham, Jonathan	Naomi Marcum	Sept. 5, 1850
Bean, William	Permelia Turner	Oct. 15, 1854
Beard, John	Elizabeth Wilson	Mar. 13, 1855
Beck, Jacob	Leaner ? Sellards	Mar. 21, 1825
Belcher, James	Elizabeth Marcum	Oct. 18, 1838
Bell, Abner	Christina Cyrus	Jan. 29, 1859
Bellomy, C. C.	Nancy Snow	Apr. 11, 1859
Bench, Lewis	Nancy Workman	Feb. 9, 1832
Benjamin, Morgan	Isabel Mead	Aug. 8, 1852
Benton, Jacob F.	Pehoebe Carter	Oct. 21, 1852
Bernard, Ira	Mary Mills	Aug. 29, 1852
Bloss, Isaac	Sarah McClure	Apr. 27, 1854
Bocook, Andrew	Sarah Roberts	Dec. 19, 1835
Bocook, Elijah	Mary Tomlin	Oct. 12, 1856
Bocook, John	Martha Sperry	Dec. 8, 1849
Bocook, John	Susan Bryant	Sept. 3, 1830
Bocook, William	Sarah Sperry	Apr. 10, 1838
Bocook, William	America Bryan	Mar. 5, 1851
Boggs, David	Sarah Holbrook	Jan. 25, 1825
Boggs, Eliphus	Martha Prince	Nov. 23, 1854
Boggs, Elisha	Catherine Gambell	Feb. 22, 1844
Boggs, Henderson	Polly Fields	Feb. 16, 1843
Boggs, James	Regina Gambell	Nov. 15, 1858
Boggs, John	Nancy Griffith	Oct. 27, 1852
Boggs, John	Mahala Griffith	Sept. 7, 1849
Boggs, John R.	Martha J. Rudd	Mar. 5, 1850
Boggs, Nelson	Elizabeth Green	Jan. 8, 1857
Boggs, William	Ann Johnson	Sept. 5, 1828
Bolt, Greenville	Mary Davis	Dec. 30, 1836
Borders, Daniel	Sarah Davis	May 25, 1845

120

Groom	Bride	Date of Marriage
Borders, John	Elizabeth Pack	May 6, 1838
Borders, John	Zarilda Preston	Dec. 29, 1842
Borders, William	Abigail Wheeler	July 30, 1845
Bowe, William	Sarah J. Caperton	July 15, 1858
Bowen, Alfred	Matilda Castle	Feb. 11, 1836
Bowen, Franklin	Margaret Carey	Apr. 21, 1859
Bowen, Henry	Mary Pack	Nov. 24, 1843
Bowen, John	Elizabeth Chapman	Feb. 28, 1830
Bowen, William	Nancy Williamson	Jan. 21, 1858
Bowling, James	Orphy Leslie	Mar. 22, 1835
Bowman, Milton	Rebecca Dilley	Sept. 5, 1843
Boyd, Greenville	Mary West	Sept. 28, 1843
Boyd, Ison	Polly Fitzpatrick	Sept. 2, 1849
Boyd, James	Abigail Brown	Dec. 29, 1824
Boyd, James	Nancy Lemaster	Jan. 17, 1836
Bradford, John	Casender Pugh	May 19, 1829
Bradley, George H.	Elizabeth Thompson	Aug. 25, 1833
Bradley, Ralph	Sarah Jane Bradley	Jan. 7, 1854
Bradley, Thomas	Mahala Thompson	Jan. 16, 1835
Brammer, Emanuel	Polly White	Mar. 3, 1823
Branham, Ben	Emaline Fluty	Sept. 16, 1855
Branham, Henderson	Miranda Fluty	Oct. 5, 1850
Branham, Riley	Lucinda Fannin	Feb. 28, 1854
Branham, W.	Julia N. Fitzpatrick	Nov. 29, 1854
Branhan, Wiley	Eliza Stewart	Aug. 22, 1855
Branham, Wiley	Rachael Fannin	May 7, 1845
Brewer, ? Isaac	Keziah Spradling	Nov. 29, 1839
Brewster?, James	....	Nov. 14, 1840
Brown, George	Lucinda Large	June 13, 1858
Brown, John	Letish Hylton	July 17, 1834
Brown, Thomas	Nancy Davis	May 17, 1833
Brown, William	Julia Stafford	Oct. 6, 1828
Bryan, David	Mary White	July 14, 1839
Bryan, James	Nancy Short	Jan. 6, 1855
Bryan, Owen	Lucinda Pack	Dec. 20, 1858
Bryant, George	Elizabeth Jobe	Oct. 28, 1845
Bryant, John	Mooring Bocook	Jan. 2, 1828
Bryant, John	....	Dec. 5, 1836
Bryant, ...	.... Thompson	May 2, 1845
Brumfield, Martin	....	July 5, 1829
Bromfield, Madison	Julina Stewart	Apr. 18, 1837
Burchett, Benard	Deresa Curnutte	June 12, 1857
Burchett, Benjamin	Elizabeth Watson	Nov. 27, 1834
Burchett, Burwell	Sarah Easterling	June 20, 1825
Burchett, Drury	Hannah Middleton	....
Burchett, Fleming	Cynthia Chapman	Oct. 6, 1859
Burchett, John	Milla Chappin? (Chapman)	May 28, 1827
Burchett, Robert	Polly Roe	Dec. 12, 1834
Burchett, William	Margaret Meek	...., 1835
Burgess, C. M.	Vienna Spencer	Nov. 30, 1832
Burgess, Samuel H.	Polly Williams	Sept. 24, 1836
Burgess, Strother F.	Polly Dyer	Feb. 10, 1827
Burk, Evan	E. Loar	Dec. 23, 1828
Burk, B.	N. Fulkerson	Feb. 18, 1836
Burns, Harvey	Mary Sulser	July 14, 1834
Burns, John M.	Keziah Clay	Apr. 24, 1843
Burns, J. L.	Julia Ann Dean	Mar. 23, 1856
Burriss, M. G.	....	July 20, 1833
Burt, Charles	Frances Stroud	June 16, 1854

Groom	Bride	Date of Marriage
Burton, Allen U.	Christina Davis	Mar. 16, 1854
Burton, David	Sarah Williams	Apr. 22, 1854
Burton, Ira	Mormer ? C. Kelly	May 20, 1856
Burton, James	Lucy G. Roberts	Sept. 25, 1854
Burton, James	Susan Moody	Jan. 22, 1852
Burton, John	Elizabeth Borders	...., 1850
Buskirk, Thomas	Sarah Lower ? (Loar)	Dec. 15, 1822
Butler, Andrew W.	Lydia Robinson	July 4, 1853

C

Cains, Thomas	Deresa Chaffin	Dec. 25, 1839
Caldwell, Andrew	Mary Roma	July 17, 1854
Calloway, James	....	Sept. 19, 1830
Canterberry, Franklin	Nancy Canterberry	Oct. 25, 1828
Canterberry, L. F.	Ruhama Damrell (Damron)	Jan. 1, 1837
Canterberry, Reuben	Elzira Mosely	Feb. 22, 1826
Canterberry, Reuben	Mrs. Frances Fulkerson	Dec. 21, 1853
Canterberry, R. F.	Lucinda Bryant	Oct. 26, 1856
Carroll, Daniel	Serena Sparks	Oct. 17, 1844
Carter, Cobuery?	Elizabeth Stewart	Apr. 18, 1838
Carter, Covey	Sarah Skeens	Sept. 6, 1849
Carter, Covey	Anna Adkins	Apr. 3, 1856
Carter, George	Emaline Hutchinson	June 19, 1856
Carter, Jackson	Jane Graham	Aug. 26, 1856
Carter, James H.	Elizabeth Thompson	Mar. 6, 1854
Carter, Jeremiah	Celia Chappin	May 17, 1829
Carter, John	Mary Jane Hutchinson	Dec. 1, 1859
Carter, W.	Winnie Cooksey	Sept. 11, 1851
Cartmill, George	Maria Hoobler	Sept. 23, 1852
Cartmell, W.	Polly Davidson	Apr. 11, 1833
Casey, David	Polly Dyer	Oct. 26, 1824
Casey, D.	Darah Dyer	Oct. 24, 1859
Casey, Henry	Catherine Crank	Dec. 1, 1828
Cazey, James	Sarah Jane Nease	Mar. 12, 1835
Castle, Claiborne	Elizabeth McKinster	Jan. 16, 1857
Castle, Henderson	Elizabeth Brown	July 30, 1835
Castle, John	Julia Boyd	Feb. 20, 1857
Castle, Lindsay	Phoebe Bowen	Jan. 1, 1835
Castle, William	Lucy Hall	Sept. 7, 1843
Castle, William	Cynthia Boggs	Dec. 25, 1852
Castle, William	Emiella Skaggs	June 5, 1850
Cecil, Kenzie B.	Lurana Helvey	Oct. 21, 1834
Chadwick, George	Deadema Lockwood	July 13, 1824
Chaffin, David C.	Patsey Adams	Apr. 24, 1854
Chaffin, James	Mary Sanders	Oct. 7, 1854
Chaffin, James	Jemima Short	Jan. 16, 1851
Chaffin, James	Juda Adkins	June 20, 1833
Chaffin, Kenas M.	Margaret Gowens	Apr. 27, 1856
Chaffin, John	Sarah Kitchen	Mar. 17, 1859
Chaffin, John	Jemima Senters	Mar. 10, 1836
Chaffin, Nathan	Dicie Justice	Feb. 25, 1836
Chaffin, Thomas	Jane Horn	Feb. 27, 1842
Chaffin, William	Nancy Curnutte	Jan. 29, 1835
Chaffin, William	Polly Taylor	Sept. 27, 1849
Chaffin, William	Amanda Jordan	Apr. 26, 1858
Chambers, Daniel	Sally L. Justice	Feb. 29, 1839
Chandler, Henry	Jennie Mott Wheeler	Mar. 26, 1835
Chandler, James	Catherine Daniel	Aug. 13, 1835

Groom	Bride	Date of Marriage
Chaney, Abel	Polly Chaffin	Dec. 13, 1822
Chapman, Andrew J.	Martha McClure	Feb. 17, 1828
Chapman, George	Charlotte Stewart	Feb. 5, 1856
Chapman, Henry	Clementine McClure	Feb. 12, 1852
Chapman, John	Rebecca Muncey	Aug. 16, 1858
Chapman, Mitchell	Emily Ball	Dec. 5, 1835
Chapman, William	Polly McClure	Dec. 16, 1823
Chapman, William	Nancy McClure	Apr. 30, 1850
Chapman, William	Lurany Hager	Dec. 31, 1855
Childers, Abram	Elizabeth Preston	Dec. 25, 1823
Childers, James	Elizabeth Harrell	Nov. 2, 1854
Childers, John	Mary Cook	Apr. 21, 1833
Childers, Russell	Pricie Stafford	Oct. 1, 1849
Chappin, Simeon	Amanda French	Aug. 26, 1832
Chappin, Stanley	Sarah Conley	Aug. 6, 1834
Christian, ...	.... Shannon	Feb. 14, 1851
Christian, William A.	Elizabeth Shannon	Aug. 18, 1850
Clark, Anderwell	Cynthia Lambert	Sept. 26, 1836
Clark, Charles	Nancy Large	May 2, 1844
Clark, Joseph	Cynthia Swearengen	Feb. 17, 1828
Clay, Evan P.	Rebecca Stith	Aug. 16, 1853
Clay, James M.	Eliza Jane Clay	Jan. 26, 1853
Clay, John	Catherine Lambert	Dec. 11, 1859
Clay, Jordan	Ollie Carr	Jan. 13, 1840
Clayton, John M.	Adelaide Allison	Mar. 20, 1852
Coburn, James	Rebecca Slusher	Nov. 5, 1843
Coburn, Joseph	Feraby Wellman	Apr. 6, 1859
Codle, (Caudill) William	Jane Wheeler	Jan. 19, 1823
Coffee, William A.	Servill Fife	Nov. 26, 1857
Coffman, Albert	Sarah Crouch	Oct. 23, 1852
Collier, Daniel	Sarah Blevins	Aug. 12, 1855
Collier, John	Polly Holbrook	Apr. 26, 1824
Collins, Hiram	Patsy Dale	May 31, 1826
Cook, John M.	Amelia A. Savain	Sept. 22, 1840
Cook, Milton	Mary A. Mainor	July 22, 1850
Cooksey, Isaac	Elizabeth Johnston	May 10, 1834
Cooksey, John	Nancy Wood	Feb. 9, 1840
Cooksey, Solomon	Exome Thompson	Apr. 17, 1851
Compton, Layne	Louise Miller	Dec. 21, 1855
Conley, Ezekiel	.... Skaggs	Sept. 3, 1849
Conley, Thomas	Nancy Skaggs	Mar. 29, 1858
Copley, Cyrus	Sarah Marcum	Mar. 15, 1838
Copley, James	Sarah Marcum	...., 1838?
Copley, James	Hannah Indicutt	Dec. 7, 1851
Copley, James	Margaret Chaffin	Feb. 9, 1837
Copley, William	Nancy Williamson	July 30, 1822
Cordiall, (Caudill) Jeremiah	Jane Cooksey	Oct. 15, 1854
Cordell, (Caudill) William	Cynthia Moody	Jan. 23, 1855
Cordell, (Caudill) William	Clarinda Fitzpatrick	Oct. 16, 1855
Cox, Bennett	Sally Nickell	Nov. 26, 1834
Cox, Bennett	Frances Baisden	May 26, 1850
Cox, John	Nancy Lowe	Mar. 15, 1838
Crabtree, Hiram	Evaline Short	Mar. 25, 1832
Crabtree, John	Elizabeth Short	Oct. 16, 1830
Crabtree, Joshua	Sarah Jarrell	Oct. 16, 1855
Craft, Tillman	Sarah Sparks	Mar. 18, 1835
Craft, Thomas	Nancy Caldwell	June 9, 1836
Crank, Nathan	Cynthia Spillman	Oct. 25, 1838
Creech, Henry	Christina Wells	Oct. 27, 1852

Groom	*Bride*	*Date of Marriage*
Crum, David	Nancy Adams	July 14, 1830
Crum, Jesse	Ruth Mills	Apr. 16, 1857
Crum, Jesse	Sarah J. Music	Mar. 24, 1859
Crum, Joel	Nancy Short	Jan. 15, 1843
Crum, John	Dicie Spalding	Dec. 3, 1851
Crum, John	Frances Alley	Sept. ...., 1859
Crum, Reuben	Alifair Ward	Jan. 16, 1834
Culver, Abraham	Patsy Hale	Sept. 3, 1838
Curnutte, David	Deadamia Lyon	Aug. 1, 1822
Curnutte, David	Bertha Sparks	Sept. 27, 1855
Curnutte, John	Sarah, Berry	Oct. 8, 1857
Curnutte, John	Sarah Ann Wellman	Sept. 21, 1855
Curnutte, Reuben	Zelpha Holbrook	Mar. 21, 1833
Curnutte, Stephen	Elizabeth Kinner	Oct. 20, 1843
Cyrus, Abraham	Feriba Hatton	Dec. 23, 1858

D

Dalton, James	Jane Workman	Nov. 8, 1845
Damron, George	Sally Preston	Feb. 16, 1826
Damron, Samuel	Dicie Chapman	Feb. 16, 1849
Damron, William	Mrs. Elizabeth Baker	Oct. 12, 1854
Daniel, A.	E. Ramey	Feb. 13, 1853
Daniel, Andrew	Susannah Hylton	July 17, 1834
Daniel, Ison	Eleanor Jaynes	May 5, 1842
Daniel, Thomas	Eunice Adams	Apr. 30, 1828
Daniel, Watt A.	Maranda Lyon	Mar. 16, 1857
Davenport, P. L.	Elizabeth Davis	June 1, 1852
Davidson, Joseph	Nancy Burgess	July 7, 1825
Davidson, Nathaniel	Olive Hart	Apr. 26, 1834
Davis, Andrew	Ellen Meek	Oct. 2, 1823
Davis, Elihu	Rachael Nelson	Aug. 31, 1826
Davis, George	Juliet Dillon	Dec. 30, 1835
Davis, Henry	Polly Muncy	Dec. 3, 1833
Davis, Henry	Nancy Preston	Mar. 26, 1853
Davis, Henry	Margaret McKay	May 14, 1856
Davis, Hezekiah	Millie Wheeler	Sept. 29, 1842
Davis, Hezekiah B.	Nancy Hickman	Aug. 19, 1858
Davis, Hickman	Nancy Compton	Apr. 3, 1850
Davis, James	Levina Haney	Nov. 23, 1822
Davis, James	Lucinda Canterberry	Sept. 3, 1829
Davis, James	Elvira Hassisage	May 25, 1854
Davis, John	Elizabeth Nelson	May 14, 1835
Davis, John	Nancy Chapman	Sept. 15, 1836
Davis, Joseph	Catherine Borders	Jan. 19, 1826
Davis, Martin P.	Catherine Spencer	Jan. 17, 1857
Davis, Michael	Mahala Adkins	Feb. 11, 1858
Davis, Nathaniel	Lucinda Buchanan	Mar. 13, 1831
Davis, William	Farusha Jane Adkins	Mar. 30, 1856
Davis, William	Pricie Kirk	Sept. 20, 1857
Davis, William	Sally Hensley	Mar. 6, 1859
Dean, John	Vina Lowe	Feb. 21, 1833
Dean, Jonathan	Mary Ann Prince	Mar. 10, 1829
Dean, Joseph H.	Emily Grubb	Mar. 31, 1856
Dean, William E.	Minerva Stewart	Jan. 4, 1859
Deboard, Jacob	Clara Wheeler	Nov. 23, 1827
Defoe, Charles	Elizabeth Manley	Oct. 4, 1834
Delong, George	Polly Moore	Sept. 3, 1839
Delong, James	Elizabeth Ward	June 1, 1834

Groom	*bride*	*Date of Marriage*
Derrifield, David	Jane Culver	Mar. 16, 1857
Derrifield, John	Mahala Berry	Jan. 21, 1850
Derrifield, William	Nancy Jordan	May 23, 1833
Diamond, Charles, Jr.	Manha ? W. Roberts	Oct. 22, 1857
Diamond, Jesse C.	Susan Stobaugh (Stambaugh)	June 4, 1827
Dillon, Micajah	Polly Ann Nelson	Feb. 23, 1849
Dingess, John	Juda Williamson	Apr. 1, 1858
Dobbins, John	Catherine Spradling	Aug. 6, 1830
Dooley, William	Martha A. McKinster	Oct. 1, 1855
Dorsey, George B.	Maranda Meek	Oct. 12, 1850
Downey, James	Jane Hatton	Dec. 25, 1858
Duley, Harrison (Dooley)	M. McDowell	Mar. 7, 1853
Dyer, James	Mary Broomfield	Sept. 19, 1856
Dyer, Owen	Rebecca Peck	Nov. 27, 1829
Dyer, William	Nancy Auxier	Sept. 14, 1823

E

Eastham, Edward	Julia A. Roberts	Feb. 13, 1851
Easton, Lewis	Elizabeth Lambert	Feb. 8, 1855
Edwards, Isaac	Elizabeth Griffith	Nov. 16, 1843
Edwards, Meredith	Sarah Osborn	Dec. 5, 1832
Edwards, William	Susanna Evans	Oct. 19, 1845
Elam, Walter	Eleanor Wheeler	July 27, 1825
Elkins, William	Emily J. McGuire	Dec. 21, 1858
Endicott, Benjamin	Elizabeth Day	Nov. 5, 1834
Endicott, Samuel	Esther Johnson	Apr. 24, 1823
Endicott, William	Elcenia Marcum	Aug. 18, 1857
Engram, Thomas	....	May 22, 1828
Estep, John	Mary Sadler	May 21, 1839
Evans, Harrison	Sarah Daniels	Oct. 23, 1828
Evans, William	Phoebe Adair	July 7, 1836
Evans, Wilson	Elizabeth Dobbins	Dec. 17, 1851

F

Fannin, Bryant	Polly Smith	Oct. 28, 1823
Fannin, Isaac	Sarah Ross	Nov. 9, 1830
Fannin, Isaac	Mary Savage	Oct. 14, 1855
Fannin, John	Margaret Furguson	Mar. 23, 1834
Fannin, Joseph	Elizabeth Kitchen	Feb. 19, 1822
Fannin, Lewis	Elizabeth W. Riffe	June 10, 1858
Fannin, William	Polly Pack	July 14, 1833
Farley, William H.	Phoebe Adair	Feb. 25, 1836
Farmer, Ephriam	Hala Brooks	Aug. 26, 1851
Ferguson, Elisha	Elizabeth Martin	Mar. 27, 1837
Ferguson, Elisha	Elizabeth Griffith	May 25, 1859
Ferguson, James	Polly Bromley	...., 1823
Ferguson, John Patton	Ann Edwards	Aug. 26, 1836
Ferguson, Moses	Margaret Skaggs	Mar. 16, 1848
Ferguson, Obadiah	Charitan Vaughan	...., 1837
Ferguson, Samuel	Malinda Meek	Mar. 29, 1832
Fields, James	Polly Deboard	...., 1835
Fields, John	Rebecca Kirk	...., 1855?
Fiffe, Joseph	Martha Skaggs	Dec. 28, 1843
Fiffe, William	Ruth Terry	Mar. 13, 1851
Finn, Mastin	Elizabeth Kiger	Feb. 28, 1823
Fitzpatrick, Burgess	Sarah A. Jarred	...., 1837
Fitzpatrick, Burgess	Maria McClure	Mar. 11, 1851

Groom	Bride	Date of Marriage
Fitzpatrick, Jameson	Jane Preston	Apr. 25, 1843
Fluty, Aaron	Mary Ann Maynard	June 1, 1843
Fluty, Frances	Mary Jarrell	July 26, 1857
Foster, ...	.... Hooser? (Van Hoose)	June 13, 1851
Foster, Alexander	Henrietta Caldwell	Sept. 4, 1849
Foster, George	Nancy Johnson	Sept. 30, 1829
Foster, Jacob	Eve Grubb	Apr. 25, 1839
Foster, William S.	Elizabeth J. Bradley	Oct. 25, 1857
Fortner, Lorenza Dow	Polly Cox	May 4, 1826
Fortner, William B.	Lucinda Prichard	Apr. 3, 1857
Fraley, Aud	Barbara White	Oct. 27, 1825
Frasher, (Frazier) John W.	Mrs. Cinderilla Price	Oct. 20, 1859
Frazier, George	Charlotte Wells	June 19, 1828
Frazier, Granville	Sallie Coffman	Mar. 13, 1858
Frazier, Jesse	Polly O'Daniel	Sept. 7, 1839
Frazier, Micajah	Lucy Gibson	May 31, 1835
Frazier, John	Polly Wolkmin (Workman)	Apr. 26, 1837
Frazier, Samuel	Polina Martin	Oct. 3, 1833
Frazier, William	Peggy Napier	Mar. 11, 1852
French, Jehue	Sarah Ann Hazlett	Aug. 2, 1855
French, John W.	Mary Ann Hazelett	Aug. 2, 1855
Fry, A. J.	Rachael Wiley	July 1, 1853
Fugett, F.	Lucretia Evans	June 30, 1845
Fugett, Moses	Mary Grubb	Feb. ...., 1836
Fuller, Obadiah	Pricie Morehead	July 19, 1835
Fultz, Morgan	Mary Warner	Feb. 25, 1828

G

Gambell, Ettison	Matilda Boggs	Oct. 6, 1855
Gambell, Hargis	Cynthis Lyons	Oct. 15, 1843
Gambell, Jesse	Eleanor Boggs	Apr. 12, 1857
Gambell, Martin	Mahala Lyons	Jan. 12, 1837
Gambell, William	Jemima Boggs	Dec. 16, 1841
Gardner, George W.	Emily Bloomer	July 27, 1834
Garred, Anderson	Elizabeth Dyer	Mar. 18, 1852
Garred, David W.	Nancy Dyer	Mar. 18, 1847
Garrett, Elliott	Deluth Randale	Jan. 21, 1851
Gavet, (Garrett) Ezekiel	Sarah Chapman	Feb. 13, 1824
Garrett, Morgan	Hannah McClure	Feb. 28, 1854
Gee, David	Sarah James	Feb. 20, 1833
Gent, William	Frankie Sparks	Sept. 20, 1834
Ghose, William G.	Lavina Graham	Oct. 28, 1853
Gill, Benjamin	Polly Neal	Aug. 3, 1852
Gillespie, Thomas	Emeretta Moore	Sept. 18, 1854
Gilliam, John	Sarah Jackson	July 7, 1857
Goble, Green	Rebecca Jones	Jan. 1, 1833
Goble, M. B.	Hester Ann Burgess	Oct. 16, 1855
Goble, Stephen	....	Feb. 19, 1835
Goff, J. B.	Mary E. Small	Feb. 4, 1858
Goodnoe, N. H.	Mary A.? Dovener	Mar. 13, 1838
Gordon, William	Elizabeth Moore	July 27, 1854
Gowens, George W.	Mary Thompson	Mar. 1, 1849
Gowens, Alexander	Polly Skidmore	June 14, 1822
Graves, Henderson	Clara E. Harrell	July 27, 1854
Graves, L.	Sallie McKinster	Feb. 22, 1829
Graham, William W.	Sarah Jane Wellman	Mar. 1, 1858
Grayham, (Graham) Jesse	Eunice Roberson	Aug. 7, 1832
Green, Burwell	Phoebe Cordell (Caudill)	Apr. 14, 1857

Groom	Bride	Date of Marriage
Green, Elias	Anna Bevins	Mar. 18, 1851
Green, George W.	Mary Webb	Jan. 13, 1853
Green, Travis	Delila Hays	July 21, 1851
Green, Walter A.	Isabel Short	Jan. 16, 1834
Griffith, Abel	Ailsey Withrow	Aug. 16, 1836
Griffith, Elzy M.	Letitia Hurst	Mar. 28, 1855
Griffith, Evan	Sarah Griffith	Aug. 13, 1857
Griffith, George	Elizabeth Hensley	May 6, 1858
Griffith, James	Elizabeth Gannards (Garred)	Mar. 20, 1824
Griffith, James A.	Margaret Woods	Apr. 10, 1856
Griffith, Jesse	Peggy Wood	Mar. 6, 1828
Griffith, Robert	Susanna Edwards	Jan. 19, 1837
Griffith, Robert	Mary Adams	Mar. 19, 1853
Griffith, William	Polly Litteral	Feb. 23, 1840
Grubb, Absolom	Elizabeth Lambert	Aug. 24, 1826
Grubb, George	Emily E. Walters	Aug. 14, 1849?
Grubb, George	Polly Curnutte	Feb. 8, 1855
Grubb, Isaac	Rebecca Stewart	Apr. 14, 1838
Grubb, James	Elizabeth Cook	Oct. 17, 1835
Guess, H. L.	Eliza Smith	Dec. 25, 1838

H

Groom	Bride	Date of Marriage
Hagerman, William	Patsy Johnson	Aug. 7, 1842
Hale, Elisha	Sarah McKinster	June 29, 1859
Hale, F.	Nancy Justice	May ...., 1850
Hale, Zachariah	Margaret Dean	May 29, 1858
Hall, Isom	Rachael Crum	Aug. 8, 1837
Hamilton, David	Nancy Grubb	Aug. 31, 1844
Hampton, R.	....	Nov. 21, 1834
Hampton, William	Sally Carter	Nov. 16, 1855
Haney, Samuel	Mahala Brown	Dec. 20, 1837
Hanley, John	Mary Mead	Mar. 7, 1849
Harbell, J. J.	Pauline Fortner	May 15, 1856
Hardin, Harvey	Sarah Hensley	Feb. 15, 1855
Hardin, John	Patsy Cox	1836 or 1837
Harding, James	Mary Turner	Dec. 21, 1849
Hardesty, George W.	Mary Ann Canterberry	Aug. 22, 1850
Hardwick, George	Polly Toler	Jan. 4, 1829
Hardwick, George	Elizabeth Williamson	Jan. 29, 1832
Hardwick, Richard	Susan Cox	Jan. 15, 1829
Harmon, Thomas	Amy F. Newman	Nov. 23, 1853
Harrison, Thomas	Elizabeth Peery	Dec. 8, 1836
Hatcher, John B.	Elizabeth Wallace	Nov. 28, 1855
Hatton, ...	.... Newman	June 14, 1845
Hatton, Allen	Elizabeth Tomlin	July 30, 1843
Hatton, Alvin	Cornilda Dyer	Mar. 12, 1857
Hatton, Edmond M.	Sarah Hatton	Sept. 29, 1842
Hatton, Jonah B.	Gidney Canterberry	Feb. 26, 1834
Hatton, Melville	America Compton	July 22, 1853
Hatton, Patrick	Nancy Chaffin	Mar. 3, 1843
Haws, Allan P.	Tabitha Preston	Jan. 12, 1850
Haws, Asbury	Catherine Taylor	Sept. 23, 1844
Hay, Henry	Dicie Skaggs	Feb. 14, 1853
Hay, William	Emily Skaggs	Dec. 20, 1858
Hays, Alemander	Polly Large	May 9, 1837
Hays, John	Elizabeth Thompson	May 28, 1853
Hays, William	Elizabeth Murray	Sept. 4, 1845
Hays, William	Margaret Carter	June 20, 1859

Groom	Bride	Date of Marriage
Hazlett, Robert	Margaret Holliday	Aug. 10, 1825
Hensley, Elijah	Elizabeth Glatts	Mar. 13, 1832
Hensley, Floyd	Rachael Parker	...., 1836
Hensley, Isom	Nancy Rose	Dec. ...., 1859
Hensley, Jacob	Danatia Hardy	Sept. 9, 1855
Hensley, Wesley	Sally Ratcliff	Apr. 8, 1852
Henry, Philip	Elizabeth Brown	Feb. 2, 1823
Hereford, B. L.	Eleanor R. Wallace	May 23, 1851
Herrell, William	Elizabeth (Sadler) Van Hoose	Feb. 9, 1858
Hewlett, H. B.	Rachael Burks	Sept. 10, 1833
Hicks, John	Elizabeth Rose	Oct. 25, 1857
Hill, Wiley B.	Malinda Holbrook	Mar. 29, 1850
Hill, William	Nancy Terry	May 27, 1844
Hinkle, Haraford	Evaline	Nov. 11, 1858
Hinkle, Wesley	Sarah Moore	July 21, 1857
Hite, Andrew J.	Susan Slusher	May 17, 1849
Hilton, Jesse	Elizabeth Ball	Nov. 10, 1831
Hilton, Nathan P.	Polly Meek	Aug. 5, 1832
Hilton, Nathan P.	Frances Yost	Feb. 2, 1843
Hobbs, James	Mary Sadler	July 17, 1837
Hobbs, John	Margaret Horn	Sept. 27, 1849
Hodge, Gabriel	Mahala Pigg	Aug. 7, 1849
Hodge, Henry	Virginia Crouch	Aug. 12, 1856
Hodge, Wilson	Lurana Foster	Sept. 6, 1844
Hogan, Andrew	Susan Burnside	Oct. 11, 1843
Hogan, Isom	Leany Clay	Feb. 1, 1827
Holbrook, Elisha	Ursley (Ursula) Triplett	Mar. 22, 1856
Holbrook, John	Rebecca Boggs	Jan. 21, 1829
Holbrook, Randleman	Polly Boggs	May 22, 1834
Holbrook, William	Sally Fife	May 23, 1833
Holt, Nathan	Elizabeth Wellman	July 14, 1828
Holt, Wade H.	Frances Dyer	Nov. 23, 1852
Holt, William	Elizabeth Walker	Jan. 9, 1823
Hood, James F.	Barbara Diamond	Nov. 3, 1852
Horn, Henry	Sarah Short	Apr. 13, 1839
Horn, James	Alafair Chaffin	Oct. 27, 1844
Horn, Joseph	Rebecca Roberts	Jan. 1, 1853
Howe? George	Sarah Fannin	Oct. 20, 1836
Hubbard, Wesley	Martha Shannon	Oct. 9, 1849
Hulett, Jeptha	Jane Crank	Apr. 15, 1837
Humphrey, Rufus	Katherine Fraley	Mar. 5, 1834
Hutchinson, Logan	Susan White	Sept. 15, 1836
Hutchinson, John A.	Almeda Bradley	Mar. 15, 1849
Hutchinson, John N.	Nancy Sparks	Mar. 21, 1857
Hutchinson, Vincent	Mrs. Luvina P. McDyer	Oct. 15, 1855
Hylton, William	Katherine Griffith	Feb. 19, 1829

I

Indicutt, (Endicott) Joseph	Barsheba Sumner	Jan. 6, 1825
Indicutt, Joshua	Hannah James	Aug. 6, 1834
Ison, Doctor	Elizabeth Fraley	May 15, 1845
Ison, Ira	Linnie Sparks	Sept. 5, 1833
Irons, ...	.... Wade	Oct. 1, 1851

J

Jackson, Elisha	Nancy Fields	Oct. 2, 1850
Jackson, Isaac	Eliza Porter	May 27, 1856

Groom	Bride	Date of Marriage
Jackson, Thomas	Sally Fields	July 22, 1849
Jacobs, John	Mahala Jordan	Mar. 12, 1839
James, Basil	Narcissus Duncan	June 17, 1827
James, David	Louise Chapman	Jan. 26, 1857
James, Edward	Pelina Jane Messer	Oct. 15, 1837
Jarrell, Harvey	Lucretia Stephenson	Mar. 21, 1852
Jarrell, John	Elizabeth Bromley	Dec. 14, 1826
Jayne, Henry	Sarah Sparks	Dec. 25, 1824
Jayne, Henry L.	Sarah Lyon	Mar. 22, 1855
Jewel, Thomas	Phoebe Muncy	Nov. 6, 1835
Jobe, Elisha	Jane Sargeant	Oct. 16, 1855
Jobe, James H.	Mary Blankenship	....
Job, John	Pricilla Young	Feb. 20, 1826
Johns, Martin H.	Mary L. Goble	Nov. 12, 1847
Johnson, Eli	Sally Copley	May 21, 1835
Johnson, Hiram	Lottie Wellman	Oct. 7, 1822
Johnson, J. A.	Elizabeth Burgess	May 13, 1858
Johnson, James	Sarah Gilbert	Mar. 25, 1859
Johnson, Jesse	Polly Biggs	Aug. 27, 1826
Johnson, John	Alafair Copley	June 19, 1836
Johnson, Martin	Martha Kazee	Dec. 7, 1849
Johnson, Samuel	Eliza Slusser	Feb. 20, 1845
Johnson, Thomas	Lucinda Muncey	Jan. 24, 1854
Johnson, W. H.	Marinda Crabtree	Mar. 8, 1849
Jones, Alfred	Nancy Jones	Jan. 16, 1823
Jones, James	Jane Mahern? (Mahan)	May 24, 1828
Jones, John W.	Sarah Jane Rice	May 8, 1856
Jones, Joshua	Millie James	1835 or 1836
Jones, Josiah	Lucretia McClure	Mar. 22, 1855
Jordan, Absolom	Sarah Prater	Apr. 8, 1840
Jordan, Benjamin	Millie Adkins	Mar. 21, 1833
Jordan, Covey	Matilda Carter	Oct. 18, 1854
Jordan, George	Abigail Pennington	Oct. 16, 1837
Jordan, H. H.	Jane Bowling	Jan. 5, 1857
Jordan, Hiram	Fanny Hays	Mar. 30, 1854
Jordan, Hiram	Margaret Berry	May 8, 1856
Jordan, James	Sarah Kitchen	Dec. 15, 1835
Jordan, John	Martha Turman	Feb. 8, 1844
Jordan, Jonas	Sidney Jobe	1835 or 1836
Jordan, Joseph	Isabella Rose	Dec. 14, 1835
Jordan, Richard	Melia Derrifield	Aug. 10, 1836
Justice, Bazzler	Sarah Wright	Jan. 19, 1844
Justice, David	Margaret Chambers	Sept. 10, 1843
Justice, Ehud	Annie Caldwell	Dec. 17, 1836
Justice, Ehud	Phoebe Pack	Jan. 25, 1852
Justice, Eli	Elizabeth Moore	Nov. 18, 1832
Justice, Hiram	Lucy Caldwell	May 17, 1827
Justice, Peyton	Lucy Bazwell	May 9, 1839
Justice, Pilate	Margaret Johnson	Feb. 4, 1849
Justice, Samuel	Mary Craft	May 23, 1842
Justice, Samuel B.	Ary Carey	Nov. 10, 1849

K

Keaton, Elijah	Mary Waddle (Waddell)	Feb. 27, 1859
Keezee, Charles	Barbara Elam	June 30, 1824
Kesee, Elias	Sophia Lyon	Apr. 13, 1855
Kesee, Harvey	Jane Griffith	Mar. 20, 1850
Kezee, Jeremiah	Elizabeth Morris	Oct. 10, 1839

Groom	Bride	Date of Marriage
Keesee, John	Susannah Griffith	Aug. 9, 1849
Keesee, Reuben	Frances Sparks	Dec. 1, 1836
Kelly, James	Mary Job	Nov. 9, 1850
Kelly, Joseph	Eliza Chadwick	Aug. 26, 1849
Kendall, James P.	Fene Whitley	Aug. 8, 1839
Kendall, Lewis W.	Sallie Harris	Apr. 12, 1855
Kinner, Greenville	Elizabeth Ann Howe	Apr. 25, 1843
Kirk, Q.	....	Apr. 10, 1831
Kirk, Thomas	Synthean James	Jan. 16, 1823
Kirk, George	Anna Leakin (Lakin)	May ...., 1842?
Kirk, Hugh	Mahala Marcum	Dec. 13, 1833
Kirk, James M.	Nancy Dingess	Oct. 26, 1843
Kirk, Thomas	Ibby Aldrige	Feb. 1, 1855
Kitchen, Alexander	Leaner Jordan	Mar. 28, 1833
Kitchen, Fleming	Rachael Webb	Apr. 3, 1845
Kitchen, Jesse L.	Elizabeth Roberts	Sept. 25, 1828
Kitchen, John	Leah Hensley	Mar. 21, 1854
Knipp, William	Viletta Roe	Nov. 25, 1835

L

Groom	Bride	Date of Marriage
Lackey, Carson	Evaline McGuire	Mar. 26, 1853
Lackey, James	Sylvia Miller	Feb. 8, 1854
Lakin, James	Eliza P. Layne	Aug. 9, 1859
Lambert, B. F.	Rebecca J. Beckenhammer (Beckelhimer)	Jan. 1, 1858
Lambert, Fannin	....	June 16, 1835
Lambert, Hiram	Polly Broomfield (Brumfield)	Mar. 7, 1851
Lambert, John	Elizabeth Stephens	July 7, 1836
Lambert, Wade H.	Nancy C. Isaacs	Jan. 16, 1854
Large, Andrew	Lucinda Chaffin	Aug. 29, 1844
Large, David	Polly Thompson	Feb. 28, 1829
Large, James	Anna Carter	Apr. 10, 1849
Large, Thomas	Nancy Lyon	Apr. 20, 1843
Layne, Isaac	Jemima Wellman	July 17, 1845
Layne, William	Sarah Sparks	July 12, 1830
Leakin, (Lakin) Joseph	Mariam Guston	Apr. 4, 1841
Lee, Jarrell	Sarah Ann Frazier	May 4, 1849
Lemaster, Francis	Rachael Read (Reed)	July 7, 1827
Lemaster, William	Sarah Gent	Mar. 6, 1834
Lesley, J. K.	Roxie Preston	May 18, 1857
Lesley, (Leslie) John B.	Maria Diana McCormick	Nov. 20, 1849
Lester, Isaac	Nancy Sparks	Feb. 4, 1858
Lester, Linzie	Nancy Pennington	Dec. 20, 1852
Lester, Linzie	Nancy Osborn	June 7, 1859
Lester, Thomas	Polly Sparks	Jan. 1, 1854
Lester, Thomas	Merna Pennington	July 27, 1854
Lewis, John	Susanna Bane?	Oct. 3, 1837
Lewis, John	Harriett McComas	Oct. 3, 1850
Lewis, John	Nancy Cox	Apr. 25, 1854
Lilly, Edward	Susan Butcher	Nov. 10, 1850
Litteral, Johnson	Polly Jobe	May 21, 1843
Lives?, John	Elizabeth White	Feb. 16, 1834
Lloyd, George	Elender McClure	July 22, 1830
Loar, Michael B.	Dulcena Parks	Mar. 27, 1837
Loar, Moses	Nancy Parker	Dec. 26, 1850
Loar, Peter	Nancy Curnutte	Mar. 3, 1837
Lockwood, Ephriam	Elizabeth White	Mar. 4, 1828
Lockwood, Jacob	Hannah Gains	Jan. 4, 1835

Groom	Bride	Date of Marriage
Lockwood, Jacob	Ruth Hazlett	June 3, 1859
Lockhart, James	Cynthia Copley	Nov. 23, 1831
Lockwood, W.	Sarah White	Feb. 6, 1832
Lovejoy, John	Polly Hogan	June 15, 1826
Lowe, Garrett	Fanny Mead	July 23, 1838
Lowe, Jacob	Jane Lesley	Jan. 30, 1835
Lowe?, John	Lyddie Chandler	Apr. 8, 1858
Lowe, Stephen	Mary Stepp?	Aug. 6, 1834
Lowe, William	Maranda Johnson	Jan. 22, 1842
Lutes, John	Caroline Bryan	Sept. 22, 1845
Lykins, Thomas	Elizabeth Sperry	Feb. 20, 1825
Lyons, Abraham	Abagail Sizemore	May 10, 1834
Lyon, Corbin	Nancy Lester	Mar. 24, 1858
Lyon, James	Nancy Large	June 8, 1822
Lyon, Jesse	Polly Wellman	June 1, 1837
Lyon, Levi	Sarah Jordan	Oct. 16, 1837
Lyon, John	Margaret Lester	Apr. 8, 1858
Lyon, John H.	Nancy Lambert	June 6, 1856
Lyon, John S.	Thurza Holbrook	Oct. 31, 1852
Lyon, Lewis	Linna Grizle (Grizell)	Sept. 16, 1823
Lyon, Lewis	Polly Sparks	Jan. 1, 1854
Lyon, William	Linnie Skaggs	Nov. 19, 1839

M

Manor, Charles	....	....
Manor, Simeon	Raney Spellman	....
Marcum, Fleming	Eliza Pack	...., 1849
Marcum, Jacob	Eliza Brewer	Feb. 1, 1838
Marcum, Jacob	Evaline Brewer	June ...., 1843
Marcum, Joseph	Polly Branham	Oct. 22, 1834
Marcum, Joshua	Mahala Fluty	Aug. 7, 1844
Marcum, Peter	Minerva Hampton	June 12, 1845
Marcum, Samuel	Demiba? Kirk	Dec. 18, 1843
Marcum, Stephen	Sarah Hampton	Sept. 20, 1833
Marcum, Stephen	Laura Farris	Jan. 19, 1835
Marcum, Stephen	Jane Damrell (Damron)	Sept. 15, 1839
Marcum, William	Nancy Crum	...., 1837
Martin, John P.	Mary E. Childers	July 8, 1854
Massey, Steel	Caroline Cantley	Nov. 16, 1855
Mathias, Daniel	Sally Copley	July 7, 1836
May, Henry	Malinda J. Diamond	July 5, 1857
May, Samuel	Nancy Spencer	Sept. ...., 1835
May, Thomas H.	Edy McGuire	Jan. 3, 1854
Maynard, Elias	Sarah Maynard	Dec. 18, 1844
Maynard, Lewis	Catherine Fluty	June 1, 1843
McCall, James	Patsy Hardwick	June 11, 1827
McCall, John	Elizabeth McSorley	Jan. 21, 1855
McCloud, John	Patsy Farmer	Mar. 24, 1857
McClure, George	Vedina Davis	Nov. 23, 1858
McClure, Nelson	Mary Jane Chapman	Jan. 27, 1858
McClure, William	Nancy Hardwick	July 4, 1858
McCormack, ...	Mary Dyer	July 19, 1855
McCormack, James	Esther McCoy	Apr. 10, 1855
McCormack, Micajah	Rhoda Munsey	Apr. 9, 1854
McCormack, Wiley	Perlina Waller	Jan. 18, 1856
McCoy, George	Tabitha Auxier	June 7, 1822
McCoy, James	Elizabeth Derrifield	Sept. 7, 1840
McCoy, Pleasant	Vicie Chapman	Dec. 20, 1843

Groom	Bride	Date of Marriage
McCrosky, ...	.... Canterberry	Jan. 28, 1845
McDaniel, John	Sarah White	Dec. 10, 1823
McDowell, John	Nancy Matthews	July 28, 1835
McDowell, John	Nancy Gibbs	Mar. 21, 1837
McDowell, Peter	Dicie Chaffin	Nov. 7, 1855
McDyer, F. A.	Lucinda Huff	June 12, 1856
McDyer, John	Lavena Hutchinson	Apr. 20, 1849
McGrannahan, L. D.	Nancy Miller	Mar. 12, 1854
McGrannahan, John F.	Permitta Burgess	Jan. 4, 1831
McGraw, Charles	Julina Bromfield	Feb. 28, 1855
McGuire, James	Elizabeth Haney	Sept. 23, 1852
McGuire, Joseph	Eliza Ann Wiley	Feb. 24, 1856
McGuire, Robert	Peace Kennedy	Mar. 15, 1838
McHunter, Samuel	Rebecca Pennington	Aug. 1, 1833
McIntire, John	Mahala Thompson	...., 1824
McKenzie, Robert	Amanda Rice	July 15, 1858
McKinster, Allen	Betsy Ann Spencer	Jan. 24, 1850
McKinster, H. J.	Elizabeth Carter	Sept. 21, 1856
McKinster, John	Elizabeth Van Hoose	Jan. 2, 1852
McKinster, William	Temperance Packwood	Aug. 20, 1827
McKinster, William	Patsy Mead	Mar. 16, 1854
McMaster, John	Elizabeth Neill	Jan. 13, 1859
McNight, Ervin	....	....
Mead, Abraham	Jane Reily	Aug. 2, 1837
Mead, A.	Elizabeth Smith	June 7, 1859
Mead, Ambrose	Polly Spencer	Aug. 24, 1852
Mead, Andrew	Elizabeth Austin	July 12, 1858
Mead, Henry	Polly McKinster	July 19, 1829
Mead, Henry	Malinda Stewart	Feb. 3, 1837
Mead, Jesse	Elizabeth McKinster	Nov. 20, 1828
Mead, Jesse	Nancy Spencer	Nov. 16, 1838
Mead, John	Ellen Murray	Mar. 4, 1859
Mead, Robert	Eleanor Spencer	Mar. 4, 1852
Medley, John F.	Elizabeth Jones	Apr. 10, 1854
Meek, Edward	Ellen Chapman	Jan. 6, 1851
Meek, Jesse	Martha Goble	Aug. 9, 1859
Meek, Madison	Sarah Van Hoose	Nov. 2, 1854
Meek, William	Elizabeth White	Sept. 5, 1833
Meek, William	Sarah Syck	Jan. 1, 1856
Mellon, William P.	Ellen S. Clark	May 21, 1856
Merrell, J. C.	Levisa J. Buchanan	May 27, 1856
Messer, Jacob	Pricilla Gallahue	Nov. 15, 1836
Messer, Morgan	Elizabeth Williamson	Oct. 2, 1857
Middleton, James	Larcus Skaggs	June 6, 1844
Middaugh, Jesse C.	Mary Ann Van Hoose	Apr. 28, 1854
Miller, A. H.	Amanda Shannon	Nov. 10, 1857
Miller, Edward B.	Charlotte Crockett	Nov. 19, 1838
Miller, Garland	Nancy Hinkle	Sept. 15, 1850
Miller, James A.	Polly Hinkle	Sept. 2, 1850
Miller, James C.	Elizabeth Miller	Oct. 16, 1856
Miller, James C.	Elizabeth Murray	Aug. 12, 1859
Miller, John B.	Judith Hall	Feb. 21, 1851
Miller, J. T.	....	Aug. 3, 1828
Miller, Robert	Elizabeth Cooksey	Oct. 15, 1838
Miller, Samuel	Elizabeth Hinkle	Dec. 18, 1849
Miller, Thompson	Susanna Mead	Nov. 2, 1854
Mills, John	Elizabeth Copley	Nov. 10, 1859
Mills, Martin	Elizabeth Sammons	June 22, 1856
Mims, Martin	Abagail Johnston	Dec. 21, 1830

Groom	Bride	Date of Marriage
Mobley, Samuel	Tabitha	Aug. 16, 1822
Mollett, Hiram C.	Elizabeth Collins	Nov. 1, 1835
Moore, Arthur	Nancy Sagraves	May 26, 1855
Moore, David	Polly Nelson	July 18, 1822
Moore, David	Lucinda Ball	Oct. 4, 1844
Moore, David N.	Angeline Thompson	Nov. 22, 1858
Moore, Elisha	Elsa Jordan	....
Moore, Harvey	Nancy Thompson	Aug. 28, 1850
Moore, James	Nancy J. Haney	Feb. 15, 1855
Moore, James H.	Mahala Carter	Dec. 21, 1857
Moore, John	Rebecca Bowling	May 20, 1853
Moore, Joseph	Nancy Thompson	Jan. 16, 1855
Moore, Samuel	Thurza Hardin	...., 1837
Moore, William	Cinda Miller	May 2, 1824
Moore, William	Delila Hale	Jan. 17, 1839
Moore, Wesley	Ladocia McKinster	Feb. 16, 1857
Moore, William	Eleanor Thompson	Jan. 30, 1854
Morgan, Benjamin	Isabel Mead	Aug. 8, 1852
Morris, Benjamin	Frances Griffith	Aug. 24, 1844
Morris, Benjamin	Louisa Griffith	Oct. 7, 1852
Morris, David	Susan Clevenger	Jan. 26, 1859
Morris, Henry	Cynthia Price	Nov. 2, 1843
Morris, Henry	Elizabeth Bailey	Oct. 26, 1853
Morris, Matthew	Margaret Rice	Nov. 14, 1849
Morrow, Daniel	Polly Artrip	May 27, 1859
Mullett, James G.	Margaret Blevins	Mar. 16, 1834
Mullineaux, George	Jane Muncy	Jan. 25, 1852
Mullins, Isaac	Sarah Travis	Nov. 4, 1859
Mullins, Isham	Lena Kitchen	...., 1826
Mullins, John W.	Mary Adams	Feb. 27, 1854
Muncey, David W.	Jemima Muncey	Aug. 14, 1849
Muncey, Samuel	Sallie Chapman	Oct. 22, 1835
Muncey, Samuel	Dicie Spalding	Nov. 24, 1839
Muncey, William	Peggy Hensley	Sept. 2, 1828
Murphy, Archibald	Susanna Ratcliffe	Feb. ...., 1851
Murphy, John	Mary Ann Rose	Mar. 10, 1849
Murray, Rhoderick	Fannie Borders	Feb. 1, 1843
Music, Elechu?	Susannah Wilson	Oct. 9, 1851

N

Napier, Edmond	Ella Watts	June 8, 1825
Napier, Patrick	Perlina Watts	May 5. 1829
Nelson, Gabriel	Elizabeth Short	May 12, 1836
Nelson, William H.	Nancy Harris	Dec. 13, 1839
Newman, Greenville	Mary Ann Kelly	July 14, 1842
Newman, Moses	Elizabeth Stewart	Feb. 21, 1854
Newman, Reynolds	Malinda Canterberry	May 29, 1830
Newton, Sylvester	Elizabeth Thacker	May 22, 1858
Nicks, Elisha	Matilda Young	Dec. 23, 1822
Nichols, Newman	Luran Artrip	Mar. 16, 1835
Nipp, (Knipp) Robert	Elizabeth Rice	Apr. 15, 1838
Norman, E. G.	Barbara Cyrus	Mar. 21, 1852
Norton, David	Emily Davidson	July 25, 1830

O

O'Brien, Isaac	Susanna Short	July 1, 1855
Old, William	Nancy M. Bevans	Mar. 25, 1854

Groom	Bride	Date of Marriage
O'Roark, James	Elizabeth Muncey	Feb. 5, 1852
Osburn, Edmond	Nancy C. Evans	June 21, 1855
Osburn, Thomas	Millie Dean	Jan. 30, 1830
Osburn, Thomas	Phoebe Holbrook	Jan. 21, 1851
Osburn, Walter	Sallie Edwards	May 24, 1824
Oxier, (Auxier) Jackson	Nancy Nolin	June 24, 1841

P

Groom	Bride	Date of Marriage
Pack, Archibald	Mary Calloway	Aug. 30, 1830
Pack, Archibald	Mary Muncey	Nov. 9, 1843
Pack, Bartley	Anna Fluty	April 25, 1839
Pack, Berry	Rebecca Blevins	Feb. 9, 1840
Pack, Cornelius	Nancy Evans	Aug. 16, 1834
Pack, Daniel	Julia A. Thompson	Sept. 27, 1858
Pack, George	....	Apr. 21, 1833
Pack, George	Anna Fannin	Dec. 8, 1842
Pack, John	Sarah Ann Endicott	Apr. 4, 1844
Pack, John	Jane Wheeler	Apr. 24, 1851
Pack, Leander	Oma Hanley	Mar. 15, 1856
Pack, William	Matilda Bowens	Nov. 25, 1830
Pack, Samuel	Mary Evans	May 16, 1839
Paisley, Jesse	Sallie Marcum	Feb. 2, 1843
Paisley, Moses, Jr.	Maria Chapman	July 5, 1849
Paisley, Ryburn	Penelope Copley	Jan. 23, 1840
Paisley, Samuel	Mary Pruitt	Mar. 27, 1859
Pardon, Hiram	Fannie Hays	Mar. 30, 1854
Parker, Samuel	Mary Berry	Jan. 14, 1857
Parks, Micajah	Jane Sisson	Dec. 18, 1858
Parks, Shelton	Susan Frazier	Feb. 3, 1831
Parsley, (Paisley) William	Nancy Chaffin	Apr. 4, 1839
Peck, George C.	Emily Stafford	Feb. 22, 1838
Pelfrey, William	Sarah (Sally) Rose	Oct. 16, 1852
Penix, ...	.... McDowell	May 28, 1852
Pennington, John W.	Aggie Webb	Nov. 11, 1849
Pennington, John J.	E. R. Murphy	Apr. 14, 1853
Pennington, William	Nancy Kelley	Aug. 11, 1839
Pennington, William	Margaret Ann Murphy	Mar. 15, 1847
Pennington, W. P.	Rebecca French	Nov. 1, 1854
Pennington, William T.	Sarah Pennington	Nov. 2, 1854
Pennington, William I.	Margaret Bailey	Dec. 15, 1856
Perry, ...	.... Marcum	Sept. 23, 1845
Perry, Abraham	Eba Williamson	June 10, 1838
Perry, Russell	Margaret Cook	June 18, 1838
Perry, Thomas	Narcissa Canterberry	Jan. 15, 1834
Perry, William, Sr.	Mary Farmer	Aug. 24, 1843
Peters, Jacob	Jane See	Oct. 19, 1837
Pigg, George	Mary Chapman	Feb. 12, 1852
Pigg, John	Elizabeth Wellman	Aug. 28, 1844
Pigg, William	Elizabeth B. Chapman	Feb. 3, 1853
Pitts, ...	.... Fannin	Feb. 13, 1845
Plumm, John	Elizabeth Evans	Apr. 24, 1854
Pool, Lewis	Amanda Skeens	Aug. 20, 1856
Porter, Alexander	Rebecca Porter	Sept. 19, 1839
Porter, Alex	Polly Mutter	Dec. 16, 1843
Porter, Elijah	Amanda Hardin	Dec. 21, 1854
Porter, John	Margaret Jackson	July 1, 1876
Potts, Joseph	Sarah Rice	June 18, 1822

Groom	Bride	Date of Marriage
Preston, Albert	Hulda Childers	Sept. 9, 1849
Preston, Arthur	Nancy Miller	Oct. 26, 1828
Preston, Boteman	Julia Ann Picklesimer	Nov. 7, 1854
Preston, Henry	Elizabeth Cains	Jan. 18, 1827
Preston, Hereford	Elizabeth Hurt	Mar. 26, 1854
Preston, James	Levina Murray	Mar. 12, 1840
Preston, James	Linna Price	Oct. 6, 1854
Preston, John	Keziah West	July 20, 1842
Preston, Reuben	Eastin Evans	Jan. 14, 1836
Preston, Robert	Matilda West	July 20, 1842
Preston, Stephen	Pricilla Miller	Jan. 14, 1824
Preston, William	Susan Murray	Nov. 25, 1845
Prichard, A. J.	Nancy B. Burgess	Apr. 17, 1858
Prichard, George	Olivia A. Bolt	Sept. 21, 1843
Prichard, Wiley	Elizabeth Bolt	Jan. 25, 1855
Prichard, William	Mary Lyon	Apr. 28, 1833
Price, Henry	Elizabeth Wellman	Aug. 6, 1835
Price, James	Ruth A. Stewart	Dec. 21, 1827
Price, James	Emily Blevins	Mar. 5, 1843
Price, Jesse	Dicie Salyers	July 30, 1845
Price, John	Sally Fitzpatrick	Feb. 2, 1837
Price, Robert	Nancy Thompson	June 30, 1825
Price, Washington	Sarah Borders	Sept. 30, 1830
Price, Wood	Wood? Fitzpatrick	July 16, 1859
Prince, James	Elizabeth Hensley	....
Prin (c) e, James McHenry	Nancy Frederick	Mar. 29, 1855
Prince, John	Lavina Griffith	Apr. 7, 1840
Prince, John W.	Emily Fugett	June 1, 1854
Prince, Nicholas	Charity Rigsby	Jan. 4, 1830
Prince, Miles	Nancy Rigsby	Apr. 21, 1853
Prince, (Price) Van	Mary Ann Massey	Jan. 31, 1856
Prong, Henry	A. M. Porter	Dec. 20, 1852
Pulley, David	Amanda Willis	Feb. 6, 1852
Pulaski, Maxmillan	Mary S. Owsley	Sept. 10, 1855

Q

Queen, James	Millie Manor	Sept. 9, 1839
Queen, John	Sarah Lambert	June 12, 1856
Queen, Walter	Julina Riffe	Apr. 13, 1852

R

Ramey, Thaddeus	Jannie Caldwell	Apr. 2, 1835
Ratcliff, David	Sarah Eldridge	July 26, 1853
Ratcliff, Harvey	James Garred	...., 1826
Ratcliff, Lorenzo D.	Fanne Morris	June 18, 1856
Ratcliff, Richard	Martha Hardin	Sept. 14, 1829
Ratcliff, William	Nancy Garred	Feb. 20, 1823
Ratcliff, William	Polly Skaggs	Feb. 22, 1854
Ratcliff, William	Elizabeth Lemon	About 1850
Ratcliff, Zachariah	Nancy Griffith	Feb. 18, 1832
Ratcliff, Zachariah	Polly Griffith	Dec. 8, 1849
Reed, William	Nancy Jackson	Mar. 6, 1837
Rice, Anderson	Susan Griffith	Aug. 27, 1829
Rice, David K.	Nancy Curnutte	Oct. 9, 1855
Rice, E.	Ruth Prince	Sept. 6, 1835
Rice, Ezekiel	Peggy Rice	Feb. 19, 1837
Rice, George	Peggy Harvey	Nov. 19, 1832

Groom	Bride	Date of Marriage
Rice, Hezekiah	Ruth Prince	Sept. 17, 1835
Rice, Jacob	Amanda Grannahan	May 3, 1835
Rice, Jacob	Adelaide Crabtree	Aug. 8, 1850
Rice, James	Rebecca Stewart	June 11, 1822
Rice, James	Jane Burns	Sept. 18, 1823
Rice, James M.	Mary M. Brown	Mar. 19, 1840
Rice, James R.	Delilah Hutchinson	May 31, 1853
Rice, Mathias	Fannie Bond	Feb. 22, 1827
Rice, Sherard	Margaret Morris	Dec. 2, 1828
Rice, William	Nancy Akers	Feb. 25, 1850
Rice, William	Peggy Spalding	Aug. 7, 1853
Ridge, John	Nancy Holiday	Feb. 26, 1823
Riffe, William	Elizabeth Short	Dec. 19, 1850
Rigglesby, Lewis	Rebecca Burgess	Dec. 21, 1826
Riggsby, Drury	Nancy Rose	Feb. 27, 1834
Riggsby, Francis	Ary Privette	Jan. 17, 1833
Riggsby, Henry	Nancy Skaggs	June 16, 1853
Riggsby, Thomas	Linna Deboard	Jan. 5, 1839
Riggsby, Willis	Mary Skaggs	July 28, 1853
Right, (Wright) Elkanah	Sarah Large	Apr. 2, 1859
Right, (Wright) Patterson	Susannah Sagraves	Aug. 3, 1854
Right, (Wright) William	Sarah Rose	June 19, 1853
Roach, Edward	Margaret Stewart	May 19, 1838
Roberts, George W.	Julina Burton	Dec. 31, 1833
Roberts, George H.	Amanda Carter	Nov. 24, 1838
Roberts, Isaac	Phoebe Workman	July 31, 1822
Roberts, Isaac	Cynthis Ann Pack	Aug. 19, 1843
Robertson, ...	.... Shannon	Oct. 26, 1852
Robertson, Hudson B.	Nancy Shannon	Oct. 24, 1851
Robertson, Isaac	Elizabeth Runion	Mar. 9, 1833
Robinson, George	Venoy Gibson	Aug. 3, 1851
Robinson, Richard	Matilda Thompson	Feb. 29, 1828
Rollins, William	Margaret Neely	Feb. 6, 1851
Rose, Jones	Polly Betty Murphy	Nov. 28, 1852
Rose, Madison	Juliana Amos	July 22, 1832
Rose, Thomas	Rhoda Fife	Oct. 8, 1840
Rose, Zachariah	Peggy Auxier	Aug. 28, 1825
Ross, Granville	Margaret Pinson	Jan. 1, 1839
Ross, J. D.	Susan Lockwood	Aug. 15, 1833
Ross, John D.	Martha J. Leslie	Apr. 15, 1857
Rudd, Thomas	Nancy Evans	Feb. 21, 1850
Ruggles, Robert	Elizabeth Stewart	Jan. 5, 1855
Runion, Adron	Hester Ann Smith	About 1840
Russell, Lewis	Jane Davidson	Feb. 11, 1822
Russell, Rhomas	Jane Yates	Sept. 6, 1851

S

Sagraves, Joseph	....	Sept. 13, 1832
Sagraves, William	Charlotte Mitchell	Sept. 17, 1835
Salyers, Thomas	Mary Creech	Oct. 18, 1857
Sammons, David	Mary Magdalin?	Apr. 5, 1849
Sammons, Roland, Jr.	Lucinda Hensley	Oct. 29, 1854
Sammons, Thomas	Emily Hammond	Jan. 9, 1851
Sansom, Elias	Tamsey Hardin	Jan. 2, 1840
Sansom, William	....	Feb. 7, 1824
Sargent, Stephen D.	Lavena Young	Aug. 17, 1850
Sargent,? William	Cinda Pennington	Apr. 6, 1854
Savage, Andrew J.	Polly Stewart	Oct. 15, 1852

Groom	Bride	Date of Marriage
Savage, Chrisley	Rebecca C. Riffe	Aug. 30, 1849
Savage, John	Martha Thompson	Aug. 15, 1827
Savage, John D.	Mary Riffe	June 1, 1843
Scisson, Alamander?	Clarinda Chaffin	Aug. 3, 1856
Scisson, Emanuel	Martha Jane Strother	Feb. 25, 1854
Scisson, Joseph	Elizabeth Webb	July 15, 1850
Scott, John	Polly Helvy	Mar. 9, 1834
Seagraves, Zachariah	Anna Johnson	Apr. 13, 1858
See, Jarred	Catherine Maynard	Aug. 31, 1857
See, Michael	Elizabeth Peck	Dec. 22, 1859
Seedmore? (Skidmore) James	Cynthiann Flynn	July 17, 1822
Sellards, Elias	Elmina Muirhead	June 20, 1834
Sellards, Samuel	....	Oct. 22, 1833
Sellards, Samuel	Polly Lowe	Feb. 15, 1834
Shannon, John	Martha Ann Hatton	Aug. 4, 1842
Shannon, Joseph	Frances Howe?	Mar. 21, 1845
Shannon, Mitchell B.	Margaret Justice	Feb. 22, 1855
Shannon, Thomas	Mary Wallace	Jan. 30, 1828
Shannon, Thomas	Marian? Kelly	Apr. 13, 1854
Shannon, William H.	Caroline McGrannahan	Dec. 25, 1832
Shelton, William S. H.	Malissa P. Jackson	Jan. 11, 1859
Short, Daniel	Dinah Justice	Dec. 25, 1834
Short, James	E. Taylor	Aug. 6, 1840
Short, James	Martha Chaffin	Jan. 23, 1849
Short, John	Louanna Casteel (Castle)	Apr. 14, 1836
Short, John	Martha Parker	July 16, 1850
Short, Samuel	Elizabeth Rice	Sept. 11, 1845
Short, Samuel	Hannah Hays	Nov. 6, 1851
Short, William	Emily See	Mar. 13, 1832
Simpson, George	Elizabeth Isaacs	Nov. 4, 1852
Skaggs, A.	....	Nov. 20, 1825
Skaggs, Christian	Elizabeth Peery	Feb. 24, 1829
Skaggs, John	Margaret Holbrook	...., 1842
Skaggs, John	Mary Lester	May 22, 1844
Skaggs, John	Polly Fiffe	Oct. 24, 1844
Skaggs, John	Lucinda Riggsby	Oct. 10, 1850
Skaggs, Peter	Cler(i)nda Prince	Mar. 20, 1823
Skaggs, Peter	Marian Holbrook	Apr. 10, 1834
Skaggs, Martin	Elizabeth Fyffe	Jan. 16, 1853
Skaggs, Solomon	Tabitha Middleton	Jan. 25, 1838
Skaggs, Solomon	Nellie Riggsby	Sept. 20, 1855
Skaggs, Squire	Mahala Chaffin	Aug. 15, 1837
Skeens, James	Nancy B. Moore	Dec. 4, 1854
Skeens, John	Nancy Lyon	Jan. 30, 1838
Skidmore, John	Prudentia Arnold	July 22, 1822
Slack, ...	.... Crouch	Jan. 16, 1851
Sloan, Alden	Sarah Bryant	Jan. 24, 1853
Sloan, Patrick	Clementine McKinster	Sept. 19, 1855
Smith, Abram	....	....
Smith, David	....	Feb. 3, 1824
Smith, Edmond	Jane Curnutte	Feb. 9, 1843
Smith, F.	Nancy Balmone (Bellomy)	June 6, 1852
Smith, Henry	Anna Wellman	May 9, 1852
Smith, John	Susan Maynard	Apr. 23, 1843
Smith, Joshua	Elizabeth Fraley	Mar. 29, 1838
Smith, Vinson	Sophronia C. Coffman	May 31, 1851
Smith, William	Sarrilda Roberts	Jan. 28, 1852
Snealdredge, Perry	Marilda Hatton	Feb. 3, 1850
Soliday, ...	.... Dean	May 13, 1852

137

Groom	Bride	Date of Marriage
Solomon, James	Sally Price	Apr. 7, 1849
Spalding, Charles	Elizabeth Thompson	Apr. 5, 1849
Spalding, Jackson	Mahala Kirk	...., 1837
Spalding, James	Joni ? Evans	Oct. 11, 1855
Spalding, William	Nancy Wellman	June 4, 1844
Sparks, ...	.... Green	Dec. 21, 1845
Sparks, Alfred	Mary Ann Green	Dec. 30, 1852
Sparks, Calvin	Sally Lyon	June 19, 1828
Sparks, Daniel	Sarah Jayne	July 31, 1832
Sparks, David	Eleanor Cordell	July 5, 1859
Sparks, Elias	Susanna Pridemore	Dec. 24, 1834?
Sparks, George	Nancy Short	Aug. 7, 1822
Sparks, Jarrett	Elizabeth Boggs	Sept. 22, 1825
Sparks, Matthew	Hannah Adkins	Jan. 18, 1852
Sparks, Reuben	Elizabeth Deal	July 6, 1849
Sparks, Reuben	Mary Curnutte	Dec. 18, 1857
Sparks, Thomas	Katherine Jayne	Dec. 24, 1823
Sparks, Wesley	Nancy Keen	Aug. 22, 1835
Spencer, Charles	Rebecca Thompson	Dec. 7, 1829
Spencer, James	Lucy Nelson	Apr. 19, 1822
Spencer, Jesse	Polly Thompson	Mar. 1, 1849
Spencer, Jesse	Mary Mead	Dec. 22, 1853
Spencer, James	Keziah Jane Davis	June 29, 1845
Spencer, James	Polly Spencer	Mar. 20, 1857
Spencer, John	Matilda Borders	Sept. 11, 1834
Spencer, John	Julia Ann Hays	Apr. 23, 1851
Spencer, John	Frances Davis	June 6, 1859
Spencer, Lewis B.	Fannie Spencer	Apr. 4, 1850
Spencer, O. M.	Nancy Williams	Dec. 17, 1832
Spencer, Thomas	Rebecca Griffith	Sept. 15, 1842
Spencer, William	Mahulda McKinster	May 25, 1858
Sperry, Andrew J.	Lurana Bradley	Sept. 20, 1855
Sperry, Benjamin	Elizabeth Delia?	Nov. 30, 1839
Sperry, James	Cynthia Canterberry	Sept. 30, 1822
Sperry, James	Pelynia Canterberry	Mar. 21, 1827
Sperry, John	Susan Workman	Feb. 6, 1855
Sperry, Rudolph	Nancy Canterberry	Sept. 24, 1825
Spillman, John	Sarah Berry	Aug. 21, 1854
Spriggs, Robert	Polly Castle	Jan. 26, 1837
Spurlock, Francic M.	Frances Hatton	Aug. 24, 1850
Stafford, John	Mary Garitt	Oct. 29, 1845
Stafford, Ralph	Julia Miller	Dec. 6, 1829
Stafford, Ralph M.	Cynthia Ann Burgess	June 18, 1837
Stambaugh, John	Martha Skaggs	Oct. 31, 1841
Stapleton, Basil	Polly Bowen	Sept. 26, 1830
Stapleton, Jacob	Nancy Evans	Nov. 24, 1834
Stapleton, Joseph	Elizabeth Sellards	Aug. 8, 1829
Stapleton, Zedekiah	Sally Fugett	Dec. 25, 1826
Stepp, John	Susanna Porter	May 25, 1837
Stepp, Moses	Mary L. Paisley	Jan. 3, 1850
Stepp, Moses	Sarah Bowen	Dec. 8, 1859
Stepp, William	Phoebe Dingess	May 23, 1857
Stevenson, Calvin	Elizabeth Boyd	Jan. 28, 1847
Stephenson, David	Mary Scott	May 17, 1855
Stephenson, William	Sarah Spellman	Dec. 15, 1835
Stewart, Absolom	Rachael Hager	July 10, 1828
Stewart, Absolom	Amy Fannin	Dec. 18, 1838
Stewart, Charley	Sarah Grubb	June 20, 1833
Stewart, James	Amanda Crank	Sept. 17, 1838

Groom	Bride	Date of Marriage
Stewart, James	Sarah Leakin	Mar. 1, 1839
Stewart, John	Lucinda Evans	June 29, 1834
Stewart, John	America Sperry	Nov. 20, 1843
Stewart, John	Dorothy Richardson	Aug. 22, 1858
Stewart, Mitchell	Cynthia Mead	Apr. 20, 1859
Stewart, Ralph	America Canterberry	July ...., 1829
Stewart, Robinson	Nancy McSurley	Dec. 17, 1850
Stewart, Thomas H.	July Grubb	May 14, 1853
Stewart, William	Polly Holliday	May 27, 1828
Stith, Jesse	Eliza B. Hatton	Dec. 8, 1851
Stobaugh, (Stambaugh) Henry	Hila Moore	Mar. 10, 1825
Stobaugh (Stambaugh) Isaac	Nancy Williams	May 16, 1832
Stoddard, David	....	Feb. 8, 1823
Stonebraker, Joseph	Louisa Chaffin	May 3, 1843
Strahan, ...	....	Sept. 4, 1832
Stratton, Cornelius	Margaret Davis	May 24, 1834
Stratton, Henry	Rhoda Finley	Jan. 20, 1839
Stratton, John	Mary Ann Vermillion	Apr. 4, 1859
Stratton, William	Nancy Akers	Sept. 2, 1852
Strother, John	Julia Ann Cyrus	Dec. 23, 1859
Strother, Stephen	Katherine Lower (Loar)	Sept. 18, 1822
Sturgill, Alven	Nancy Fraley	Feb. 14, 1830
Swearengen, Samuel	Sarah Artrip	Oct. 4, 1827
Swetnam, C. L.	Deresa Wellman	Apr. 27, 1837
Swetnam, Elzy M.	Cynthia Preston	Jan. 31, 1839
Swim, Daniel	(Mrs.) Martha Rider	Jan. 9, 1853

T

Taylor, Ellis	Mahala Stewart	Apr. 30, 1855
Terrell, Charles	(Mrs.) Leah Spillman	July 13, 1855
Terry, Isaac	Rebecca Anboned?(Ann Bond)	July 12, 1825
Thomas, William	Sarah Thompson	Apr. 19, 1856
Thompson, Alley	Elizabeth Webb	Apr. 29, 1828
Thompson, Andrew	Sally Daniels	May 20, 1839
Thompson, Andrew J.	Mary Jane Spencer	Sept. 10, 1850
Thompson, David	Fennie Pennington	Aug. 16, 1855
Thompson, David	Malinda Thompson	Jan. 29, 1837
Thompson, David H.	Elizabeth Loar	May 15, 1845
Thompson, George	....	June 30, 1825
Thompson, George	Mary Lambert	Dec. 4, 1827
Thompson, Granville	Elizabeth Ann Leakin	July 11, 1844
Thompson, Isaac P.	Deresa Berry	Aug. 4, 1859
Thompson, James	Patsy Lambert	Apr. 25, 1833
Thompson, James	Sallie Young	June 22, 1852
Thompson, Jeremiah	Mahala Derrifield	Feb. 2, 1854
Thompson, John	Nancy Messer	Oct. 16, 1837
Thompson, John	Eliza Muirhead	Jan. 22, 1837
Thompson, John	Abigail Webb	Dec. 20, 1849
Thompson, John	Jane F. Chapman	Feb. 27, 1857
Thompson, Johnson	Polly Pack	Nov. 3, 1832
Thompson, Martin	Ann Large	Dec. 15, 1823
Thompson, Michael	Nancy Spencer	May 6, 1856
Thompson, Owen	Elizabeth Justice	Aug. 8, 1858
Thompson, Parmer	Matilda Derrifield	Feb. 2, 1854
Thompson, Robert	....	July 23, 1833
Thompson, Russell	Fannie Nelson	Nov. 27, 1829
Thompson, Russell S.	Amanda Moore	Aug. 3, 1854
Thompson, Samuel	Emeretta Thompson	Jan. 8, 1859

Groom	Bride	Date of Marriage
Thompson, Samuel	Sarah Wallen	Apr. 30, 1843
Thompson, Squire	Minta Mead	May 21, 1856
Thompson, Steven	Elizabeth Marcum	Mar. 30, 1831
Thompson, Thomas	Nancy Ball	Mar. 12, 1853
Thompson, Wesley	Polly Spencer	Feb. 5, 1829
Thompson, Wesley	Esther Pack	Sept. 29, 1835
Thompson, Wesley, Jr.	Elizabeth Thompson	July 28, 1852
Thompson, William	Mellie Borders	June 21, 1837
Thompson, William	Jane Wells	Nov. 30, 1833
Thornhill, James	Sarah Justice	Feb. 9, 1847
Toler, Robert	Juliet Keech	Sept. 7, 1826
Tomlin, Alex	Eliza B. Hoover	June 8, 1837
Tomlin, James	Eliza B. Clay	Sept. 18, 1851
Tomlin, John	Sarah Hoover	Feb. 22, 1838
Tomlin, Solomon	Julina Fannin	Apr. 1, 1849
Travis, George	Elizabeth McClure	Aug. 13, 1856
Travis, Robert	Permella Ramey	Feb. 23, 1859
Treadway, John	Janthie E. Taylor	May 31, 1859
Truman, James L.	Margaret Rous	Dec. 18, 1845
Turner, Bow?	(Mrs.) Sarah Hatton	June 10, 1855
Tyree, Zachariah	Barbara Gallihue	Aug. 7, 1827

V

Van Hoose, Henry J.	Priciller Young	Jan. 15, 1868
Van Hoose, John	Polly Hogan	June 15, 1826
Van Hoose, John W.	Hiley Ann Roberts	Jan. 30, 1850
Van Hoose, Levi	Elizabeth Saddler (Damron)	Nov. 23, 1828
Van Hoose, Moses	Mariam Hays	Jan. 19, 1854
Van Horn, Franklin	Nancy Morrow	Aug. 6, 1852
Van Horn, John	Nancy White	Apr. 29, 1823
Vermillion, John	Susanna Moore	Sept. 3, 1839
Vinson, William	Jane Chambers	Sept. ...., 1835

W

Walker, Holbert	Susanna Baker	Nov. 12, 1854
Walker, William	Jane Holt	Jan. 9, 1823
Wallace, John	Fanny Walkeson?	Mar. 29, 1824
Wallace, John	Sally Stephens	Feb. 9, 1833
Waller, Henry	....	Dec. 31, 1826
Waller, John	Caroline Gowens	Sept. 17, 1854
Walters, John	Elizabeth Ratcliff	Aug. 13, 1855
Walters, Robert	Louisa Swetnam	Feb. 26, 1824
Ward, Ambrose	Polly Spencer	Aug. 4, 1852
Ward, Emmannuel	Matilda Mosely	Aug. 25, 1858
Ward, James	Cynthia Young	Jan. 8, 1840
Ward, James	Nancy Blevins	Jan. 23, 1851
Ward, Joseph	Jessie Thanks	Dec. 18, 1833
Ward, Solomon, Jr.	Lucilin? Porter	Apr. 3, 1843
Ward, Wells	Sarah Preston	Aug. 31, 1843
Warnock, William	Jane Preston	Dec. 25, 1853
Watson, Andrew	Nancy Thompson	Feb. 15, 1858
Watson, James	Hannah Stanley	Feb. 28, 1838
Watts, Elias	Sarah Donithan	June 17, 1822
Watts, Harkins	Nancy Adkins	Mar. 27, 1827
Watts, William	Elender Adams	Jan. 10, 1827
Watts, William	Emily Faulkner	Feb. 10, 1853
Weathers, William	Rebecca Lillard	Apr. 15, 1827

Groom	Bride	Date of Marriage
Webb, ...	.... Pennington	...., 1844?
Webb, David	Rachael Garrell	July 10, 1833
Webb, William Riley	Patsy Jordan	Sept. 11, 1836
Webb, William	Sarah Farris	Sept. 18, 1858
Weddington, James	Catherine Mead	Aug. 25, 1825
Weddington, William	Cynthia Kirk	July 12, 1855
Welch, Jerome	Cassandra C. Drake	July 12, 1857
Wellman, Bennett	Mariah Burton	Mar. 30, 1837
Wellman, Cornelius	Lydia Burchett	May 20, 1853
Wellman, David	Rebecca Wilson	Oct. 26, 1824
Wellman, David	Mary Holbrook	Nov. 28, 1850
Wellman, James, Jr.	Flora See	Oct. 16, 1851
Wellman, John	Lyddia Marcum	Apr. 26, 1827
Wellman, Lewis F.	Rebecca Kelly	Jan. 1, 1851
Wellman, McGinnis	Polly Lowe	Jan. 29, 1832
Wellman, Michael	Ailsy White	Mar. 2, 1853
Wellman, Samuel	Lucusa Burchett	........, 1834
Wellman, William	Anna Chapman	Dec. 24, 1845
Wells, Lewis	Lucinda Johnson	Oct. 28, 1849
Wheeler, Amos H.	Hannah Morris	May 25, 1834
Wheeler, Daniel	Eliza Graham	Mar. 7, 1858
Wheeler, James	Carrulet Graham	Nov. 17, 1853
Wheeler, William	Elizabeth Borders	Sept. 17, 1829
Wheeler, William	Mary Moore	June 10, 1858
White, Daniel	Polly Stewart	Feb. 2, 1829
White, Francis J.	Nancy Meek	July 3, 1835?
White, John	Juda Clay	Oct. 12, 1856
White, Nelson	Nancy Sparks	Jan. 8, 1857
White, Solomon	(Mrs.) Dorcas Prichard	Feb. 10, 1825
White, Sylvester	Mary Jobe	Sept. 20, 1858
White, William H.	Jemima Bradley	Mar. 1, 1855
Whitley, Jackson	Rachael Kelly	May 30, 1844
Whitten, Daniel	Phoebe Boggs	June 15, 1823
Wilbur? (n), Wilson or Wm.	Mary Wilson	Apr. 5, 1854
Williams, Amos	Hannah Preece	Nov. 8, 1859
Williams, Burrell	Nancy Ann James	Oct. 15, 1837
Williams, Henry J.	Frances A. Goodwin	Jan. 29, 1857
Williams, Jacob	Phoebe Boggs	Apr. 23, 1850
Williams, Jefferson	Mary Griffith	Mar. 28, 1839
Williams, Jonathan	Polly Cazey	May 6, 1827
Williams, Neng? (Ney)	Selby Evans	Apr. 13, 1853
Williams, Shadrack	Dicie Smith	...., ...
Williams, Thomas	Susanna Ross	Mar. 31, 1836
Williams, William	Rebecca Burton	Feb. 22, 1852
Williamson, Ald (en) or Alex	....	Oct. 14, 1833
Williamson, Elias	....	June 28, 1828
Williamson, Elijah	Lucinda Miller	Jan. 9, 1840
Williamson, J. B.	Visa Maynard	June 8, 1859
Williamson, James	Polly Clay	June 19, 1834
Williamson, James	....	Nov. 20, 1834
Williamson, Owen	Peggy McNeely	Apr. 20, 1843
Williamson, Solomon	Polly Spriggs	Feb. 6, 1851
Williamson, William	Pamela Evans	Aug. 6, 1834
Williamson, William	Peggy Price	June 20, 1844
Wilson, ...	.... Clay	Mar. 30, 1854
Wilson, Morris	Mahala Stapleton	June 10, 1851
Wilson, William	Rachael Blevins	Mar. 8, 1836
Witherow, ...	Martha J. Rose	Mar. 30, 1854
Witherow, Alfred	Judith Jobe	June 19, 1854

141

Groom	Bride	Date of Marriage
Witherow, Samuel	Susan Ward	Oct. 4, 1849
Woods, Aaron	Susannah Griffith	Jan. 1, 1852
Woods, Andrew	Keziah Lambert	Dec. 19, 1838
Woods, James	Polly Cains	Mar. 18, 1828
Wooten, Castle	Keziah Justice	Dec. 17, 1850
Wooten, Silas	Julina Chapman	Aug. 28, 1833
Wooten, Thomas A.	Jane Castle	Aug. 1, 1827
Workman, Alderson	Rebecca McClure	Apr. 24, 1850
Workman, Alfred	Loctiory ? Adkins	Nov. 16, 1854
Workman, Harvey	Ellen McClure	Apr. 24, 1850
Workman, Jesse	Elizabeth Marcum	May 21, 1828
Workman, Spencer	Sarah Webb	Sept. 19, 1858
Wright, Elkanah	Sarah Large	Apr. 2, 1849
Wright, Joseph	Elizabeth J. Powell	Oct. 17, 1850
Wright, Patterson	Susanna Sagraves	Aug. 3, 1854
Wright, William	Sarah Rose	June 19, 1853

Y

Young, A. J.	Sarah England	Apr. 28, 1854
Young, Alfred R.	Emaline Blevins	Dec. 31, 1858
Young, Franklin J.	Hilan Van Horn	Oct. 16, 1858
Young, James	Jane White	Nov. 5, 1823
Young, James	Elizabeth Pennington	Nov. 8, 1855
Young, Jesse	Rachael Adkins	Apr. 12, 1824
Young, John	Anna Wright	About 1839
Young, Paschal	Jane Hall	July 28, 1853
Young, Samuel	Sally Graham	Nov. 30, 1835
Young, William	Fannie Adkins	Apr. 1, 1858
Yates, Thomas	Nancy Pennington	Mar. 20, 1853

Z

Zeller, William	Caroline Docteptin	Oct. 8, 1850

142

CHAPTER VII

PIKE COUNTY, KENTUCKY

ORGANIZATION

March Court, 1822—First Day.

Be it remembered that at the house of Spencer Adkins on Monday the fourth day of March in the year of our Lord one thousand eight hundred and twenty two (it being the first Monday in said month of March) Simeon Justice, James Roberts, Reuben Retherford, John Hunt and John Bevins produced commissions from under the hand of John Adair, Governor of the Commonwealth of Kentucky, with the seal of the said Commonwealth thereto affixed, appointing them * * * justices of the peace in and for the said county of Pike; and thereupon the said Simeon Justice, the first numbered in the said commissions, before the said James Roberts, the second numbered in said commissions, did, on the Holy Evangelist of Almighty God, took (take) as well the oath to support the constitution of the United States and of this State as the oath of justice of the peace together with the oath prescribed by the act of assembly entitled "An Act More Effectually to Suppress the Practice of Duelling"; and then the said Simeon Justice administered, on the Holy Evangelist of Almighty God, to the said James Roberts, Reuben Retherford, John Hunt and John Bevins, the persons in the said commissions, as well the (oath) to support the constitution of the United States and of this State as the oath of a justice of the peace together with the oath prescribed by the act of assembly entitled "An Act More Effectually to Suppress the Practice of Duelling"; and thereupon a court was formed for the said county of Pike. And now here at a court held agreeable to the Act of Assembly establishing the county of Pike approved the nineteenth day of December one thousand eight hundred and twenty one, at the house of Spencer Adkins as aforesaid on Monday the fourth day of March (being the first Monday therein) anno domini, one thousand Eight hundred and twenty two and in the thirtieth year of the Commonwealth of Kentucky.

Present: Simeon Justice, James Roberts, Reuben Retherford, John Hunt and John Bevins, Esquires, Gentlemen Justices.

* * *

James Honaker produced a commission from under the hand of John Adair, Governor of the said Commonwealth, with the seal of the said Commonwealth thereto affixed, appointing him sheriff of this county. Whereupon Simeon Justice, the presiding justice of this court, administered (to) the said James Honaker on the Holy Evangelist of Almighty God, as well the oath to support the constitution of the United States and of this State as the oath of sheriff together with the oath prescribed by the late Act of Assembly More Effectually to surpress (sic) the Practice of Duelling; and thereupon the said James Honaker together with Richard Damron, Abram Beavers, and Barnabas Johnson, his securities (sureties) entered into and acknowledged their bonds in the penalty of three thousand dollars, agreeable to the law.

* * *

Spencer Adkins is unanimously appointed clerk of this court, *pro tem*, who took as well the oath to support the constitution of the United States and of this State as the oath of county clerk together with the oath prescribed by the Act of Assembly entitled "An Act

More Effectually to Surpress (sic) the Practice of Duelling"; and who together with Richard Damron, Abram Beavers, William Ratliff, Sr., William Tackett, Thomas May and Thomas Owings, his securities (sureties), entered into and acknowledged their bonds (in) the penalty of one thousand pounds, conditioned agreeable to law * * *

* * *

On motion of Spencer Adkins, Clerk of the Court, Jacob Mayo (was) admited (sic) and sworn as his deputy in this county.

* * *

William Triplett who made it appear to the satisfaction of the court that he had license to practice as an attorney-at-law came into court and qualified as such (and) who took as well the oath to support the constitution of the United States and of this State as the oath of an Attorney-at-law together with the oath more effectually to surpress (sic) the practice of duelling.

* * *

Elijah Adkins produced a commission from under the hand of John Adair, Governor of the Commonwealth of Kentucky, with the seal of the Commonwealth thereto affixed, appointing (him) coroner in this county. Whereupon he took as well the oath to support the constitution of the United States and of this State as the oath of a coroner together with the oath more effectually to surpress (sic) the practice of duelling; and together with William Ratliff, Jr., Joseph Adkins, William Mullins and Samuel Mayres (Myers?), his security (sureties) entered into and acknowledged their bonds in the penalty of one thousand pounds conditioned agreeable to law.

* * *

William Triplett is appointed prosecuting attorney of the pleas of this county during the pleasure of the court.

* * *

Elijah Adkins is appointed commissioner of the revenue of this county for the year of our Lord one thousand eight hundred and twenty-two

* * *

Richard Damron and Joseph Adkins are recommended to the Executive as proper and fit persons to fill the office of surveyor in this county, a majority of the justices of the peace in said county concurring in this recommendation.

* * *

Ordered that this court be adjourned till nine o'clock, A. M.
(Signed) Simeon Justice

MARRIAGES 1822-1865

Marriage Records of Pike County, Kentucky, from organization of the County in 1822 to 1865, inclusive:

Groom	Bride	Date of Marriage
A		
Aarons, Theodore	Josophene Butcher	June 15, 1857
Abshire, Jackson	Vina Bishop	Jan. 4, 1865

Groom	Bride	Date of Marriage
Adams, Allen	Jennie Mullins	Mar. 21, 1861
Adams, Bartholomew	Elizabeth Slone	Feb. 15, 1847
Adams, Constantine	Frances Stowers	Sept. 23, 1833
Adams, Henderson	Anna Pinson	Jan. 27, 1858
Adams, Isaac	Elizabeth Justice	Dec. 23, 1860
Adams, John	Pricilla Bentley	July 23, 1849
Adams, Lewis	Catherine Leek	Oct. 21, 1856
Adams, William	Louisa Hall	Jan. 7, 1857
Adkins, Absolom	Delilah Elswick	Sept. 9, 1830
Adkins, Allen D.	Matilda Williams	Mar. 20, 1834
Adkins, Anderson	Nancy Thornsberry	Apr. 15, 1832
Adkins, Anderson	Martha Adams	May 29, 1859
Adkins, Anderson	Sally Rowe	Feb. 7, 1861
Adkins, Andrew Jackson	Abigail Fanny Ramey	Dec. 26, 1850
Adkins, Caleb	Siltaney ? Newsom	Nov. 17, 1859
Adkins, Daniel	Susanna Fry	Apr. 14, 1836
Adkins, Daniel	Nancy Ann Blair	Apr. 15, 1858
Adkins, Eli	Margaret McClannahan	March 13, 1850
Adkins, Elias	Nancy Hackney	Aug. 4, 1824
Adkins, Elisha	Margery Adkins	Aug. 14, 1823
Adkins, Elisha	Delila Boney	May 6, 1829
Adkins, Elisha	Serena May	May 11, 1848
Adkins, George W.	Polly Ann Ford	Mar. 23, 1850
Adkins, Gilbert	Malinda Dye	Aug. 16, 1860
Adkins, Henley	Sally Bevins	Sept. 25, 1850
Adkins, Henry	Betsy Thacker	Feb. 5, 1824
Adkins, Henry	Jerusha Coleman	May 21, 1826
Adkins, Henry	Malinda Adkins	Mar. 31, 1854
Adkins, Henry D.	Bethany Hopkins	Feb. 7, 1856
Adkins, Isham	Jane McCombs	Aug. 23, 1846
Adkins, James H.	Mary Keen	Dec. 25, 1847
Adkins, Jesse	Sarah Boney	June 11, 1831
Adkins, Jesse	Elizabeth Hopkins	Sept. 4, 1834
Adkins, Jesse	Elizabeth Boney	Aug. 5, 1838
Adkins, Jesse	Lucy Cox	Apr. 21, 1859
Adkins, Joel	Polly Adkins	Mar. 25, 1829
Adkins, John	Sarah Adkins	Aug. 14, 1823
Adkins, John	Nancy Thacker	Sept. 24, 1830
Adkins, John	Millie Bowling	Aug. 16, 1844
Adkins, Joseph, Jr.	Polly Fuller	Oct. 16, 1825
Adkins, Joseph	Elizabeth Adkins	Dec. 10, 1848
Adkins, Joseph	Elizabeth Adkins	Oct. 10, 1848
Adkins, Melleton	Sallie Thacker	Apr. 25, 1829
Adkins, Nathaniel	Elizabeth Justice	June 20, 1845
Adkins, Nathaniel	Farendy Adkins	Dec. 29, 1864
Adkins, Peter	Louizan Belcher	Mar. 25, 1858
Adkins, Riley	Polly Magee (McGee)	Mar. 5, 1851
Adkins, Riley	Barbara Rowe	Aug. 5, 1854
Adkins, Riley	Anna Slone	Dec. 26, 1856
Adkins, Sam	Catherine Elswick	Oct. 8, 1855
Adkins, Samuel	Sarah Damron	Oct. 28, 1855
Adkins, Stephen	Fannie Rowe	Mar. 31, 1852
Adkins, Wilburn	Mary Jane Gillespie	Feb. 16, 1865
Adkins, William	Nancy Hamilton	July 29, 1823
Adkins, William	Nancy Damron	Jan. 14, 1824
Adkins, William	Sarah May	Dec. 14, 1839
Adkins, William	Anna Thacker	Jan. 1, 1840
Adkins, Winright	Sarah Boney	Mar. 3, 1844

Groom	Bride	Date of Marriage
Adkins, Winright	Sally Mullins	July 5, 1849
Adkins, Winright	Nancy Gillespie	Sept. 24, 1855
Adkins, Winright	Mary Kidd	May 31, 1858
Adkins, Winright	Nancy Phillips	Sept. 24, 1860
Adkins, Winston	Hannah Coleman	Feb. 3, 1828
Akers, Andrew	Polly Branham	Jan. 24, 1828
Akers, David	Mary Marshall	Oct. 20, 1859
Akers, James W.	Lucinda Ray	Mar. 22, 1852
Akers, Joseph	Phena Elliott	Sept. 18, 1851
Akers, Stephen	Sarah Hamilton	Nov. 15, 1847
Akers, Tolbert	Polly Sturgill	Dec. 8, 1831
Akers, Valentine	Hannah Blankenship	July 7, 1847
Aleshire, Peter	Ardilda Justice	Sept. 29, 1857
Allan, John A.	Debora Hayten	Jan. 15, 1857
Alley, Ben W.	Elizabeth Prewitt	Oct. 29, 1849
Alley, Peter H.	Sarah Stanley	Dec. 21, 1854
Alley, Simeon	Edy Sturgill	Feb. 19, 1846
Allison, James	Mary Gannon	Sept. 20, 1849
Allison, John	Amy Johnson	Sept. 15, 1850
Anders, Russell	Juda Stowards?	Mar. 20, 1835
Anderson, Charles	Elizabeth Owens	Jan. 10, 1839
Anderson, Charles, Sr.	Hannah White	May 17, 1842
Anderson, David, Jr.	Millie Justice	Feb. 1, 1838
Anderson, George W.	Mary Jane Morgan	Jan. 6, 1859
Anderson, Hiram	Spicy Tackett	Feb. 6, 1845
Anderson, Jesse	Sally Edwards	Sept. 18, 1845
Anderson, John	Nancy White	Aug. 25, 1841
Artrip, James	Lucinda Sykes	Feb. 2, 1860
Austin, Henderson	Elizabeth Gannon	Jan. 19, 1853
Auxier, Joseph K.	Elizabeth Jane Walker	Dec. 5, 1850

B

Groom	Bride	Date of Marriage
Bailey, Thompson P.	Mary Fain	Dec. 2, 1858
Baldridge, William	Nancy E. Gillespie	Mar. 23, 1843
Baldwin, Alex	Christina Hall	Jan. 19, 1859
Baldwin, Fielding	Pricilla Estep	Apr. 18, 1830
Baldwin, Jesse	Lucy Estep	Mar. 18, 1832
Baldwin, John W.	Elvina Blankenship	Mar. 16, 1861
Ball, James	Nancy Whitt	Dec. 26, 1847
Bartley, James	Mary Jane Walls	Apr. 16, 1860
Bartley, Levi	Ann Mullins	June 21, 1865
Baswell, Elias	Elizabeth Ratcliff	May 10, 1827
Bebley, William	Louisa Raynes	Oct. 9, 1856
Belcher, Ali	Polly Purson ? (Person)	Apr. 24, 1824
Belcher, George	Sally Taylor	Jan. 13, 1830
Belcher, George W.	Frances Ramey	Nov. 19, 1847
Belcher, James Davidson	Nancy Bishop	Mar. 11, 1849
Belcher, James	Polly McCombs	...., 1822
Belcher, John	Mary Elswick	Dec. 13, 1849
Belcher, John	Celia Adkins	Apr. 6, 1840
Belcher, John	Jane Taylor	June 24, 1822
Belcher, Joseph	Nancy Ramey	Apr. 5, 1831
Belcher, Moses	Almeda Elswick	Feb. 7, 1856
Belcher, William	Cynthia Adkins	Aug. 19, 1824
Belcher, William	Polly Powell	Dec. 11, 1831
Belcher, Wesley	Anna Moore	Dec. 18, 1832
Belcher, William Riley	Lyddia Hunt	Feb. 21, 1850
Bentley, Ben	Anna Ramey	May 8, 1845

Groom	Bride	Date of Marriage
Bentley, Daniel	Maranda Ramey	May 8, 1845
Bentley, Moses	Martha Blankenship	Feb. 23, 1837
Bentley, Samuel	Mahala Hall	Mar. 13, 1845
Bentley, William	Rebecca Ramey	...., ...
Beverly, Freeman	Nicey Ramsey	Nov. 2, 1830
Beverley, Sam	Nancy Polley	Sept. 29, 1823
Bevins, Allen P.	Louisa Stacy	Mar. 15, 1865
Bevins, George	Nancy Williamson	Dec. 3, 1829
Bevins, George W.	Nancy Wuson	Oct. 28, 1855
Bevins, Hiram	Luney Leslie	Dec. 10, 1835
Bevins, James	Elizabeth Justice	Mar. 12, 1831
Bevins, James	Polly Pinson	Aug. 14, 1836
Bevins, James	Susan Walker	Mar. 17, 1853
Bevins, James M.	Mary Jane Hamilton	Jan. 1, 1860
Bevins, John	Nancy Ratcliff	Feb. 4, 1858
Bevins, Joseph	Mary Wuson	July 28, 1832
Bevins, Madison	Nancy Smith	Dec. 7, 1848
Bevins, Thomas, Jr.	Elizabeth Williamson	July 23, 1833
Bevins, Thomas	Lyddia Ratliff	July 23, 1835
Bevins, Thomas J.	Elizabeth Boger	Feb. 21, 1861
Bishop, Aaron	Jane King	Sept. 9, 1841
Bishop, Riley	Millie Abshire	Sept. 6, 1860
Bishop, William	Polly Justice	May 15, 1831
Bishop, William	Jane Hackney	Apr. 2, 1840
Blackburn, Daniel	Nancy Maynard	Jan. 15, 1846
Blackburn, George	Nancy McCoy	Sept. 25, 1856
Blackburn, George	Nancy Raynes	June 24, 1858
Blackburn, George	Elizabeth C. Bevins	Aug. 30, 1860
Blackburn, Greenville R.	Tabitha May	May 12, 1861
Blackburn, Harmon	Barbara Plymale	Nov. 27, 1851
Blackburn, Henry	Lucinda Blevins	Dec. 20, 1860
Blackburn, Hutson	Mary Roman	Oct. 22, 1834
Blackburn, Isom R.	Nancy Jane Reeds	Apr. 13, 1865
Blackburn, James	Margaret Roman	Nov. 10, 1839
Blackburn, Jacob	Elizabeth Stafford	Oct. 3, 1847
Blackburn, John	Lyddia Blankenship	Oct. 11, 1834
Blackburn, John	Pricie Justice	Apr. 17, 1856
Blackburn, John H.	Malinda Smith	May 25, 1865
Blackburn, John W	Martha Blankenship	Mar. 16, 1861
Blackburn, Nathaniel	Elizabeth Plymale	July 19, 1860
Blackburn, Peyton	Linna Whitt	Mar. 22, 1846
Blackburn, Thomas	Elizabeth Deal	June 20, 1865
Blackburn, William	Rebecca Scott	Nov. 15, 1843
Blackburn, William	Judith Phillips	June 12, 1846
Blackburn, William	Elizabeth Scalf	Oct. 27, 1850
Blair, Anderson	Louisa McCoy	Sept. 19, 1850
Blair, John	Polly Raisden	May 10, 1823
Blair, John	Polly Damron	Feb. 21, 1861
Blair, Joseph	Gerusha Collins	Mar. 13, 1828
Blair, William T.	Wirena Adkins	Feb. 22, 1865
Blankenship, Barnett	Sarah Branham	Sept. 17, 1835
Blankenship, Ben	Isabella Gillespie	Apr. 20, 1848
Blankenship, Ben	Dorothy Rich	Jan. 8, 1857
Blankenship, Francis M.	Millie Phillips	May 15, 1862
Blankenship, Henry	Elizabeth Adams	July 14, 1839
Blankenship, Hiram	Elizabeth Deal	July 13, 1830
Blankenship, Isham	Martha White	Aug. 25, 1824
Blankenship, Obediah	Sarah Frederick	Aug. 20, 1851
Blankenship, Oliver	Louisa Oliver	Feb. 13, 1860

Groom	Bride	Date of Marriage
Blankenship, Presley	Polly Lockhart	July 16, 1840
Blankenship, Sol	Kate Daniel	June 8, 1823
Blankenship, Zachariah	Dorcas Lester	Aug. 28, 1824
Blankenship, William	Spicy McCown	Oct. 27, 1836
Blevins, Dan	Mary Ann Belcher	Dec. 10, 1846
Blevins, Jacob	Elizabeth Belcher	Oct. 3, 1847
Blevins, John	Rebecca Rhoten	Aug. 25, 1852
Boger, Joseph	Nancy Morris	Sept. 16, 1858
Bollings, Ezekiel	Nancy Baker	Apr. 19, 1849
Bolling, Henry	Susanna Adkins	Sept. 20, 1846
Bolling, Henry	Rebecca Ratcliff	Feb. 20, 1851
Bolling, John R.	Louisa Porter	Dec. 26, 1850
Boney, Hiram	Nancy Crabtree	Feb. 3, 1830
Booker, Thomas B.	Matilda Estep	July 5, 1852
Bowles, Orlando C.	Pauline Cecil	June 8, 1862
Branham, Alfred	Celia Blair	Mar. 16, 1865
Branham, Andrew	Sabra Estep	Feb. 2, 1826
Branham, David	Bets Adkins	Feb. 7, 1828
Branham, David	Catherine Kinney	May 30, 1839
Branham, Edward	Mary McBryer	June 23, 1840
Branham, Edward	Elizabeth Osborn	Aug. 6, 1847
Branham, Elias	Peggy Vanover	Dec. 31, 1854
Branham, James	Fannie Branham	Mar. 25, 1823
Branham, James	Fannie Damron	Jan. 3, 1860
Branham, James	Leccie Tackett	Dec. 4, 1865
Branham, John	Mahala Mosely	Jan. 6, 1842
Branham, John	Usley Branham	Feb. 17, 1843
Branham, Jonathan	Polly Gilliam	Nov. 5, 1829
Branham, Joseph	Elizabeth Morgan	Apr. 2, 1835
Branham, Lewis	Margaret Vanover	Aug. 31, 1850
Branham, Reuben	Harriett Francisco	Mar. 21, 1850
Branham, Sam	Millie Ratliff	Aug. 15, 1848
Branham, Turner	Mary Gibson	Nov. 23, 1826
Branham, Turner	Malinda McKenzie	Nov. 16, 1846
Branham, William	Elizabeth Johnson	June 19, 1828
Branham, William	Sukie Foulkes	Jan. 14, 1862
Breeding, Albert	Elizabeth King	Mar. 15, 1851
Breeding, George	Sally Colley	Aug. 21, 1826
Breeding, J. W.	Miriam Adkins	Aug. 8, 1841
Brown, G. N.	Mariah Poage	Nov. 16, 1857
Brown, Jeremiah	Mollie Blackburn	Feb. 26, 1854
Brown, John	Mary Allison	Dec. 17, 1854
Brown, William	Rachael Tolley	Oct. 6, 1834
Brown, William M.	Pernetta Hall	Mar. 8, 1860
Brown, William S.	Delia Blackburn	June 21, 1860
Brown, George N.	Sophia Cecil	Nov. 17, 1847
Browning, Elias	Sally Ann Smith	Feb. 14, 1861
Bryant, Allan	Polly Johnson	Dec. 26, 1848
Bryant, David	Polly Lavina Mullins	Mar. 28, 1830
Bryant, James	Nancy Venters	May 22, 1839
Bryant, Joseph	Elizabeth Venters	May 22, 1839
Bryant, William	Mary Mullins	July 31, 1828
Buckley, William	Frances Sword	June 15, 1850
Burchett, Jesse B.	Louisa Bevins	Apr. 9, 1857
Burk, Charles	Westeny Rice	Apr. 13, 1826
Burk, Charles	Nancy Adams	Apr. 12, 1855
Burk, Green V.	Lourena Hall	Jan. 16, 1859
Burk, Isaac	Nancy Ramey	Apr. 5, 1831

Groom	Bride	Date of Marriage
Burk, John	Rachael Owens	Nov. 9, 1825
Burk, Jonathan	Elizabeth Bryant	Apr. 24, 1855
Burk, Nathaniel	Jennie Johnson	Feb. 5, 1860
Burk, Richard	Sarah Tackett	Nov. 5, 1835
Burks, James	Virginia Sword	Aug. 2, 1859
Burks, Robin	Rebecca Mullins	June 8, 1844
Burks, William	Nancy Hall	Mar. 4, 1857
Burress, Daniel	Lackey McCoy	May 7, 1858
Burress, James	Isabel Francic	Feb. 11, 1849
Burton, Andrew	Susanna Shockey	Dec. 5, 1822
Bush, James D.	Mary Ferguson	July 27, 1865

C

Cain, Olmer W.	Nancy Ann Whitt	Mar. 30, 1856
Cains, Richard	Arminda Elkins	July 20, 1865
Cain, Thomas	Nancy McColley	Sept. 6, 1832
Campbell, David	Nancy Beverly	Mar. 19, 1829
Campbell, William W.	Mary Slone	Feb. 15, 1835
Canada, Alley	Christina Whitt	Apr. 15, 1848
Canada, Andrew	Peggy Hatfield	Jan. 29, 1824
Canada, Andrew J.	Anna Varney	Mar. 31, 1861
Canada, Eli	Susan Toler	Sept. 13, 1833
Canada, Elijah	Catherine Mead	Apr. 24, 1828
Canada, Hammond	Reecie Fields	Feb. 14, 1850
Canada, Hammond	Jane Muson	May 31, 1857
Canada, Richard	Mina Burcham	Nov. 29, 1848
Canada, Sam	Nancy Charles	Mar. 26, 1846
Cantrell, Abraham, Jr.	Sarah Kilgore	Mar. 20, 1828
Cantrell, Abraham	Elizabeth Campbell	Apr. 25, 1855
Cantrell, Hiram	Nancy Mullins	Mar. 14, 1833
Cantrell, Isaac	Artie Sanders	May 14, 1854
Cantrell, John	Aggie Phipps	Mar. 20, 1828
Carey, Asa H.	Louisa Retherford	July 5, 1851
Carey, William	Jennie McCoy	July 27, 1865
Carter, Charles	Rhoda Smith	Feb. 12, 1846
Carter, Edmond	Nancy Warren	Nov. 5, 1856
Carter, Henry S.	Rachael Charles	Dec. 18, 1851
Carter, Morgan	Mary Pinson	Sept. 7, 1847
Carter, Quinton	Hettie Jones	Dec. 5, 1844
Cartwright, Thomas C. P.	Frances Murphy	Aug. 30, 1830
Case, James	Jane Ramey	Apr. 28, 1844
Casebolt, David	Matilda Ray	Mar. 15, 1860
Casebolt, John J.	Polly Sanders	May 4, 1843
Casebolt, John L.	Sarah Ann Ramey	Sept. 17, 1858
Casey, Elijah	Amanda Fields	Aug. 9, 1849
Cassidy, James	Mahala Blackburn	Feb. 5, 1845
Cassidy, James	Sarah Ann Thurston	Mar. 30, 1851
Castle, H. Wilson	Oma Moore	Aug. 25, 1841
Castle, Henry	Susanna May	Sept. 2, 1850
Castle, James	Sarah Sword	Mar. 22, 1841
Castle, James	Cynthia Moore	May 17, 1842
Castle, William	Nancy Runyon	Dec. 29, 1829
Caudill, Matthew	Elizabeth Tackett	Apr. 5, 1855
Caudill, Stephen	Elizabeth Casebolt	May 1, 1828
Cavins, William	Rachael White	Sept. 28, 1854
Cecil, Kenzie B.	Elizabeth Mutors (Mutters)	Mar. 6, 1849
Cecil, William	Elizabeth Ratcliff	May 8, 1828

Groom	Bride	Date of Marriage
Chadwell, John A.	Tamsey Miller	Apr. 21, 1836
Chaffin, Nathan	Matilda Varney	Oct. 19, 1837
Chaffin, William	Sally Deskins	Nov. 9, 1836
Chaney, Abner	Lottie Goff	Apr. 14, 1853
Cheney, Charles	Elizabeth Fletcher	Dec. 9, 1847
Chaney, Charles	Elizabeth Slone	Apr. 24, 1853
Chaney, Charles	Elizabeth Kendrick	Feb. 19, 1855
Chaney, Harvey G.	Polly Moore	Jan. 24, 1861
Chaney, John	Amanda Adkins	Sept. 23, 1858
Chaney, Mark	Jane McCombs	May 2, 1837
Chaney, Mark	Louise Adams	Oct. 3, 1837
Chaney, John W.	Corcas Moore	May 10, 1859
Chaney, Jonathan	Ibby Raines	Mar. 30, 1862
Chaney, Thomas	Sophia Campbell	Jan. 28, 1834
Chaney, William P.	Malinda Sword	Apr. 1, 1858
Chapman, Edward	Elizabeth Hunt	Jan. 6, 1842
Chapman, Thomas	Polly Farley	July 19, 1829
Chapman, Thomas	Mary Harris	Sept. 28, 1854
Charles, Andrew J.	Louisa Ramey	Mar. 27, 1856
Charles, David	Sarah Cline	Dec. 8, 1823
Charles, David	Elizabeth Goff	Mar. 31, 1853
Charles, Frederick	Elizabeth McColley	May 26, 1825
Charles, Frederick	Malinda McCoy	June 2, 1853
Charles, George	Abigail Payne	Aug. 10, 1823
Charles, George	Charlotte Chaney	Aug. 11, 1835
Charles, George	Keziah Daugherty	Aug. 3, 1860
Charles, Greenville	Isabella Goff	Aug. 16, 1855
Charles, Greenville	Margaret Bevins	Apr. 24, 1859
Charles, Greenville	Louisa Jane Maynard	Aug. 20, 1857
Charles, Harvey George	Elizabeth Phipps	Mar. 4, 1858
Charles, John, Jr.	Elizabeth Hinkle	July 20, 1847
Charles, John J.	Sarah Ann Francis	May 4, 1841
Charles, John	Elizabeth Smith	Mar. 6, 1853
Charles, Thomas	Elizabeth Cain	Oct. 24, 1852
Childers, Alex	Nancy Ann Ratcliff	Oct. 20, 1860
Childers, John	Charlotte Ratcliff	Aug. 9, 1849
Childer, Loven	Rebecca Ratcliff	Feb. 7, 1861
Childers, Miles	Ebbin Plynell?	Jan. 17, 1856
Childers, Nathaniel	Serena Taylor	Mar. 29, 1850
Childers, Nathaniel	Mary J. Ratcliff	Jan. 17, 1859
Childers, Pleasant	Frances Johns	Apr. 28, 1828
Childers, Pleasant	Polly McClannahan	Nov. 30, 1837
Church, Joel, Jr.	Nancy Layne	Feb. 10, 1837
Clark, Daniel R.	Frances Etter?	Sept. 19, 1852
Clark, Edmond	Millie Ramey	July 1, 1825
Clark, Hiram	Eleanor Lewis	May 27, 1837
Clark, Jackson	Malden Stratton	............, 1859
Clark, Reuben	Sylvia Sipple	Feb. 5, 1861
Clay, Andrew	Elizabeth McGee	Feb. 6, 1857
Clay, Caleb	Zilpha Akers	Dec. 23, 1824
Clay, Flemmon	Emeriah Collinsworth	June 28, 1859
Clay, Henry	Mary Anderson	Aug. 2, 1838
Clay, James	Malinda Akers	July 20, 1826
Clay, John	Anna Elswick	Apr. 18, 1824
Clay, Mitchell	Louisa Huffman	Aug. 31, 1848
Clay, Mitchell	Eliza Nunnery	July 17, 1853
Clendennen, Robert	Amanda Hinchman	July 13, 1827
Clevenger, John	Mary Stilton	Oct. 1, 1829

Groom	Bride	Date of Marriage
Clevenger, Levi	Nancy Hamilton	May 22, 1842
Clevenger, Levi Thomas	Sarah Blackburn	Aug. 15, 1847
Clevenger, Pinson	Rebecca McColley	Apr. 25, 1859
Clevenger, Pleasant	Margaret Hamilton	May 22, 1842
Clevenger, Russell	Elizabeth Pinson	May 28, 1823
Clevenger, Silas	Jane Simpkins	Apr. 4, 1865
Cline, Jacob	Nancy Fuller	Jan. 13, 1826
Cline, Jacob	Rebecca Taylor	Nov. 2, 1865
Cline, John	Keziah Mead	Nov. 21, 1822
Cole, James	Susanna Runyon	May 16, 1830
Cole, Parkinson	Elizabeth Walker	Jan. 18, 1862
Cole, Thompson	Elizabeth Slone	June 21, 1861
Coleman, Abraham	Rebecca Adkins	May 8, 1840
Coleman, Abraham	Millie O'Quinn	Aug. 4, 1859
Coleman, Crockett	Mary Ann Thacker	Aug. 31, 1865
Coleman, Curtis	Matilda Estep	Mar. 19, 1835
Coleman, Daniel	Mary Evans	Nov. 13, 1835
Coleman, Daniel	Bethena Adkins	June 9, 1842
Coleman, Daniel	Sarah Smith	Feb. 3, 1848
Coleman, Dan B.	Marian Smith	Mar. 17, 1858
Coleman, David	Elizabeth Ann Cox	Dec. 7, 1844
Coleman, Elexious	Sarah Smith	Jan. 5, 1860
Coleman, George	Frances Powell	July 16, 1861
Coleman, Hammond	Melvina Coleman	Nov. 14, 1857
Coleman, Henry	Sarah May	Sept. 1, 1840
Coleman, Isaac	Mary Coleman	July 6, 1843
Coleman, Isaac	Mary Whitt	July 6, 1861
Coleman, John	Elizabeth Thornsberry	Jan. 26, 1837
Coleman, Mathias	Lucinda Ratliff	July 13, 1854
Coleman, Miles	Jane Childers	Nov. 3, 1860
Coleman, Moses	Biddy Bevins	Jan. 28, 1830
Coleman, Moses	Louisa May	Aug. 3, 1848
Coleman, Moses	Rachael Dotson	June 3, 1854
Coleman, Nathaniel	Ann Coleman	Apr. 7, 1861
Coleman, Peters	Sarah Dale	Aug. 6, 1836
Coleman, Richard D.	Nancy King	Feb. 18, 1847
Coleman, Riley	Lucy Conway	Nov. 21, 1865
Coleman, Stephen	Lucy Adkins	Mar. 30, 1833
Coleman, Stephen	Rachael McAllister	July 9, 1853
Coleman, Winright	Rebecca Newsom	Jan. 16, 1861
Coleman, William	Pricie Charles	June 19, 1855
Coleman, William	Mary Scarberry	Apr. 23, 1856
Coleman, William	Sibrena Powell	Aug. 2, 1858
Collier, Elias	Elizabeth Green	Apr. 6, 1851
Collier, Patrick	Rachael Davis	Mar. 26, 1827
Collier, Richard	Mary Caudill	Aug. 30, 1832
Collins, Andrew	Elizabeth Smith	Sept. 7, 1845
Collins, Archibald	Peggy Coots?	May 18, 1824
Collins, Caleb	Polly Osborn	Mar. 10, 1836
Collins, Edward	Anna Justice	June 26, 1834
Collins, George	Patsy Elswick	June 17, 1836
Collins, Jacob	Nancy Riffe	July 23, 1843
Collins, Jacob	Elizabeth Ann Corrius?	Jan. 11, 1847
Collins, James	Susie Holliday	Oct. 15, 1824
Collins, John	Eliza Justice	Aug. 2, 1839
Collins, James H.	Rachael McGinn	Oct. 2, 1851
Collins, Leonard	Nathemiah Price	June 30, 1831
Collins, Levi	Nancy Johnson	Oct. 2, 1836

Groom	Bride	Date of Marriage
Collins, Thomas	Elizabeth Cook	Jan. 7, 1843
Collins, William	Polly Mullins	Mar. 22, 1829
Collins, William	Polly J. Hurley	Apr. 18, 1861
Collinsworth, Anderson	Lucinda Lewis	Nov. 29, 1830
Compton, Bartemus	Catherine Stilton	Jan. 12, 1837
Compton, James T.	Sallie McCown	Jan. 31, 1857
Compton, Lee	Elsie Damron	Oct. 22, 1837
Compton, William F.	Polly Sword	Mar. 30, 1851
Conway, John	Polly Campbell	Jan. 5, 1836
Conway, John	Lucinda Ratcliff	Dec. 23, 1847
Conway, Michael	Barsheba Ratcliff	Sept. 29, 1847
Cook, James	Rebecca Tackett	May 22, 1823
Cook, James	Polly Lawson	May ...., 1849
Cook, John	Betsy Cinrantaffy	Oct. 10, 1822
Cook, Solomon	Polly Hall	Oct. 21, 1830
Cook, William	Polly Rumyn (Runyon)	July 12, 1846
Cool, James	Nancy Moore	Aug. 13, 1857
Cordell, Jesse	Elender Estep	Aug. 6, 1834
Cox, John	Amanda Adkins	Apr. 18, 1858
Crabtree, Solomon	Mary Hatfield	Feb. 22, 1861
Crabtree, William	Elizabeth Watson	Nov. 3, 1853
Crabtree, John	Sarah Ann Keathly	May 1, 1851
Crabtree, James S.	Elizabeth Stanley	Nov. 3, 1848
Curry, Barnabas	Elizabeth Browning	Feb. 28, 1831

D

Groom	Bride	Date of Marriage
Dale, Joseph	Rebecca Fields	Oct. 24, 1854
Damron, Abraham	Sarah Branham	July 6, 1835
Damron, Abraham	Pricie Roberts	Apr. 18, 1853
Damron, Christian	Matilda Blair	Jan. 4, 1860
Damron, Elisha	Sarah Elswick	Jan. 23, 1845
Damron, Harvey	Mary Ann Maynard	Aug. 11, 1855
Damron, Jackson	Spicey Roberts	Sept. 7, 1848
Damron, James	Polly Adkins	May 1, 1836
Damron, John W.	Elizabeth McCown	Feb. 2, 1857
Damron, Lazarus	Jane May	Jan. 7, 1839
Damron, Lazarus	Rebecca Ratliff	Dec. 31, 1846
Damron, Moses	Charity Adkins	Aug. 3, 1837
Damron, Moses D.	Artie Sturgill	Mar. 20, 1861
Damron, Robert	Rebecca Damron	Jan. 6, 1859
Damron, Solomon	Frances Sword	Jan. 4, 1849
Damron, Spurlock	Sarah Trout	Aug. 4, 1836
Damron, Spurlock	Maranda Roberts	Jan. 11, 1857
Damron, William	Ruth Ramsey	Feb. 17, 1847
Damron, William M.	Elizabeth Branham	Sept. 15, 1860
Danes?, John M.	Nancy Phillips	Apr. 4, 1861
Daniels, Richard	Margaret Charles	Oct. 28, 1842
Daniel, Samuel	Lucy Smith	July 26, 1842
Daugherty, Hiram	Mary Coleman	Aug. 2, 1854
Davis, Baxter	Lillie Branham	Aug. 28, 1825
Davis, Harrison	Rebecca Stacy	Oct. 6, 1861
Davis, Henry	Celia Stotts	July 11, 1846
Davis, James	Mary Charles	Jan. 9, 1845
Davis, John	Anna Pinson	Jan. 11, 1840
Davis, John	Rebecca Elkins	Feb. ...., 1845
Dawson, Vincent	Lyddia Ratcliff	Feb. 20, 1848
Dawson, William	Susan Ratcliff	Oct. 16, 1839

Groom	Bride	Date of Marriage
Deal, Reuben	Elizabeth Stilton	Jan. 6, 1853
Deal, John	Sally Ball	Oct. 10, 1830
Deal, Joiner	Lucy Prichett	Aug. 1, 1823
Deal, Solomon	Jane Shepherd	Mar. 19, 1851
Debush, James	Nancy Bishop	Jan. 26, 1835
Dempsey, Lewis	Nancy Stepp	Oct. 21, 1852
Deskins, Harrison	Armath Ferguson	May 25, 1854
Deskins, James	Isabel Hibbard	Jan. 10, 1841
Deskins, John	Martha Devins	Oct. 15, 1840
Deskins, John	Sarah Jones	Aug. 24, 1845
Deskins, Lewis	Martha Jane Williams	Feb. 15, 1849
Deskins, Nathaniel	Sarah Phillips	May 10, 1849
Dials, George	Sarah May	Mar. 9, 1854
Dials, James	Mary Ann Smith	Feb. 18, 1860
Dials, John	Rebecca May	May 7, 1857
Dials, Moses	Nancy Welch	Aug. 17, 1856
Dillon, William	Emeriba Neely	Sept. 3, 1829
Dials, Absolom	Nancy Maynard	Oct. 17, 1827
Dills, John	Ann Ratcliff	Nov. 6, 1842
Dotson, Daniel	Lauanza Estep	May 4, 1847
Donley, (Donnelly) James	Liddy M. Johnson	Jan. 26, 1856
Dotson, Elijah	Elizabeth Charles	May 19, 1853
Dotson, George W.	Nancy J. Daugherty	Aug. 1, 1861
Dotson, John	Sarah Charles	Apr. 5, 1849
Dotson, Jordan	Rhoda Stump	June 9, 1865
Dotson, Reuben	Matilda Ann Coleman	Mar. 23, 1851
Dotson, Riley	Jane Estep	Feb. 5, 1846
Drake, Alfred	Elizabeth Breeding	July 31, 1831
Drake, Isaac	Betsy Adkins	June 15, 1826
Drake, Isaac	Peggy Bishop	Mar. 11, 1830
Drake, Solomon	Jane Elswick	Oct. 15, 1829
Duncan, Mark P.	Anna Canada	Nov. 2, 1829

E

Groom	Bride	Date of Marriage
Edmonds, Preston	Frances Mims	Aug. 24, 1858
Edwards, Humphrey	Jane Carty	July 13, 1847
Edwards, Isham	Emiel C. Ford	Aug. 20, 1843
Elkins, Booker	Christina Johns	Jan. 25, 1861
Elkins, James	Barbara E. Clevenger	Aug. 5, 1852
Elkins, James	Julia A. F. Walker	Dec. 10, 1865
Elkins, John H.	Sarrilda Shortridge	Nov. 8, 1860
Elkins, S. J.	Catherine McCarty	Sept. 15, 1859
Elkins, William F.	Elizabeth L. Lyons	Nov. 23, 1848
Elliott, Granville	Nancy Hall	Apr. 24, 1852
Elliott, John	Elizabeth Francis	June 27, 1827
Elliott, John	Anna Bentley	Mar. 2, 1837
Ellis, Anderson J.	Jennett Debord	Oct. 17, 1848
Elswick, A. Jackson	Sarah McCarthy	Dec. 24, 1857
Elswick, Bradley, Jr.	Patsey Tackett	Sept. 19, 1851
Elswick, George W.	Eliza Branham	Feb. 22, 1860
Elswick, H.	M. Bryant	Aug. 8, 1856
Elswick, Harvey G.	Amanda B. Eppling	Mar. 1, 1859
Elswick, Jonathan	Polly Mullins	Apr. 17, 1858
Elswick, John	Sally Kinney	Dec. 31, 1835
Elswick, John	Polly Hackney	Feb. 20, 1837
Elswick, Louis	Pricie M. Hackney	Feb. 25, 1857
Elswick, Robert	Maria A. Miller	June 22, 1865

Groom	Bride	Date of Marriage
Elswick, Thomas	Sarah Hackney	Dec. 14, 1865
Elswick, Wesley	Peggy Kinney	Dec. 28, 1844
Elswick, William, Jr.	Polly Mahan	July 29, 1827
Elswick, W. M.	Nancy Kinney	Feb. 12, 1835
Emmert, John W.	Frances Brown	Oct. 24, 1849
England, George	Rachael Tackett	Feb. 21, 1861
England, Ruel	Pricie Clay	May 1, 1850
England, Sherwood	Sally Cook	Feb. 13, 1845
Eppling, Henry H.	Jane Hunt	Mar. 25, 1852
Eppling, Isaac	Morning A. Taylor	June 20, 1826
Eppling, Isaac	Anna Polley	Aug. 24, 1852
Eppling, Isiah	Nancy Hackney	Dec. 27, 1846
Eppling, James H.	Clementine Rains	July 1, 1858
Eppling, John B.	Mary A. Rowe	Dec. 29, 1860
Estep, Andrew J.	Pricie Lester	May 18, 1860
Estep, David	Pricie Slone	July 3, 1856
Estep, James	Sarah Frazier	July 7, 1823
Estep, John	Lucinda Prater	Nov. 5, 1857
Estep, John	Polly McCoy	May 1, 1851
Estep, John	Mary Blankenship	June 28, 1865
Estep, Martin	Sarah Ann Lowe	Aug. 5, 1855
Estep, Samuel	Susanna Mullins	Feb. 15, 1830
Estep, William	Elizabeth Blankenship	Jan. 5, 1866
Evans. Thomas	Susue Davis	Nov. 21, 1822

F

Groom	Bride	Date of Marriage
Farley, Henry	Polly Stare?	Aug. 10, 1822
Farley, Jesse	Elizabeth McCoy	Apr. 12, 1849
Farley, John	Matilda Stafford	June 30, 1833
Farley, John	Polly Alley	June 3, 1847
Farley, Nimrod	Juliet Clendennen	Aug. 10, 1822
Farley, Samuel	Matilda Taylor	Apr. 14, 1839
Farley, Sam G.	Mary Ann Varney	Nov. 9, 1865
Farley, Thomas	Nancy Maynard	May 6, 1841
Farley, Thomas	Nancy C. Pinson	Dec. 25, 1860
Farley, Thomas G.	Lucy Retherford	Feb. 28, 1861
Farley, W. H.	Betsey Phillips	Aug. 6, 1823
Farley, William	Polly Runyon	Aug. 6, 1846
Farmer, John	Mary Mullins	Apr. 25, 1861
Farmer, Osman L.	Pricie Victoria Coleman	Feb. 5, 1865
Farris, James	Nancy Burgett	Feb. 2, 1857
Faulkner, James	Louisa Ratliff	Dec. 3, 1847
Ferguson, Harvey	Lucinda Ratcliff	Aug. 21, 1861
Ferguson, James	Rachael McCoy	Nov. 10, 1832
Ferguson, Joseph	Eliza Damron	June 14, 1835
Ferguson, Malachi	Nancy Owens	July 19, 1826
Ferguson, Samuel	Lurissa Ratcliff	Oct. 26, 1852
Ferguson, Stephen M.	Lucinda Weddington	May 13, 1847
Ferguson, William	Thurza Jane Ratliff	May 2, 1852
Ferrell, Andrew	Mary Slater	Apr. 30, 1835
Ferrell, Elijah	Sarah Justice	Sept. 28, 1837
Ferrell, John	Elizabeth Coleman	Feb. 14, 1828
Ferrell, Richard J.	Sarah Ann Sansom	Sept. 15, 1865
Fidler, John F.	Malinda Sword	July 30, 1857
Fields, Cummings	Polly Ann Lawson	July 29, 1851
Fields, Jason	Mary Jewel	July 19, 1849
Fields, Jason	Nancy Williamson	Sept. 17, 1854

Groom	Bride	Date of Marriage
Fields, Joseph	Rebecca Pinson	Feb. 1, 1845
Fields, Reuben	Matilda Porter	Jan. 5, 1860
Fields, Robert	Mary Usley Reed	Dec. 31, 1840
Fields, William	Frances Reed	Feb. 25, 1841
Fife, Edward A.	Peggy Sanders	July 28, 1836
Fife, George W.	Sophia King	Sept. 15, 1861
Fife, Thomas	Permelia Syck	Mar. 11, 1865
Fleming, Frederick	Amy Wright	June 18, 1840
Fleming, John	Mary Mullins	Jan. 31, 1833
Fleming, Philip	Minerva Mullins	July 5, 1838
Fleming, Robert Jeff	Lettie Mullins	Dec. 16, 1846
Fleming, William	Elizabeth Mullins	Sept. 26, 1841
Fletcher, Joseph	Nancy Ramey	Apr. 5, 1831
Fletcher, Major L.	Nancy E. Hunt	May 15, 1845
Ford, Harrison	May Dawson	Jan. 19, 1854
Ford, Jackson	Rachael Newsom	Aug. 22, 1850
Ford, William	Malinda McGee	June 28, 1840
Fraley, Henry P.	Artie Taylor	Dec. 9, 1858
Fraley, Hezekiah	Elizabeth Helvey	Aug. 30, 1828
France, William	Delila Quillen	Apr. 18, 1829
Francis, Andrew	Elizabeth Hopkins	Jan. 6, 1853
Francis, Andrew J.	Hannah Cline	Dec. 28, 1857
Francis, David	Juda Gibson	Oct. 4, 1836
Francis, Elijah	Charity Smith	Aug. 24, 1848
Francis, George	Franky McCoy	Aug. 30, 1854
Francis, James	Lucy Daniel	Apr. 4, 1847
Francis, James M.	Maria S. Daugherty	July 19, 1860
Francis, William, Jr.	Peggy Boner	Oct. 27, 1855
Francisco, George W.	Zarilda Osborn	June 10, 1852
Francisco, John	Polly Varney	Oct. 7, 1858
Frasher, (Frazier) Robert	Frances Hall	Mar. 7, 1833
Frederick, John	Patsy Boney	June 9, 1825
Frederick, John	Pricilla Retherford	Apr. 22, 1849
Frederick, John	Sally Retherford	Dec. 8, 1850
Frederick, Martin	Runniah Neeley	Sept. 6, 1835
Frederick, Martin	Polly Retherford	Nov. 1, 1855
Frederick, Nathan	Polly Blankenship	Sept. 7, 1848
Frederick, Nathan	Morning Retherford	June 12, 1852
Frederick, Peter	Polly Collins	May 20, 1831
Fry, Jackson	Elvina Frances Ratcliff	Dec. 19, 1850
Fulkerson, Martin	Elizabeth Mims	Jan. 18, 1847
Fuller, Calvin	Margaret McCauley	Feb. 23, 1834
Fuller, Elijah	Frances Thompson	Mar. 5, 1838
Fuller, John	Selah Anderson	Oct. 1, 1840
Fuller, John W.	Rebecca Ford	Aug. 20, 1856
Fuller, Thomas	Elizabeth Warrick	Jan. 31, 1845

G

Galling, ? John	Nancy Stair	Sept. 19, 1865
Gannon, Barnabas	Betsey Adkins	May 18, 1843
Gannon, Jonathan	Perliced? E. E. Williamson	Dec. 29, 1859
Gannon, William	Mary Ann Wuson	Apr. 17, 1823
Garrell (Jarrel) Thomas	Sally Phillips	Dec. 30, 1839
Gess, John	Sarah Rowe	Apr. 14, 1844
Gibson, David	Sylvia Bolling	Mar. 26, 1857
Gibson, Elijah	Nancy McGee	Feb. 26, 1824
Gibson, Elijah	Evaline Slone	Sept. 3, 1849

Groom	Bride	Date of Marriage
Gibson, Elijah	Delila Smith	Mar. 15, 1845
Gibson, Ison	Evaline Slone	Sept. 3, 1849
Gibson, Ison	Margaret Jane Burk	Aug. 4, 1854
Gibson, James	Evaline Gibson	Nov. 26, 1860
Gibson, Joel	Polly Spears	May 20, 1829
Gibson, Joel	Rhoda Raynes	Aug. 10, 1865
Gibson, John	Polly Blanton	Oct. 4, 1825
Gibson, John	Tazzy Bailey	Feb. 16, 1855
Gibson, John W.	Polly Ann Morgan	Aug. 12, 1850
Gibson, Martin, Jr.	Matilda Davis	July 6, 1833
Gibson, Robert	Elizabeth Moore	Mar. 29, 1832
Gibson, Thomas	Susan Bartley	Nov. 25, 1860
Gibson, William	Martha Bartley	Dec. 5, 1860
Gibson, Zachariah	Elizabeth McGee	...., 1822
Gilbert, George	Lydia Morgan	Sept. 23, 1844
Gilbert, Sam J.	Mary Hunt	Sept. 20, 1847
Gilliam, Berry	Elizabeth Sword	Dec. 22, 1851
Gilliam, Nathaniel	Amanda Steele	...., ...
Gillsepie, James	Lucinda McCown	Mar. 3, 1845
Gillespie, Matthew	Eliza Ross	July 29, 1858
Gillespie, William	Nancy McCown	Mar. 14, 1847
Goff, Edward	Isabel Coleman	May 22, 1823
Goff, George	Nancy Parsons	Dec. 21, 1849
Goff, John	Nancy Ramsey	Mar. 18, 1852
Goff, Martin V.	Rebecca Ramey	Dec. 28, 1858
Goff, William	Polly Ramey	Feb. 25, 1851
Good, John	Cynthia Fields	Dec. 25, 1860
Good, Marshall	Sana Childers	Jan. 5, 1856
Goosling, Ambrose	Millie Kesee	May 14, 1826
Goosling, Hammond	Jane Hunt	Nov. 30, 1848
Goosling, John	Cynthia Smith	Dec. 28, 1848
Grant, William	Rebecca Runley	May 21, 1857
Greer, Philip	Mary Greer	Jan. 8, 1865
Griffith, David	Jane Compton	July 12, 1849
Griffith, George W.	Nancy Blackburn	Jan. 3, 1850
Griffith, John W.	Hulda Slone	Jan. 10, 1847
Griffith, Richard	Malvina Slone	Jan. 21, 1847
Gross, Jarred	Margaret Clevenger	June 21, 1853
Guess, Moses	Victoria E. Rowe	July 19, 1859

H

Hackney, Anderson	Polly Adkins	Dec. 7, 1848
Hackney, Charles	Morning Stilton	Mar. 23, 1848
Hackney, Ephraim	Sarah Elswick	Mar. 18, 1852
Hackney, John	France Hurley	Sept. 21, 1842
Hackney, Ruel P.	Westeny Adkins	Dec. 8, 1849
Hackworth, Jesse	Polly Ratcliff	Oct. 7, 1830
Hackworth, Pleasant	Rachael Ratcliff	Sept. 25, 1827
Hackworth, Preston	Nancy Branham	Feb. 19, 1828
Hackworth, Tolbert	Lettie Front	Aug. 31, 1826
Hagey?, Jacob	Dorcas Eppling	Dec. 24, 1826
Hale, John	Rhoda Elkins	Mar. 20, 1854
Hale, John B.	Martha Jane Compton	June 6, 1865
Hall, Alex	Susanna Morgan	Jan. 7, 1830
Hall, Alex	Polly Johnson	June 20, 1865
Hall, David	Spicy Hall	Aug. 21, 1860

Groom	*Bride*	*Date of Marriage*
Hall, Elijah	Margaret Clark	July 13, 1829
Hall, Harmon	Frances M. Elliott	Feb. 17, 1851
Hall, Henry	Agatha Branham	Jan. 2, 1840
Hall, Isaac	Lucy Cole	Dec. 26, 1839
Hall, James	Mary Osborn	Jan. 22, 1846
Hall, Jarvey	Elizabeth Elliott	July 20, 1825
Hall, Jonathan, Jr.	Polly Cook	Sept. 6, 1850
Hall, Masias	Cadence Tackett	Apr. 17, 1846
Hall, Morgan	Lesty Cook	Aug. 17, 1848
Hall, Owen	Catherine Hall	June 11, 1840
Hall, Raleigh	Jane Cook	Sept. 1, 1825
Hall, Randall	Kate Johnson	May 31, 1827
Hall, Reuben	Mahala Bentley	Mar. 23, 1837
Hall, Richard	Sally Tackett	July 22, 1830
Hall, Riley, Jr.	Lucinda Cook	May 27, 1842
Hall, Riley	.... Tackett	Aug. 27, 1851
Hall, Riley	Mary Ann Adams	Dec. 31, 1853
Hall, Riley	Lucy Johnson	Apr. 1, 1862
Hall, Robert	Nancy Akers	Feb. 5, 1846
Hall, Sam, Jr.	Malinda Edwards	June 10, 1847
Hall, Samuel	Nancy Little	June 23, 1853
Hall, Samuel	Mary Newsom	Feb. 21, 1861
Hall, Wilburn	Rachael Osborn	Aug. 23, 1865
Hall, William	Elizabeth Johnson	Mar. 10, 1836
Hall, William	Nancy Osborn	Aug. 13, 1854
Hamilton, James	Patsy Ratliff	Sept. 15, 1837
Hamilton, Jesse	Pherina Hall	July 28, 1825
Hamilton, Nelson	Almeda Belcher	Dec. 26, 1839
Hamilton, Preston	Matilda Edwards	June 10, 1847
Hamilton, Sam	Jane Bryant	June 8, 1828
Hamilton, Thomas	Margaret Newsome	June 24, 1842
Hamilton, William	Elizabeth Frazier	Apr. 10, 1834
Hamilton, William	Millie Ray	...., ...
Hamilton, Wyatt	Almeda Mutters	June 14, 1855
Hammons, Ephraim	Winnie Little	Dec. 22, 1842
Hammons, Joe	Polly Ingleton	Apr. 25, 1839
Hanover, John	Nancy Johnson	Aug. 27, 1835
Hargis, Thomas	Jane Weddington	June 27, 1818?
Harless, Aaron	Elizabeth Huston	July 23, 1830
Harless, George J.	Cyrena Rowe	Jan. 27, 1853
Harmon, Daniel	Emeriah Runyon	Mar. 10, 1844
Harmon, Elias W.	Mary May	Nov. 15, 1849
Harris, James	Peggy Pinson	Aug. 15, 1844
Harris, Thomas	Ellen Harmon	May 16, 1844
Harris, William	Lucy Tackett	Mar. 16, 1849
Harrison, Daniel J.	L. E. Elkins	July 21, 1858
Harrison, Hezekiah	Sarah Ann Marrs	Aug. 24, 1858
Hatcher, John L.	Elizabeth Weddington	Feb. 6, 1855
Hatfield, Anderson	Polly Runyon	Aug. 2, 1855
Hatfield, Bazil	Nancy J. Lowe	Dec. 17, 1858
Hatfield, Eli	Anna Evans	Sept. 20, 1827
Hatfield, Ellison	Sarah Ann Staten	Sept. 3, 1865
Hatfield, Ephraim	Nancy Vance	Aug. 28, 1828
Hatfield, Ephraim	Anna Bundy	Nov. 28, 1830
Hatfield, Ephraim	Eliza McCoy	May 10, 1859
Hatfield, Ferrell	Juda Ball	Oct. 14, 1838
Hatfield, James	Mary Blackburn	Mar. 18, 1858

Groom	Bride	Date of Marriage
Hatfield, John	Mary A. Crabtree	Dec. 20, 1849
Hatfield, John H.	Sarah A. Ferrell	Jan. 24, 1856
Hatfield, Joseph	Nancy Evans	Sept. 20, 1827
Hatfield, Joseph	Mary Justice	Nov. 21, 1852
Hatfield, Ransom	Tabitha Taylor	Nov. 28, 1850
Hatfield, Richard	Polly Venters	Aug. 25, 1842
Hatfield, Valentine	Jane Maynard	Aug. 29, 1853
Hawkins, Elihu	Christina Bush	Nov. 2, 1848
Haynes, Joseph	Barbara Porter	July 5, 1860
Hayton, Jacob	Hannah Fife	Dec. 5, 1845
Hayton, Johnson	Polly Allen	Nov. 3, 1842
Hayton, Joseph	Martha A. Fife	Feb. 24, 1852
Hayton, Moses	Sarah Fuller	July 15, 1852
Hayton, Thomas	Elizabeth Sanders	Aug. 19, 1852
Heaberlin, Jacob	Rosanna Hawyer	June 9, 1822
Helvey, Henry	Miriam Justice	Dec. 30, 1832
Helvey, William M.	Martha Jane Sparks	July 19, 1856
Hensley, Aaron	Patsy Ball	Dec. 28, 1848
Hensley, Abraham	Jane Ball	Nov. 28, 1848
Hensley, Daniel	Easter Coleman	July 17, 1824
Hensley, Sam D.	Macindy Ball	Mar. 19, 1857
Herndon, James H.	Pricie M. Williamson	Dec. 18, 1850
Herriford, James H.	Meriba Ratcliff	June 16, 1840
Hibbitts, Joseph	Sarah Ratcliff	July 17, 1865
Hill, John M.	Mary A. Anderson	Jan. 2, 1847
Hillman, James	Louisa Weddington	Mar. 28, 1839
Hilton, James	Minta Coleman	Oct. 21, 1852
Hinkle, Lorenzo D.	Mary Jane Sparks	...., ...
Hinton, Richard	Millie Owens	Sept. 22, 1858
Hopkins, Elisha	Phoebe Adkins	Mar. 4, 1833
Hopkins, George	Victoria Hopkins	Oct. 29, 1865
Hopkins, John	Elizabeth Francis	Sept. 15, 1854
Hopkins, Joseph	Lucinda Morgan	Feb. 8, 1841
Horn, Henry	Eliza Johnson	Nov. 11, 1857
House, John	Delila Ramey	Oct. 16, 1833
Howard, Delaney	Elizabeth Pinson	Feb. 16, 1855
Howard, Thomas	Nancy May	Nov. 20, 1842
Howard, William	Dorcas Thacker	Feb. 26, 1829
Howell, James	Dillie Collier	Oct. 14, 1827
Howell, John	Pamelia Reynolds	Nov. 8, 1832
Howell, Samuel	Kate Ratcliff	Aug. 11, 1831
Huffman, Albert	Hannah E. Robinson	Mar. 4, 1850
Huffman, Anderson	Matilda Ford	Feb. 8, 1849
Huffman, Archelaus	Levisa Robinson	Jan. 4, 1845
Huffman, James	Amanda Helms	Jan. 23, 1845
Huffman, John	Hannah Robinson	Apr. 13, 1860
Hunt, Absolom	Elizabeth Bevins	June 29, 1849
Hunt, Adam	Polly Keen	Oct. 6, 1836
Hunt, Elijah	Bethany Fields	May 14, 1865
Hunt, George	Celia Breeding	Apr. 2, 1826
Hunt, Henry	Sarah Lowe	Apr. 14, 1842
Hunt, Henry	Phoebe McCoy	May 14, 1857
Hunt, Henry	Mary Ann Hunt	June 11, 1865
Hunt, John, Jr.	Dicie Taylor	Apr. 16, 1832
Hunt, John, Jr.	Margaret Eppling	Mar. 24, 1865
Hunt, John, Jr.	Cecelia Ellen Whitt	June 2, 1861
Hunt, John	Gernia McCoy	Jan. 6, 1861

Groom	Bride	Date of Marriage
Hunt, Lazarus	Elizabeth Ramey	Nov. 9, 1837
Hunt, Moses	Polly Bishop	Aug. 28, 1836
Hunt, Moses	Rebecca Runyon	Oct. 1, 1846
Hunt, Thomas	Jane West	Aug. 10, 1858
Hunt, Thomas	Caroline M. Varney	Feb. 24, 1853
Hunt, William	Pricie Bishop	Sept. 1, 1856
Hunt, Aaron	Kizzie Ann Fields	May 15, 1860
Hurley, John	Cusey ? Mounts	Jan. 25, 1860
Hurley, Jonathan	Ruth Estep	Mar. 2, 1854
Hurley, Moses	Valey Hackney	June 10, 1840
Hurley, Peyton	Elizabeth Mounts	Aug. 4, 1856
Hurley, Sam	Mary Charles	May 7, 1860
Hurley, William	Isabel Breeding	Sept. 9, 1843
Hurt, Creed F.	Sarah Wuson	Mar. 13, 1861
Hurt, Robert	Easter Leslie	Oct. 5, 1854
Hutson, James	Sarah Sword	Sept. 12, 1841
Hylton, Charles	Elizabeth Sweeney	Feb. 15, 1855
Hylton, Hiram	Elizabeth Gibson	June 1, 1860
Hylton, James	Susan Griffith	Oct. 20, 1850

I

Groom	Bride	Date of Marriage
Irick, William	Lyddia Clay	Aug. 8, 1843
Isbell, Ezekiel	Elizabeth Wilburn	June 1, 1853
Isbell, William	Lucinda Stidham	Dec. 23, 1851

J

Groom	Bride	Date of Marriage
Jackson, David	Malinda Prewitt	Dec. 22, 1853
Jackson, Hawkins F.	Elizabeth Keith	May 24, 1845
Jackson, Isaac	Elizabeth Leslie	Jan. 20, 1837
Jackson, James M.	Naomi Leslie	May 11, 1843
Jackson, James M.	Esther M. Milam	June 13, 1852
James, Abner	Margaret Campbell	Apr. 20, 1823
James, Abner	Millie Young	Jan. 24, 1856
James, Isaac	Betsy Spriggs	Oct. 15, 1826
Johnson, Andrew J.	Margaret J. Robinson	May 3, 1849
Johnson, Bailey	Rebecca Johnson	Aug. 14, 1851
Johnson, Cornelius	Millie Ratcliff	Mar. 6, 1862
Johns, Dan W.	Anna Adkins	Dec. 25, 1842
Johnson, Isaac	Mary McPeek	Jan. 29, 1846
Johnson, James E.	Margaret Ramsey	Dec. 5, 1850
Johnson, James W.	Rebecca Sword	Aug. 14, 1852
Johnson, Jacob	Elizabeth Osborn	Mar. 1, 1838
Johnson, John	Mary Lawson	Mar. 11, 1841
Johnson, John	Rebecca Clay	May 11, 1848
Johnson, John	Elizabeth Ratliff	Jan. 16, 1859
Johnson, Madison	Catherine Tackett	Dec. 26, 1848
Johnson, Martin	Susanna Anderson	Nov. 26, 1843
Johnson, Peter	Susan C. Crabtree	Aug. 3, 1843
Johnson, Peyton	Susanna Mounts	Mar. 14, 1858
Johnson, Peyton	Anna Justice	Aug. 4, 1836
Johnson, Pleasant	Anna Burk	Feb. 15, 1848
Johnson, Robert	Easter Branham	May 11, 1842
Johnson, Thomas R.	Martha Gillespie	June 13, 1853
Johnson, Thomas	Catherine Robinson	May 22, 1860
Johnson, William	Nancy Deal	Sept. 21, 1824

Groom	Bride	Date of Marriage
Johnson, William	Elizabeth Branham	June 19, 1828
Johnson, William	Matilda Mullins	May 13, 1830
Johnson, William	Nancy Warrick	Dec. 16, 1835
Johnson, William	Elizabeth Ramey	Dec. 9, 1844
Johnson, William	Sarah Mounts	Dec. 8, 1854
Johnson, William	Armintie Sowards	Dec. 6, 1860
Jones, John	Phoebe Sturgill	Nov. 27, 1845
Jones, John	Sarah Stepp	July 18, 1848
Jones, John	Mary Lyons	Jan. 15, 1856
Jones, Junius C.	Pricie McClune	July 17, 1851
Jones, Nathaniel	Mary McCowan	Feb. 16, 1851
Jones, William	Catenena Payne	Dec. 27, 1827
Justice, Abner	Martha Thacker	Dec. 23, 1841
Justice, Abshire	Sarah Wuson	Oct. 20, 1844
Justice, Alex	Margaret King	July 22, 1830
Justice, Andrew	Rachael Phillips	Feb. 6, 1836
Justice, Booker	Gidia Thacker	Mar. 7, 1833
Justice, Claiborne	Frances Stanley	Sept. 20, 1846
Justice, Colbert	Martha Kendrick	Aug. 24, 1865
Justice, Ezra	Matilda Keen	Feb. 21, 1849
Justice, Fleming	Lucinda Blackburn	Jan. 26, 1851
Justice, Flemmon	Mary Ann Gilbert	May 25, 1856
Justice, George	Patsy Herrell	June 16, 1827
Justice, George, Jr.	Nancy Campbell	...., ...
Justice, George W.	Mary Ann McGee	Mar. 19, 1857
Justice, Gilmore	Polly Payne	Apr. 7, 1850
Justice, Hammond	Lucinda Blackburn	Jan. 26, 1857
Justice, Harvey	Rebecca Wuson	Oct. 20, 1844
Justice, Hiram	Nancy Clevenger	Dec. 14, 1837
Justice, James	Elizabeth James	...., 1822
Justice, James M.	Mahala Stanley	Dec. 26, 1864
Justice, Joab	Sarah Charles	Dec. 11, 1846
Justice, John	Nancy Blackburn	Oct. 11, 1860
Justice, John W.	Luraney Smith	July 16, 1865
Justice, John W.	Dorcas Thacker	Feb. 9, 1865
Justice, Peyton	Elizabeth Keen	Apr. 20, 1838
Justice, Simon	Susan Lawson	Aug. 18, 1842
Justice, Simeon	Barbara Wilson	Oct. 3, 1844
Justice, Simeon	Elizabeth Robinson	Mar. 2, 1852
Justice, Simeon	Mary May	July 21, 1859
Justice, Thomas	Polly Thacker	Apr. 22, 1848
Justice, Thomas	Polly Justice	Oct. 18, 1865
Justice, William	Jane Maynard	Jan. 21, 1837
Justice, William	Mary A. Thacker	Nov. 19, 1840
Justice, William	Mary Ann Blackburn	Jan. 6, 1848
Justice, William	Almeda Sipple	Mar. 17, 1850
Justice, William A.	Dorcas Brown	June 17, 1852
Justice, William	Nancy Thacker	May 3, 1860

K

Keathley, Henry	Nancy Trout	Dec. 28, 1834
Keathley, Oliver G.	Rebecca M. Keathley	Dec. 28, 1858
Keathley, Simpkins	Patsy Akers	Nov. 6, 1828
Keathley, Simpkins	Malinda Charles	Aug. 16, 1860
Keathley, Simpkins, Jr.	Cynthia Ann Lee	Dec. 4, 1840
Keel, Samuel	Cynthia Ray	Aug. 22, 1850

Groom	Bride	Date of Marriage
Keen, Harper	Elizabeth Phillips	Nov. 14, 1839
Keen, Harper	Rebecca Blevins	May 1, 1856
Keen, John	Charlotte Griffith	Jan. 20, 1848
Keen, Lewis	Susan Mutter	Mar. 15, 1849
Kelly, Joseph T.	Mary Ferguson	Jan. ...., 1845
Kendrick, Dan L.	Clarinda Adkins	Mar. 1, 1865
Kendrick, Harvey P.	Sarah Slone	Oct. 27, 1844
Kendrick, James M.	Rhoda M. Justice	Jan. 22, 1865
Kendrick, Milton G.	Elizabeth Slone	Jan. 18, 1835
Kendrick, William H.	Elizabeth Thacker	Aug. 12, 1858
Kennedy, Thomas	Delila Bevins	Sept. 16, 1829
Kesee, Booker	Mary Lowe	Oct. 4, 1840
Keesee, John	Lucinda Bevins	Mar. 11, 1824
King, Andrew J.	Millie Phillips	Dec. 7, 1853
King, David B.	Delila Clark	July 15, 1841
King, Harrison	Docia Ann Sarah Lowe	Oct. 16, 1851
King, John	Sarah Collins	July 5, 1838
King, John	Sally Branham	May 8, 1822
King, John	Lavina Pinson	Apr. 9, 1855
King, Lewis	Polly Phillips	July 22, 1827
King, Samuel	Delila Pinson	Sept. 12, 1827
Kinney, Leonard	Johnson, J.	Nov. 10, 1853
Kinney, Leonard	Martha Ann McCown	Sept. 17, 1857
Kinney, John	Polly Branham	June 19, 1834
Kinney, William	Sarah Robinson	May 7, 1853
Kirk, William	Nancy Williams	Mar. 2, 1835
Kirk, William	Elizabeth Collins	Nov. 1, 1848
Kunard, (Kennard), James A.	Martha Sword	Aug. 26, 1852

L

Groom	Bride	Date of Marriage
Lawrence, William J.	Sophia Vandikes	May 10, 1856
Lawson, Emly	Elizabeth Maynard	Dec. 9, 1858
Layne, Austin	Catherine Ratcliff	Jan. 20, 1839
Layne, Daniel	Polly Robinette	June 12, 1851
Layne, John N.	Mary Honaker	Oct. 10, 1842
Layne, John	Elizabeth McCoy	June 29, 1848
Layne, John L.	Sarah Walters	June 16, 1855
Layne, Merida	Margaret Phillips	Nov. 14, 1839
Layne, Meredith	Daisy ? Blankenship	Sept. 17, 1854
Layne, Thomas	Angeline Weddington	July 30, 1860
Layne, William	Sarah Ratliff	Jan. 6, 1843
Layne, William	Piety Hackworth	Apr. 24, 1823
Lee, John	Malinda Layne	Oct. 16, 1843
Leech, Peter	Elizabeth Stotts	Apr. 7, 1831
Leedy, Abraham	Jane Ratcliff	Dec. 24, 1857
Leedy, Randolph	Depoline Ratliff	Oct. 2, 1850
Leslie, Edmond	Sallie Stilton	Dec. 11, 1825
Leslie, Pharmer	Mary Bevins	July 12, 1829
Lester, Calvin	Lucinda Estep	Dec. 25, 1865
Lester, Elisha	Melvina McClannahan	Sept. 9, 1852
Lester, Jacob	Susue Matney	Feb. 16, 1848
Lester, James	Sidney Payne	Feb. 28, 1828
Lester, John C.	Rebecca Elliott	Nov. 8, 1829
Lester, John	Ruth Yates	Aug. 25, 1830
Lewis, Ben	Anna Jesse	Feb. 4, 1840

Groom	Bride	Date of Marriage
Lewis, John	Margaret Sanders	Mar. 6, 1843
Lewis, Thomas	Delila Blankenship	Mar. 4, 1832
Lewis, William	Lucinda Shockey	Jan. 18, 1829
Lile, Richard	Nancy Fuller	Nov. 30, 1851
Little, David	Lyddia Johnson	June 14, 1849
Little, Isaac	Lucinda Caudill	Aug. 26, 1841
Little, James	Mary Caudill	Oct. 4, 1847
Little, John	Mary Burk	June 23, 1853
Little, Marion	Hulda Branham	Sept. 21, 1854
Little, Moses	Daisy Osborn	Mar. 2, 1852
Little, Reuben	Jane Warrick	Dec. 6, 1860
Little, William	Elizabeth Sweeney	June 8, 1828
Little, William	Polly Crabtree	Mar. 5, 1840
Lockhart, Bird	Jane Staten	Jan. 21, 1833
Looney, John	Cynthia Stiltner	Feb. 1, 1826
Looney, John	Mary Ann Childers	Nov. 30, 1848
Looney, John	Emerita Rowe	Oct. 6, 1853
Looney, Joseph	Polly Looney	June 14, 1829
Looney, Joseph	Louisa Childers	Nov. 16, 1848
Lowe, Fountain B.	Sudy Staten	Dec. 18, 1856
Lowe, James F.	Lyddia E. Taylor	Sept. 13, 1852
Low (e), James	Mary Ann Retherford	Sept. 3, 1846
Lowe, James	Daisy Blankenship	Oct. 9, 1858
Lowe, Nathaniel	Eva Maynard	June 9, 1861
Lowe, O. B. M.	Elizabeth Runyon	Sept. 2, 1858
Lowe, William	Maria Davis	June 14, 1822
Lowe, William	Elizabeth King	Oct. 3, 1831
Lowe, William L.	Jane Varney	Aug. 26, 1860
Lycans, John	Betsy Syck	Feb. 2, 1823
Lycans, Moses	Sophia Havens	Apr. 29, 1860
Lycans, John D.	Lyddia Maynard	Feb. 27, 1848
Lycans, William	Chaney Smith	May 27, 1852

M

Mainor, Lindsay	Martha J. Rider	Sept. 3, 1854
Mann, J. Richard	Patsy Hamilton	June 22, 1865
Marrs, Harmon	Virginia Edmonds	June 3, 1858
Marrs, John	Cynthia May	Nov. 22, 1833
Martin, Lindsay	Elizabeth Ray	Oct. 20, 1852
Martin, Sylvester	Mary Hopkins	Jan. 27, 1859
Mathis, Reuben	Hannah Smith	Nov. 18, 1830
Matney, Alex	Jane Hamilton	Dec. 23, 1848
Matney, David	Mary Elswick	Sept. 10, 1829
Matthews, Forester	Patsy Ratcliff	May 29, 1831
Matthews, James	Nancy Castle	Feb. 17, 1825
May, Alexander	Sarah Ann Smith	Mar. 19, 1857
May, Daniel	Polly Stotts	Aug. 18, 1846
May, Gideon	Malinda Hylton	Dec. 30, 1830
May, Harvey	Juda Retherford	Sept. 10, 1857
May, Isaac	Tabitha Jane Presley	Dec. 30, 1849
May, James	Nancy Ball	June 11, 1843
May, James	Sarah Coleman	Mar. 15, 1849
May, John A.	Nancy Smith	Dec. 23, 1852
May, Jonathan	Eliza Howell	Apr. 7, 1842
May, Joseph	Polly Farley	Mar. 15, 1851

Groom	Bride	Date of Marriage
May, Reuben	Emeriah Honaker	Mar. 5, 1835
May, Thomas	Elizabeth Leslie	Mar. 4, 1841
May, Washington	Matilda Retherford	Mar. 19, 1851
May, William C.	Nancy C. Runyon	May 1, 1856
May, W. J.	Cerepta Retherford	Jan. 8, 1857
Maynard, Allen	Nancy Cains	Apr. 16, 1840
Maynard, Alvis	Harriett Taylor	Feb. 28, 1828
Maynard, Barnabas	Lucy Fuller	June 26, 1833
Maynard, Barnabas	Pricie Robinson	Jan. 6, 1859
Maynard, Ben	Elizabeth Deskins	Dec. 19, 1839
Maynard, Christopher	Eve Shockey	Sept. 9, 1839
Maynard, David	Sally Spriggs	June 16, 1840
Maynard, David	Margaret Hylton	Dec. 22, 1841
Maynard, David A.	Jane Ramey	Jan. 1, 1865
Maynard, Decatur	Louisa C. Fletcher	June 20, 1861
Maynard, Edward	Anna Lykins	Nov. 15, 1843
Maynard, George	Martha Smith	Aug. 4, 1824
Maynard, George W.	Sarah Cains	Sept. 10, 1857
Maynard, Hammon	Elizabeth Taylor	Oct. 12, 1848
Maynard, Henderson	Lucinda McCoy	Mar. 17, 1842
Maynard, Henry	Nancy Spry	Mar. 14, 1824
Maynard, Isaac	Polly Smith	Nov. 23, 1823
Maynard, Isaac	Charity Maynard	May 28, 1861
Maynard, James	Sallie Fuller	Jan. 5, 1829
Maynard, James	Sophia Spry	Nov. 20, 1830
Maynard, James	Elizabeth Damron	Feb. 9, 1833
Maynard, James	Sophia Finley	Nov. 15, 1838
Maynard, Jarred	Martha A. Tummier	Nov. 11, 1856
Maynard, John H.	Comfort Sansom	Sept. 6, 1855
Maynard, Jordan	Wina Nichols	Sept. 16, 1853
Maynard, Mark	Charity Maynard	...., 1824
Maynard, Moses	Chloe Francis	July 26, 1838
Maynard, Moses	Levisa Varney	Sept. ...., 1840
Maynard, Richard	Martha Pinson	Sept. 1, 1829
Maynard, Richard	Charlotte Taylor	...., 1833
Maynard, Stephen	Polly Stepp	Oct. 26, 1837
Maynard, Thomas	Sallie Phillips	Aug. 5, 1847
Maynard, Thompson	Betsy Jones	June 6, 1833
Maynard, William	Louvina Retherford	Mar. 7, 1844
Maynard, William	Nancy Alley	Mar. 16, 1848
Maynard, William	Malinda Hunt	June 28, 1849
Maynard, William	Nancy Lykins	June 24, 1852
Maynard, William T.	Polly Stair	Nov. 10, 1859
Mays, Ehud	Fanny Rowe	Feb. 11, 1829
Mays, James	Amazelia Ratcliff	Jan. 31, 1836
McClannahan, David	Mahala Justice	Jan. 2, 1844
McColly, Thomas	Nancy Scott	Aug. 14, 1823
McColly, James	Polly Fuller	Mar. 25, 1827
McConnell, Thomas P.	Linda Mire Phillips	Aug. 31, 1826
McCown, Hugh	Rebecca Carter	Aug. 25, 1831
McCown, Hugh	Susanna Gillespie	Sept. 13, 1851
McCown, Linzie	Mary A. Bowling	July 29, 1849
McCoy, Addison	Mary A. May	Mar. 24, 1861
McCoy, Allen	Elizabeth Blankenship	Sept. 9, 1841
McCoy, Andrew	Nancy Justice	Aug. 31, 1837
McCoy, Asa	Eleanor Burriss	Sept. 14, 1832

Groom	Bride	Date of Marriage
McCoy, Asa P.	Nancy Caroline Pike	Sept. 6, 1855
McCoy, Ben	Phoebe McCoy	Oct. 31, 1839
McCoy, Ben	Nancy Robinett	Sept. 28, 1851
McCoy, George	Mary Daniel	July 15, 1827
McCoy, Hiram	Chloe Sansom	Sept. 12, 1837
McCoy, John, Jr.	Peggy Burriss	Dec. 2, 1827
McCoy, John	Nancy Roman	Mar. 30, 1845
McCoy, John R.	Rachael Blankenship	June 30, 1859
McCoy, Pyrrhus	Malinda Hunt	Nov. 5, 1846
McCoy, Randolph	Mary Ann Stafford	Nov. 20, 1823
McCoy, Randolph	Elizabeth Sansom	Apr. 16, 1846
McCoy, Randolph	Sarah McCoy	Dec. 9, 1849
McCoy, Richard	Jane Allen	Aug. 3, 1851
McCoy, Richard	Mary Ann Chaney	May 25, 1836
McCoy, Samuel	Nancy Williamson	Sept. 12, 1841
McCoy, Samuel	Elizabeth Fletcher	Mar. 6, 1853
McCoy, Sam	Reecie Whitt	May 19, 1861
McCoy, Selkirk	Nancy Blankenship	June 25, 1861
McCoy, Selkirk	Louisa Williamson	Sept. ...., 1850
McCoy, Uriah	Elizabeth Retherford	May 23, 1850
McCoy, William E.	Elizabeth Roten	July 7, 1861
McCoy, William H.	Nancy Jane Taylor	Oct. 7, 1855
McCoy, William H.	Daly Ann Allen	Aug. 23, 1859
McCoy, William	Sarah Runyon	Apr. 6, 1843
McCoy, William	Mary A. Burriss	Apr. 27, 1831
McCoy, William	Sarah James	Dec. 23, 1836
McCray, James	Louisa Yonts	Oct. 11, 1838
McGee, Fuller	Rebecca Fuller	Sept. 22, 1844
McGinnis, Gordon	Amelia Workman	Apr. 5, 1857
McGinnis, James H.	Mary Williams	Aug. 6, 1851
McKinney, James	Mary Jane Slone	Feb. 16, 1860
McKinney, Robert	Polly Ann Keathley	Dec. 20, 1855
McNeely, Thomas	Arminda Staten	Sept. 9, 1851
Meade, Ben	Patsy Perry	Nov. 9, 1839
Meade, Daniel	Jane Jarrell	Jan. 3, 1839
Meade, Reuben	Martha Weddington	Oct. 12, 1837
Meade, Rhodes	Talitha Sparks	June 15, 1848
Meade, Rhodes	Emeriah Elkins	Jan. 21, 1849
Meade, Robert	Margaret Robinette	Feb. 3, 1840
Mead, McDonald	Elizabeth McCoy	June 20, 1865
Mead, Riley	Lucy Johnson	Apr. 1, 1862
Mead, Solomon	Mary Perry	Sept. 21, 1840
Mead, Thomas	Polly Hall	Mar. 28, 1822
Mead, Tolbert	Lucretia Nicewander	Nov. 21, 1853
Mead, William	Elender Retherford	Sept. 14, 1823
Mead, William	Barbara Pinson	Feb. 7, 1841
Mead, William	Caroline M. R. Robinson	Nov. 11, 1852
Meek, Jesse P.	Abigail Weddington	Sept. 28, 1837
Mercer, Levi	Mary Bartlett	June 16, 1865
Millard, Abraham	Rachael Burgett	Feb. 23, 1854
Millard, Andrew J.	Ruth E. Slayton	May 5, 1859
Millard, Ben W.	Josephene Sleyton	Jan. 22, 1859
Millard, Elijah	Mary Jane Walker	Feb. 22, 1846
Miller, Abraham	Elizabeth Wooten	...., ...
Miller, Charles	Tabitha Sweeney	Jan. 22, 1829
Miller, John	Eleanor Griffith	Oct. 11, 1843

Groom	Bride	Date of Marriage
Mills, Columbus	Nancy B. Scalf	Nov. 13, 1855
Mills, William	Julia Ann Barnard	Jan. 16, 1854
Mills, William	Sarah James	Sept. 18, 1855
Mims, John D.	Pricie Adkins	Feb. 10, 1830
Mitchell, Enoch	Lettie Mullins	Feb. 19, 1855
Mitchell, Jonathan J.	Matilda Jane Branham	Apr. 5, 1849
Moore, Aaron	Lyddia Elswick	Apr. 16, 1840
Moore, Annanias	Susanna Ramey	Feb. 2, 1830
Moore, Enoch	Cynthia Reed	Dec. 4, 1848
Moore, Isaac, Jr.	Mary Clevenger	Feb. 11, 1841
Moore, Isaac	Rebecca Mullins	Mar. 21, 1842
Moore, Langford	Elizabeth Jane Robinson	Aug. 1, 1850
Moore, Reece	Allie Mullins	Nov. 7, 1837
Moore, William M.	Lucy Clevenger	Sept. 26, 1833
Moore, William	Elizabeth Muncey	Sept. 13, 1832
Moore, William C.	Jane Mullins	Mar. 15, 1838
Moore, William C.	Sarah Tackett	Nov. 11, 1854
Morgan, Isham	Elizabeth Branham	Apr. 6, 1837
Morgan, James	Elizabeth Hinch?	May 1, 1836
Morgan, James	Nancy Rowe	Aug. 5, 1838
Morgan, William	Nancy Aldridge	June 13, 1836
Morgan, William H.	Lydia Ratliff	May 18, 1842
Morgan, William	Spicy Gibson	Oct. 7, 1854
Morris, Ambrose	Polly Bevins	Jan. 18, 1837
Morris, James	Jane Blackburn	Mar. 14, 1861
Morris, Kenas	Nancy Charles	Mar. 2, 1865
Morrison, James R.	Sallie Clay	July 15, 1829
Mounts, Charles W.	Polly Cline	Apr. 29, 1853
Mounts, Elijah	Delila Francis	May 23, 1861
Mounts, Jackson	Arsena Evans	Jan. 2, 1861
Mullett, William	Elizabeth Branham	Dec. 23, 1860
Mullins, Alexander	Peggy Fleming	Apr. 15, 1827
Mullins, Alex	Marilda Osborn	Oct. 28, 1855
Mullins, Alex	Mary Osborn	June 20, 1865
Mullins, Ambrose	Marra Mullins	July 14, 1822
Mullins, Booker	Polly Newsome	Dec. 3, 1829
Mullins, Booker	Nancy Potter	July 9, 1835
Mullins, Eli	Elizabeth Short	Jan. 3, 1824
Mullins, Isham	Rosanna Hawyer	June 9, 1822
Mullins, Isham	Cadence Osborn	Oct. 30, 1838
Mullins, James	Polly Newsom	Aug. 19, 1837
Mullins, James S.	Judy Bolling	Sept. 20, 1849
Mullins, Jefferson	Didiemay Sowards	Oct. 20, 1859
Mullins, John	Mary Elkins	Sept. 17, 1865
Mullins, John	Elizabeth Mullins	June 6, 1822
Mullins, John	Dorcas Osborn	Apr. 6, 1837
Mullins, John, Jr.	Ollie Short	Sept. 1, 1830
Mullins, John	Polly Mullins	Mar. 12, 1846
Mullins, John	Maria Reed	Dec. 25, 1850
Mullins, Johnson	Lovena Fleming	Jan. 9, 1840
Mullins, Marshall	Rebecca Vanover	Nov. 28, 1841
Mullins, Martin	Amanda Miller	Oct. 19, 1865
Mullins, Nelson	Matilda Elswick	Jan. 19, 1854
Mullins, Owen	Jane Potter	Oct. 11, 1846
Mullins, Richard	Lucinda Tackett	Aug. 30, 1842
Mullins, Sanders	Mahala Morgan	Apr. 1, 1833

Groom	Bride	Date of Marriage
Mullins, Sherwood	Catherine P. Moore	May 11, 1860
Mullins, Smith	Peggy Newsome	Apr. 19, 1833
Mullins, Solomon	Dorcas Kelly	Apr. 26, 1832
Mullins, Solomon	Nancy Wilcox	Feb. 27, 1848
Mullins, Spencer	Elizabeth Johnson	Sept. 24, 1853
Mullins, William	Sarah Waltrip	Sept. 9, 1824
Mullins, William	Elizabeth Culpepper Justice	Mar. 12, 1832
Mullins, William	Sarah Tackett	June 27, 1839
Mullins, William	Sarah Stanley	Mar. 12, 1852
Mullins, William B. H.	Delilah Branham	Aug. 2, 1850
Muncy, Thomas	Marian Burgett	Apr. 6, 1854
Murphy, Alex	Biddy McCoy	Apr. 13, 1848
Murphy, Anderson	Judith Retherford	Nov. 24, 1842
Murphy, Edmond	Susanna Clevenger	Sept. 1, 1823
Murphy, Gabriel	Hannah Phillips	Mar. 2, 1848
Murphy, John	Mary A. Ramey	Aug. 18, 1853
Murphy, William	Clara White	Mar. 14, 1861
Murray, Hiram	Nancy Kennedy	Feb. 12, 1827
Murray, Hiram	Nancy Quillen	Aug. 7, 1839
Music, Alex	Sarah McCoy	Nov. 22, 1849
Music, James C.	Mary Barnard	June 8, 1852
Mutter, Adam	Betsey Findley	Mar. 13, 1834
Mutter, George W.	Lydia Miller	July 9, 1860
Mutters, John	Polly Hunt	Apr. 2, 1826
Mutters, Thomas	Elender Miller	Mar. 25, 1852

N

Neely, William	Barbara Jackson	Oct. 1, 1829
New, John	Nancy Davis	Aug. 3, 1800
Newsom, Frederick	Ansy Hall	Jan. 22, 1835
Newsom, George W.	Matilda Elkins	Sept. 8, 1859
Newsom, Harrison	Mary Hall	Feb. 11, 1834
Newsom, Hart	Rebecca Maynard	Apr. 25, 1861
Newsom, Hartwell	Jennie Mullins	May 5, 1825
Newsom, Hartwell	Sally Tolbey	Mar. 13, 1831
Newsom, Henry	Patsy Branham	Feb. 9, 1831
Newsom, Portwell	Marinda Bryant	Nov. 6, 1837
Newsom, Portwell	Amanda Jane Hamilton	Apr. 8, 1858
Newsom, Wilson	Ruth Osborn	Nov. 22, 1855
Nicholas, Fleming	Mary Ann Harold	Feb. 28, 1861
Nipp, (Knipp) Samuel	Nancy Smith	Aug. 13, 1827
Nix, James	Emaline Johnson	Nov. 26, 1822
Noonkister, Michael	Delimoa Anderson	Nov. 30, 1851
Nunnery, Mitchell	Elizabeth Porter	Mar. 14, 1850

O

Oney, John	Arminda Hinkle	Oct. 28, 1840
Osborn, Cornelius	Rhoda Hammond	Nov. 18, 1850
Osborn, George	Clarinda Burk	Dec. 14, 1854
Osborn, Jeremiah	Mary Moore	Nov. 17, 1836
Osborn, Jesse	Sarah Johnson	July 13, 1858
Osborn, Lewis	Mary Marshall	Feb. 18, 1851
Osborn, Shadrack	Elizabeth Robertson	Feb. 5, 1846
Osborn, Sherd	Phoebe Reynolds	Nov. 25, 1838
Osborn, Stephen	Nancy Mullins	July 2, 1840

Groom	Bride	Date of Marriage
Owens, Andrew	Armanda Ramey	Mar. 16, 1837
Owens, James	Louisa Whitten	Mar. 18, 1834
Owens, James	Pricie Ramey	Mar. 27, 1842
Owens, John	Nancy Baldridge	July 22, 1827
Owens, Rhodes	Nancy P. Ratcliff	Oct. 27, 1844
Owens, Silas W. R.	Dorcas May	July 21, 1847
Owens, Thomas, Jr.	Sarah Damron	Oct. 24, 1833
Owens, Thomas J.	Mary H. C. Draper	Jan. 8, 1845
Owens, William F.	Louisa Jane Branham	Dec. 10, 1846

P

Groom	Bride	Date of Marriage
Paisley, Alex	Elizabeth Smith	Oct. 25, 1838
Parsons, C.	Sarah Johnson	Feb. 10, 1865
Parsons, David	Nancy Reed	Dec. 21, 1856
Parsons, Gabriel	Mollie Clevenger	Feb. 18, 1844
Parsons, Richard	Lydia Campbell	Mar. 13, 1832
Patterson, William	Easter McCoy	May 22, 1862
Patton, John	Barbara Thompson	June 10, 1847
Pauley, John S.	C. A. Bogar	June 15, 1862
Pauley, Joseph S.	Mary Stepp	Apr. 7, 1859
Payne, George M.	Phoebe Ray	Feb. 23, 1848
Payne, James	Sally Harper	Dec. 5, 1831
Payne, John	Susanna Lester	July 30, 1825
Payne, Simeon	Aggie Smith	Dec. 5, 1831
Peery, Andrew	Dorcas Syck	Jan. 7, 1839
Perkins, George C.	Elizabeth Baldridge	July 25, 1865
Perry, George	Rebecca Syck	Nov. 29, 1829
Perry, George	Rebecca Lawson	Nov. 3, 1836
Peters, Thompson M.	Sarah Sword	June 22, 1858
Phillips, Abraham	Jane Prater	Nov. 11, 1858
Phillips, Jacob	Elizabeth Kesee	Dec. 5, 1822
Phillips, Jesse	Nancy Keen	July 13, 1832
Phillips, John W.	Eady Smith	Nov. 13, 1856
Phillips, Richard	Lavina Scott	Jan. 2, 1859
Phillips, Thompson	Anna Keen	Jan. 11, 1835
Phillips, William	Malinda Ratliff	Nov. 15, 1844
Phillips, William	Mary King	Dec. 8, 1854
Phillips, Zachariah	Clarinda Adkins	Jan. 22, 1846
Pinson, Aaron	Ellen ? King	Apr. 9, 1847
Pinson, Allen	Elizabeth Smith	July 6, 1843
Pinson, George	Sally Bevins	July 9, 1840
Pinson, Henry	Polly Whitt	Nov. 12, 1835
Pinson, Henry	Rebecca Huffman	Jan. 13, 1842
Pinson, John C.	Elvira J. Young	Feb. 27, 1859
Pinson, Sam	Topsie Dawson	Mar. 21, 1855
Pinson, Samuel	T. J. Lawson	Mar. 24, 1853
Pinson, Jarrett	Dilly Howard	June 23, 1860
Pinson, Thomas	Sarah E. M. Hunt	June 18, 1857
Plymale, Hugh	Dulcena Adkins	Feb. 19, 1850
Plymale, Isaac	Mary Rowe	May 27, 1830
Polly, (Pauley) David, Jr.	Anna Thornsberry	Mar. 19, 1829
Polly, John	Elizabeth Eppling	June 2, 1853
Porter, Elijah	Mary Scott	Feb. 6, 1825
Porter, Elijah	Nancy Ramey	Feb. 3, 1840
Porter, James	Rebecca Stotts	Apr. 1, 1824
Porter, Joseph	Polly Ann Horn	Nov. 19, 1841
Porter, William I.	Barbara E. Walters	Apr. 3, 1856
Potter, Andrew	Elizabeth Bolling	July 25, 1858

167

Groom	Bride	Date of Marriage
Potter, George	Polly Jane Belcher	Feb. 7, 1856
Potter, Henry	Cynthia Mullins	July 22, 1855
Potter, Isham	Mary Ann Sanders	Feb. 10, 1842
Potter, James A.	Mary C. Weddington	June 21, 1859
Potter, John	Elizabeth Ramey	July 16, 1846
Potter, John	Susanna Sanders	Mar. 27, 1851
Potter, Levi	Sally Cantrell	Jan. 7, 1839
Potter, Richard	Mary Ramey	Jan. 20, 1825
Powell, David	Almeda Harless	Apr. 21, 1836
Powell, George	Nancy Polly (Payley)	Oct. 9, 1828
Powell, George	Hannah Anderson	Oct. 27, 1853
Powell, Thomas	Mary Adkins	Oct. 25, 1859
Prater, Daniel	Polly McCoy	Mar. 19, 1846
Prater, James	Elizabeth Ratliff	Feb. 3, 1847
Preston, Thomas	Anna Pinson	May 29, 1823
Prewitt, Alfred	Martha Templeton	Oct. 31, 1837
Price, James R.	Sarah Marrs	Dec. 4, 1856
Price, Neely	Susan Cooley	June 29, 1836
Price, Thomas	Nancy Ratcliff	May 14, 1828
Price, William C.	Elizabeth Weddington	Nov. 15, 1849
Priest, William	Nancy Weddington	Oct. 31, 1858
Price, William	Rebecca Hayton	Oct. 3, 1837
Prichett, William	Rhoda Justice	Mar. 12, 1839
Priest, William	Elizabeth Giddens	Mar. 22, 1825

Q

Quillen, William	Catherine Hall	June 15, 1834
Quillen, Anderson	Charlotte Sanders	Apr. 4, 1837

R

Ramey, Andrew	Ann Potter	Jan. 5, 1860
Ramey, Charles	Nancy Case	Jan. 27, 1840
Ramey, Charles	Susanna Henson	Jan. 2, 1859
Ramey, Daniel	Lucinda Carty	Feb. 13, 1840
Ramey, James	Pricie Elswick	Feb. 7, 1831
Ramey, John	Malinda Powell	Mar. 13, 1834
Ramey, John	Dicie Owens	Dec. 17, 1843
Ramey, John	Emily Stratton	Mar. 15, 1846
Ramey, Matthew	Charity Bentley	Aug. 27, 1840
Ramey, Moses	Jane Fuller	Mar. 29, 1838
Ramey, Perry	Malinda Bentley	Mar. 5, 1866
Ramey, Robert	Nancy Clark	Apr. 17, 1825
Ramey, William	Elizabeth Stapleton	Aug. 25, 1855
Ramey, William	Polly Henson	July 24, 1859
Ramsey, Charles	Lucinda Rose	Sept. 24, 1843
Ramsey, Daniel	Sarah Ann Lee	May ...., 1849
Ramsey, Daniel	Letitia Sowards	Oct. 7, 1824
Ramsey, G. W.	Ruth Polly (Pauley)	July 11, 1833
Ramsey, James W.	Emaline Austin	Sept. 27, 1855
Ramsey, John F.	Mary Adkins	Dec. 28, 1846
Ramsey, Nathan	Jennie Hall	Aug. 20, 1826
Ramsey, Whitley	Elizabeth Matney	Dec. 9, 1841
Ramsey, William, Jr.	Mary Fuller	Mar. 7, 1852
Ratliff, Algeree	Louisa Little	June 6, 1862
Ratliff, Alex	Elizabeth Hylton	Aug. 13, 1837
Ratliff, Andrew	Margaret Sparks	Aug. 22, 1861
Ratliff, Andrew J.	Ruthie Mullins	June 26, 1865
Ratliff, Colbert	Bethena Bolling	Jan. 7, 1861

Groom	Bride	Date of Marriage
Ratliff, Esquire	Rosama Maynard	June 23, 1836
Ratliff, Frederick	Susanna Cole	Feb. 15, 1825
Ratliff, Harvey	Hannah Johnson	Apr. 10, 1859
Ratliff, Harrison	Louisa Coleman	Dec. 13, 1855
Ratliff, Jacob	Kesiah Sparks	Dec. 2, 1852
Ratliff, James	Frances Strother	Apr. 2, 1835
Ratliff, James	Emla Ratliff	Dec. 27, 1855
Ratliff, James L.	Dorcas Adkins	Jan. 30, 1857
Ratliff, James T.	Elizabeth Ratliff	Nov. 8, 1861
Ratliff, Joel	Elizabeth Coleman	Dec. 22, 1859
Ratliff, John	Malinda Slone	Jan. 20, 1862
Ratcliff, John	Nancy Cox	Nov. 19, 1849
Ratliff, John S.	Elizabeth A. Ross	Feb. 1, 1861
Ratliff, Joseph E.	Jane Ferguson	Dec. 3, 1859
Ratliff, John, Jr.	Tamsey Adkins	Dec. 16, 1842
Ratliff, Moses	Susanna Stilton	Apr. 5, 1848
Ratliff, Nathan	Matilda Case	May 15, 1834
Ratliff, Nathan	Adeline Lynn	Dec. 17, 1849
Ratliff, Noah	Elizabeth J. Riley	Feb. 7, 1859
Ratliff, Paul	Emeriah Hall	Mar. 9, 1865
Ratliff, Richard	Polly Syck	Sept. 7, 1841
Ratliff, Richard	Louisa Hillman	Feb. 2, 1844
Ratliff, Robert	Mary Edwards	Oct. 6, 1839
Ratliff, Silas, Jr.	Mary Howell	Oct. 23, 1833
Ratliff, Silas	Mary Justice	Feb. 8, 1844
Ratliff, Silas W.	Mary Jane Weddington	Dec. 9, 1852
Ratliff, Silas	Ollie Moore	Feb. 7, 1861
Ratliff, Thomas	Deborah Owens	Dec. 16, 1827
Ratliff, Thompson	Elizabeth Ann Powell	Oct. 29, 1850
Ratliff, Tyre	Nancy Ratliff	Mar. 20, 1856
Ratliff, William	Malinda Huston	Sept. 8, 1836
Ratliff, William	Lydia Ford	Dec. 3, 1840
Ratliff, William, Jr.	Catherine Compton	Feb. 15, 1847
Ratliff, William	Eliza Crabtree	Mar. 28, 1851
Ratliff, William F.	Caroline Marrs	Apr. 4, 1854
Ratliff, William	Polly Ratliff	Oct. 18, 1855
Ratliff, William A.	Louisa Ratliff	Oct. 29, 1857
Ratliff, William J.	Tempa Smith	May 19, 1858
Ratliff, William	Cynthia Little	May 25, 1861
Ray, Ben	Sally Jones	Feb. 23, 1830
Ray, Daniel	Martha Barnett	Feb. 11, 1836
Ray, Eli	Susanna Clay	Mar. 21, 1860
Ray, James	Polly Maynard	Apr. 5, 1838
Ray, John W.	Rebecca Tackett	May 30, 1833
Raynes, Charles	Rhoda Haynes	about 1856
Raynes, Charles Henry	Lucinda Justice	Jan. 20, 1853
Raynes, Christopher	Mary Jane Eliza Slone	Feb. 24, 1853
Raynes, John	Sally Justice	Oct. 14, 1830
Raynes, John, Jr.	Sophia Conway	Dec. 10, 1857
Reed, Harmon	Anna Smith	Dec. 12, 1844
Reed, Gilbert	Lyddia Retherford	July 2, 1840
Reed, James	Elizabeth J. C. Honaker	Sept. 17, 1845
Reed, Lorenzo Dow	Juda Fields	Feb. 1, 1849
Retherford, James	Sallie Kennedy	...., 1831
Retherford, John	Louvisa Runyon	Mar. 17, 1853
Retherford, Joseph	Millie Kesee	July 20, 1829
Retherford, Robert	Jane Kennedy	May 19, 1822
Reynolds, Henry G.	Anna Ratliff	July 24, 1857
Reynolds, John	Cynthia Ratliff	Aug. 28, 1834

Groom	Bride	Date of Marriage
Reynolds, William M.	Anna D. Clevenger	June 4, 1843
Rice, James M.	Louisa Sword	Sept. 20, 1859
Richardson, John N.	Zila Robinson	Aug. 19, 1834
Richardson, John N.	Caroline M. Ratliff	Apr. 2, 1840
Riffe, Elijah	Malinda Robinson	Apr. 30, 1841
Riffe, Gordon	Sally Mullins	Nov. 27, 1838
Right (Wright) Augustus	Phoebe Evans	Dec. 13, 1843
Riley, Daniel	Nancy Jane Cole	May 2, 1861
Robards, Thomas	Mary E. McCoy	Jan. 17, 1861
Robinett, John	Diedemay Jones	Sept. 7, 1853
Robinett, Stephen	Elizabeth Francis	Aug. 31, 1848
Robinett, William	Polly Scabuary (Scarberry)	Dec. 11, 1844
Roberts, Isaac	Dorcas Kelly	Jan. 26, 1837
Roberts, James	Rebecca Mullins	May 13, 1838
Roberts, James, Jr.	Nancy Boney	July 27, 1826
Roberts, Jesse	Hannah Stanley	Feb. 25, 1841
Roberts, John P.	Sarah M. Mullins	Dec. 20, 1860
Roberts, Owen	Delila Caudill	May 27, 1841
Roberts, Ricely	Mary A. Taylor	Aug. 3, 1859
Roberts, Riley	Jane McCoy	Aug. 3, 1855
Robertson, George	Martha Ratliff	Oct. 19, 1837
Robertson, John	Susanna Ratliff	Sept. 10, 1833
Robertson, John	Nancy Thacker	June 2, 1844
Robertson, John	Susan Ratliff	Sept. 22, 1836
Robertson, William	Sallie Branham	May 12, 1825
Robinson, Anderson J.	Phoebe Compton	Sept. 6, 1861
Robinson, George	Margaret Adams	Mar. ...., 1857
Robinson, George	Frances Ward	Jan. 22, 1856
Robinson, Harvey	Jane Mullins	Mar. 4, 1858
Robinson, James	Sarah McGee	Dec. 8, 1845
Robinson, James	Rachael Clark	June 21, 1847
Robinson, James	Phoebe Huffman	Sept. 11, 1853
Robinson, John	Louisa Damron	May 1, 1856
Robinson, John W. P.	Nancy Caldwell	Sept. 11, 1856
Robinson, R. P., Jr.	Martha Helms	Feb. 21, 1848
Robinson, Richard	Elizabeth Justice	June 4, 1840
Robinson, Richard P.	Elizabeth Thornsberry	Oct. 13, 1861
Robinson, Samuel	Cynthia Elkins	Nov. 4, 1841
Robinson, Samuel	Mrs. Hannah S. Gilbert	Dec. 18, 1846
Robinson, William	Pricie M. Hamilton	Feb. 10, 1859
Roman, Isham	Charity Coleman	.........., 1834
Roman, James	Mary Smith	Jan. 19, 1836
Roman, Greenville L.	Elizabeth Morris	Nov. 2, 1861
Roman, Levi	Nancy Adkins	Feb. 28, 1839
Roman, William	Nancy Smith	Jan. 19, 1836
Roman, William, Jr.	Nancy Smith	Sept. 19, 1836
Rose, Reece	Aggie Adkins	Sept. 11, 1823
Ross, Reece A.	Isabel Anderson	Sept. 9, 1830
Rowe, Charles	Pricie Justice	Sept. 22, 1828
Rowe, Charles	Catherine Rowe	Nov. 21, 1849
Rowe, Francis M.	Frances Hurley	July 20, 1865
Rowe, Franklin	Lettie Ratliff	Apr. 29, 1841
Rowe, Henderson	Nancy P. Thornsberry	Dec. 1, 1859
Rowe, Huffman	Malissa Slone	Jan. 21, 1850
Rowe, James	Aggie Mays	Jan. 8, 1824
Rowe, John	Polly Hammond	Sept. 9, 1824
Rowe, John	Sarah Slone	July 4, 1844
Rowe, John	Polly Lane	Mar. 24, 1850
Rowe, Lloyd	Wyrena Adkins	Dec. 8, 1849

Groom	Bride	Date of Marriage
Rowe, Reuben	Sarah Eppling	June 8, 1861
Rowe, Robert	Hannah Slone	July 19, 1854
Rowe, Solomon	Melvina Breeding	Jan. 17, 1845
Rowe, Stephen	Jane Breeding	Apr. 13, 1832
Rowe, Stephen	Frances May	Sept. 20, 1846
Rowe, Stephen	Winnie Columbia Slone	May 25, 1853
Rowe, Stephen, Jr.	Polly Branham	Nov. 9, 1854
Ruffman, Elias	Nancy Phillips	Nov. 1, 1827
Runyon, Adam, Jr.	Martha Harris	Sept. 10, 1825
Runyon, Adam	Waltha Aldridge	Sept. 14, 1839
Runyon, Addon?	Jennie Maynard	Dec. 23, 1824
Runyon, Alex	Sarah Starr	July 2, 1827
Runyon, Asa	Sarah Smith	Dec. 13, 1851
Runyon, George	Juda Maynard	Dec. 11, 1865
Runyon, Harvey	Polly Stotts	Apr. 15, 1831
Runyon, Henry, Jr.	Polly Blackburn	Sept. 5, 1841
Runyon, John C.	Reecie Bevins	Aug. 5, 1852
Runyon, Mitchell	Margaret Taylor	Jan. 6, 1848
Runyon, Thomas	Millie Havens	June 19, 1856
Runyon, Thomas H.	Permelia E. Lowe	June 10, 1860
Runyon, William	Polly Maynard	June 3, 1830
Russell, Henry	Louvina Adkins	July 9, 1857
Rutherford, ...	Isabel Canada	May 14, 1846

S

Groom	Bride	Date of Marriage
Salisberry, Hiram	Nancy Owen Hall	July 23, 1833
Salisberry, Lackey	Margaret Justice	Apr. 20, 1848
Salisberry, W. T.	Susanna M. J. Keathley	Nov. 15, 1865
Sanders, Charles	Mary Elizabeth McGee	July 5, 1865
Sanders, Granville	Rhoda Potter	Jan. 15, 1845
Sanders, Elisha	Ollie Adkins	May 21, 1831
Sanders, Ichabod	Elizabeth Francisco	Feb. 5, 1849
Sanders, Jacob	Louisa Gillespie	Mar. 10, 1858
Sanders, Jacob	Mahulda Ison	May 26, 1861
Sanders, John	P. Baldridge	Apr. 6, 1844
Sanders, William	Nancy Ramey	Dec. 24, 1856
Sandridge, John E.	Elizabeth Miller	June 27, 1847
Sansom, James	Cloe Chapman	Jan. 2, 1823
Sansom, John	Paulina Stafford	May 5, 1833
Sayers, Augustus B.	Rhoda Justice	May 24, 1855
Scarberry, David	Eleanor Estep	Aug. 5, 1852
Scarberry, John	Mary Carter	Dec. 24, 1860
Scarberry, Robin	Polly Smith	Feb. 25, 1849
Scarberry, William	Rachael Carter	Jan. 10, 1856
Scott, Andrew	Margaret Pinson	May 13, 1830
Scott, Axton	Ruth Bevins	Oct. 27, 1836
Scott, Daniel	Nancy Stafford	July 10, 1836
Scott, Evan	Martha Ratliff	July 11, 1842
Scott, Henderson	Rebecca Maynard	Sept. 26, 1861
Scott, James	Levina Stafford	Aug. 31, 1843
Scott, James H.	Lydia Bevins	Oct. 30, 1859
Scott, James M.	Emily Retherford	May 17, 1860
Scott, John H.	Harriett Farley	Aug. 29, 1861
Scott, Mitchell	Malinda J. Reynolds	Apr. 30, 1857
Scott, William M.	Kentucky Sowards	Sept. 14, 1860
Scott, William C.	Basheba Retherford	Apr. 1, 1857
Scott, William	Manda M. Stratton	July 7, 1865
Sellards, James	Emaline Shortridge	June 19, 1859

Groom	Bride	Date of Marriage
Setser, James W.	Elvira Dials	June 15, 1854
Sexton, John	Susie Collins	May 26, 1822
Sexton, Jonathan	Mary J. Whitt	June 4, 1865
Shockey, Henry	Rachael Giddens	Oct. 1, 1827
Short, William	Bethany Slone	Nov. 25, 1856
Shortridge, Miles	Jane Hackney	Jan. 23, 1851
Sipple, Leroy B.	Isabel Justice	Dec. 10, 1857
Slater, Jackson	Polly Harris	Sept. 5, 1839
Slater, William	Elizabeth Harris	Dec. 4, 1835
Slone, Archibald	Susan Hobbs	May 28, 1824
Slone, Arch	Nancy Justice	May 15, 1834
Slone, Arch, Jr.	Anna Blackburn	May 11, 1845
Slone, Arch	Mariam Bishop	Aug. 9, 1860
Slone, David	Sallie Maynard	July 2, 1825
Slone, Elijah	Nancy Conway	July 27, 1847
Slone, Elijah	Mary Coleman	Feb. 7, 1860
Slone, Franklin	Margaret Estep	Jan. 31, 1850
Slone, Frederick	Lucinda Bennett	Feb. 23, 1829
Slone, George	Elizabeth Justice	May 18, 1822
Slone, Gordon	Polly Slone	Sept. 23, 1861
Slone, Isham	Charlotte Keen	June 24, 1865
Slone, Ison	Rebecca Anderson	Dec. 23, 1852
Slone, Jacob	Martha Raynes	May 3, 1861
Slone, James	Mary Havens	Aug. 25, 1844
Slone, John	Jane Rowe	Jan. 20, 1848
Slone, John	Winnie Fields	Dec. 17, 1825
Slone, John	Elizabeth Raynes	Mar. 23, 1855
Slone, Mitchell	Mary Justice	Oct. 17, 1844
Slone, Mitchell	Pricie Justice	July 17, 1848
Slone, Morgan	Charlotte Raynes	May 4, 1854
Slone, Morgan	Nellie Slone	June 24, 1858
Slone, Shadrack	Susan Hale	Dec. 30, 1832
Slone, Spencer	Elizabeth Rowe	Mar. 30, 1848
Slone, Spencer	Emily McKinney	Oct. 6, 1859
Slone, William	Margaret Pinson	July 7, 1839
Slone, William	Sally Rowe	May 4, 1826
Slone, William	Martha Adams	May 15, 1853
Slone, William	Polly Terry	Apr. 13, 1857
Smallwood, Elijah	Mary Ratliff	Oct. 22, 1840
Smiley, Alex A.	Sarah Justice	Nov. 11, 1847
Smiley, Fred A.	Rhoda A. Bishop	Sept. 18, 1856
Smith, Aaron	Jane Justice	July 24, 1842
Smith, Aaron	Elizabeth Slone	Dec. 28, 1865
Smith, Absolom	Katy Hinager	July 4, 1827
Smith, Absolom	Kate Blankenship	Nov. 28, 1830
Smith, Callahan	Sarah Phillips	Apr. 3, 1856
Smith, Charles	Sarah Lykins	July 20, 1848
Smith, David	Melvina Prewitt	May 14, 1851
Smith, Frederick	Perlina Young	Nov. 3, 1853
Smith, George	Elizabeth Daugherty	Apr. 4, 1850
Smith, George W.	Amy Reece	Apr. 13, 1865
Smith, Harrison	Mary Ann Casey	Nov. 9, 1865
Smith, Hawkins F.	Mary Taylor	Dec. 6, 1860
Smith, Henry	Matilda Owens	Aug. 1, 1833
Smith, Henry	Mahala Elliott	Apr. 26, 1838
Smith, Henry	Lucretia Bevins	Apr. 21, 1847
Smith, Isaac	Mary Ann Coleman	Aug. 17, 1837
Smith, Isaac	Mahala Alexander	Sept. 20, 1849
Smith, Isaac	Rachael Edmonds	Apr. 1, 1855

Groom	Bride	Date of Marriage
Smith, Isiah	Ure ? West	Oct. 28, 1852
Smith, Isiah	Villa West	Mar. 19, 1857
Smith, Jacob	Lucinda Lawson	Dec. 13, 1839
Smith, Jacob	Jane Stanley	Apr. 3, 1855
Smith, James	Delila Hylton	Mar. 25, 1838
Smith, James	Mintie Adkins	Aug. 8, 1841
Smith, James	America West	Feb. 17, 1848
Smith, Jeremiah	Susan Maynard	Aug. 12, 1824
Smith, Jesse	Hester West	Feb. 21, 1850
Smith, John	Kate Charles	May 27, 1827
Smith, John	Dianah Retherford	Nov. 22, 1858
Smith, Jonathan	Lonnemiah Daugherty	Apr. 14, 1850
Smith, Joseph	Sarah Hunt	Mar. 22, 1857
Smith, Martin	Nancy Jane Layne	June 15, 1845
Smith, Martin	Celia Ann Bevins	Feb. 23, 1852
Smith, Milton	Mary Magdaline Edmonds	Dec. 5, 1865
Smith, Richard	Rebecca Ramey	Apr. 18, 1861
Smith, Robert	Elzira Young	Aug. 9, 1855
Smith, Wilburn	Nancy May	Aug. 30, 1855
Smith, William	Elizabeth Ford	Jan. 12, 1865
Southard, Bluford	Charity Damron	July 5, 1854
Southard, James	Louisa Saddler	Dec. 11, 1834
Sowards, Lewis	Ollie Morgan	July 4, 1833
Sowards, Martin	Melvina Mullins	Mar. 4, 1858
Sowards, Morgan C.	Manesuey ? Adkins	June 22, 1865
Sowards, Moses	Louisa Branham	Sept. 7, 1837
Sowards, Thomas	Stella Justice	Jan. 22, 1824
Sparks, Richard	Mary Johnson	Jan. 24, 1849
Sparks, Richard	Rebecca Davis	Mar. 15, 1865
Spears, Arnett C.	Helen Clair	Dec. 19, 1865
Spears, George	Mary Fuller	Dec. 21, 1843
Spotts, Chapman A.	Louisa M. Daugherty	Nov. 3, 1858
Spruce, Ben	Matilda Thacker	Jan. 24, 1824
Spurlock, John	Polly Branham	Oct. 31, 1822
Stacy, Harvey	Levisa Roberts	June 22, 1850
Stacy, Simon	Polly Mullins	Dec. 19, 1850
Stafford, Compton	Eleanor McCoy	May 22, 1833
Stafford, Flemmon	Elizabeth Evans	Aug. 22, 1841
Stafford, Harmon	Mary Jane McCoy	Aug. 16, 1855
Stafford, John	Louisa Spratt	July 12, 1830
Stafford, Montreville	Mary Ann Farley	Mar. 27, 1832
Stafford, Thomas	Jane Staten	Mar. 21, 1861
Stair, John	Juliet Taylor	July 9, 1839
Stanley, Claiborne	Susan McCown	Sept. 26, 1833
Stanley, John L.	Sarah Scarberry	July 28, 1847
Stanley, John R.	Nancy Justice	Aug. 30, 1865
Stanley, Joseph	Nancy Crabtree	Nov. 12, 1846
Stanley, Joseph P.	Jane Justice	Aug. 18, 1859
Stanley, Rickles?	Delania Kirk	Aug. 10, 1836
Stanley, William	Sarah Ann Scott	Dec. 1, 1853
Stapleton, David	Polly Potter	Jan. 12, 1859
Stark, Fielding	Louisa Draper	May 2, 1850
Starr, James	E. Cantrell	Apr. 22, 1855
Starr, Sam	Nancy Hensley	Mar. 10, 1846
Staten, Avery	Levisa Varney	June 24, 1860
Staten, Booker	Levisa Canada	Dec. 30, 1855
Staten, Malachi	Margaret White	Aug. 11, 1833
Staten, Richard	Malinda Bevins	Aug. 3, 1852
Staten, William	Nancy McCoy	July 27, 1834

173

Groom	Bride	Date of Marriage
Steele, Paris	Sarah J. Reynolds	Nov. 30, 1865
Steele, Ralph	Lucy Ferrell	June 29, 1823
Steele, William W.	Elizabeth Dawson	Jan. 23, 1860
Steele, William W.	Mary M. E. May	June 5, 1862
Stepp, Aaron	Parlee Jane Maynard	Dec. 20, 1855
Stepp, David	Rebecca Stair	May 23, 1854
Stepp, James	Elizabeth Bevans	Nov. 16, 1837
Stepp, James	Leaner Maynard	Jan. 10, 1841
Stepp, Robert	Charity Maynard	Dec. 4, 1843
Stepp, Thomas	Charity Runyon	Oct. 26, 1865
Stewart, Robert B.	Peggy Robinson	Mar. 26, 1832
Stewart, Thomas	S. Lunce	Oct. 24, 1841
Stilton, David	Nancy Prichett	July 25, 1826
Stilton, Elijah	Lettie Zettie Elswick	Oct. 26, 1837
Stone, Buckawin	Sarah Fields	Mar. 7, 1852
Stone, Lewis	Pernetta Reed	June 12, 1845
Stone, Moses D.	Pricilla Ratliff	June 4, 1858
Stotts, John, Jr.	Elizabeth Cox	May 6, 1822
Stovall, George	Garlena Huffman	Oct. 25, 1859
Stratton, Harry	Martha McGuire	Feb. 26, 1829
Stratton, Harry	Anna Adkins	Dec. 21, 1843
Stratton, Hezekiah	Nancy A. Ross	Oct. 18, 1855
Stratton, Hiram	Mary Pinson	Sept. 2, 1834
Stratton, John S.	Malissa Ellen Burk	June 15, 1853
Stratton, Milton	Martha B. Leslie	Sept. 17, 1829
Stratton, Richard	Susan Howard	Aug. 17, 1853
Stratton, Tandy	Millie King	May 27, 1862
Stratton, William	Dicie Spurlock	Apr. 3, 1824
Stratton, William H.	Nancy J. Hensley	Feb. 5, 1856
Stratton, William H. H.	Lucinda Ross	May 23, 1861
Stump, George	Elizabeth Williams	Dec. 31, 1840
Stump, George	Rebecca Bevins	Aug. 23, 1865
Sturgill, Blackburn	Lucinda Clay	Feb. 17, 1845
Sturgill, Eli	Belinda Clark	May 28, 1845
Sturgill, Elijah	Ruth Mollett?	Jan. 16, 1834
Sturgill, Lewis	Hulda Damron	July 29, 1847
Sturgill, William	Rebecca Gilliam	Nov. 20, 1860
Sweeney, James	Sally Ratliff	Nov. 23, 1829
Swinney, Joshua	Martilda McCown	Feb. 4, 1850
Swinney, Riley	Catherine Cavins	Aug. 11, 1853
Sweeney, Riley	Causby Gibson	May 29, 1859
Sweeney, Spencer	Mary Moore	Dec. 6, 1855
Sword, Francis	Susan Clark	Mar. 13, 1823
Sword, Francis M.	Mary Robinson	Jan. 15, 1853
Sword, Henry	Polly May	Sept. 1, 1825
Sword, James	Cena Compton	July 17, 1848
Sword, John W.	Matilda Clay	Apr. 1, 1861
Sword, Lucas	Malinda Robinson	June 5, 1828
Sword, L. B.	Mary Ann Miller	Dec. 6, 1858
Sword, Richard	Phoebe Hall	Feb. 26, 1844
Sword, Richard P.	Susan Lycans	Nov. 22, 1859
Sword, William J.	Mrs. Pricie M. Herrington	Oct. 1, 1854
Sword, William H. H.	Crissa Robinson	July ...., 1860
Sword, William	Crissie Ramley?	Mar. 25, 1841
Syck, Jacob	Polly Ratliff	Oct. 17, 1832
Syck, Jacob	Nancy Taylor	Oct. 14, 1865
Syck, James	Sarah Maynard	Aug. 24, 1843
Syck, Richard	Sarah Gannon	Sept. 8, 1859
Syck, William	Elender Clevenger	Oct. 19, 1837

Groom	Bride	Date of Marriage

T

Groom	Bride	Date of Marriage
Tackett, Abel	Rebecca Caudill	Feb. 22, 1855
Tackett, Benjamin	Sarah Adkins	Jan. 16, 1856
Tackett, Greenville	Rebecca Hall	May 6, 1854
Tackett, George	Hannah Osborn	May 11, 1823
Tackett, George	Rachael Caudill	Sept. 9, 1855
Tackett, George	Eliza Kinney	July 30, 1858
Tackett, Harvey	Mary Ann Kinney	Apr. 19, 1855
Tackett, Hiram	Elizabeth Newsom	Dec. 8, 1850
Tackett, Isaac	Juda Mullins	Nov. 3, 1840
Tackett, James	Delila Osborn	Dec. 5, 1850
Tackett, John	Elizabeth Leadenham	Aug. 17, 1828
Tackett, Joshua	Elizabeth Mullins	June 25, 1840
Tackett, Moses	Peggy Dicie Osborn	Apr. 17, 1831
Tackett, Philip	Charity Branham	Apr. 4, 1836
Tackett, Solomon	Angeline Robinson	Dec. 25, 1848
Tackett, Solomon	Mariba Hall	May 6, 1854
Tackett, Tapley	Elizabeth Hamilton	Jan. 23, 1845
Tackett, William	Sallie Caudill	Mar. 2, 1828
Tackett, William	Sarah Osborn	Jan. 22, 1846
Tackett, William	Nancy Robinson	May ...., 1849
Taylor, Allen	Jemima Prewitt	Oct. 28, 1837
Taylor, Alvis	Savinia Smith	Aug. 15, 1859
Taylor, Azandrions	Sarah Vance	Jan. 12, 1837
Taylor, Azander	Cynthia Ann Taylor	June 13, 1853
Taylor, Benjamin	Elizabeth Burgett	Jan. 5, 1854
Taylor, Burgess	Fannie Hardin	Aug. 5, 1822
Taylor, Dary?	Letha Miller	July 21, 1865
Taylor, Henry	Elizabeth Maynard	Mar. 29, 1855
Taylor, James	Lucretia Wuson	Sept. 23, 1832
Taylor, James	Isabel Maynard	Jan. 6, 1862
Taylor, Jesse	Frankie Lucas	Jan. 2, 1823
Taylor, John	Cynthia Maynard	Sept. 29, 1832
Taylor, John H.	T. J. Phillips	Sept. 16, 1860
Taylor, John	Mary Dean	June 19, 1843
Taylor, Kelsey	Mary A. Collinsworth	Mar. 8, 1855
Taylor, Nathaniel	Louisa Nichols	Feb. 2, 1854
Taylor, William	Sally Slone	June 10, 1832
Taylor, William	Nancy Hunt	Feb. 13, 1862
Terry, Friend L.	Emily Rowe	Nov. 13, 1836
Thacker, Absolom	Polly Slone	Mar. 30, 1845
Thacker, Elisha	Florinda Justice	Dec. 7, 1837
Thacker, Emmanuel	Eleanor Thacker	Jan. 15, 1851
Thacker, Ferrell	Mary A. Chaney	Jan. 22, 1865
Thacker, George	Sarah Parsons	Dec. 4, 1851
Thacker, Greenville	Dorcas Adkins	May 3, 1848
Thacker, Greenville	Lyddia Conway	Aug. 17, 1865
Thacker, Joseph	Martha E. Black	Feb. 19, 1855
Thacker, Joseph	Elizabeth Robinson	Aug. 14, 1865
Thacker, John	Emily Adkins	Aug. 18, 1836
Thacker, John A.	Nancy Ann Stanley	Feb. 24, 1852
Thacker, John	Malinda Blackburn	Feb. 14, 1839
Thacker, Randolph	Patsy Adkins	...., 1831
Thacker, Reuben	Malinda Justice	Sept. 4, 1828
Thacker, Reuben, Jr.	Artie Justice	Sept. 20, 1865
Thacker, Thomas	Polly Parsons	Mar. 15, 1861
Thacker, William	Ruth Adkins	Sept. 2, 1841
Thompson, Albert	Mary Stratton	July 24, 1855
Thompson, James	Cynthia Jane Chapman	Mar. 24, 1849

Groom	Bride	Date of Marriage
Thompson, John	Sally Slater	Apr. 17, 1828
Thompson, Samuel	Sarah Ann Syck	Aug. 2, 1855
Thompson, Will	Mary White	Jan. 20, 1849
Thompson, William	America Mills	July 14, 1848
Thompson, Willis	Nancy Whitt	Dec. 21, 1849
Thompson, William	Nancy Helvey	Oct. 17, 1827
Thornsberry, James M.	Mary Jane Stump	Aug. 23, 1860
Thornsberry, John	Elizabeth Polly (Pauley)	Feb. 15, 1838
Thornsberry, Levi	Lottie Ford	July 23, 1843
Thornsberry, Martin	Nancy Campbell	Aug. 12, 1852
Thornsberry, Walter	Mary Childers	Sept. 2, 1852
Thorp, William	Mary Cole	Dec. 22, 1839
Tiller, William	Rachael Ferrell	July 8, 1832
Totten, William	Nancy Russell	May 5, 1839
Trent, Humphrey	Martha Smith	June 15, 1865
Trout, Charles	Jane Damron	July 20, 1837
Trout, Stephen	Maria Hunt	Aug. 26, 1853

V

Vance, Alex	Millie Justice	Jan. 29, 1861
Vanover, Cornelius	Peggy Johnson	Dec. 23, 1841
Vanover, William	Sarah Ann Estep	Dec. 21, 1849
Varney, Alexander	Susan Payne	Jan. 2, 1853
Varney, Alex	Louisa Pinson	Dec. 6, 1860
Varney, Andrew	Nancy Retherford	Mar. 1, 1838
Varney, Asa	Loyisa Retherford	July 15, 1851
Varney, Francis	Polly Williamson	Mar. 17, 1839
Varney, Henry	Lydia Blackburn	Apr. 13, 1865
Varney, John	Anna Roman	Sept. 5, 1833
Varney, Madison	Piety Staten	June 6, 1852
Varney, William Anderson	Jane Blackburn	Apr. 6, 1856
Venters, George Martin	Susanna Clevenger	Jan. 1, 1845
Venters, John	Elizabeth Clevenger	Jan. 4, 1844

W

Wadkins, John N.	Lyddia Jane Ratliff	Oct. 5, 1865
Waggoner, Tobias	Caroline M. Price	Oct. 19, 1858
Walker, Joseph G.	America Sowards	Aug. 1, 1861
Walker, William A.	Rebecca Bevins	May 8, 1861
Wallace, Levi	Elizabeth Francis	Mar. 3, 1861
Walters, Wilburn	Mary Sword	July 1, 1856
Walters, Zachariah	Peggy Owens	Jan. 3, 1825
Walton, Lorenzo	Mary Jane Nunner	Apr. 1, 1847
Weddington, Henry	Susan Ratliff	July 3, 1860
Weddington, Jacob	Therry Hunt	Mar. 6, 1845
Weddington, Jacob	Nancy Smith	Jan. 15, 1860
Weddington, John T.	Hannah Meade	June 6, 1836
Weddington, William	Polly Meade	Jan. 27, 1828
Weddington, William	Susanna Ratliff	Sept. 11, 1856
Weddington, William J.	Frances Tibbs	Feb. 13, 1865
Wemerer, ? Samuel	Polly Smith	Oct. 1, 1836
West, Greenville	Celia Smith	July 27, 1850
White, Arthur	Rebecca Millard	Jan. 22, 1824
White, Harrison	Elizabeth Murphy	Feb. 18, 1861
White, Henley	Polly Jane Rowe	Aug. 2, 1859
White, John	Hannah Osborn	Sept. 26, 1839
White, John D.	Rebecca Howell	Dec. 5, 1850

Groom	Bride	Date of Marriage
Whitt, Merida	Sallie Adkins	July 18, 1822
Whitt, William	Nancy Blackburn	Sept. 11, 1853
Whitt, John	Polly Lewis	Apr. 11, 1830
Williams, Achilles	Nancy McCoy	May 15, 1845
Williams, James T.	Palina Hensley	Sept. 26, 1836
Williams, William, Jr.	Selby R. Sword	Mar. 30, 1848
Williamson, Ben	Susanna Walker	Mar. 12, 1835
Williamson, Elijah	Jane King	May 30, 1824
Williamson, Hibbard	Caroline Ratliff	Nov. 12, 1856
Williamson, John	Charlotte Lowe	Oct. 20, 1839
Williamson, John M.	Nancy Jewell	Feb. 25, 1841
Williamson, John M.	Charlotte Millard	July 31, 1851
Williamson, Jonah	Mary Ann Bevins	Nov. 3, 1853
Williamson, Joseph	Sarah Ray	Feb. 11, 1859
Williamson, Moses	Elizabeth Jones	Feb. 5, 1850
Williamson, Richard	Susanna Miller	Sept. 13, 1835
Wilson, Asa	Nancy Hatfield	June 17, 1861
Wilson, Harvey	Sallie Carter	Apr. 20, 1846
Wilson, Thomas M.	Barbara McColley	July 20, 1838
Wingo, James	Nancy Ann Stratton	Apr. 9, 1851
Wolfington, Jerry H.	Sarah Branham	Aug. 5, 1847
Wolford, Andrew	Elender Hurley	June 7, 1849
Wolford, Daniel	Sarah Dotson	May 4, 1851
Wolford, Frederick	Peggy Mounts	Aug. 23, 1849
Wolford, George	Abigail Coleman	July 9, 1837
Wolford, George	Sarah Prater	June 7, 1849
Wolford, John	Keziah Davis	Mar. 16, 1837
Wooten, Jordan	Dorcas Wuson	Apr. 20, 1823
Wooten, Silas	Elizabeth Williamson	Aug. 12, 1827
Wuson, Ben	Esther Deskins	May 8, 1829
Wuson, Ben	Mary Smith	Aug. 25, 1836
Wuson, Braxton	Hulda Adkins	Mar. 4, 1830
Wuson, Ferrell	Sarah Pinson	Aug. 28, 1845
Wuson, Franklin	Louisa Mart	Nov. 11, 1841
Wuson, Freeman	Matilda Scott	Feb. 1, 1855
Wuson, Hammon, Jr.	Anna Bevins	Oct. 14, 1830
Wuson, Hammond	Nancy Jane Burnett	Oct. 5, 1865
Wuson, Hibbard	Polly Ann Walters	Sept. 29, 1842
Wuson, Hiram M.	Matilda Jane Maynard	July 6, 1858
Wuson, James	Polly Millard	July 11, 1843
Wuson, James H.	Mary Boyer	Mar. 15, 1854
Wuson, James H.	Sarah Jane Hunt	Apr. 15, 1865
Wuson, James W.	Eliza Blackburn	May 5, 1861
Wuson, Jeremiah	Mary Ann Parsons	Aug. 27, 1855
Wuson, Jeremiah	Nancy Blackburn	Mar. 30, 1859
Wuson, John	Ann Bevins	Oct. 16, 1834
Wuson, John II.	Jemima Bevins	Oct. 14, 1843
Wyrick, Harvey	Elizabeth Hunt	about 1848

Y

Yates, Richard	Pricie Polly (Pauley)	about 1850
Yonts, William	Nancy Ray	Jan. 21, 1830
Young, George W.	Sarah Burgett	July 9, 1861
Young, James E.	Elizabeth Smith	Apr. 22, 1860
Young, John	Nancy Ann Mary Jane Clevenger	Mar. 19, 1850
Young, John	Elizabeth Cravens	Aug. 22, 1860

CHAPTER VIII

CARTER COUNTY, KENTUCKY

FORMATION

CARTER COUNTY, the 88th in order of establishment, was formed in 1838 from Greenup and Lawrence Counties and was named in honor of Colonel William Grayson Carter, the then State Senator in the Kentucky Legislature from the district composed of the Counties of Lewis, Greenup and Lawrence. (See Carter Family). Grayson, the seat of justice, was named for Colonel Robert Grayson, uncle to Colonel William Grayson Carter. (See Grayson Family).

SETTLEMENT

The exact period of the first settlement of what is now Carter County is not certainly known. It is generally believed to have been about 1808 at the Sandy River salines near present Grayson by persons engaged in making salt, the most prominent of whom was Captain Thomas Scott of Lexington, Kentucky, who died in 1870, aged 93. At these works considerable quantities of salt was made at one time and transported to market by wagons over the Lexington turnpike to the towns of the blue grass region and by flatboats down the Little Sandy River to the Ohio.

EARLIEST AVAILABLE COURT ORDER

March Term 1846.

At a county court commenced and held in and for Carter County in Grayson at the Court House March the 9th 1846. Present: James McGuire, Harris W. Thompson, Hiram S. Booten, Thomas Williams, Thomas Scott, James Offill, Gent (lemen) justices.

Thomas Williams this day produced a commission from the Governor of this Commonwealth appointing [him] justice of the peace for this county with a certificate of qualification thereon endorsed, and thereupon he took his seat as a justice of this court.

This day Charles W. Honaker produced a commission from the Governor of this Commonwealth appointing him sheriff of this county, and thereupon he, together with Jackson B. Ward, George W. Ward, George W. Biggs, Samuel Everman, Jacob Kibbey, Benjamin F. Crawford, George W. Crawford and Charles N. Lewis, his sureties, entered into and acknowledged two bonds conditioned according to law and took the oath required by law.

On motion of Charles W. Honaker, sheriff of this county, Charles N. Lewis was introduced and sworn as his deputy.

Ordered that it be certified to the Governor of this Commonwealth that John Plummer and Jacob Kibbey are recommended as fit persons to fill the office of justice of peace in this county in the place of Charles W. Honaker who is commissioned and sworn as high sheriff of this county, a majority of all the justices in commission being present and concurring therein.

Ordered that court adjourn till court in course.

[Signed] Z. Tyree.

MARRIAGES 1838—1853

Earliest marriage records, Carter County, from organization of county in 1838 to 1853.

Groom	Bride	Date	By Whom

A

Armstrong, William	Susan Nethercutt	Dec. 15, 1843	Daniel Carroll
Adams, Charles	Sarah Bays	Oct. 8, 1846	Elder Rufus Humphreys
Adams, Thomas	Martha Selvage	June 13, 1849	H. S. Booten
Armstrong, James H.	Eliza Jane Watson	Nov. 6, 1851	Elzaphan Rucker
Alexander, Robert	Minerva Fannin	July 8, 1851	Archibald Rice
Adams, Sylvester	Jane Bays	Oct. 8, 1852	Elzaphan Rucker
Alexander, William	Sarah Jane Prince	May 9, 1848	H. S. Booten
Amis (Amos), John	Mary Ann Evans	Oct. 13, 1852	C. H. Stewart

B

Burton, Henderson	Rosa B. Sexton	Apr. 14, 1839	Archibald Rice
Buckner, George	Millie Pruitt	Mar. 31, 1839	Zachariah Hale
Boggs, Harrison	Jacintha Buckner	July 11, 1841	Zachariah Hale
Beckwith, Arthur C.	Louisa Duncan	May 26, 1842	Philip Strother
Bare (Baer), Ambrose A.	Mahala Skaggs	Sept. 9, 1843	D. Carroll
Buckner, James	Sarah Rose	....	Zachariah Tyree
Barker, William	Minnie Holbrook	Aug. 26, 1843	Elder J. T. Wilburn
Brinegar, Gova	Patsy Henderson	Oct. 24, 1844	Zachariah Tyree
Brammer, William	Polly Ann Offill	Jan. 9, 1844	Z. Tyree
Broadburn, Jackson	Jane Alexander	Apr. 10, 1845	Z. Tyree
Bush, William	Anna McGlone	Dec. 31, 1846	Thomas Abrams
Byrd, Thomas J.	Levina DeHart	Dec. 23, 1846	Z. Tyree
Brumfield, Floyd	Rebecca Loots (Luts)	Oct. 16, 1849	A. Rice
Bradford, William	Jaybidda Bellew	Sept. 30, 1847	E. Rucker
Blankenship, William	Amanda B. Dawson	Nov. 9, 1847	Archibald Rice
Bradshaw, George	Sarah Jane Bradford	Dec. 12, 1848	Philip Strother

Groom	Bride	Date	By Whom
Bocook, John	Eliza Jane Henderson	Feb. 17, 1848	Philip Strother
Black, Benjamin C.	Ann L. Thompson	Dec. 5, 1848	Philip Strother
Blankenship, Obediah	Elizabeth Thomas	Apr. 8, 1849	Daniel Trout
Baer, Reuben	Mary Mullins	May 26, 1850	P. Humphreys
Bench, Oliver	Martha Chapman	Apr. 22, 1850	Z. Tyree
Biggs, Benjamin	Louisa Tanner	Oct. 16, 1850	Z. Tyree
Brown, William A.	Margaret J. Alexander	Dec. 25, 1851	Z. Tyree
Baker, Tipton	Margaret Wilburn	Mar. 1, 1851	S. Rice
Brodburn, John	Evaline Keathley	Dec. 26, 1850	John A. Short
Blankenship, Johnson	Jemima Kibbey	Apr. 9, 1844	P. Strother
Boggs, Hugh	Rebecca Cox	Jan. 9, 1853	
Boggs, Whit	Martha Ellen Jessee	June 10, 1872	
Boggs, Ephraim	Sarah A. Counts	Dec. 27, 1871	

C

Clark, Joseph	Mary Thomas	Apr. 30, 1840	Archibald Rice
Campbell, Thomas M.	Nancy Williams	Sept. 3, 1840	J. B. Lawhun
Clain, John	Telithia Swim	Feb. 8, 1841	Z. Tyree
Carver, Morgan	Lettie Johnson	Apr. 12, 1841	Z. Tyree
Crawford, B. F.	Mary Elizabeth Burks	June 27, 1843	P. Strother
Clark, Isaac	Lucinda Howard	Apr. 24, 1842	Z. Tyree
Clark, Joseph	Jane Watson	June 30, 1843	Elzaphan Rucker
Cooper, Cyrus	Cynthia Stamper	Mar. 14, 1844	Z. Tyree
Conley, Elijah	Nancy Jones	Sept. 26, 1844	James Lampton
Carroll, Nelson	Angeline Harper	Feb. 13, 1845	Daniel Carroll
Cannifax, Calvin	Reecie R. Duncan	Mar. 24, 1848	H. S. Booten
Cole, Jeremiah	Polly Rice	May 12, 1849	H. S. Booten
Carpenter, Fielding	Mary E. W. Rister	May 19, 1849	J. B. Lawhun
Cooley, John	Millie Cozzell	Apr. 16, 1849	
Cook, Joel	Eliza M. Carver	Nov. 8, 1850	Z. Tyree
Coburn, James	Fannie Robertson	Mar. 1, 1851	A. Rice
Colegrove, Edwin	Sidney, Crone	Nov. 18, 1851	D. Carroll
Combs, Wylie	Polly Fields	Jan. 26, 1851	D. Duff

D

Dawson, Henry	Nancy Hall	Aug. 25, 1844	Jas. Lampton, J. P.
Devore, John	Martha Nunnelly	Aug. 26, 1847	Philip Strother
Davis, Benjamin F.	Pamelia Williams	July 4, 1848	Z. Tyree
Dismore, Fletcher	Nancy Ann Brammer	Sept. 8, 1848	Z. Tyree
Day, John L.	Eliza Richards		
Duff, Daniel	Ellender Roe	Mar. 16, 1851	R. Humphreys
Duncan, John W.	Judith Burton	Oct. 16, 1851	Jas. H. Wright
Dean, Clifton	Susan D. Rucker	Jan. 1, 1852	
Darnell, William R.	Nancy E. Taylor	Feb. 10, 1852	E. Rucker
Dean, John S.	Martha S. Everman	Oct. 28, 1847	P. Strother
Davis, W. A.	Castaria Prichard	Feb. 27, 1872	
Duly, John Z.	Hebe S. Hord	Nov. 29, 1855	

Groom	Bride	Date	By Whom

E

Enochs, Alfred	Mary Ann Miller	Nov. 18, 1838	A. Sanders
Everman, Elzy	Evaline Plummer	Mar. 2, 1840	J. B. Lawhun
Elliott, George	Mary Ann		
	Brammer	May 1, 1843	E. Howard
Erwin, Thomas	Martha Stamper	Dec. 1, 1844	Z. Tyree
Evans, Ralph	Mildred F. Locker	Aug. 15, 1847	Barabus F. Kinder
Eastham, John	Elizabeth Davis	Apr. 5, 1848	Caleb F. Hill
Ernest, David	Jane Kidd	June 10, 1849	Joel Cook
Everman, Jacob	Elizabeth Dearing	Jan. 26, 1850	D. Duff
England, William J.	Rebecca S. Everman	Mar. 22, 1851	P. Thorpe
Elliott, William K.	Delilia A. Vincent	Feb. 28, 1856	
Elliott, Ben.	Nancy Kegley	Aug. 12, 1858	
Elliott, John M.	Phoebe E. Horton	Sept. 19, 1860	
Elliott James H.	Callie S. King	Feb. 11, 1868	

F

Fults, Joseph	Elizabeth Smith	Nov. 22, 1838	J. B. Lauhun
Fults, Wesley	Sylva Stamper	Jan. 28, 1840	J. B. Lauhun
Fraley, Wilson	Priscilla Fults	Dec. 24, 1846	R. Humphreys
Fisher, William R.	Mary J. Kirk	Apr. 25, 1848	John Fannin
Fannin, John	Sarah McGlone	Jan. 12, 1849	Z. Tyree
Fults, Arthur	Rachel Presley	Sept. 25, 1850	D. Carroll
Fannin, Burrell	Nancy Stamper	Dec. 19, 1850	
Frayler, Greenberry	Margarite Rice	Oct. 8, 1850	Samuel Kibby
Fisher, Alfred	Rebecca Wallace	July 30, 1850	D. Duff
Fannin, Joseph	Mary Mullins	Feb. 25, 1851	D. Duff
Fults, Hezekiah	Matilda Fannin	Dec. 18, 1851	Z. Tyree
Flannagin, Valentine	Mary James	Dec. 8, 1851	P. Strother
Fisher, Joseph	Susan Kirk	Sept. 13, 1851	P. Thorp
Fields, James M.	Mary Ann Boggs	Dec. 19, 1852	Elzaphan Rucker
Filson, Ulysses P. C.	Grace McIntyre	Mar. 25, 1847	Z. Tyree

G

Glover, Thomas J.	Margaret Lambert	May 7, 1841	Jos. Fannin
Gilkey, David	Margaret Bellomy	Dec. 10, 1843	P. Strother
Gully, James	Martha Ann Evans	Feb. 2, 1843	Z. Tyree
Gallion, Jonathan	Elizabeth Adkins	Oct. 5, 1843	A. Rice
Gillum, Zachariah	Amelia Buckner	June 23, 1845	Z. Tyree
Gullett, Daniel	Nancy Jane Thomas	Jan. 7, 1848	A. Rice
Gilbert, John	Dorcas Cornett	Mar. 20, 1848	P. Strother
Griffey (Griffith), Huston	Martha Jones	Dec. 28, 1848	Z. Tyree
Gillum, Charles	Odanna Fraley	Feb. 4, 1849	R. Humphreys
Gilbert, Samuel	Nancy Jacobs	Sept. 1, 1849	H. S. Booten
Goodin, C. P.	Rebecca Stafford	Aug. 5, 1850	P. Strother
Gillum, James	Delilah Patrick		
Gee, Robert	Celetha Jacobs	Dec. 25, 1860	

H

| Henderson, James H. | Margaret Henderson | Sept. 27, 1838 | A. Sanders |
| Horton, Travis | Rebecca Cox | Dec. 24, 1841 | D. Carroll |

Groom	Bride	Date	By Whom
Horsley, James	Elizabeth Broomfield	Apr. 10, 1843	Z. Tyree
Harris, L. T.	Mary J. Elliott	Oct. 31, 1843	D. Carroll
Hall, James	Susan Lusk	Feb. 15, 1843	A. Rice
Ham, James H.	Sarah Gosvens	Sept. 20, 1843	E. Rucker
Hensley, Stephen	Sally M. Murphy	Aug. 13, 1843	Eli Howard
Hicks, Nathan	Ruth Sherman	Mar. 19, 1844	John J. Wallace
Hall, James	Matilda Fraley	Mar. 6, 1844	J. J. Wallace
Hunter, Squire H.	Polly Ann Adams	Aug. 31, 1845	R. Humphreys
Hensley, John	Crecyann Coburn	May 13, 1847	P. Strother
Howard, David J.	Jemima DeHart	Sept. 1, 1847	Z. Tyree
Holbrook, Robert	Frances Holbrook	Feb. 18, 1848	R. Humphreys
Howard, Roley M.	Jemima Jones	May 26, 1848	Z. Tyree
Holbrook, Jesse	Mary Holbrook	Oct. 26, 1848	R. Humphreys
Huntsman, James E.	Ellender Littleton	Jan. 5, 1848	Phores Thorp
Hall, Elkanah	Elizabeth Savage	Dec. 19, 1849	R. Humphreys
Hartley, John	Elizabeth Hartley	Oct. 2, 1849	H. S. Booten
Henderson, Harvey	Elzira Tyree		
Howe, James	Elvaline Pope	June 12, 1850	D. Carroll
Horsley, William	Elizabeth Rhoden	Sept. 28, 1850	Joseph Thorp
Holbrook, John	Louanna Holbrook	Dec. 23, 1850	D. Duff
Hill, Thomas	Delilah McClurg		
Hale, Andrew J.	Mary Ann Jones		
Holbrook, Allen	Nancy McFarland	July 2, 1852	D. Carroll
Hinton, Charles	Clarinda Horsley		
Hicks, John	Heebe Kezee	July 31, 1856	
Horton, James K. P.	Elizabeth Boggs	Oct. 9, 1867	
Horton, John T.	Lovina M. Rice	Sept. 15, 1870	
Horton, Jarvis H.	Talitha E. Mobley	July 29, 1871	
Hilton, Willson P.	Nancy Wright	Apr. 27, 1867	
Hilton, Nathan	Violet Pennington	May 4, 1873	

I

Ison, Isom	Hannah Boggs	Oct. 21, 1849	E. Rucker
Ingram, Sylvanius	Nancy Angeline Bocook	Feb. 7, 1850	Z. Tyree
Irwin, John B.	Susan Ramey	Mar. 26, 1850	Z. Tyree

J

Jordan, Levi	Catharine Brammer	Apr. 21, 1842	Z. Tyree
Jones, Stephen	Nancy Landsdown	Mar. 13, 1842	Z. Tyree
Jones, John	Evaline Jones	Jan. 11, 1843	Z. Tyree
James, John	Margaret Ross	Sept. 5, 1844	Z. Tyree
Jones, Levi H.	Sarah H. Ridgeway	July 22, 1848	Z. Tyree
Jenkins, James	Frances Robinson	May 1, 1849	A. Rice
Jarvis, Solomon	Susan Wallace	May 16, 1849	D. Carroll
Jordan, John	Susan Hall	Feb. 13, 1851	D. Duff
Jefferson, Thomas	Gerusha Lewis	Mar. 6, 1851	R. Humphreys
Johnson, William	Vicie Williams	Dec. 13, 1852	P. Strother
Jacobs, Ira	Martha Gee	Dec. 3, 1856	

K

Kennedy, Milton	Ellender Boggs	Aug. 8, 1842	A. Rice
Kelley, Samuel	Mary Jane Rice	Mar. 11, 1845	Philip Strother
Kitchen, Nehemiah	Martha Fannin	Dec. 3, 1846	L. H. Jones

Groom	Bride	Date	By Whom
Kibbey, William	Mary Scott	June 28, 1847	Wm. P. Read
Keathley, William	Mary Gilbert	Jan. 3, 1849	H. S. Booten
Kelley, John	Nancy Whitt	Sept. 14, 1849	P. Humphreys
Kezee (Kozee), Jesse	Nancy Ward	Jan. 31, 1856	
Kozee, Andrew	Susan Kozee	June 23, 1853	
Kozee, William E.	Dorissa Carnutte	Nov. 12, 1853	
Keesee, Elias	Talitha Jane ˙Savage	July 3, 1856	
Kozee, George W.	Selina Jane (Hylton) Wright	June 5, 1873	
Kitchen, William R.	Nancy E. Shearer	Oct. 11, 1866	
Kitchen, John M.	Mary W. Shearer	June 13, 1871	
King, Elias	Sabrina Bryant	Sept. 22, 1866	
King, John W.	Elizabeth Bledsoe	Dec. 24, 1865	
King, James H.	Louisa Roe	Oct. 2, 1867	
King, Van B.	Nancy Counts	Jan. 8, 1873	
Kibbey, John	Mary L. Morris	Nov. 3, 1858	
Kibbey, William	Edy McGlone	Oct. 30, 1860	

L

Lange (Large), William	Nancy Thompson	June 28, 1840	A. Rice
Litteral, James	Martha Sparks	Mar. 11, 1842	Joel Cook
Lyons, Nathaniel A. P.	Jane Carroll	July 14, 1842	D. Carroll
Lansdown, St. Clair	Nancy Ann Tyree	Apr. 10, 1843	Z. Tyree
Lowe, Alfred N.	Sarilda Baker	Feb. 9, 1845	P. Strother
Long, John H.	Tillie Coburn	Nov. 28, 1846	H. S. Booten
Lunsford, James	Fannie Jones	Nov. 24, 1848	H. S. Booten
Lewis, Edward P.	Nancy Ann Trumbo	Jan. 13, 1848	B. F. Kinder
Lambert, Job	Clarinda Cole	Mar. 31, 1849	John Fannin
Lewis, Jeremiah	Delilah Branham	Feb. 22, 1849	P. Humphrey
Littleton, George T.	Mary Saulsberry	May 13, 1850	Pharis Throp
Lambert, John W.	Sarah A. Plummer	Nov. 15, 1851	Z. Tyree
Lemaster, Zachariah	Edy Yates	Oct. 23, 1851	Z. Tyree
Lewis, Andrew	Hannah Skaggs	Feb. 26, 1864	P. Humphreys
Lewis, Andrew	Juda Branham	Dec. 29, 1851	P. Humphreys

M

Messer, Reuben	Sarah Laws	Jan. 30, 1839	A. Rice
Moore, Nicholas	Nancy Ann Dummit	Apr. 2, 1840	Z. Hale
McFarland, Miles	Hannah Whitt	Dec. 18, 1841	D. Carroll
McClurg, William M.	Lucinda Williams	Dec. 7, 1842	
McGuire, Robert	Margaret Banfield	Dec. 27, 1843	E. Rucker
McGlothlan, Jacob	Margaret J. Swim	Dec. 28, 1843	Z. Tyree
Mullins, Elias	Eleanor Rice	Aug. 28, 1843	Elzaphan Rucker
McDavid, John	Pamelia Armstrong	Jan. 11, 1844	E. Rucker
Mobley, Harris W.	Malinda Lowe	July 17, 1849	D. Carroll
McGuinnis, Thomas	Sarah Lunsford	Oct. 27, 1849	P. Strother
Moore, Forman	Rebecca Hooker	Mar. 22, 1849	H. S. Booten
Manning, Isaac	Louisa Manning	May 1, 1850	Z. Tyree
Mullins, Sampson	Elizabeth Parsons	Mar. 3, 1851	R. Humphreys
McCleese, Thomas	Cynthia Ann Cooper	Aug. 13, 1851	
Mabry, Colvin	Martha Branham	July 10, 1851	R. Humphreys
Moore, Thomas	Sarah Ann Fraley	June 26, 1851	R. Humphreys

Groom	Bride	Date	By Whom
Mowry (Maury), John	Mosing M. Fisher	April 25, 1852	D. Carroll
McSwinney, O. L.	Eliza Stafford	Nov. 10, 1851	Phileas Throap
Mobley, William	Amanda S. Elliott	Dec. 10, 1855	....
Morris, Henry C.	Nancy Burchett	Sept. 3, 1852	....
Morris, Henry C.	Margaret A. Underwood	May 18, 1884	....

N

Nicholas, Benjamin B.	Ann Dickerson	Feb. 1, 1844	James Lampton
Nethercutt, Moses	Catherine Mauk	Oct. 5, 1848	Z. Tyree
Nethercutt, George	Sarah Curnute	Jan. 3, 1850	Z. Tyree

P

Plummer, Reuben	Louisa Virgin	Apr. 16, 1840	Philip Strother
Pennington, James	Dideamay Sturgeon (Sturgill)	Apr. 6, 1843	Daniel Carroll
Prince, Zachariah	Sarilda Jane Hays	Aug. 10, 1846	H. S. Booten
Prince, Thomas	Mary Jacobs	Oct. 8, 1846	A. Rice
Pigot, Eli	Hulda Drake	Aug. 27, 1851	Philip Strother
Parsons, John	Hannah Ann White	May 22, 1851	P. Humphreys

R

Roe, Isom	Ellen H. Gilbert	Mar. 25, 1841	Zachariah Tyree
Rice, W. W.	Martha A. Thompson	May 29, 1842	P. Strother
Richards, J. P.	M. Elliott	Feb. 6, 1842	P. Strother
Richards, Robert	Lucretia Duncan	Dec. 19, 1843	Z. Tyree
Rice, James M., Jr.	Jane Goad	Oct. 30, 1845	A. Rice
Roberts, Joseph	Fanny Smith	July 29, 1847	Thos. Abrams
Reynolds, Pleasant A.	Nancy M. Barker	Aug. 10, 1848	P. Humphreys
Rhoden, William	Rebecca Prewitt	Apr. 5, 1848	L. H. Jones
Rowe, James	Sarah Crone	Aug. 10, 1849	Daniel Carroll
Ray, John W.	Sally Ann Tyree	Mar. 10, 1850	Z. Tyree
Rice, William S.	Mary Haney	June 10, 1851	A. Rice
Raybourn, Enoch R.	Mary Penlam	Dec. 28, 1852	B. J. Kinder
Raybourn, Samuel	Mary Jane Irwin	....	
Rice, William M.	Nancy Rogers	....	
Roe, James H.	Margaret Ann Johnson	Nov. 16, 1852	D. Duff
Riley, Jacob	Susan Cooley	Oct. 13, 1852	N. Moore
Rose, Henderson	Lodisa Whitt	Aug. 31, 1852	P. Humphreys
Rice, A. G.	Phoebe Horton	Sept. 15, 1870	....

S

Smith, William	Catherine Evans	May 29, 1838	J. B. Lawhun
Sherman, William	Cynthiann Fults	Nov. 22, 1838	....
Stewart, Andrew	Rachel Cook	Dec. 25, 1838	Joel Cook
Shearer, Walter	Nancy Rice	July 16, 1840	Philip Strother
Sprinkle, Jacob	Elizabeth DeHart	May 22, 1841	Z. Tyree
Smith, Abraham	Sarah Mullins	Sept. 23, 1841	E. Rucker
Smith, Ambros	Nancy Fults	Mar. 13, 1842	Z. Tyree

Groom	Bride	Date	By Whom
Sparks, James	Susan Whitt	Apr. 13, 1843	J. F. Wilburn
Sparks, Nelson	Margaret Means	Mar. 16, 1843	D. Carroll
Siers, James	Jane Boggs	Dec. 15, 1843	Daniel Carroll
Setters, John	Harriet Ford	Nov. 12, 1843	Z. Tyree
Savage, John	Hannah Oney	July 31, 1843	E. Rucker
Stewart, James	Nancy Thompson	Nov. 20, 1843	A. Rice
Stamper, George	Catherine Dyer	Oct. 24, 1844	Z. Tyree
Sparks, John	Emily Henderson	Feb. 15, 1844	P. Strother
Savage, Isaac M.	Cynthia Ann Stewart	Jan. 25, 1844	A. Rice
Setters, Thompson	Mary Pennington	Feb. 20, 1844	Z. Tyree
Sexton, William	Frances Nipp	Jan. 28, 1844	D. Carroll
Swearingen, William	Frances Hall	Feb. 11, 1845	James Lampton
Stephens, Riley	Jane Stephens	Apr. 5, 1846	P. Strother
Scott, Andrew J.	Rhoda Morris	Apr. 5, 1846	P. Strother
Stewart, H. T.	Arminta Blankenship	June 17, 1847	A. Rice
Stone, Enoch	Polly Horsley	July 24, 1847	H. S. Booten
Swearingen, William	Elizabeth Davis	Sept. 14, 1848	....
Stephens, Daniel	Nancy Stephens	Mar. 26, 1848	P. Humphreys
Stephens, James	Susannah Buckner	July 10, 1849	D. Carroll
Siers, James	Polly Clark	July 8, 1849	Lewis Skaggs
Sparks, Isaac	Mary N. Jones	Feb. 22, 1849	Z. Tyree
Strother, A. S.	Aurena Reeves	Nov. 10, 1850	Z. Tyree
Sadler, Valentine	Mary McCoy	Apr. 23, 1850	A. Rice
Smith, Samuel A.	Rose Ann Zornes	Mar. 4, 1850	Z. Tyree
Shepherd, John T.	Harriet Kibby	Aug. 20, 1850	J. B. Lawhun
Smith, Caswell	Celia Burress	Apr. 21, 1850	Z. Tyree
Savage, James N.	Sarah Bellomy	May 2, 1850	Z. Tyree
Stamper, Jackson	Susan Fannin	Dec. 22, 1850	Z. Tyree
Stone, Ezekiel	Malinda Stafford	Dec. 26, 1850	Z. Tyree
Sparks, Jesse B.	Sarah Falkner	May 25, 1851	D. Duff
Swearnigen, LaFayette	Jane Gilbert	Sept. 23, 1851	B. F. Kinder
Spencer, Henry K.	Mary James	Sept. 13, 1852	John James
Skaggs, Moses W.	Martha J. Fraley	Oct. 28, 1852	P. Humphreys
Sparks, Daniel	Elizabeth Sparks	June 16, 1852	P. Humphreys
Stone, John	Rachel Jordan	Oct. 6, 1852	P. Strother
Swimm, John	Mary A. Knapp	Dec. 21, 1852	H. G. Sweatnam
Sparks, Hugh	Nancy Cornute	Apr. 10, 1852	D. Carroll

T

Thompson, John	Susan Shults	Sept. 9, 1840	Z. Tyree
Taber, Addison, C.	Matilda Henderson	Feb. 1, 1841	Z. Tyree
Tolliver, Hampton	Malinda Stewart	Oct. 11, 1840	Joel Cook
Tanner, John	Levisa W. Millard	Dec. 2, 1850	P. Strother
Triplett, Elijah	Elizabeth Adams	Jan. 1, 1852	E. Rucker
Thompson, Anderson L.	Sarah Watson	Sept. 11, 1852	Z. Hale
Taber, Lauderdale L.	Pamelia Stamper	July 25, 1852	Z. Tyree

U

Underwood, Nelson	Delilah Evans	Nov. 6, 1851	B. F. Kinder

185

Groom	Bride	Date	By Whom

W

Groom	Bride	Date	By Whom
Wooton, Thomas	Nancy Henderson	Dec. 20, 1838	Aaron Sanders
Waugh, William	Louisa Evans	Jan. 13, 1840	J. B. Lawhun
Wilburn, William	Nancy Long	Mar. 8, 1842	E. Rucker
Ward, William	Thursa Virgin	Feb. 19, 1843	P. Strother
Wells, B. F.	Nancy Robinson	July 28, 1843	E. Rucker
Wallace, George	Nancy Johnson	Mar. 4, 1843	Jno. J. Wallace
Walters, Harrison	Polly Skeens	Oct. 26, 1849	P. Strother
Wade, Alfred	Mary Rucker	Aug. 25, 1847	W. P. Read
Williams, Eli	Mary L. Sturgeon	Sept. 19, 1847	P. Humphreys
Ward, Charles L.	Nancy S. Ward	July 19, 1849	P. Strother
Wolfford, Michael	Sarah Ann Rice	June 23, 1849	H. S. Booten
Waugh, Jacob P.	Martha Carroll	Nov. 26, 1850	Z. Tyree
Winegar, John	Elizabeth Wilburn	Apr. 21, 1850	Z. Tyree
Wallace, William	Cynthia Fisher	Aug. 31, 1850	D. Duff
Wooton, Thomas	Eliza Lyons	July 7, 1850	D. Carroll
Williams, Samuel P.	Malinda Lambert	Mar. 10, 1851	Phineas Throap
Wooton, Thomas	Jane Lawhun	Oct. 22, 1851	J. W. Lawhun
Walters, Mathias	Barbara A. Swim	Dec. 22, 1852	D. Duff
Waggoner, Jacob	Nancy Mullins	Nov. 6, 1846	P. Humphreys
Watson, William	Eliza Ann Bush	Jan. 9, 1860	
Wilhoit, Ephraim B.	Alice Frizzell	Aug. 30, 1867	

Z

Groom	Bride	Date	By Whom
Zornes, Martin	Lucinda Horsley	Nov. 28, 1839	J. B. Lawhun
Zornes, Philip	Rachel Zornes	Aug. 12, 1839	J. B. Lawhun

CHAPTER IX

JOHNSON COUNTY, KENTUCKY

EARLIEST AVAILABLE COURT ORDER

Johnson County Court.

June Term 1844.

At a court held for the county of Johnson at the Court House in Paintsville on the 3rd day of June 1844. Present:

"Shaderick" Preston, Elexious Howse, Constantine Conley, John Stafford [and] Francis A. Brown.

* * *

Ordered that John Howse, Clerk of the county, be allowed fifty-eight dollars for books furnished by him in the office which is ordered to [be] certified to the Auditor of Public Accounts for payment.

* * *

On motion of Daniel Hagar, high sheriff of this county, William J. Hagar was sworn as his deputy (sic) according to law.

MARRIAGES 1843—1859

Marriage Records of Johnson County, Kentucky, from organization of county, April, 1843 to 1859, inclusive, giving name of groom, bride, date of marriage, and where of record, name of minister or justice of the peace who performed the ceremony:

Groom	Bride	Date of Marriage	By Whom
A			
Absher, Jacob	Rebecca Collins	June 11, 1848	J. W. Huff, J. P.
Adams, James	Freelove O'Bryan	Nov. 25, 1848	J. W. Huff
Adams, Samuel J.	Mahala Rice	July 27, 1846	
Alley, Robert	Sarah Dixon	July 27, 1853	Isaac Collins
Arrowood, William	Nancy E. Wills	April 21, 1859	
Auxier, Daniel	Lucinda Linthicum	Nov. 13, 1846	M. L. King
B			
Bailey, Allen	Mahala Salyers	Dec. 10, 1855	
Bailey, David	Aggy Lyon	Oct. 17, 1844	
Bailey, James	Mary Magdalene McKenzie	Jan. 25, 1849	H. Jayne
Bailey, John Q. A.	Elizabeth Gullett	Apr. 28, 1851	G. W. Price
Baldwin, Anthony	Sarah Howes	Nov. 30, 1849	H. Rankin
Ball, Jesse	Jane Keith	Oct. 5, 1846	
Ball, William H.	Lucy Jane Castle	Nov. 21, 1856	

Groom	Bride	Date of Marriage	By Whom
Barker, John C.	Catherine Lemaster	Jan. 13, 1859	
Bays, James J.	Rachael Picklesimer	Nov. 6, 1849	J. Picklesimer, Minister of Baptist Church
Bays, Samuel E.	Elizabeth Picklesimer	Oct. 5, 1846	J. Picklesimer
Bays, William G.	Sarah Pelphrey	Aug. 14, 1856	
Blair, Asa J.	Minerva W. Spradlin	Feb. 13, 1853	
Blair, James	Nancy Roberson	July 26, 1847	
Blair, James H.	Mary Horn?	Jan. 24, 1850	E. Howes, Minister M. E. Church
Blair, John	Tabitha Burks	Dec. 24, 1851	Electius Howes
Blair, John	Evaline Conley	July ...., 1855	
Blair, John L.	Jane Caudill	May 4, 1854	
Blair, Wallace	Margaret Hitchcock	Dec. 25, 1856	
Blanton, James	Cynthia Ratcliff	...., 1858	
Blanton, John	Martha Conley	Sept. 10, 1858	
Blanton, Madison T.	Ailsey Blanton	Mar. 10, 1849	
Blanton, Pleasant	Clarinda Salyer	Feb. 23, 1853	
Blanton, William	Mahala Conley	May 1, 1859	
Blevins, Daniel	Nancy Osborn	Feb. 13, 1847	H. Jaynes, J. P.
Blevins, Thomas A.	Ruths Gibson	June 1, 1846	
Blevins, William	Catherine Salyers	Jan. 17, 1855	
Boggs, Randolph	Martha Holbrook	Aug. 17, 1854	
Booth, Ellis	Nellie O'Bryan	Jan. 11, 1856	
Borders, Davidson	Eleanor M. Peery	Nov. 17, 1847	G. W. Price
Borders, Hezekiah	Jemima Lemaster	Nov. 26, 1846	H. Jayne
Borders, Lewis	Rebecca Wheeler	(about) Jan. 7, 1851	
Borders, William	Sarah J. Mayo	July 10, 1849	Hugh Rankin
Bowen, Adam	Mary Gibson	Oct. 3, 1857	
Boyd, Andrew	Juliann Brown	Apr. 27, 1847	J. Borders, Minister Baptist Church
Boyd, Claiborne	Minerva Evans	...., 1858	
Bradley, Cornelius	Thurza Davis	Mar. 14, 1847	E. Bays
Bradley, Daniel	Sarah Pruitt	Aug. 4, 1853	B. P. Porter, Minister, Baptist Church
Branham, David	Lucy Ann Remy	Feb. 26, 1855	
Brook, Aaron	Nancy Absher	Jan. 26, 1849	
Brown, Andrew	Susannah Stambaugh	Apr. 5, 1846	G. W. Price
Brown, Archibald	Belinda Francis	Nov. 15, 1849	J. Borders
Brown, George W.	Eliza Sherman	...., 1857	
Burgess, James E.	Martha Porter	Oct. 18, 1859	
Burke, John W.	Angeline Blanton	Feb. 19, 1852	E. Howes
Burris, M. T.	Agatha Spears	July 27, 1854	
Burkett, Frederick	Jeriah Dale	June 13, 1847	J. W. Huff
Burkett, James R.	Elizabeth Kelly	Apr. 14, 1844	E. Howes
Butcher, William	Mary Wells	Feb. 1, 1845	
But(l)er, George W.	Athy J. Preston	June 10, 1858	

C

Canard, (Kennard) Elzy	Cynthia Litteral	Mar. 15, 1852	
Canard, Mason	Leanner Mead	...., 1856	
Cantrell, Henry	Fanny Fairchild	Dec. 27, 1847	H. Jaynes
Cantrell, John	Elizabeth Salyers	Jan. 14, 1850	H. Jaynes

Groom	Bride	Date of Marriage	By Whom
Cantrell, John	Sarah Webb	July 27, 1848	H. Jaynes
Castle, Andrew	Belinda Boyd	Aug. 13, 1851	G. Selsor
Castle, Edward	Polly Wiley	Feb. 11, 1847	G. W. Price
Castle, Hezekiah	Levina Grimm	Jan. 19, 1854	
Castle, Inman	Susan Castle	Aug. 22, 1857	
Castle, Ira	Nancy Bowling	Feb. 3, 1845	E. Bays
Castle, Israel	Susannah Grimm	Nov. 3, 1846	G. W. Price
Castle, James	Matilda Ward	Nov. 14, 1850	George Selsor
Castle, Madison	Leah Jane Preston	June 14, 1856	
Castle, Marcum	Catherine Penix	May 8, 1851	J. Borders
Castle, Niles H.	Elizabeth Wiley	Nov. 23, 1845	G. W. Price
Castle, William	Mary Jane Davis	Dec. 3, 1845	
Castle, William	Anne Gibbs	Oct. 17, 1858	
Castle, Zachariah	Polly Wyatt	Jan. 14, 1856	
Cassidy, Alex	Lucretia Ward	Jan. 30, 1847	James Delong
Cassidy, Philip	Elizabeth Copley	Mar. 9, 1851	B. P. Porter
Castner, Casper	Charlotte Preston	May 3, 1852	E. Howes
Caudill, Abel	Phoebe Hitchcock	Oct. 29, 1846	
Caudill, Abner	Mary Justice	July 24, 1849	H. Jaynes
Caudill, Amos	Jane Thompson	Mar. 9, 1849	H. Jayne
Caudill, James C.	Polly Fitzpatrick	June 14, 1846	John Picklesimer
Caudill, Mathew	Nancy Williams	Apr. 15, 1854	
Caudill, Reuben	Levisa Jane Barnett	Sept. 1, 1845	E. Bays
Chambers, Lorenzo D.	Margaret J. Auxier	May 2, 1855	
Chandler, Henry	Perlina E. Grimm	Mar. 18, 1857	
Chandler, Isaac	Eliza Green	Sept. 29, 1848	
Chandler, James	Catherine Daniels	Aug. 30, 1859	
Chandler, William	Rachael O'Bryan	Nov. 20, 1852	E. Howes
Clay, Matthew	Jane Butler	Aug. 3, 1845	E. Bays
Clay, Matthew	Lucinda Sturgill	Nov. 13, 1850	E. Howes
Coffee, Richard	Rebecca McKenzie	Dec. 15, 1858	
Coldiron, Hiram E.	Rebecca McCarty	Dec. 9, 1858	
Collingsworth, Thomas	Arty Burchett	Apr. 4, 1844	
Collins, Allen	Phoebe Ratcliff	May 20, 1857	
Collins, Amos	Nancy J? Collins	July 7, 1857	
Collins, Andrew J.	Amanda Collins	Apr. 17, 1852	A. Selsor
Collins, Elijah	Nancy J.? Ratcliff	Feb. 23, 1853	G. Selsor
Collins, George W.	Lydia Collins	Feb. 2, 1854	
Collins, Hiram	Barbara Auxier	Oct. 30, 1856	
Collins, Jefferson	Matilda Tackett	Jan. 13, 1852	E. Howes
Collins, William	Levisa Ratcliff	Dec. 20, 1851	G. Selsor
Collins, William W.	Susan L. Russell	Mar. 10, 1859	
Colvin, Asa	Polly Ann Mahan	Oct. 23, 1851	G. W. Price
Colvin, John	Mary Wheeler	Dec. 3, 1855	
Conley, Absolom	Cynthiann James	Dec. 8, 1854	
Conley, Constantine	Rebecca J. McCarthy	June 9, 1854	
Conley, David H.	Nancy Conley	Dec. 15, 1853	
Conley, Edmund	Elizabeth McCarty	Dec. 11, 1846	B. Caudill
Conley, Edmund	Mary Ann Salyer	Feb. 7, 1859	
Conley, George W.	Nancy Gullett	Oct. 18, 1852	
Conley, Harmon	Catherine Miller	Apr. 24, 1856	
Conley, Henry	Mahala Davis	June 15, 1848	G. W. Price
Conley, Hiram E.	Clarinda Rice	Oct. 20, 1853	
Conley, Isaac	Rachael Pennington	Oct. 30, 1858	
Conley, John	Cynthia Cantrell	Apr. 11, 1855	

189

Groom	Bride	Date of Marriage	By Whom
Conley, Thomas	Lydia Conley	Feb. 5, 1858	
Conley, William W.	Dicy Bailey	Mar. 23, 1850	G. W. Price
Conley, William J.	Laurena Auxier	Aug. 19, 1853	
Conley, William M.	Eliza Colvin	June 21, 1857	
Coolsey, Albert J.	Mahala Salyers	Feb. 14, 1857	
Cooper, Archibald	Polly Litteral	Sept. ...., 1857	G. W. Price
Cooper, Richard L.	Katherine Salyers	Apr. 16, 1849	
Crace, Stephen	Margaret Gullett	Aug. 25, 1849	
Crace, Stephen W.	Nancy Jane Conley	Jan. 18, 1853	G. Selsor
Craft, Wylie	Diana Sparks	Dec. 24, 1845	G. W. Price
Crum, Daniel	Rhoda Clay	Aug. 18, 1849	B. P. Porter
Crum, Eli	Clementine Porter	May 17, 1853	B. P. Porter
Crum, Pleasant	Juda Ward	Sept. 11, 1845	G. W. Price
Crum, William	Mary Mutter	Feb. 20, 1856	
Curtis, John	Abigail Remy	Apr. 13, 1850	E. Howes
Cunningham, Peter	Martha Ann Waller	Jan. 4, 1852	Isaac Goble
Cunningham, Timothy	Sarah E. Spears	...., 1858	
Cunningham, William	Eliza Waller	...., 1858	

D

Groom	Bride	Date of Marriage	By Whom
Dale, Berry	Chancy Coal (Cole)	Oct. 16, 1856	
Dale, Pleasant	Matilda Collins	June 4, 1858	
Damron, John	Charlotte Adkins	Dec. 13, 1858	
Daniel, Amos	Elizabeth Remy	Feb. 13, 1853	
Daniel, David	Sarah Jayne	Jan. 1, 1846	John Borders
Daniel, Francis	Perlina Daniel	July 21, 1853	J. Borders
Daniel, George W.	Polly Ward	Nov. 6, 1845	G. W. Price
Daniel, George W.	Zilphy Low (e)	Nov. 19, 1846	G. W. Price
Daniel, James	Elizabeth Daniel	...., 1858	
Daniel, John	Mary Van Hoose	(about) Nov. 10, 1852	
Daniel, John Oliver	Peggy Ann Castle	Mar. 17, 1848	J. Borders
Daniel, Moses	Juliann Mullett	...., 1847	
Daniel, Peter	Mary Van Hoose	Nov. 11, 1852	
Daniel, Solomon	Polly Ann Daniel	Apr. 13, 1855	
Daniel, Thomas B.	Mary Jane Castle	Jan. 26, 1854	
Daniel, Thomas	Agnes Swann	...., 1857	
Daniel, William	Katherine Stapleton	Jan. 6, 1847	J. Picklesimer
Davis, Bracken L.	Mary Conley	Nov. 13, 1856	
Davis, Harvey C.	Louisa Howes	Nov. 27, 1856	
Davis, John B.	Sarah Ward	Feb. 8, 1852	G. W. Price
Davis, Joseph	Elizabeth Borders	(about) Nov. 9, 1850	
Davis, Michael	Anna Ward	Sept. 24, 1846	John Borders
Davis, Zachariah	Mahala Stapleton	(about) June 28, 1853	
Dean, Joshua P.	.... Dorton	June 12, 1848	
Diles, (Dials) William D.	Rachael Conley	Feb. ...., 1855	
Dixon, Farmer	Sarah Conley	...., 1858	
Dixon, Henry	Jane Stafford	Feb. 13, 1849	J. W. Huff
Dixon, John Q.	Pricie Lavena Weddington	Nov. 14, 1850	T. S. Brown
Dorton, Joel	Eleanor Johnson	July 13, 1843	G. W. Price

190

Groom	Bride	Date of Marriage	By Whom
Dorton, Joel	Martha Fitzpatrick	Jan. 30, 1848	G. W. Price
Dutton, Elias	Sarah Penix	Nov. 12, 1850	B. P. Porter
Dykes, Charles	Samantha M. Nott	June 3, 1846	J. W. Huff

E

Elam, Robert D.	Arta F. Pelphrey	Nov. 29, 1853	
Elliott, John M.	Sarah Jane Smith	Sept. 23, 1848	E. Howes
Estep, Lilburn	Rachael Lemasters	July 6, 1854	
Evans, John W.	Juda Castle	Nov. 13, 1856	
Evans, Wilson	Martha Cantrell	Dec. 24, 1852	

F

Fairchild, Aaron	Dorcas Sparks	Feb. 27, 1845	
Fairchild, Abner	Lucinda Salyer	Feb. ...., 1857	
Fairchild, Benjamin	Minerva Jane Blevins	Jan. 1, 1848	H. Jaynes
Fairchild, Ebenezer	Elizabeth Hanna	Apr. 29, 1854	
Fairchild, George W.	Mary S? Davis	Nov. 7, 1859	
Fairchild, John W.	Sarah Ann Williams	Apr. 8, 1850	H. Jaynes
Fairchild, Moses	Catherine McKenzie	Nov. 4, 1849	H. Jaynes
Fairchild, Shadrack	Sarah Hannah	Apr. 1, 1846	E. Howes
Fairchild, William	Eleanor Rice	Nov. 28, 1859	
Fannin, Henry	Mary Davis	Dec. 2, 1847	J. Borders
Fannin, Jackson	Cinda Wiley	(About) Nov. ...., 1849	
Fannin, Samuel	Margaret Wiley	Nov. ...., 1854	
Ferguson, James J.	Mary M. Hill	Oct. 2, 1847	J. W. Huff
Finney, Samuel	Mary Michael	Jan. 11, 1856	
Fitzpatrick, Isaac	Mary B. Adams	Feb. 18, 1852	
Fitzpatrick, John	Ann Penix	Mar. 15, 1858	
Fitzpatrick, William	Eliza Milum	Apr. 6, 1852	
Franklin, John M.	Isabella Ferguson	Nov. 5, 1856	
Frazier, William J.	Zielpha Lemasters	June 23, 1859	
Fugett, Joseph C.	Mary Williams	Feb. 13, 1859	

G

Garred, Ulysses	Lydia Stafford	(About) Jan. 15, 1853	
George, Albert	Susan Roberson	July 24, 1851	G. Selsor
George, S. W.	Macy Jane Lewis	Feb. 21, 1845	E. Bays
Gibson, Spencer	Azie Cole	Aug. 7, 1843	
Gillum, Peter	Ann Evans	Feb. 14, 1850	E. Howes
Goble, Abraham	Louisa Jane Hanna		
Goble, Drury	Alafare Clay	Nov. 11, 1855	
Goble, Isaac	Emily Hanna	(About) Nov. 14, 1852	
Goble, Jeremiah	Mary Ann Musick	(About) Jan. 6, 1852	
Goble, John	Eliza Goble	May 1, 1855	
Goble, William	Matilda Kistner	Mar. 18, 1859	
Green, Andrew J.	Dorcas Jayne	Nov. ...., 1856	
Green, David	Lucinda Barnhardt	Oct. 2, 1847	T. S. Brown
Green, Giles	Margaret Yates	Mar. 14, 1846	W. Bailey

191

Groom	Bride	Date of Marriage	By Whom
Green, Thomas	Jemima Brown	Feb. 1, 1844	G. W. Price
Green, William G.	Louisa Dale	July 6, 1843	E. Howes
Griffith, Richard	Mary Sagraves	Nov. 22, 1853	
Grimm, Charles J.	Sarah Ann Stambaugh	July 21, 1859	
Grimm, Frederick M.	Emaline Castle	Apr. 28, 1857	
Grimm, John F.	Frances Brown	Feb. 6, 1851	J. Borders
Grizzle, John	Arminta Robertson	Aug. ...., 1855	
Gullett, Ira	Lydia Pelphrey	Jan. 8, 1846	W. Bailey
Gullett, Joseph	Serena Stambaugh	Nov. 22, 1851	E. Howes
Gullett, Martin	Juda Hampton	Apr. 11, 1850	W. Bailey
Gullett, Wylie	Jane Pelphry	Dec. 25, 1843	

H

Groom	Bride	Date of Marriage	By Whom
Hager, Henry	Nancy J. Franklin	Nov. 19, 1846	J. W. Huff
Hager, William J.	Phoebe A. Roach	Mar. 16, 1853	A. W. Thompson
Hamilton, Benjamin	Catherine Fairchild	Apr. 30, 1850	E. Howes
Hamilton, Samuel	Cynthia Hill	Apr. 13, 1843	E. Howes
Hamon?(d), Joseph	Susan Shaver	About Nov. 9, 1850	
Hanna, Andrew J.	Rachael F. Spradlin	Apr. 20, 1853	E. Howes
Hannah, Ebenezer	Nancy Fairchild	Oct. 7, 1852	E. Howes
Hannah, Elzy	Cynthiann Litteral	About Mar. 18, 1852	
Hanna, George W.	Elizabeth Davis	Oct. 16, 1854	
Hannah, Joseph	Susanna Picklesimer	July 17, 1848	T. S. Brown
Hanna, William B.	Elizabeth Blair	May 17, 1854	
Harkins, Hugh	Martha Murphy	Nov. 25, 1851	T. S. Brown
Harris, John	Elizabeth Lawson	Oct. 1, 1843	W. Bailey
Haw, ? John W.	Sarah Dixon	Dec. 12, 1853	
Hays, Isaac	Catherine Van Hoose	Aug. 31, 1848	J. Borders
Herald, Robert	Elizabeth Dixon	Oct. 30, 1853	
Hinkle, John	Elizabeth Crum	Nov. 6, 1847	James Delong
Hitchcock, John	Clarinda Pelphrey	Dec. 21, 1853	
Hitchcock, Nimrod	Mary Pelphrey	Oct. 17, 1847	J. Picklesimer
Hitchcock, Parker	Sophia Salyer	Apr. 21, 1856	
Hitchcock, Rowland J.	Elizabeth Marshall	Nov. 20, 1856	
Holbrook, Campbell	Susan Holbrook	Apr. ...., 1856	
Holbrook, John K.	Elizabeth Salyers	Apr. 4, 1847	L. Skaggs
Horne, John	Mary Fairchild	Apr. 30, 1850	E. Howes
House, James	Serilda Remy	Feb. 10, 1852	
House, James M.	Jane Hager	June 14, 1843	E. Bays
Howard, Thomas	Polly Perkins	Mar. 3, 1845	E. Bays
Howes, William W.	Mary Susan Witten	Jan. 18, 1849	T. S. Brown
Howes, William W.	Mary Kelly	Dec. 15, 1854	
Hylton, Eliphus P.	Sarah Green	Sept. 19, 1844	G. W. Price
Hylton, Eliphus P. S.	Nancy Castle	Nov. 8, 1855	

J

Groom	Bride	Date of Marriage	By Whom
Jackson, Samuel	Lidy Elizabeth Collins	Mar. 25, 1845	J. W. Huff
Jayne, Daniel	Mary Ross	Oct. 1, 1853	

Groom	Bride	Date of Marriage	By Whom
Jayne, Daniel J. V.	Serrena Salyer	July 17, 1859	
Jayne, William W.	Lydia Williams	June 19, 1852	
Jenkins, Henry	Rosanna Blevins	Feb. 26, 1850	H. Jaynes
Jenkins, Isaac	Ailsey Hill	June 18, 1843	W. Bailey
Johnson, Francis	Juliann Castle	Oct. 17, 1856	
Johnson, John	Surilla Sagraves	Jan. 2, 1857	
Joseph, John	Bary Blanton	Feb. 9, 1854	
Justice, Abram	Peggy Bays	Apr. 22, 1852	
Justice, Ehud	Mary E. Rhoten	Feb. 22, 1859	

K

Groom	Bride	Date of Marriage	By Whom
Keaton, Houston	Keziah Price	Mar. 25, 1848	J. W. Huff
Keeler, John W.	Matilda Dean	May 10, 1849	J. W. Huff
Kezee, John	Polly (Mary) Brummett	Aug. 25, 1848	H. Jayne
Keith, James	Sarah Lemaster	Oct. 27, 1845	J. W. Huff
Kelly, Mathias J.	Tempy Prince	Oct. 19, 1854	
Kesner, Casper	Charlotte Preston	May 3, 1852	
Kimbler, Silas	Sarah Boyd	May 15, 1858	
Kimbler, Solomon	Lucinda Picklesimer	Jan. 24, 1846	J. Picklesimer
Kimbler, William	Nancy Picklesimer	Mar. 2, 1844	E. Bays
King, Rev. Narcus L.	Catherine Stafford	Mar. 18, 1845	Wm. B. Landrum

L

Groom	Bride	Date of Marriage	By Whom
Lavender, Edward	Eliza Hager	Feb. 21, 1849	E. Howes
Lemaster, Alexander	Martha Lemaster	Oct. 27, 1851	J. Pelphrey
Lemaster, Ambrose	Fanny Shaver	About Feb. 1, 1851	
Lemaster, Benjamin F.	Emily J. Murphy ?	Feb. 15, 1846	
Lemaster, Daniel	Nancy Chandler	Mar. 15, 1855	
Lemaster, Daniel	Catherine Salyer	Oct. 20, 1856	
Lemaster, Daniel P.	Phoebe Bays	Dec. 23, 1851	J. Pelphrey
Lemaster, Francis	Rebecca Fairchild	May 1, 1856	
Lemaster, George	Susanna Davis	Nov. 23, 1853	
Lemaster, James E.	Lydia M. Tackett	........., 1857	
Lemaster, John	Mary Davis	May 3, 1855	
Lemaster, John B.	Margaret Curtis	Feb. 2, 1850	J. Pelphrey
Lemaster, Lewis	Anna Salyer	June 1, 1846	H. Jaynes
Lemaster, Stephen	Elizabeth McKenzie	Apr. 6, 1854	
Lemaster, Sylvester	Nancy Reed	Jan. 5, 1857	
Lemaster, Thomas	Polly Cantrell	July 6, 1848	H. Jayne
Lemaster, William	Narcissus Salyer	Aug. 6, 1849	H. Jayne
Leslie, Martin	Sarah B. Mayo	Jan. ...., 1844	James Reed
Litteral, Daniel	Elizabeth Burks	July 15, 1844	E. Bays
Litteral, George W.	Matilda Huff		
Litteral, Harrison	Elizabeth Ward	Nov. 15, 1856	
Litteral, James W.	Elizabeth Pace	Oct. 18, 1855	
Litteral, Milton	Minerva Salyer	Jan. 31, 1856	
Litteral, Wiley	Rebecca Pace	Aug. 16, 1855	
Littleton, James M.	Margaret Waller	Feb. 12, 1853	I. Goble
Livingston, B. F.	Sarah Hager	Sept. 14, 1844	E. Bays
Livingston, Harry A.	Mary Ann Dixon	Sept. 2, 1844	E. Howes

Groom	Bride	Date of Marriage	By Whom
Lowe, William	Cynthiann Roberts	Oct. 5, 1857	
Lunsford, John	Matilda House	July 10, 1854	
Lyon, James	Jemima Wheeler	Jan. 23, 1851	H. Jayne
Lyon, Kauson	Dicy Ward	Oct. 14, 1852	
Lyon, Marion	Angeline Jayne	Jan. 24, 1850	

M

Groom	Bride	Date of Marriage	By Whom
Maginnis, George	Lydia Bannister	Jan. 6, 1859	
Mahann, Johnnie	Rebecca Colvin	Oct. 18, 1846	Benj. Caudill
Mahan, John	Irene Stafford	Oct. 24, 1846	
Mallett, David	Martha J. Damron	...., 1858	
Mallett, David	Mary Adkins	Oct. 21, 1859	
Mankins, John	Nancy J. Witten	Mar. 23, 1853	G. Selsor
Manor, Isaac	Matilda Newsom	Nov. 2, 1851	B. P. Porter
Manor, Jonathan	Nancy Stepp	Jan. 12, 1850	J. Borders
Manor, Lewis	Lucretia Pauly	Nov. 20, 1852	B. P. Porter
Manus, Thomas	Elizabeth Musick	Jan. 25, 1849	J. W. Huff
Marshall, John	Sarah Ann Ferguson	Oct. 9, 1856	
Martin, John W.	Mary J. Hager	Apr. 22, 1857	
Martin, Morgan	Sarah Craft	May 13, 1847	M. L. King
Martin, Morgan	Bethany? Justice	Jan. 1, 1853	Enoch Green
Matney, John	Lucinda Dean	Dec. 12, 1844	Marcus L. King
Matthews, Elijah	Ann Eliza Porter	July 29, 1852	Benj. P. Porter
May, Caleb	Sarah Pelphrey	Nov. 2, 1843	E. Bays
May, Robert W.	Elender Conley	Oct. 8, 1857	
Maynard, Lewis	Jane Young	Jan. 8, 1844	
Maynard, William	Mary Cassiday	June 21, 1847	J. Delong
McCarty, Nelson	Louisa Blanton	June 6, 1856	
McCarty, Thomas	Tempy McCallister	May ...., 1856	
McDaniel, William	Mary Bailey	July 21, 1846	H. Jayne
McDowell, James	Ary Deboard	July 25, 1849	H. Jayne
McGlothlin, David	Belinda Ward	July 19, 1853	B. P. Porter
McGuire, John	Ruthy Jane Spears	Nov. 11, 1856	
McHenry, John	Caroline Dean	July 14, 1853	Orson Long
McKenzie, Andrew J.	Frances Lemaster	Nov. 9, 1852	J. Pelphrey
McKenzie, Andrew J.	Rebecca Fairchild	June 25, 1857	
McKenzie, Henry	Lerena Vanover	Nov. 14, 1858	
McKenzie, Henry P.	Sarah J. Bays	About Mar. 4, 1853	
McKenzie, Lafayette	Mary Ann Sparks	July 17, 1859	
McKenzie, Lemuel	Mary Lemaster	Jan. 26, 1854	
McKenzie, Martin	Lydia Sparks	Apr. 7, 1859	
McKenzie, Thomas J.	Elizabeth Ross	Jan. 4, 1858	
McKemzie, William	Nancy Rice	Mar. 4, 1852	J. Pelphrey
McNeely, Benjamin	Rebecca Clay	Aug. 24, 1848	B. P. Porter
Mead, John	Mary Jane Salyer	Aug. 18, 1859	
Mead, Robert	Mary Holy	Feb. 8, 1849	Jas. Delong
Meadows, Ephriam	Rebecca McGlothlin	Aug. 11, 1856	
Meadows, Johnson	Margaret Davis	July 17, 1856	
Meadows, Thomas T.	Mary Ann Davis	Nov. 23, 1853	
Meek, John	Percilla Jobe	Mar. 30, 1846	G. W. Price
Meek, John	Catherine Miller	May 23, 1859	

Groom	Bride	Date of Marriage	By Whom
Meek, Nathan	Elizabethann Pack	Jan. 9, 1857	
Meek, Richard	Amanda M. Ward	July 10, 1859	
Meek, Zepheniah	Jane Davis	Nov. 18, 1853	
Moore, John	Cynthia Delong	July 17, 1851	B. P. Porter
Moore, Sampson	Elizabeth Preest	Feb. 10, 1853	B. P. Porter
Murray, George W	Margery Ward	July 6, 1846	
Murray, Jesse	Fanny Davis	Aug. 8, 1843	
Mutter, Christopher	Barbara Bannister	Feb. 21, 1856	
Musick, Abraham	Rachael Collins	July 3, 1856	
Musick, Andrew	Martha Goble	Mar. 27, 1856	
Musick, Andrew L.	Emily Bowen	Dec. 7, 1856	
Musick, John	Minerva Baldridge	Nov. 22, 1851	

N

Groom	Bride	Date of Marriage	By Whom
Nelson, Manuel	Anna Burton	June 29, 1848	J. Borders
Nibert, James	Arminta Auxier	Nov. 6, 1849	
Nickell, Alexander W.	Katherine Salyers	Feb. 4, 1847	H. Jaynes
Nickell, George J.	Civiller S. Salyers	Jan. 17, 1849	E. Howes
Nickell, Shelby	Margaretann Welch	Dec. 26, 1850	G. Selsor
Noe, William	Mahala J. Johnson	about Apr. 9, 1853	

O

Groom	Bride	Date of Marriage	By Whom
O'Brien, James, Jr.	Lou Ann Bowen	Jan. 25, 1849	J. W. Huff
O'Bryan, James	Agnes Craft	Nov. 4, 1856	
O'Brien, Reuben H.	Elizabeth Stapleton	Aug. 20, 1844	S. Preston
O'Brien, William	Margaret Francis	Oct. 1, 1848	J. Borders
Osborn, Alfred	Cynthia Ward	Oct. 26, 1848	
Osborn, Andrew	Susan Blevins	Mar. 8, 1844	
Osborn, Calvin	Mary Jane Ward	Aug. 13, 1849	B. P. Porter
Osborn, Edmund	Palina Blevins	Mar. 27, 1845	
Osborn, Henry	Nancy Salyers	Aug. 28, 1846	J. Fugett
Osborn, Jesse	Lydia Keaton	Mar. 13, 1855	
Owens, James	Rosanna	Aug. 17, 1845	J. W. Huff
Owsley, Peter	Mary Ann Lunsford	July 12, 1859	

P

Groom	Bride	Date of Marriage	By Whom
Pace, Matthew	Elizabeth Salyers	Apr. ...., 1855	
Pack, Allen	Perlina Chandler	Dec. 2, 1857	
Pack, Charles	Levina Chandler	Feb. 10, 1858	
Pack, John	Sarah Jane Castle	Feb. ...., 1854	
Patrick, Allen	Elizabeth Litteral	Mar. 12, 1846	W. Bailey
Patrick, Elijah	Louise Rule	...., 1856	
Patrick, Jackson M.	Elizabeth Rice	Oct. 30, 1851	W. Bailey
Patrick, Jillson P.	Malinda Rice	Nov. 20, 1845	
Patrick, John W.	Abigail Salyer	Sept. 19, 1858	
Patrick, Reuben	Amanda Hager	Nov. 11, 1851	W. Bailey
Patrick, Wiley C.	Mary Huff	...., 1856	
Pelphrey Andrew J.	Naomi Salyer	Nov. 9, 1858	
Pelphrey, Daniel	Sarahann Hitchcock	Dec. 6, 1846	J. Picklesimer
Pelphrey, David A.	Mary Wheeler	Oct. 1, 1857	
Pelphrey, William R.	Serrena Van Hoose	...., 1855	
Penix, Allen	Mary Stapleton	Apr. 7, 1856	
Penix, William	Sarah Dorton	Oct. 14, 1847	G. W. Price

Groom	Bride	Date of Marriage	By Whom
Pennington, Claiborne	Sarah Lemaster	Oct. 30, 1858	
Pennington, Hiram	Sarah Lemaster	Jan. 17, 1846	H. Jayne
Pennington, James	Nancy Fairchild	Aug. 28, 1849	
Pennington, James	Celia Harris	Nov. 8, 1848	
Pennington, Levi	Elizabeth Pratt	Nov. 20, 1851	J. Pelphrey
Pennington, Levi	Michal Lemaster	Jan. 21, 1858	
Perry, George W.	Thurza Skaggs	Apr. 23, 1858	
Pinson, Aaron	Elizabeth Boyd	Mar. 10, 1849	
Pool, Robert H.	Martha Ann Robertson	May 5, 1851	
Porter, Benjamin	Nancy Cassidy	Mar. 15, 1844	
Porter, Benjamin B.	Elizabeth Crumm	...., 1855	
Porter, Henry D.	Irany Stafford	Feb. 8, 1849	J. W. Huff
Porter, Joseph	Eunice Mutter	July 29, 1852	B. P. Porter
Porter, Kenada	Polly Crumm	Aug. 19, 1853	
Porter, Samuel	Pricilla Mutter	Dec. 14, 1852	B. P. Porter
Porter, Samuel	Mary Jane Collins	Apr. 11, 1847	J. W. Huff
Porter, William G.	Jane Ferguson	Dec. 14, 1854	
Picklesimer, Andrew	Martha McKenzie	May 23, 1843	J. Picklesimer
Picklesimer, David	Polly Barrett	Oct. 10, 1843	E. Bays
Picklesimer, Francis M.	Minerva Bays	Feb. 2, 1852	
Picklesimer, Nathaniel	Nancy C. Boyd	Oct. 5, 1846	
Picklesimer, Phillip	Eliza Salyer	Nov. 23, 1857	
Picklesimer, Samuel	Phoebe Rice	Mar. 21, 1857	
Pratt, Enoch	Jeanette Webb	Apr. 15, 1847	H. Jayne
Prater, Thomas	Rebecca Auxier	Aug. 29, 1846	J. Fugett
Preece, William	Bertha Maynard	Nov. 23, 1852	
Preston, Atcheson	Rebecca Witten	Oct. 12, 1850	
Preston, Burgess	Elizabeth Porter	Apr. 3, 1844	S. Hanna
Preston, Eliphus	Zina Ward	July 30, 1849	
Preston, Eliphus	Lucinda Preston	Sept. 5, 1845	E. Bays
Preston, Eliphus	Nancy Jane Grimm	Oct. 9, 1845	G. W. Price
Preston, Eliphus Jr.	Malinda Louise Witten	Oct. 8, 1850	
Preston, Franklin	Emily E. Hager	Jan. 28, 1857	
Preston, James M.	Rhoda Spence	Aug. 26, 1852	
Preston, James W.	Delila Gilmon	About Dec. 8, 1849	
Preston, James W.	Sarah Barnhart	...., 1857	
Preston, Martin	Julia Brown	Nov. 20, 1856	
Preston, Moses	Martha Van Hoose	Jan. 21, 1857	
Preston, Nathan	Angeline Preston	Apr. 27, 1846	W. Bailey
Preston, Nathaniel	Lucinda Stapleton	Aug. 2, 1857	
Preston, Redford	Betsy Ann Price	Dec. 9, 1845	G. W. Price
Preston, Samuel	Mahala Ward	Aug. 8, 1854	
Preston, Thomas	Rhoda Preston	Oct. 1, 1843	B. Preston
Preston, Thomas	Elizabeth Castle	Aug. 17, 1856	
Price, C. C.	Sarah Meek	July 10, 1857	
Price, David	Delilah Mankins	Nov. 4, 1847	
Price, Hamilton	Eveline Salyers	Oct. 26, 1853	
Price, Harrison	Zena Ward	July 30, 1849	B. P. Porter
Price, William	Bitha Maynard	Nov. 23, 1852	
Price, Elias	Susan Rigsby	Nov. 18, 1858	
Prince, John	Celia Caldwell	Nov. 4, 1856	

Groom	Bride	Date of Marriage	By Whom

Q

Quillen, Marion S.	Cynthia Ann Dean	...., 1857	....

R

Groom	Bride	Date of Marriage	By Whom
Reed, William	Lydia Rice	Oct. 23, 1846	J. Picklesimer
Rice, Martin	Lucinda Evans	Mar. 20, 1856	....
Rice, Robert	Sarah Morris	Oct. 13, 1853	....
Rice, Samuel	Katherine Reed	Oct. 22, 1846	J. Picklesimer
Right, (Wright) Bayless	Isabel Gent	Mar. 13, 1844	E. Bays
Right, (Wright) Henry	Matilda Pennington	Mar. 8, 1844	E. Bays
Roberson, James H.	Clarinda Spears	June 3, 1859	....
Roberts, John W.	Louisa Ferguson	Aug. 12, 1852	....
Ross, Joseph	Perlina Dobings (Dobyns)	Mar. 21, 1855	....
Rudd, Thomas	Sarah Roberson	Mar. 6, 1856	....
Russell, Fleming M.	Margaret Pennington	Dec. 16, 1857	....

S

Groom	Bride	Date of Marriage	By Whom
Sagraves, Walter	Charity Conley	Nov. 15, 1855	....
Sagraves, Wilburn	Hetta McKenzie	July 11, 1856	....
Sagraves, William	Catherine Johnson	....	....
Salyers, Asa	Elizabeth Cantrell	Apr. 12, 1849	....
Salyers, Benjamin	Martha Salyers	Aug. 13, 1848	J. Picklesimer
Salyers, Benjamin	Eliza Stapleton	Nov. 10, 1857	....
Salyers, Henderson	Elizabeth Williams	Dec. 4, 1843	H. Jaynes
Salyers, Jackson	Eleanor Lemaster	Oct. 5, 1846	H. Jaynes
Salyers, Jeremiah	Elizabeth Conley	Sept. 17, 1845	E. Howes
Salyers, Joseph	Catherine Stapleton	Aug. 27, 1853	....
Salyers, Levi	Sarah M. McKenzie	Feb. 7, 1858	....
Salyers, Samuel P.	Ursly (Ursula) Evans	Jan. 5, 1852	J. Pelphrey
Salyers, Samuel B.	Arminta Sturgill	Apr. 13, 1850	E. Howes
Salyers, William	Recie Justice	Nov. 12, 1857	....
Salyers, Wiley	Christine Lemaster	May 28, 1857	....
Scaggs, Andrew	Juda Holbrook	Aug. 13, 1857	....
Scaggs, James	Mary Holbrook	Feb. 20, 1851	L. Scaggs
Scaggs, John	Lucy Sparks	Dec. 25, 1858	....
Scaggs, Peter	Sarah Sparks	Oct. 20, 1858	....
Selsor, James P.	Tabitha Ferguson	Feb. 14, 1853	G. Selsor
Senters, Willis	Rachael Tackett	Nov. 22, 1851	G. W. Price
Shaver, James	Cynthiann Chandler	Oct. 20, 1846	J. Picklesimer
Shaver, Ransom	Delia Picklesimer	Mar. 6, 1855	....
Short, Granderson	Mary Mead	Feb. 26, 1849	J. W. Huff
Smith, David	Fanny Holbrook	Aug. 11, 1852	....
Smith, Hugh	Lucy Salyers	June 10, 1858	....
Smith, Thomas	Mahala Ann Shelton	Nov. 20, 1856	....
Sparks, Henry	Mary Conley	Nov. ?, 1857	....
Sparks, Thomas	Peggy Johnson	Oct. 10, 1858	....
Sparks, William	Martha Salyer	Dec. 14, 1859	....
Spears, Enoch	Malinda Williams	Nov. 9, 1855	....
Spears, Samuel	Clarinda Roberson	Apr. 3, 1856	....
Spears, Samuel	Elizabeth Price	May 17, 1855	....
Spears, Samuel	Eliza Jane Welch	Apr. 13, 1851	I. Goble

Groom	Bride	Date of Marriage	By Whom
Spears, Thomas J.	Mary D. Musick	Aug. 18, 1859	
Spears, Thomas W.	Rebecca Gains	July 26, 1847	
Spears, Vincent	Isabel Welch	July 16, 1853	I. Goble
Spears, Wallace W.	Mary Roberson	Nov. 17, 1859	
Spears, Wiley	Elizabeth Butcher	Dec. 12, 1846	
Spears, Wiley	Eliza Crider	Dec. 11, 1854	
Spence, Andrew	Alafare Bannister	Aug. 5, 1853	
Spradlin, Benjamin F.	Permelia Howes	May 6, 1855	
Spradlin, Evan	Emaline May	Jan. 24, 1848	
Spradlin, James	Amanda Stafford	Dec. 30, 1852	G. Selsor
Spradlin, James	Tempa Hitchcock	Dec. 2, 1843	E. Bays
Spradlin, James	Jane Wheeler	July 1, 1858	
Spradlin, Jasper	Elizabeth Horn ?	May 20, 1849	
Spencer, John	Martha J. McGlothlin	Nov. 1, 1855	
Spradlin, Solomon	Susan Fairchild	Nov. 22, 1851	E. Howes
Spradlin, Solomon	Harriett Moles	June 29, 1857	
Spradlin, William	Mahala Conley	Mar. 5, 1857	
Stacy, George W.	Chaney Manor	Aug. 24, 1851	B. P. Porter
Stafford, Davis	Malinda Carson	About Nov. 26, 1860	
Stafford, James	Cynthia Dixon	Dec. 27, 1844	S. Preston
Stafford, Ralph	Amanda Hager	Feb. 22, 1849	E. Howes
Stambaugh, Frederick	Sarah Short	Aug. 14, 1853	
Stambaugh, Frederick	Martha Lemaster	Feb. 22, 1852	J. Pelphrey
Stambaugh, James	Martha Turner	Mar. 13, 1848	J. W. Huff
Stambaugh, John W.	Clarinda Blair	Apr. 4, 1852	E. Howes
Stambaugh, Philip	Mary Jane McKenzie	Apr. 9, 1848	
Stambaugh, Robert J.	Savilla Payne	Nov. 16, 1859	
Stambaugh, Sylvester	Remember Rowland	July 22, 1847	E. Howes
Stapleton, Charles	Elizabeth Salyers	Oct. 3, 1856	
Stapleton, Edward	Elizabeth Salyers	July 3, 1856	
Stapleton, Israel	Nancy Ann Wood	Aug. ...., 1857	
Stapleton, Richard	Nancy Daniel	Jan. 19, 1848	J. W. Huff
Stepp, Elias	Margaret Mead	May 5, 1856	
Sundys, Kendrick	Nancy S. Hager	June 18, 1846	J. W. Huff

T

Groom	Bride	Date of Marriage	By Whom
Tackett, Hiram	Lucinda Shaver	Mar. 22, 1846	J. Picklesimer
Tackett, James M.	Eliza Workman	Aug. 1, 1852	W. Bailey
Tackett, James M.	Sarah Bowen	July 7, 1856	
Tackett, Levi	Susanna Tackett	June 10, 1844	E. Howes
Trimble, James	Sarah Baldwin	Nov. 14, 1859	
Trimble, William	Clarinda Picklesimer	Mar. 19, 1853	
Trimble, William	Susan Bynyan	Mar. 9, 1853	
Turner, Joseph	Mary J. Collins	Feb. 22, 1857	
Turner, Samuel F.	Cynthia E. Rule	Apr. 12, 1853	

V

Groom	Bride	Date of Marriage	By Whom
Van Hoose, Bracken	Anna Davis	Dec. 18, 1859	
Van Hoose, Jesse	Keziah Van Hoose	Nov. 29, 1845	E. Howes

Groom	Bride	Date of Marriage	By Whom
Van Hoose, Levi	Nancy Dixon	Jan. 11, 1851	A. Rice
Van Hoose, Nathan	Lydia Pelphrey	About June 30, 1852	
Vincent, Gabriel M.	Surrilda Derossett	Nov. 5, 1844	E. Howes
Vaughan, Alexander	Perlina Alexander	Apr. 16, 1858	
Vaughan, Henry S.	Mary J. Turner	July 20, 1851	G. Selsor
Vaughan, William	Rachael Baldwin	Jan. 17, 1850	E. Howes

W

Groom	Bride	Date of Marriage	By Whom
Walter, Shadrack	Elizabeth Litteral	Apr. 2, 1853	G. Selsor
Ward, Andrew	Mary Sturgill	May 4, 1854	
Ward, Andrew J.	Clarinda Webb	Feb. 15, 1856	
Ward, Andrew J.	Lydia Litteral	Feb. 27, 1858	
Ward, Charles A.	Katherine Howes	Jan. 1, 1852	
Ward, David	Clarinda Stapleton	About Nov. 27, 1852	
Ward, James	Juliann Van Hoose	Aug. 3, 1854	
Ward, James	Mariah Vines?	Feb. 28, 1858	
Ward, James	Nancy Sturgill	About Jan. 5, 1853	
Ward, John	Serilda Blevins	June 8, 1848	B. P. Porter
Ward, John	Nancy Preston	Nov. ...., 1847	
Ward, John	Perlina Meek	Apr. 2, 1853	G. Selsor
Ward, Solomom	Elizabeth Van Hoose	Jan. 27, 1847	G. W. Price
Ward, Solomom	Mahala Jane Porter	Dec. 27, 1849	B. P. Porter
Ward, Solomom	Mary Jane Mullett	Apr. 3, 1856	
Ward, Thompson	Phoebe S. Blevins	About Mar. 10, 1852	
Ward, William	Nancy E. Stambaugh	Nov. 25, 1847	J. Borders
Ward, Washington	Mary McGlothlin	Aug. 31, 1854	
Ward, William S.	Arminta Barnhart	June 18, 1858	
Walker, George R.	Elizabeth Baldwin	Feb. 2, 1850	E. Howes
Walker, Henry W.	Martha J. Auxier	July 19, 1855	
Waller, Greenville	Drusilla C. Childress	Jan. 30, 1851	I. Goble
Waller, Henderson	Sarah B. Hanna	Dec. 27, 1847	
Walters, John M.	Sarah Litterall	...., ...	
Walters, Winfrey	Elizabeth Preston	Oct. 11, 1854	
Walton, Lorenzo Dow	Miranda S. Mayo	Nov. 22, 1850	H. Rankin
Watkins, Rice	Sarah Stambaugh	May 25, 1851	E. Howes
Webb, John	Phoebe Butler	Jan. 29, 1846	I. Goble
Webb, Sylvester	Nancy J. Ward	Feb. 5, 1857	
Webb, Thomas J.	Frances J. Spears	Oct. 3, 1856	
Wellman, Jeremiah	Elizabeth Ramey	Nov. 5, 1850	Reuben W. McCormick
Wells, Alexander	Martha Wells	Dec. ?, 1855	
Wells, George	Nancy Butcher	May 19, 1853	I. Goble
Wells, William	Mary Ann Cary	Aug. 16, 1848	J. Delong
Wheeler, Daniel	Mary Salyer	Dec. 30, 1852	Enoch Green
Wheeler, John	Martha Green	May 29, 1845	J. Borders
Wheeler, John W.	Katherine R. Wheeler	June 28, 1853	J. Borders
Wheeler, Martin	Julia A. Price	Nov. 10, 1859	
Wheeler, Stephen	Jemima Wheeler	Apr. 19, 1855	
Wheeler, Stephen	Eliza Chandler	Nov. 8, 1853	
Wheeler, Stephen H.	Elizabeth Bowman	July 12, 1856	
Wheeler, William	Juda Green	Nov. 4, 1853	
Wilcox, Andrew J.	Angeline Lemaster	Feb. 9, 1859	

Groom	Bride	Date of Marriage	By Whom
Wiley, Andrew	Nancy Eveline Tackett	Oct. 26, 1849	
Wiley, John	Sarah House	July 17, 1848	T. S. Brown
Wiley, Richard	Cynthia Lowe	Nov. 19, 1846	G. W. Price
Wiley, William	Ropieann Adkins	Aug. 5, 1844	G. W. Price
Wiley, William	Nancy Tackett	...., ...	
Williams, Andrew	Clarinda Picklesimer	Mar. 8, 1853	
Williams, David	Lydia Webb	Nov. 4, 1856	
Williams, Elliott	Eda Van Hoose	May ...., 1856	
Williams, Jacob	Elizabeth Butler	Apr. 26, 1847	
Williams, James	Katherine Hill	Nov. 15, 1851	J. Pelphrey
Williams, Lewis	Margaret Salyer	Nov. 13, 1851	J. Pelphrey
Williams, Moses	Emily J. Webb	May 15, 1856	
Williams, Noah	Ellen Webb	Feb. 16, 1854	
Williams, Robert	Nancy Picklesimer	Mar. 19, 1848	H. Jaynes
Williams, Sylvester	Minerva L. Webb	Nov. 10, 1858	
Williams, Thomason	Malissa Stafford	July 15, 1856	
Williamson, Stephen	Ellen Blevins	Feb. 21, 1850	B. P. Porter
Williamson, ...	Sarah Ann Copley	Oct. 15, 1851	B. P. Porter
Wilson, Henry	Calista Stafford	Dec. 5, 1858	
Witten, George H.	Martha A. Butler	Nov. 24, 1847	J. W. Ridgell
Witten, Isaac Quin	Elizabeth Hackworth	Jan. 27, 1848	E. Howes
Witten, John W.	Lydia Berry	Mar. 15, 1846	J. W. Huff
Witten, William	Mary Jane Dixon	Nov. 11, 1856	
Wood, James	Louisa Boyd	Dec. 4, 1855	
Wood, John W.	Amacetta S. Derossett	June ...., 1848	E. Howes
Wood, William	Lucinda Stafford	Nov. 9, 1852	
Wright, Willis	Martesia Sagraves	Mar. 27, 1846	

Y

Groom	Bride	Date of Marriage	By Whom
Yates, John P.	Lydia Salyer	July 22, 1859	
Young, Harrison	Mary Burton	About Oct. 5, 1850	
Young, John	Elizabeth Pack	Jan. 10, 1850	J. Borders
Young, William	Jane Chandler	Oct. 24, 1850	T. S. Brown

CHAPTER X

MORGAN COUNTY, KENTUCKY

ORGANIZATION, EARLIEST COURT RECORDS

State of Kentucky (
Morgan County (Sct.

Be it remembered that at the house of Edward Wells in the county of Morgan pursuant to an act of the General Assembly of the Commonwealth of Kentucky, establishing a county and appointing a time for holding courts therein, on Monday the tenth day of March in the year 1823, it being the second Monday, and in the 31st year of the Commonwealth, commissions of the peace for the said county from the Governor of this State directed to Mason Williams, Edward Wells, Isaac Lycans, Hollaway Power, John Hammond, William Lewis, John S. Oakley, John Williams, Thomas Mickle, Joseph Carroll, Fielding Hanks (and) William Biddle (?), were severally produced. Whereupon the aforesaid persons were appointed and authorized to hold a county court for the said county and discharge the duties of justice of the peace in manner and form prescribed by law. Whereupon Isaac Lycan was appointed to administer the oath, required by the first section of the seventh article of the constitution, to Mason Williams who took the same. Then the said Mason Williams to the rest of the said justices who took the same oath. The court being this far constituted, James Cash (Kash), produced a commission from his Excellency John Adair, Esqr., Governor of the Commonwealth of Kentucky, appointing him sheriff of the county during the time prescribed by law (which commission bears date the 11th day of December, 1822). Whereupon the said James Cash took the oath of office, the oath of fidelity to this State and the oath to support the constitution of the United States, (and) entered into and acknowledged his bond with Isaac Lycan, Holloway Power and John Cox, his securities (sureties) in the penal sum of three thousand dollars conditioned as the law directs, which bond is ordered to be recorded. And thereupon a county court was held for Morgan County. Present: Edward Wells, Isaac Lycan, Halloway Power, John Hammond, William Lewis, John S. Oakley, John Williams, Thomas Nickle, Joseph Carroll, Fielding Hanks and William Bedell.

James G. Hazelrigg produced a certificate from a majority of the judges of the court of appeals that he had been examined by their clerk in their presence and under their direction and that they judge him to be well qualified to discharge the duties of the office of clerk; and thereupon he is appointed clerk of this court during good behavior, whereupon he took the oath required by law (and) entered into bond with Thomas Fletcher and William M. Sudduth his securities (sureties) in the penalty of $10,000 (?) conditioned according to law * * *

William M. Sudduth, Henry Chiles, William Triplett, (and) Robert Walker, Esquires, produced license severally permitting them to practice law in courts in this Commonwealth, Whereupon they took the several oaths prescribed by law and the oath of an attorney and thereupon they are admitted to practice accordingly in this court.

On motion of James Kash, Esq., sheriff of this county, Caleb Kash is appointed deputy under him and thereupon he took the oath of office.

Peter Amyx and John Elliott, Esq., are recommended to his Excellency, the Governor of this State, as proper persons to fill the office of surveyor in this county, a majority of the justices concurring in this recommendation.

William Triplett, Esquire, is appointed commonwealth's Attorney to prosecute in this court in behalf of the Commonwealth.

* * *

Ordered that court be adjourned until court in course.

(Signed)   Mason Williams.

MARRIAGES 1823-1827

Groom	Bride	Date of Marriage
A		
Adams, William	Elizabeth Williams	Dec. 21, 1826
B		
Black, Mitchell C.	Polly Cummingham	Sept. 30, 1824
Brown, Elijah	Ailsey Coffee	...., 1824
Brown, John T.	Polly Carr	Feb. 13, 1825
Brinegar, John	Polly Dorothy	Oct. ...., 1824
Blair, William	Lydia Caskey	May 17, 1827
C		
Cox, Solomon	Louisa Trimble	Sept. 11, 1823
Craig, William	Rosanna Day	Dec. 25, 1823
Connelly, Edward	Jane Phelphrey	July 1, 1824
Cock, James H.	Dolly Gallion	June 27, 1824
Casteel, John	Elizabeth Willson	Jan. 11, 1825
Cooper, Henry	Rachel Lycans	Jan. ...., 1826
Cassidy, Jesse	Susan Law	...., 1826
Clark, George	Nancy Cook	July ...., 1826
Cox, William	Cynthia Reed	Aug. ...., 1826
D		
Day, William	Perlina Stewart	Nov. 10, 1824
Davis, Joseph	Polly Williams	Jan. 13, 1825
Day, Archibald	Celia Spurlock	Oct. 29, 1826
Dotson, James	Polly Sadler	June 4, 1827
E		
Elam, James	Rebecca McGuire	Sept. 11, 1823
Ellington, John	Polly DeWitt	...., ...
Easterling, Thomas	Joannah Gallion	...., ...
F		
Fugate, Granville	Mary Perry	Aug. 3, 1826

Groom	*Bride*	*Date of Marriage*
G		
Gost, James	Jane Barker	Mar. 10, 1824
Gillum (Gilliam), Jeremiah	....	July 8, 1824
Gallion, Master (?)	Mahala Gowin	...., ...
H		
Hoskins, Preston	Rebecca Day	Aug. 6, 1823
Hill, Wesley	Polly Robbins	Feb. 7, 1824
Hadley, James	Anne Kincaid	Nov. 30, 1826
Hardin, Samuel (?)	Patsy Brown	Feb. 23, 1825
Hunt, Samuel H.	Sally Lawson	...., 1825
I		
Ison, Charles	Lucy Day	Mar. 25, 1824
Ison, William	Esther Hambleton	May 8, 1826
J		
James, (?) Thomas	Minerva Eldridge (?)	Feb. 16, 1825
K		
Kash, James	Sally Crea	Mar. 26, 1827
Kennard, David	Nancy Coffee	Aug. 9, 1823
Keeton, Marshall S.	Nancy Woods	June 4, 1827
L		
Leach, Enos	Elizabeth G. Montgomery	Aug. 6, 1823
Lawson, William	Mary Dennis (Denues)	Dec. 17, 1824
Little, Peter	Hannah Minton	Mar. 24, 1824
Lumpkins, Joseph	Priscilla Barker	Oct. 21, 1824
Little, Charles	Charlotte Bryant	June 30, 1824
Lewis, Gardner H.	Polly Amyx	Oct. 5, 1825
Large, John	Jane L. Vest	Oct. 5, 1826
Lewis, Francis	Eleanor Caskey	Dec. 3, 1826
Lewis, Edmund Price	Cynthia Cox	Nov. 25, 1824
M		
McGuire, William	Rebecca Elam	Oct. 16, 1823
May, Samuel	Eliza Hammonds (?)	Dec. 7, 1824
May, William	Dolly Linden	Jan. 25, 1824
Maddox, John	Mahala Gilmore	June 17, 1825
McClintock, Hezekiah	Polly Barker	May 16, 1825
Mannin, John	Sally Mannin	Dec. 22, 1825
Montgomery, John B.	Lettice Howard (?)	May ...., 1826
McGuire, John	Mary Cook	Mar. 8, 1827
N		
Nickel, Andrew	Rachel Kash	Sept. 9, 1824
O		
Oxley, Prior	Isabella Neal	...., 1825
Osborn, Stephen	Betsy Lewis	June 3, 1824
Osborn, James	Elizabeth Smith	July 6, 1826

Groom	Bride	Date of Marriage
P		
Pence, Andrew	.... Holland (?)	Aug. 4, 1823
Pendleton, Alexander	Charity Price	May 6, 1824
Phipps, John	Cynthia Howard	...., 1825
R		
Reed, Sanford	Mary Williams	Sept. 14, 1826
S		
Stewart, Archibald	Lucy Willson	...., 1825
Stout, Joseph	Polly Lykans	Feb. 2, 1826
Sherman, Daniel	Rebecca Day	Sept. 5, 1826
Stephens, James	Catharine Winkell	Oct. 12, 1826
Shelton, Marshall	....	...., ...
T		
Tyre, Ben	Polly Sadler	...., ...
Tipton, Joshua	Sarah Hadley	July 1, 1824
Toliver, Elijah	Martha Mannin (?)	Oct. 5, 1825
W		
Willson, Andrew	Lucy Kash	Sept. 27, 1823
Willson, Joshua	Elizabeth Lycans	Oct. 14, 1823
Whitely, George	Rebecca Davis	Apr. 15, 1824
Wells, John	Jane Caskey	Sept. 16, 1824
Williams, Caleb	Belinda Davis	May ...., 1826
Williams, Joshua	Hannah Dyer	Jan. 4, 1827
Ward, Cyrus	Nancy Mannin	Apr. 4, 1827

CHAPTER XI

PERRY COUNTY, KENTUCKY

EARLIEST AVAILABLE COURT ORDER

November Term 1823.

At a county court commenced and held at the Courthouse in Hazard on Monday, the 10th day of November, 1823.

Present: Jesse Boling, Robert Hicks, Jeremiah Combs, Joseph Cockrel, Samuel Hurley, Abel Pennington, James Turner, Daniel Duff, Robert S. Breashears and Elijah Combs Esquires.

* * * and Jesse Boling and Abel Pennington be and is [are] appointed to settle with the sheriff and they are further appointed by a majority of the court to receive the delinquent list from (words illegible) and receive the receipt of the Court of Claims to January term, 1824.

* * *

Ordered that court adjourn untill (sic) court in course.

(Signed)   Jesse Boling

CHAPTER XII

WHITLEY COUNTY, KENTUCKY

Organization, Early Court Orders

At the house of Samuel Cox in the county of Whitley on Monday the 20th day of April, in the year of our Lord one thousand eight hundred and eighteen and of the twenty-sixth year of the Commonwealth of Kentucky, it being the time and place appointed by the General Assembly of Kentucky for holding the first court for the county of Whitley aforesaid, commissions from his Excellency Gabriel Slaughter, Lieutenant Governor and acting as Governor of the Commonwealth of Kentucky, directed to Edward Riley, John Berry, Uriah Parks, Francis Faulkner, Lamme Clarke, Samuel Cox, and Isaac King, appointing them justices of the peace in and for the said county of Whitley; and thereupon, pursuant to law Edward Riley, Esq., administered the oath of office and fidelity to Samuel Cox, John Berry, Uriah Parks, Francis Faulkner, Lamme Clarke and Isaac King, justices of the peace for said county and then John Berry, Esquire, administered the oath of office and fidelity to Edward Riley, Esq., as a justice of the peace for said county.

Benton Litten produced a commission from his Excellency Gabriel Slaughter, Lieutenant Governor and Acting Governor, appointing him sheriff of Whitley county which commission was read and thereupon the said Benton Litten entered into bond in the penalty of three thousand dollars with Edward Riley, Samuel Cox, and Francis Faulkner as his securities (sureties) conditioned as the law directs. Whereupon the oath of office was administered to him as the law directs by Edward Riley, Esq. The sheriff then opened the court as the law directs. Present: Edward Reilly, John Berry, Uriah Parke, Lamme Clarke, Samuel Cox, Francis Faulkner and Isaac King, Gentlemen Justices.

A certificate was produced in court by Edward Reilly, Esq., certifying that he had administered the oath required by law to John Berry, Uriah Parks, Francis Faulkner, Samuel Cox, Lamme Clarke, and Isaac King as justices of the peace of this county; also, to Benton Litten as sheriff of this county.

A certificate was produced in court by John Berry, Esq., certifying that he had administered the oath required by law to Edward Reilly, as a justice of the peace.

The court being constituted agreeable to law proceeded to elect their clerk *pro tempore* and Milton Eve was found to be duly elected, whereupon the said Milton Eve entered into bond in the penalty of five ,thousand dollars with Joseph Eve, Lamme Clarke, Hiram Jones and Joseph Parsons as his securities (sureties) conditioned as the law directs. Whereupon Edward Reilly, Esq., administered to him the oath of office required by law.

On motion of William Roe, he is appointed constable in the bounds of Capt. Allison's old company of Militia. Whereupon he entered into bond in the penalty of $1,000 with Hiram Jones and Francis Faulkner as his securities (sureties) * * * .

On motion of Baker E. Watkins, he is appointed constable in the bounds of Capt. Richards' old company of Militia. Whereupon he entered into bond in the penalty of $1,000 conditioned as the law directs with Joel A. Watkins as his security (surety) * * .

On motion of Thomas Foley, he is appointed constable in the bounds of Capt. George Tye's company of Militia. Whereupon he entered into bond in the penalty of $1,000 conditioned as the law directs with Lamme Clarke and Andrew Evans as his securities (sureties) * * * .

On motion of John Ross, he is appointed constable in the bounds of Capt. Jacoway's company of Militia. Whereupon the said Ross entered into bond in the penalty of $1,000 conditioned as the law directs with Angus Ross as his security (surety) * * * .

On motion of William Edwards, he is appointed * * * constable in the bounds of Capt. Steele's company of Militia, whereupon he entered into bond in the penalty of $1,000 with Benjamin Tuggle, Hiram Jones and Joseph Parsons as his securities (sureties) * * * .

On motion of John L. ? Laughlin, he is appointed constable in the bounds of Capt. Steele's company of Militia. Whereupon he entered into bond in the penalty of $1,000 with George Tye, Charles Rockhold and Joseph Parsons as his securities (sureties) * * * .

It is ordered by the court that George Gill Eve be appointed counsellor and Attorney of the Commonwealth in and for this county.

Ordered that court be adjourned untill (sic) 10 o'clock tomorrow morning.

(Signed) Edward Reilly.

* * *

Court having met agreeable to adjournment, on Tuesday the 21st day of April 1818:

Present: Edward Reilly, John Berry, Uriah Parks, Francis Faulkner, Samuel Cox, Isaac King, and Lamme Clarke, Gentlemen Justices.

On motion of William Davis, he is appointed constable in the bounds of Capt. Medders' (Middaugh or Meadows) company of Militia; and thereupon the said Davis entered into bond in the penalty of $1,000 with John Medders and Peter Snider as his securities (sureties).

On motion of Nathan Cox, he is appointed constable in the bounds of Capt. Medders' company of Militia. Whereupon he entered into bond in the penalty of $1,000 with Samuel Cox and Benton Litten as his securities (sureties) * * * .

Ordered by the court that Joseph Gillis and Thomas Laughlin be recommended to his Excellency, the Acting Governor of Kentucky, as fit persons to fill the office of surveyor of Whitley county, a majority of the justices of the peace of said court being present and concurring in this recommendation.

* * *

Ordered that court be adjourned untill (sic) in course.

(Signed) Edward Reilly.

MARRIAGES 1818-1823

Groom	Bride	Date of Marriage
A		
Allen, James	Elizabeth Hufft	Sept. 25, 1821
Atkins, Hargis	Ollivia Sexton	Dec. 27, 1822
Arthur, Elias	Patsy Arthur	...., 1823
B		
Bryant, Absolam	Aggie Johnson	Aug. 3, 1818
Bennett, Amos	Sally Hamlin	June 29, 1818
Blevins, Elisha	Polly McKee	Aug. 16, 1819
Blake, Benjamin	Rachel Arthur	Mar. 12, 1819
Ballinger, John	Elizabeth Benge	Mar. 27, 1819
Broils, Aaron	Hannah Hays	Dec. 31, 1818
Brown, William	Elizabeth Levier (Sevier)	Sept. 11, 1820
Breck, Joshua	Betty Benge	Nov. 27, 1821
Bryant, John	Levie Heaton	Mar. 9, 1821
Ballew, James	Franky Jones	Jan. 27, 1821
Blevins, Daniel	Franky Blevins (Corder)	Mar. 23, 1822
Bryant, Howell	Nancy Jones	Feb. 2, 1822
Bryant, William	Ann Heaton	Apr. 27, 1833
Berry, Francis	Pamelia Mahan	Nov. 2, 1823
Brown, James A.	Nancy P. Wilson	Sept. 29, 1823
C		
Cox, Enoch	Nancy Davis	Jan. 24, 1819
Cox, Daniel	Ainsia Cox	Aug. 23, 1824
Cox, Nathan	Polly Cox	Aug. 21, 1826
Campbell, Jeremiah	Millie Wilson	Jan. 29, 1820
Creekmore, William B.	Susan Porch	Mar. 14, 1820
Creekmore, Raskey	Luranna Meadow	Mar. 6, 1821
Cummings, James	Sally Gatliff	Mar. 11, 1822
Caldwell, Daniel	Celia Lovett	Jan. 14, 1823
D		
Duncan, Henry B.	Eliza Laughlin	Oct. 12, 1820
Davis, John	Frances	Apr. 16, 1821
E		
Eaton, Brian	Free Sexton	Dec. 18, 1818
Edwards, John	Clara Grubbs	Sept. 24, 1822
Evans, William	Rebecca Levere (Severe)	Aug. 14, 1822
F		
Foley, Thomas	....	Apr. 30, 1818
Findlay (Finley)	Anna Gatliff	Jan. 25, 1820
G		
Garner, Thomas	Susan Carr	May 5, 1823
Gilreath, Gideon	Betty Ann Harmon	May 21, 1821
Gatliff, William	Delilah Blackburn	Aug. 10, 1822
Garland, Samuel	Christina Pennington	May 18, 1823

Groom	*Bride*	*Date of Marriage*

H

Hill, Aquilla	Elizabeth Tillotson	Dec. 19, 1820
Hackler, Jacob	Jane Skeen	Sept. 17, 1821
Harman, Thomas	Katie Barnard	June 29, 1823

J

Johnston, Hugh	Rebecca Gatliff	Mar. 11, 1822
Johnson, Joseph	Polly Cummings	Nov. 26, 1820

L

Laskly, Amour	Sarah Worley	Dec. 15, 1823
Laughlin, Joseph D.	Jane Duncan	Jan. 15, 1820
Lawrence, John	Jennie Morgan	Oct. 8, 1822
Lawrence, Horace	Jane Wilder	Sept. 14, 1823

M

McCormack, John	Mourning Gibson	June 22, 1819
Mead, Thomas M.	Catherine Matthews	Dec. 15, 1823
Miller, James	Catharine Mahan	Sept. 3, 1820
Meadows (Middaugh), Jacob	Jane Harmon	Apr. 16, 1821
Monholland, Samuel	Elizabeth Meadows	July 17, 1821
Meadows, Isham	Sarah Meadows	Aug. 31, 1822
Miller, Isaac	Thursa Ann Watkins	Mar. 22, 1823
Meadows, William	Sally Harmon	Oct. 19, 1823

N

Night, (Knight), George	Susan Day	June 4, 1820

O

Osborn, James	Nancy Ayres	June 13, 1822

P

Parks, Moses	Abigail Eaton	Nov. 15, 1820
Parks, Reuben	Polly Davis	Aug. 17, 1820
Perkins, William	Peggy McKee	Mar. 15, 1821
Parris, William	Nancy Freeman	Apr. 21, 1823

R

Roberts, Hamilton	Dolly Cheshire	Aug. 2, 1819
Reed, Mathias	Cassie Hamlin	Sept. 14, 1820
Rose, Benjamin	Elizabeth Powers	Sept. 2, 1820
Rogers, William	Sally Sumner	Feb. 9, 1820
Reed, Mathias	Mahala Hoof (Huff)	Feb. 26, 1821
Ross, Robert	Sally Gray	Mar. 10, 1822

S

Sumner, George	Katie Eaton	May 5, 1819
Sears, John	Mary Stanfield	Feb. 15, 1819
Smith, Elijah	Lucretia Jones	June 7, 1822

Groom	Bride	Date of Marriage
Sexton, Archer	Jane Ballinger	May 29, 1820
Sexton, William	Jane Bishop	Sept. 2, 1819
Sullivan, John W.	Ann Griffiths	...., ...
Steele, Andrew	Dalila Wells	Apr. 16, 1821
Sumner, Mark	Lucy Bryant	Dec. 18, 1821
Stringer, Missouri	Maria Ham	Mar. 7, 1822
Standfield, William	Rebecca Ellison	Dec. 19, 1822
Standfield, Sampson	Rhoda Ellison	Mar. 25, 1822
Strunk, David	Honor Pennington	Mar. 9, 1822
Stinson, Jacob	Elizabeth Wells	Aug. 4, 1823
Smith, Elijah	Lucretia Jones	June 7, 1823
Starr, Joel	Charlotte Wells	Oct. 10, 1823
Smithhert, Darby	Betsy Polly	Nov. 13, 1823
Smith, Isaac	Matilda Ross	Jan. 11, 1823
Sears, James	Polly Foley	Apr. 20, 1818

T

Tillotson, Augustus	Margaret Hill	Nov. 15, 1819
Turnbull, Nicholas	Sidney Petry	July 11, 1822

W

Wyatt, Vincent	Jemima Duncan	Sept. 19, 1819
Walker, Jesse	Peggy Bishop	Aug. 7, 1820
Watkins, Baker	Sally Berry	Apr. 4, 1822
Wells, Abraham	Nancy Sears	July 4, 1822
Walker, Joel	Cynthia Sharp	July 2, 1822
Wilson, David	Mary Wilson	Dec. 14, 1822
West, Solomon	Katharine Crecelius ?	Feb. 23, 1823

CHAPTER XIII

ELLIOTT COUNTY, KENTUCKY

ORGANIZATION

ELLIOTT COUNTY, the 114th in order of creation, was created by an act of the General Assembly of Kentucky, approved January 26, 1869, from parts of Carter, Lawrence and Morgan Counties. On April 5, 1869, the county was divided into justices' districts by a commission composed of W. H. Van Sant, J. K. Howard, G. W. Stamper and Travis Horton. (A. Ison, a member of the commission failed to act.) On the same day a committee composed of W. H. Cox, William Mynhier, W. L. Holbrook and D. D. Sublett selected the site for the county seat. The county seat town, Martinsburg, was named for Hon. John P. Martin, a distinguished pioneer of Floyd County, who had served as Representative in Congress and held many other public offices of honor and trust.

FIRST COUNTY COURT

The first session of the County Court was held May 24, 1869, presided over by the Hon. James K. Hunter, who produced his commission from His Excellency John W. Stephenson, Governor of the Commonwealth of Kentucky, which contained an endorsement thereon showing that the oath of office previously had been administered to him.

FIRST COUNTY OFFICERS

At the first session of the County Court (May 22, 1869) the county officers, who had been commissioned by the Governor, took the oaths of office and entered upon their respective duties. These officers were:

County Court Clerk, J. G. Whitt
County Attorney, James W. Hannah.
School Commissioner, Daniel C. DeHart
Circuit Court Clerk, Houston King
Sheriff, Henry D. Porter
Jailer, Joel Kegley
Coroner, Alfred Sparks
Assessor, A. J. Crisp

FIRST JUSTICES OF THE PEACE

John Hood, Milton L. Carter, Odon Cox, M. F. Adkins, Nelson Sparks, Martin Whitt, Reuben C. Sparks, Ison Wagoner, Pleasant Gillum, Charles W. Carter.

FIRST CONSTABLES

Samuel Ison, Jacob Horton, A. J. Jarrell, James M. Green.

CHAPTER XIV

MARRIAGES — FLEMING, HARLAN, LETCHER AND MASON COUNTIES

FLEMING COUNTY MARRIAGES 1798-1800

Earliest Marriage Records of Fleming County, from the organization of the County March 1, 1798, to June 30, 1800, organization of Floyd County:

Groom	*Bride*	*Date of Marriage*
A		
Alexander, John	Catherine Gilbert	May 3, 1799
Alexander, Robert	Eleanor Royce	Jan. 16, 1800
Applegate, Jacob	Hannah Roman	June 20, 1800
B		
Barnes, Joseph	Phoebe Stockton	Feb. 20, 1800
Bateman, Owen	Patience Havens	Jan. 10, 1800
Belt, Marshom	Margaret Norman	May 29, 1800
Bird, Edward	Ann Trimble	Apr. 12, 1798
Bradshaw, James	Anne Wilson	Jan. 10, 1800
Brown, Asa	Anna Alexander	Mar. 20, 1800
Builderback, Gabriel	Rachel Ferguson	Feb. 14, 1799
Builderback, William	Mary McAllister	Sept. 18, 1799
Burriss, Charles	Elizabeth Plummer	Oct. 29, 1799
Butcher, Isaac	Elizabeth Clark	Mar. 10, 1799
C		
Callahan, Anderson	Patty Reeves	Dec. 18, 1800
Choate, Edward	Hannah Frazier	Sept. 28, 1799
Correl ?, Bartholomew	Frances Clark	Dec. 19, 1799
D		
Dale, Uriah	Mary Gardner	June 13, 1799
Davis, Joseph	Polly McKee	Apr. 18, 1799
DeMoss, James ?	Sarah Burris	.... 11, 1798
Donohue, John	Elizabeth Williams	Mar. 28, 1798
F		
Finley, John	Mary Loughead	June 1, 1799
Fitzherald, James	Fannie Hughes	Apr. 27, 1800
Fletcher, Jilson	Rhoda Heffling ?	June 11, 1799
G		
Gooding, Samuel	Peggy Hinton	Nov. 8, 1800
Goodard, Abbott	Fanny Lewis	Oct. 10, 1800

Groom	Bride	Date of Marriage

L

Lapos ?, William	Geresel ? Jameson	Mar. 26, 1789?
		Mar. 26, 1798?
Linney, George	Patsy McDowell	Nov. ...., 1798

M

Mahan, John	Susannah Fellett	Sept. 18, 1799
Markwell, John	Jane Faris	Sept. 12, 1799
Morgan, George	Elizabeth Montgomery	May ...., 1798
Murphy, Robert	Elizabeth Clifford	Nov. 7, 1799
McCullough, John	Jane Robinson	Apr. 30, 1798
McKee, Robert	Elizabeth Tout ?	Sept. 3, 1799

O

| Oliver, John | Mary Burriss | Jan. 29, 1800 |

P

Pearce, Thomas	Elizabeth Collins	July 7, 1799
Pickrell, Henry	Sarah Gilkerson	Oct. 9, 1799
Plummer, Thomas	Jane Ruggles	Dec. 31, 1790 ?

R

Ramey, Enoch	Susannah Miller	Sept. 26, 1799
Ray, Jesse	Mourning Hughes	May 28, 1798
Rawlings, Jonathan	Ann Walker	Feb. 17, 1800
Reeves, Elijah, Jr.	Nancy Blemmer (Plummer)	July 1, 1800
Rhoden, Thomas	Susanna Beatty	Jan. 17, 1799
Roe, James	Abigail Mershon	July 18, 1798

S

Scott, Joseph	Margaret Newcomb	Jan. 31, 1799
Shanklin, Gordon	Ann Hart	Apr. 30, 1798
Shields, William	Elizabeth Davis	Aug. 8, 1798
Smith, John	Mary Kelly	Jan. 1, 1797
Steele, Joseph	Jane Lee	Aug. 24, 1794 ?
Stephens, Samuel	Rebecca Reed	Nov. 6, 1798
Summers, George	Aggy Heffling	Jan. 12, 1799
Sutherland, Ebenezer	Margaret McArthur	Oct. 17, 1798
Sweet, James	Elizabeth Firman	Apr. 18, 1799

T

Taylor, George	Nancy McFarland	Nov. ...., 1798
Tharp, Levi	Elizabeth Quinans ?	May 12, 1799
Thompson, John	Nancy McAllister	Apr. 16, 1799
Tucker, Benjamin	Jane Givens	Nov. 26, 1799

W

Waddell, Samuel	Eleanor Beard	May 7, 1794 ?
Wills, Samuel	Margaret Jameson	May ...., 1798
Willson, William	Lettice Willson	Feb. 7, 1794?
Winans, Jacob	Rachel Beacraft	June 27, 1799

HARLAN COUNTY MARRIAGES 1856-1863

Groom	Bride	Date of Marriage	By Whom
A			
Allen, Daniel	Obedience Huff	Sept. 6, 1857	Alexander Kelly, M.C.
Asher, John P. M.	Elizabeth Howard	May 11, 1858	John Wilson, J. P.
B			
Blanton, George	Mary Lewis	Apr. 5, 1857	A. S. Hall, Bap. Ch.
Browning, Wilson	Rebecca Osborn	Mar. 5, 1857	Noble Smith, J. P.
Buckhart, James	Sally Osborn	Aug. 29, 1857	Noble Smith, J. P.
Burns, David	Sylvania Slusher	Mar. ...., 1858	Alexander Lock, J. P.
Brock, Calvin	Margaret Long	Apr. 17, 1861	Nathan H. Noe, B. C.
Brock, Jordan	Margaret Caldwell	Feb. 17, 1858	Robert Helton, J. P.
Barnett, Joseph H.	Nancy J. Saylor	May 18, 1862	Joseph Wilder
Burchett, James W.	Louisa J. Harris	Jan. 21, 1861	John H. Farmer, J. P
Ball, Brittain	Margaret L. Pitman	May 17, 1860	William Bailey, MCS
Barnett, James	Sarah J. Robbins	July 15, 1857	Esan Piercefield, J. P.
Bailey, Jesse	Jane Howard	Nov. 15, 1860	Joseph Bailey
Bailey, Elisha	Martha Jameson	Oct. ...., 1857	Alexander Kelly
Brummett, William	Jemima Helton	Mar. 1, 1860	N. H. Noe, Elder, B. C.
Blanton, James	Martha J. Simpson	Feb. 7, 1860	David Bailey
Bailey, E. C.	Jane Lankford	3, 1861	William Middleton
Blanton, Jackson	Elizabeth Murray	Mar. 5, 1861	T. H. Noe
Burkhert (Burkhart), Walter T.?	Selma Spurlock	Apr. 6, 1861	John H. Farmer
Brock, Jonathan	Polly Saylor	May 7, 1859	Robert Helton
Belcher, Wylie	Susannah Coldiron	Feb. 24, 1859	A. S. Hall
Bailey, Minter	Sarah B. Bailey	Mar. 13, 1862	J. K. Bailey
Bailey, Solomon	Rebecca Brock	Sept. 1, 1858	N. Durham, J. P.
Baker, John	Mary Rice	June 4, 1860	A. Lock, J. P.
Bailey, J. K.	Louise Ann Jones	Jan. 21, 1863	William Middleton
Brummett, Peyton	Sylvania Osborn	Dec. 14, 1863	T. H. Noe
Blanton, Josiah	Joannah Step	Nov. 18, 1862	T. H. Noe
Baker, Henry T.	Jane Lewis	Jan. 29, 1863	Abner Lewis
Ball, Andrew J.	Louisa S. Pope	Aug. 4, 1863	William Middleton
Ball, Gibson	Nicey Ball	May 23, 1861	Solomon Pope
Ball, Evan	Juda Crider	Jan. 19, 1862	Solomon Pope
Brown, Matt	Jane Fields	Sept. 29, 1859	J. K. Bailey
C			
Carroll, John	Martha Lewis	Jan. 20, 1857	Hiram S. Powell
Creech, Daniel B.	Nancy Metcalf	Jan. 29, 1857	....
Clem, John	Louisa Osborn	Mar. 11, 1858	Alfred S. Hall, B. C.
Caywood, Stephen	Louisa Turner	July 7, 1859	Solomon Pope
Caywood, Stephen	Virginia Calloway	June 25, 1861	David Bailey
Creech, Harrison	Fanny Smith	May 12, 1861	Jonathan K. Bailey
Caldwell, Samuel S.	Idress Brock	Feb. 18, 1858	Robert Helton
Collins, John	Nancy Roark	Oct. 29, 1856	Robert Helton, J. P.
Colier, David M.	M. A. Bazwell	Jan. 24, 1860	H. S. Powell
Cornett, Samuel	Rachel Jenkins	Nov. 28, 1861	Abner Lewis
Cuder, John	Nancy A. Pope	Jan. 26, 1862	S. Pope
Clay, Elijah	Susannah Sergent	May 15, 1860	H. S. Powell
Coots, William	Elizabeth Turner	Feb. 15, 1862	A. C. Turner, J. P.
Causey, Stephen	Juda Lewis	Jan. 2, 1862	A. C. Turner
Causey, C. B.	Mary J. Dishoner	.... 18, 1858	Elihu Wells
Creech, Jonathan	Leander Lewis	Sept. 20, 1858	Elijah Creech, J. P.

Groom	Bride	Date of Marriage	By Whom

D

Groom	Bride	Date of Marriage	By Whom
Denny, Joseph	Sarah J. Hurst	Feb. 8, 1859	N. Durham, J. P.
Day, Ira	Eliza Skidmore	July 22, 1860	A. L. Hall, B. C.
Daniel, Isaiah	Elizabeth Helton	Jan. 14, 1861	David Bailey
Dean, John	Eliza Hall	Aug. 19, 1860	Wm. Middleton, J. P.
Davis, Daniel	Sarah Hoskins	Nov. 1, 1858	Alexander Lock
Day, Henry	Mary Maggard	Sept. 14, 1862	Abner Lewis, J. P.
Day, John	Savanna Skidmore	May 1, 1859	Solomon Pope

E

Groom	Bride	Date of Marriage	By Whom
Ely, Ervin	Mary Cox	Mar. 10, 1857	Leroy Ely, M. E. Ch.
Ely, Mark J. K.	Sarah Cox	Mar. 10, 1857	Leroy Ely, M. E. Ch.
Ely, Isaac	Ludamy Howard	Mar. 14, 1860	Wm. G. Howard, J. P.
Ernest, David	Esther Wilson	Dec. 2, 1861	Solomon Pope

F

Groom	Bride	Date of Marriage	By Whom
Failer, William	Tennessee Johnson	Feb. 19, 1857	Wilkerson, Howard, J. P.
Farler, John K.	Sally Clem	Aug. 30, 1858	Alfred S. Hall, B. C.
Flanery, Arvy	Eliza Daugherty	Feb. ...., 1858	Winston Huff, M. C.
French, Giles W.	June Failer	Apr. 17, 1857	Wm. Middleton
Farmer, Leonard	Fanny Jones	Mar. 29, 1860	Wm. Middleton
Flanery, Jacob	Martha Hartsock	May 29, 1862	John H. Farmer, J. P.
Fields, James	Elizabeth Noe	July 25, 1861	A. S. Hall, B. C.
Farmer, Felix	Shartell Helton	Feb. ...., 1859	Robert Helton, J. P.
Farmer, Dillon A.	Elizabeth Wilson	......., 8, 1860	Jacob Burkhart
Fouch, Alexander	Doreas Fields	.... 17, 1860	A. S. Hall
Farler, Green	Elizabeth Napier	Jan. 3, 1862	A. C. Turner, J. P.
Fee, Henderson	Sarah Osborn	Apr. 21, 1861	A. S. Hall
Forrister, John W.	Nancy Howard	Mar. 7, 1859	A. S. Hall

G

Groom	Bride	Date of Marriage	By Whom
Green, Barnett	Nancy Mircle	Feb. 24, 1857	Henry Wilson, J. P.
Griffith, Jacob	Nancy Failer	Nov. 29, 1857	Noble Smith, J. P.
Grimes, Joshua	Minerva McCabe	July 26, 1859	Solomon Pope, M. C.
Gates, Andrew	Hester Madden	Mar. 10, 1858	Wilkerson Howard
Gross, John	Ailsey Simpson	Mar. 23, 1858	Elisha A. Helton, J. P.
Guy, Edward	Marinda Barrett	Dec. 10, 1858	Henry Pennington, J.P.
Green, William	Elizabeth Hoskins	Nov. 12, 1861	Joseph Wilder
Grabell, Josephus	Sarah Carter	Jan. 15, 1859	Rev. S. H. Martin
Green, Elias	Sarah Jackson	Apr. 11, 1858	Henry Wilson, J. P.
Green, James	Margaret Miricle	Feb. 18, 1862	John H. Farmer
Griffith, Jacob	Nancy Estep	Apr. 9, 1863	Abner Lewis

H

Groom	Bride	Date of Marriage	By Whom
Howard, Larkin	Barbara Ely	Oct. 21, 1856	John Wilson, J. P.
Hoskins, Andrew I.	Thursday (Thursa) Marion	Nov. 13, 1856	Robert Helton, J. P.
Hoskins, John	Delilah Green	Dec. 20, 1857	William Bailey, M. C.
Howard, Daniel G.	Judith Wilson	...., ...	....
Huff, Hiram	Elizabeth Clem	Aug. 8, 1858	Wm. Middleton
Hoskins, Reuben	Hannah Griffith?	Apr. 29, 1858	W. Howard
Huff, William W.	Stacy Smith	Sept. 12, 1858	Winston Huff, M. C.

Groom	Bride	Date of Marriage	By Whom
Hulett, John	Jinsey Dean	Mar. 11, 1858	Noble Smith, J. P.
Howard, Wilkerson A.	Margaret Piercefield	June 20, 1861	David Bailey, J. P.
Hurst, Helvy	Sarah C. Piercefield	Dec. 21, 1858	Nelson Durham, J. P.
Hoover, Jacob	M. F. Gray	Jan. 13, 1859	H. S. Powell, J. P.
Hoskins, Irvine	Rebecca Garrison	Mar. 18, 1859	Elijah Creek, J. P.
Howard, Elijah S.	Nancy C. Howard	Mar. 25, 1860	Wm. G. Howard
Hensley, Wilson	Nancy Hensley	Aug. 8, 1860	A. S. Hall
Huff, Allen	Elizabeth Creech	Apr. 29, 1860	Jonathan Bailey
Hoskins, Braxter	Mary Arnett	...., ...	....
Howard, Dallas Dudley	Emily Jones	Apr. 17, 1862	Wm. Middleton
Hendricks, John	Mary Crawford	Jan. 9, 1861	E. McGuire
Howard, Hiram B.	Jane Coldiron	Jan. 10, 1861	....
Hutchins, Elijah	Elizabeth Bingham	Dec. 22, 1859	William Nouh
Hensley, Wash.	Sally Smith	July 21, 1861	Solomon Pope
Hurst, Solomon	Elizabeth Piercefield	Apr. 26, 1859	H. Wilson
Hoskins, Gabriel	Arena Davis	July 1, 1859	R. Bingham, J. P.
Howard, Wilson	Susan Lewis	July 15, 1860	J. Burkhart
Hall, M. S. P.	Susannah Shook	Jan. 2, 1862	Jno. H. Farmer
Hensley, G. W.	Sally Lewis	Jan. 22, 1860	T. H. Noe
Hargis, G. W.	Sabrina? Hurst	Nov. 27, 1854	....
Hoskins, Ezekiel	Anna Miricle	Aug. 5, 1861	Joseph Wilder
Hoskins, James	Catherine Miricle	Sept. 4, 1861	Joseph Wilder
Hoskins, Gabriel	Malinda Burns	Jan. 9, 1861	William North
Howard, William M.	Rachel Fee	Apr. 11, 1861	T. H. Noe
Howard, John C.	Nancy Lewis	Jan. 31, 1861	T. H. Noe
Howard, Hiram	Alice Jennings	June 9, 1859	T. H. Noe
Hendrickson, Jeff	Rosanna Rice	May 23, 1859	Alexander Lock
Helton (Hilton, Hylton), Ephraim	Margaret Taylor (Saylor?)	....	Jacob Burkhart
Hall, William C.	Sarah Ward	Oct. 13, 1859	A. S. Hall
Hall, Francis	Esther Caywood	Feb. 4, 1858	A. S. Hall
Hall, B. F.	Barbara D. Short	May 20, 1859	A. S. Hall
Huff, Milton	Nancy McKinney	Sept. 7, 1861	Wm. Bailey
Hutchins, ...	Mahala Burns	...., 1863	James Culton
Hoskins, Crittenden	Sarah Miricle	Nov. 23, 1862	....
Hall, Andrew	Levia Step	Jan. 22, 1863	William Bailey
Howard, Aaron B.	Mary Lewis	Feb. 17, 1863	Abner Lewis
Huff, Coleb	Nancy Lewis	Feb. 5, 1863	Abner Lewis, J. P.
Hall, Nathan	Louisa Noe	Mar. 22, 1863	Alfred Hall
Howard, Samuel M.	Lucy R. Noe	Aug. 2, 1863	N. T. Noe

I

Irvine, Mahlon	Jane Creech	July 26, 1862	William Middleton

J

Jones, Larkin	Letitia Jones	.... 10, 1859	A. S. Hall, B. C.
Johnson, Andrew	Nancy J. Burns	May 24, 1860	Alexander Lock
Johnson, Levi	Mary Johnson	Oct. 23, 1862	Samuel Hargis, J. P.
Johnson, Richard	M. Jane Roark	Mar. 3, 1860	Thomas B. Noe

K

Kelly, Silas W.	Rebecca Smith	Apr. 1, 1856	....
Kelly, James	Eliza Jane Johnson	Sept. 7, 1862	William Bailey

Groom	Bride	Date of Marriage	By Whom

L

Long, Lewis	Elizabeth Lansdown	Dec. 27, 1857	....
Leforce, James M.	Millie J. Bingham	Nov. 3, 1857	David Green, J. P.
Lewis, Wilson	Fanny Jones	Oct. 25, 1860	Elihu Wells, C. C.
Lawson, Samuel	Sarah Burns	Mar. 3, 1859	Robert Helton
Long, J. D.	Jane Ball	July 1, 1861	Nathan H. Noe
Lee, Larkin	S. J. Daniel	Oct. 4, 1861	Solomon Pope
Lock, Parks	Mary Miller	Mar. 13, 1857	R. Bingham
Lewis, Abner	Letitia Lewis	.... 22, 1860	John Ludge, Judge H. C. C.
Ledford, George W.	Elizabeth Howard	Dec. 5, 1861	David Bailey, J. P.
Lewis, William	Rebecca Hensley	May 14, 1857	WilkersonHoward,J.P.
Lefevre, Lyman	Nancy Baker	Sept. 8, 1859	Alexander Lock
Lefevre, John	Nancy Hoskins	Sept. 17, 1859	....
Lee, William	Elizabeth Wilder	Sept. 12, 1858	William Bailey
Ledford, Beatty	Louise Howard	Jan. 6, 1859	A. S. Hall
Lewis, John	Lucy Smith	Jan. 25, 1863	A. C. Turner, J. P.
Lee, Arthur M. C.	Margaret A. Denny	........, ..., 1861	Wm. Bailey

M

McGeorge, James	Sarah Jennings	May 24, 1857	Elisha A. Helton, J. P.
Metcalf, James	Annie Creech	Mar. 8, 1857	Joseph S. Kelly, M. C.
Muncy, Samuel L.	Martha Nance	June 24, 1857	Elisha Wells
Middleton, Benjamin	Sally Blevins	Mar. 14, 1858	William Middleton
McKnight, John G.	Celia Creech	July 29, 1862	Abner Lewis
Morris, John K.	Catherine Gillund (Gilliam)	May 13, 1859	H. S. Powell
Maynard, Joseph	Louisa Bailey	May 11, 1859	James Napier
Marion, Cornelius	Sarah Caldwell	.... 8, 1859	....
Miles, William	Lettie Blair	.... 19, 1859	Abner Lewis
Mirircle, James C.	Elizabeth Hoskins	Sept. 14, 1861	Joseph Wilder
Maggard, James	Martha Creech	...., 1861	H. S. Powell
Miller, Hogan	Elizabeth Howell	July 27, 1860	R. Bingham
Mirircle, James	Janie Mirircle	Dec. 29, 1858	William Bailey
Mirircle, Robert	Sarah Wilder	May 7, 1861	William Bailey
Mirircle, John M.	Mary Wilder	Dec. 3, 1859	Joseph Wilder

N

Napier, James	Elizabeth Jackson	Oct. 23, 1857	Robert Helton, J. P.
Napier, Samuel	Jane Marion	....	....
Nolen, James	Catherine Dixon	Dec. 30, 1858	H. S. Powell
Nance, James	Rachel Saylor	May 11, 1862	Abner Lewis
Noe, Calvin	Rebecca Browning	Sept. 29, 1861	James Blevins, B. C.
Niel, James	Eliza J. Ward	Sept. 30, 1858	Alexander Lock
Napier, Gabriel	Elizabeth North	Dec. 3, 1858	Robert Helton
Napier, James	Leah North	.... 7, 1860	Jacob Burkhart, J. P.
Napier, E. V.	Sarah Blanton	...., 1861	Thomas H. Noe
Nolen, A. H.	Alabama Jennings	Apr. 16, 1861	William Middleton
Noe, James	Maranda Gray	Jan. 23, 1858	H. S. Powell
Napier, George	Abigail Slusher	Feb. ...., 1857	A. S. Hall
Noe, Nathan H.	Martha Blanton	Mar. 5, 1857	A. S. Hall
Nolen, Chadwell	Louisa Turner	...., ...	....

Groom	Bride	Date of Marriage	By Whom

O

Osborn, Claborn?	Eliza Hensley	Aug. ...., 1860	....
Osborn, Levi	Polly Simpson	Sept. 5, 1858	John Wilson, J. P.
Osborn, Jeremiah	Polly Hensley	Feb. 19, 1857	A. S. Hall
Osborn, Andrew	Lucy Osborn	July 1, 1863	John H. Farmer
Osborn, William F.	Nancy Caywood	Apr. 1, 1858	Alfred S. Hall

P

Pickard, Doctor H.	Almira Hutchins	Sept. 27, 1857	Robert Helton
Pace, Francis	Luvana Forrister	Oct. 19, 1858	Alfred S. Hall
Pennington, William	Lavena Turner	Sept. 1, 1859	Solomon Pope
Piercefield, John C.	Nancy Mirircle	May 17, 1861	Joseph Wilder
Pope, John J.	Joanna Turner	Dec. ...., 1860	....
Powell, Amborse	Margaret Smith	...., 1862	Elias Smith, M. C.
Pennington, Edward	Annie York	Oct. 24, 1861	Elihu Wells
Philips, W. H.	Jane Osborn	May 13, 1858	A. S. Hall

R

Roark, Aaron	Emily Brown	Dec. 25, 1857	Robert Helton
Rice, B. A.	Tabitha Miller	Aug. 11, 1860	William North
Rolly (Raleigh), James	Sarah Mirircle	July 8, 1859	Nelson Durham
Reddick, Abraham	Dolly Messer	June 28, 1858	N. Durham

S

Salyers, Cracy	Elizabeth Hoskins	Sept. 26, 1857	Robert B
Saylor, Green V.	Matilda Helton	Oct. 11, 1856	John Wilson
Saylor, William	Lelithacomy Woollum	July 16, 1857	Stephen Rice
Simpson, William	Margaret Gambrill	July 15, 1857	Stephen Rice
Stapleton, Silas B.	Eliza J. Parsons	July 16, 1857	Joseph S. Kelly
Smith, Elias	Rebecca Creech	June 18, 1857	Elijah Creech, J. P.
Saylor, Ervine	Mary A. Saylor	Mar. 7, 1858	L. D. Ely
Sergent, John	Fanny Noe	Nov. 18, 1857	William Middleton
Smith, Hugh H.	Narcissa Ball	July 24, 1859	Solomon Pope
Stewart, Albert	Emily King	June 13, 1861	Solomon Pope, M. C.
Stolks (Stokes), James Riley	Julia A. Slusher	May 19, 1861	William G. Howard
Skidmore, John	Patsy Stepp	May 11, 1859	A. S. Hall
Skidmore, Albert	Mary Jones	May 5, 1859	Solomon Pope
Smith, John H.	Lucinda McDaniel	Nov. 16, 1860	Abner Lewis
Smith, Noah	Nancy Robbins	Nov. 1, 1860	William Bailey
Smith, Elias	Rebecca Creech	June 18, 1857	Elijah Creech
Smith, David	Polly Smith	Jan. 30, 1861	....
Saylor, Henry	Lucinda Osborn	July 10, 1861	Nathan H. Noe
Skidmore, A. C.	Louisa Forrister	.... 8, 1860	John H. Farmer
Stepp, Jacob	Joanna Hall	Sept. 28, 1860	A. S. Hall
Stamper, J. W.	Elizabeth Gillum	Jan. 10, 1861	H. S. Powell
Simpson, Isaac	Jemima Brock	Feb. 25, 1861	Thomas H. Noe
Sergent, Stephen	Elizabeth Powell	Apr. 3, 1861	John H. Farmer
Simpson, Calloway	Julia Blanton	Feb. 23, 1858	T. H. Noe
Stidham, Samuel	Clora Creech	May 7, 1857	Elijah Creech
Sergent, Allen	Nancy Smith	Feb. 20, 1862	J. K. Bailey
Shackleford, William	Nancy Fields	Dec. 4, 1857	A. S. Hall

Groom	Bride	Date of Marriage	By Whom
Shepherd, John	Lucy Osborn	March 15, 1857	A. S. Hall
Setser, Thomas H.	Mary Yearry	Feb. 4, 1857	Alexander Kelly
Saylor, Levi B.	Sally Pitmon?	Dec. 3, 1857	Joseph Wilder
Smith, George W.	Jerusha Unhank?	Jan. 27, 1859	S. Pope
Short, Charles	Margaret Gilbert	Nov. 6, 1862	William Bailey
Saylor, Silas W.	Nancy M. Johnson	Dec. 18, 1862	Joseph Meder
Sampson, Newton	Nancy Jane Crawford	Dec. 25, 1862	Samuel H
Stepp, Carlo B.	Polly Jackson, alias Helton	July 30, 1862	T. H. Noe
Sergent, Jackson	Nancy Browning	Feb. 9, 1863	....
Sergent, Andrew	Elizabeth Parsons	....,	.... William Bailey

T

Groom	Bride	Date of Marriage	By Whom
Thomas, Joseph	Cynthia Parsons	Jan. 5, 1859	William Middleton
Trent, Calvin	Sarah Sergent	Apr. 20, 1860	S. Pope
Templeton, John	Elizabeth Napier	Sept. 8, 1861	William Middleton
Thacker, Valentine	Sarah Taylor	Mar. 18, 1861	David Bailey
Templeton, James	Jennie Lewis	May 1, 1862	Elihu Wells
Taylor, William R.	Sally Vaughan	Apr. ...., 1861	....
Turner, John L.	Louisa Hensley	Jan. 14, 1858	W. Howard
Turner, David	Stacy Turner	Jan. 5, 1863	Abner Lewis
Turner, William	Louvana Upton	Nov. 19, 1862	Elisha Wells

U

Groom	Bride	Date of Marriage	By Whom
Unshank?, Milton	Josaphine Moore	Feb. 3, 1859	N. Durham

W

Groom	Bride	Date of Marriage	By Whom
Wilder, James B.	Rosanna Wilson	Nov. 24, 1857	Henry Wilson
Wynn, Achiles P.	Allafair Ledford	Feb. 24, 1857	S. Pope
Wilson, Peter	Sarah Howard	Feb. 24, 1859	Robert Helton
Wilder, Levi H.	Mary Jane Mirircle	Dec. 13, 1859	William Bailey
Weaver, Nathan	Nancy Flannery	Feb. 8, 1861	Jonathan Bailey
Wilson, Richard	Mary Hurst	July 25, 1859	Samuel Hargis
Wilson, Simeon	Sarah Niel	Feb. 17, 1860	Jacob Burhart
Wells, Larkin	Catherine Lewis	.... 3, 1861	Elihu Wells
Williams, Bogle	Elizabeth Creech	Feb. ...., 1861	H. S. Powell
Wilson, John	Angellella?, Wilson	Jan. 20,	Jacob Burkhart
Worms, Clark	Catherine K. Hall	Jan. 15, 1863	James Bulton
Wilson, Green	Mary Nunn	Aug. 18, 1862	Samuel Hargis, J. P.
Wilson, William H.	Sabra Brock	Nov. 5, 1862	Joseph Wilder
Wilson, William M. F.	Jane Hall	May 21, 1857	Alexander Lock

LETCHER COUNTY MARRIAGES 1843-1846

Marriage Records from organization to December, 1846

Groom	Bride	Date of Marriage	By Whom

A

Groom	Bride	Date of Marriage	By Whom
Amburgy, William	Hannah Bentley	Jan. 8, 1846	James Collins, M. C.
Adams, Spencer	Celia Church	Mar. 19, ...	Hiram Hogg

Groom	Bride	Date of Marriage	By Whom
Adams, John	Anna Adams	Oct. 20, 1844	John Caudill
Adams, John	Nancy Owings	Nov. 24, 1845	Solomon Yants, M. C.
Adams, Jesse	Polly Crofte	July 24, 1845	John Caudill
Adams, William	Mary Kinser?	Sept. 7, 1846	P. H. Collier
Adams, Jesse	Margaret Linkins?	Aug. 20, 1846	Joseph Crofte
Alington,(Ellington), Charles	Elizabeth Kilgore	Dec. 14, 1843	A. Cantrill

B

Bentley, Joseph	Anna Justice?	Mar. 13, 1843	Abram Cantrill, M. G.
Bates, John A.	Sarah Woldege	May 12, 1845	John Caudill
Back (Bach), Henry	Frances Blair	Mar. 23, 1843	David Maggard
Blair, Elihu	Celia Adams	Mar. 5, 1846	Preston H. Collier
Breeding, Wesley	Jinsey Pritchett	Apr. 1, 1846	P. H. Collier
Bentley, William	Elizabeth Amburgy	Feb. 19, 1846	....
Bates, James	Elizabeth Adams	Jan. 26, 1843	John Caudill
Bolling, Hosea	Levina Hays	...., 1846	John Caudill
Bolling, James	Polly Hammons	...., 1844	John Caudill
Burley ?, Jesse	Rachel Cornette	Nov. 12, 1843	Harrison J. Huff
Boggs, William	Rebecca Shepherd	Oct. 9, 1844	David Maggard
Bowens, William	Rebecca Williams	...., 1843	John Caudill
Back, Samuel	Rosa Malinda Day	Mar. 10, 1844	Hiram Hogg
Brown, Benjamin	Polly Blair	Sept. 25, 1845	John Caudill
Bolling, Delany	Matilda Brooks	Feb. 16, 1843	H. Hogg

C

Caudill, Henry	Jane Adams	Feb. 26, 1846	John Caudill, M. G.
Crofte?, Henry	Elizabeth Dillian	Mar. 15, 1846	P. H. Collier
Caudill, Isham	Eliza Cox	July 13, 1843	John Caudill
Combs, Edward	Lydia Adams	...., 1844	John Caudill
Caudill, Electius	Sally Madden	...., 1843	John Caudill
Collins, Thomas	Catherine Thomas	Feb. 2, 1845	James Collins
Caudill, William	Margaret Amburgy	Oct. 17, 1844	John Caudill
Caudill, William	Polly Brown	Mar. 6, 1845	David Maggard
Caudill, J.	A. Hampton	May 11, 1843	John Caudill
Collins, Charles	Lucy Gibson	July 30, 1844	James Collins
Cordelle, Alfred	Ora Sturgill	Dec. 18, 1845	P. H. Collier
Cordelle, Abel	Polly Creese?	...., 1842	J. Cordelle
Cordelle, Watson	Elizabeth Smith	...., ...	J. Cordelle
Cassady?, Thomas	Laura Richmond	May 10, 1845	P. H. Collier
Collins, Robert	Anna Banks	Mar. 16, 1844	James Collins
Cordelle, Jesse	Mary Back	Apr. 4, 1844	J. Cordelle
Creech, Gilbert	Elizabeth Maggard	July 13, 1843	D. Maggard

D

Dickerson, Little	Franky Calhoun	Jan. 1, 1843	H. J. Huff
Day, John	Susannah Collier	June 6, 1844	David Maggard
Day, David	Rebecca Back	...., 1845	John Caudill
Day, Moses	Juda Coates	Dec. 18, 1845	P. H. Collier

E

Elswick, Jacob	Sanders	Mar. 12, 1846	A. Cantrill

F

Field, Sanford L.	Ruta Young	July 25, 1843	John Caudill

Groom	Bride	Date of Marriage	By Whom
G			
Gibson, William	Hannah Gibson	Apr. 12, 1844	James Collins
H			
Hazen, James	Nancy Hall	Oct. 12, 1843	James Collins
Hall, Reuben	Nancy Hall	Mar. 24, 1846	James Collins
Hammons, Martin	Elizabeth Crofte	Feb. 19, 1846	P. H. Collier
Huff, James	Arra Wills	Aug. 20, 1844	David Maggard
Hinton, Richard	Nancy Stanley	Apr. 25, 1844	H. Hogg
Hogg, James	Dicie Frazier	Dec. 28, 1842	H. Hogg
Hubbard, Robert	Sarah Bolling	Apr. 13, 1843	H. Hogg
Hale, William	Mary Sloane	June 4, 1844	....
Hammons, Larkin	Sarah Crofte	...., 1844	J. Caudill
Hampton, Sylvester	Elizabeth Caudill	...., 1844	J. Caudill
L			
Lewis, Jonathan	Retta Polly	Feb. 22, 1844	Hiram Hogg
Lucas, Emanuel	Lottie Moore	Sept. 15, 1844	John Caudill
Lucas, Willis	Elizabeth Quillen	Sept. 15, 1845	John Caudill
Lewis, Bazil	Rebecca Maggard	Oct. 30, 1845	....
M			
Mullins, Thomas	Dicie Keel?	Nov. 14, 1846	Abram Cantrill
Maggard, John H.	Savilla Mullins	Mar. 19, 1846	D. Maggard
Maggard, James	Elizabeth Sturgill	Mar. 16, 1843	D. Maggard
McKinzie?, John	Nancy Withot?	Jan. 14, 1844	H. Hogg
Maggard, Sampson	Elizabeth Bolling	Aug. 27, 1845	D. Maggard
Maggard, David	Cussa? Morris	May 5, 1844	D. Maggard
Mastain, Benjamin	Levina Hagans	Jan. 18, 1844	H. Hogg
Mullins, Wilson	Rebecca Maggard	Feb. 5, 1846	D. Maggard
Maggard, John	Nancy Bolling	June 30, 1846	D. Maggard
O			
Osborn, John W.	Sena Moore	May 1, 1844	John Caudill
P			
Polly, James	Margaret Combs	Jan. 25, 1844	H. Hogg
Prophet, Stephen	Rebecca Cordelle	Mar. 24, 1844	J. Caudill
Pigman, Wesley	Sarah Adams	...., ...	R. Calhoun, M. G.
Pigman, John B.	Nancy Cornette	Mar. 10, 1843	Harrison J. Huff, M. G.
Potter, Marshall	Eliza Mullins	Sept. 28, 1846	Joseph Crofte
Q			
Quillen, Henry	Elizabeth Hall	Sept. 7, 1844	Abram Cantrill
Quillen, William	Nancy Yants	Oct. 9, 1843	Marcus L. King
R			
Roark, Carter	Mary Adams	Dec. 10, 1845	R. H. Collier

Groom	Bride	Date of Marriage	By Whom
S			
Sexton, Stephen	Crissie Fields	...., 1846	P. H. Collier
Sadler, Samuel	Nancy Gibson	Nov. 23, 1843	H. J. Huff
Smith, John H.	Sarah Adams	...., 1842	John Caudill
Senter, James	Amelia Macon?	Nov. 24, 1844	A. Cantrill
Short, Alexander	Caroline Brooks	Oct. 4, 1845	D. Maggard
Sexton, Isaac	Jane Sexton	July 7, 1846	James Collins
T			
Triplett, John	Mary Emaline Hall	Nov. 26, 1846	John Morris?
Thomason, Greenburg	.... Sexton	Dec. 21, 1844	J. Collins
Terry?, David	Mary Thomason	...., ...	John Caudill
W			
Wright, James	Susannah England	Mar. 17, 1843	Abram Cantrill, M. G.
Webb, Miles W.	Mary Holbrook	...., 1844	John Caudill
Wright, Andrew	Harriet Adams	June 13, ...	Joseph Crofte
Wright, John	Anna Elliott	Nov. ...., 1844	John Caudill

MASON COUNTY MARRIAGES 1789-1804

A partial list of the marriages of Mason County, Kentucky from date of organization, May 1, 1789 to February 1, 1804, the date of organization of Greenup County.

Groom	Bride	Date of Marriage
A		
Abbot, Peter	Elizabeth Helm	July 12, 1802
Acquilla, John	Elizabeth Nott	April 23, 1796
Adair, John	Eleanor Overfield	Dec. 5, 1796
Adams, Robert	Rachael Hall	Mar. 10, 1796
Adams, William	Ann Lawrence	May 18, 1800
Adamson, James	Sally Carter	Dec. 23, 1802
Alexander, James	Mary Payne	Dec. 29, 1800
Allen, Adam	Nancy Kiser	Jan. 28, 1795
Allen, John	Elizabeth Brooks	Mar. 26, 1802
Allen, Thomas	Patsy Meirs (Myers)	Nov. 13, 1795
Allen, Thomas	Elizabeth Fletcher	Sept. 26, 1803
Allison, Arthur	Sara Smith	Aug. 6, 1793
Allison, Frederick	Rebecca Woody	Sept. 13, 1800
Ambrose, William	Isabella Harrison	Jan. 15, 1803
Anno, Henry	Elizabeth Arrowsmith	Mar. 8, 1798
Anno, John	Hannah Arrowsmith	Dec. 27, 1798
Anno, William	Rebecca Pollard	Dec. 7, 1803
Applegate, Zebulon	Sabetha Preston	Apr. 22, 1802
Armstrong, Edward	Jane Chamberlain	Jan. 27, 1803
Armstrong, John	Letitia Dye	Mar. 6, 1800
Armstrong, Robert	Mary Bowens	June 29, 1797

Groom	Bride	Date of Marriage
Armstrong, William	Naomi Norris	Aug. 16, 1804
Arrowsmith, Ezekiel	Elizabeth Kenton	Apr. 6, 1797
Asberry, (Asbury) William	Sarah Taylor	Sept. 20, 1802

B

Baker, Abraham	Elizabeth Fife	Mar. 18, 1800
Baker, Joshua	Susannah Lewis	June 5, 1790
Baker, Francis	Mary Brandenburg	Aug. 30, 1802
Baker, Simon	Mary Edwards	Feb. 27, 1804
Banfield, Thomas	Prewdy Williams	Oct. 20, 1796
Barnaby, George	Susannah Slack	Nov. 5, 1795
Barnes, James	Silence Montgomery	Mar. 25, 1795
Barton, James	Hannah McNamarie	July 30, 1796
Bartley, Robert	Rachael Callen	May 30, 1803
Bassett, Benjamin	Ann Stout	June 28, 1799
Bayles, Benjamin	Betsy Wood	Sept. 25, 1798
Bayless, Platt	Anne Pool	Aug. 26, 1799
Bean, Berry	Farinetta Johnston	Mar. 28, 1802
Bean, Phillip	Mary Can (Kahn)	Feb. 2, 1804
Beasley, John	Sarah West	May 19, 1792
Beckley, William	Sarah Lewis	Sept. 3, 1790
Bell, Benjamin	Mary O'Hannon	Nov. 29, 1803
Bell, Elijah	Susannah Runyan	Dec. 8, 1800
Bennett, Archibald	Martha Duvall	July 26, 1790
Bennett, Tunis	Rachael Fowler	Nov. 24, 1791
Berkelow, Derrick	Rachael Carurine?	Oct. 30, 1802
Berry, Henry	Mary Berry	Mar. 30, 1795
Black, Charles	Sally Delaney	Aug. 20, 1802
Blackburn, Thomas	Nancy Callan	May 5, 1804
Blackburn, Thomas	Hannah Kennard	Apr. 7, 1800
Boone Levi	Sarah Duling	Aug. 2, 1800
Bowland, Edward	Anne Dawson	Sept. 14, 1795
Bowles, Stephen	Ann Thomas	Jan. 18, 1800
Bows, Ephriam	Hannah Heald	Aug. 28, 1797
Boyd, John	Sarah Wilson	Apr. 29, 1802
Boyd, Samuel	Betsy Grimes	May 14, 1804
Bradley, Robert	Polly Johnston	June 26, 1802
Bratton, Robert	Betsey Purcell	July 30, 1799
Briton, Nathan	Patsey Hatfield	July 31, 1802
Bronaugh, William	Fanny Caroll	Mar. 5, 1804
Brooks, James	Mary White	Jan. 28, 1790
Brown, Absolom	Sarah Acton	Mar. 26, 1800
Brown, Daniel	Mary Quilgease (Killgeese)	July 23, 1803
Brown, James	Frances Dobyns	Feb. 6, 1804
Brown, James	Nancy Thompson	Jan. 6, 1796
Brown, James	Betsey Thornton	Aug. 18, 1799
Brown, John	Lute West	Oct. 29, 1791
Brown, John	Nancy Hannah	Feb. 3, 1795
Browning, Meshack	Elizabeth Vantreese	Apr. 6, 1803
Bruce, Henry	Eleanor Thrailkill	Dec. 25, 1797
Bryant, Anderson	Margaret Clifton	Nov. 30, 1793
Bullitt, Wilson	Betty Hurley	June 11, 1802
Bunnell, David	Elizabeth Price	Mar. 19, 1796
Bunnell, Nathaniel	Elizabeth Donivan	Jan. 15, 1800
Bunnell, Stephen	Freelove Williams	Mar. 1, 1797
Burke, Kelly	Sarah Beck	Nov. 24, 1791
Burns, William	Sarah Jackson	Dec. 24, 1800

MARRIAGES—FLEMING, HARLAN, LETCHER, MASON COUNTIES

Groom	Bride	Date of Marriage
Burris, Ignatius	Margaret Rankin	Mar. 13, 1802
Burris, John	Elizabeth McMickel	Oct. 16, 1797
Burris, William	Elizabeth Plummer	Oct. 29, 1799
Burton, Aaron	Rebecca Lemon	May 17, 1802
Butler, John	Mary Kebby	Apr. 17, 1804

C

Groom	Bride	Date of Marriage
Calderwood, Adam	Nancy Lawson	Mar. 24, 1804
Callan, James	Annie Wells	Feb. 28, 1796
Callen, John	Annie Simpson	Sept. 4, 1797
Calvert, Gerrard	Rosanna Mc'lvain	Mar. 18, 1798
Calvert, Walter	Elizabeth Holland	Apr. 2, 1804
Calvert, William	Polly Calvert	Jan. 29, 1803
Campbell, Evan	Peggy Byers	May 9, 1803
Campbell, Jack	Lucy Botts	June 12, 1804
Campbell, James	Mary Duncan	Jan. 7, 1801
Campbell, James	Hannah Watkins	Oct. 20, 1802
Campbell, John	Sarah Dowden	Mar. 25, 1791
Campbell, William	Jane Botts	Nov. 10, 1796
Carpenter, John	Rachael Hinton	Nov. 29, 1796
Carr, William	Susannah Brandenburgh	Feb. 6, 1802
Carter, Alexander	Margaret White	July 20, 1802
Carter, Cornelius	Rhoda Goble	Apr. 10, 1800
Carter, Levi	Catherine Graham	Apr. 29, 1800
Case, Thomas	Mary Browning	Dec. 2, 1800
Chambers, John	Margaret Taylor	June 6, 1803
Chancellor, Isaac	Rebecca Purcell	Aug. 11, 1796
Chancellor, John	Elizabeth Flora	Dec. 28, 1797
Chandler, Nathaniel	Charity Peterson	Apr. 21, 1801
Chaney, Edward	Martilla Drake	Aug. 8, 1805
Chapman, Henry	Frances Crabb	Dec. 22, 1794
Charter, James	Hannah Drake	Oct. 19, 1792
Chelton, (Chilton) Joseph	Nancy Reeves	Aug. 26, 1799
Childs, Garland	Frankie Thomas	May 7, 1802
Chinn, Elijah	Polly Drake	Feb. 17, 1803
Chinnowith, Abram	Rebecca Keer (Kerr)	May 26, 1790
Clarke, Daniel	Edna Pepper	...., ...
Clarke, David	Margaret Oliver	Feb. 23, 1797
Clarke, James	Martha Brown	June 12, 1794
Clarke, Samuel	Sarah Fife	Feb. 27, 1800
Clark, Samuel	Rachael Wood	Jan. 13, 1801
Clarke, William	Mary Curtis	June 6, 1791
Clinkenbeard, John	Margaret Morgan	Feb. 23, 1797
Cochran, Andrew	Jenny Bartlett	Feb. 11, 1794
Cochran, Henry	Rachael Patton	July 20, 1791
Cole, William	Mary Whittaker	Nov. 10, 1797
Collings, (Collins) Edmund	Jane Owings	Aug. 6, 1794
Collins, Benjamin	Mary Dye	June 22, 1791
Collins, Edmund	Sally Kenton	Apr. 9, 1800
Collins, Stephen	Patsy Prater	Dec. 26, 1803
Colvin, Abram	Susannah Sidwell	Dec. 11, 1797
Colvin, George	Christiana Justice	Dec. 14, 1794
Colvin, James	Nancy Cartmell	Sept. 1, 1793
Colvin, Luther	Ruth Comrine?	Dec. 2, 1802
Colwell, (Caldwell) Andrew	Margaret Collins	May 2, 1797
Colwell, (Caldwell) Andrew	Mary Light	Aug. 15, 1797

225

Groom	Bride	Date of Marriage
Conner, James	Kiziah Burkham (Burcham)	Oct. 21, 1800
Cook, Conrad	Sarah Lake	Nov. 23, 1796
Cooper, Jacob	Sally Kinner	July 1, 1802
Cooper, Jesse	Elizabeth Cooper	Nov. 23, 1803
Cooper, Lewis	Mary Waters	Mar. 12, 1803
Cooper, Murdock	Elizabeth Parker	Jan. 7, 1895
Cooper, Richard	Mary Lewis	May 9, 1791
Cord, Jacob	Mary Mitchell	Nov. 18, 1791
Cornelius, Daniel	Judith Huff	May 14, 1804
Corwine, George	Elizabeth Wilson	May 17, 1800
Cottrell, Samuel	Jane Craighead	Apr. 21, 1801
Cox, Jeffrey	Ann Tillett	Jan. 18, 1798
Cox, Joseph	Rebecca Carter	Aug. 7, 1802
Cox, John	Sally Burkelow	July 28, 1802
Cox, Joseph	Rebecca Carter	Aug. 7, 1802
Coryell, Lewis	Sarah Vaschell	Apr. 11, 1796
Courtney, Robert	Jane Wishard	Feb. 2, 1796
Cowgill, Elisha	Jane McFarland	Nov. 10, 1797
Craig, John	Catherine Pattie	Dec. 22, 1795
Cralle, Kenner	Delilah Donivan	Dec. 22, 1802
Crawford, Samuel	Nancy McMechan	Jan. 18, 1802
Crawford, William	Nancy Dixon	Jan. 26, 1801
Craycraft, Samuel	Mary Dawson	Feb. 20, 1798
Craycraft, Thomas	Elizabeth Tarvin	June 30, 1799
Creswell, Samuel	Dolly Coppi	April 18, 1796
Cummings, Samuel	Nancy Martin	Aug. 9, 1802
Curtis, John	Eleanor Clarke	Aug. 2, 1790
Cushman, Thomas	Polly Hiatt	Aug. 10, 1803

D

Dalton, Samuel	Jane Hurst	May 25, 1802
Davidson, George	Mary Marsh	Apr. 10, 1800
Davis, Alben	Sarah Dean	Mar. 20, 1798
Davis, Joseph	Sarah Masters	July 20, 1801
Davis, Phillip	Mary McKenny	Mar. 20, 1794
Davis, Samuel	Nancy Flora	Apr. 18, 1789
Davis, Samuel	Elizabeth Smith	Aug. 21, 1793
Davis, Walter	Polly Boyd	Jan. 25, 1800
Davis, Walter	Betsy McDonald	May 2, 1801
Dean, James	Nancy Wilson	May 20, 1802
Dennan, David	Sarah Thompson	...., ...
Dent, Lawrence	Dorcas Hobbs	Apr. 13, 1797
Derbin, Amos	Susannah White	Mar. 23, 1797
Desha, John	Rebecca Overfield	July 1, 1790
Devour (Devore) Nicholas	Polly Hall	Jan. 18, 1798
Dicks, John	Elizabeth Fagan	Feb. 2, 1802
Dickson, Robert	Elizabeth Thompson	Mar. 27, 1800
Dills, Harmonius	Betsy Kennard	Sept. 10, 1801
Dills, Solomon	Susannah McGinnis	June 20, 1791
Dirzan, (Duzan) Abram	Elizabeth Anno	Dec. 16, 1795
Dixon, John	Rachael Rogers	Jan. 10, 1797
Dixon, Robert	Elizabeth Means	Jan. 31, 1797
Dobyns, Charles	Betsy Porter	Sept. 6, 1803
Dobyns, Edward	Lucy Pepper	Apr. 23, 1800
Dobyns, Enoch	Elizabeth Berry	Jan. 23, 1804
Dodge, Abraham	Sally Thompson	Mar. 14, 1800
Donovan, Acquilla	Peggy Campbell	Nov. 25, 1801

Groom	Bride	Date of Marriage
Donovan, Amos	Marcha Caldwell	Oct. 13, 1803
Donivan, J. P.	Milly Bell	Feb. 16, 1800
Downing, Elias	Dorcas Downing	Feb. 4, 1792
Downing, James	Charity Furr	Aug. 13, 1793
Downing, Joseph	Sarah Peddicord	Mar. 27, 1799
Drake, Cornelius	Fanny Witherspoon	Oct. 19, 1803
Dugan, Peter	Elizabeth Eubanke	...., 1790
Duvall, John P.	Frances Dobyns	Apr. 12, 1798
Duvall, Silas	Betsey Dobyns	Sept. 29, 1803
Dye, John	Christiana Davis	Apr. 11, 1797
Dye, Montier	Elsey Glenn	Dec. 13, 1798
Dye, William	Jemima Shelby	Nov. 16, 1802
Dye, William	Hannah Lamb	Sept. 2, 1794

E

Earl, David	Margaret Wood	Mar. 5, 1792
Earl, Thomas	Rebecca Dorety (Daugherty)	Mar. 14, 1795
Early, David	Betsy Lynn	Sept. 25, 1801
Ebert, Phillip	Jane Marshall	Feb. 10, 1795
Edwards, George	Susannah Downing	Aug. 20, 1794
Edwards, James	Anne Scott	Mar. 28, 1793
Elliott, Burgess	Sarah Acklin	June 28, 1796
Ellis, Daniel	Susannah Dyer	July 1, 1800
Ellis, James	Betsey Overfield	Jan. 11, 1803
Ellis, John	Kesiah Brooks	June 22, 1803
Ellison, Ezra	Jane Long	Jan. 27, 1803
Evans, Amos	Elizabeth Wilson	Nov. 22, 1798
Evans, Daniel	Mary Rowland	Sept. 25, 1800
Evans, David	Susannah Collins	Jan. 22, 1797
Everman, John	Mary Forgey	Apr. 27, 1800
Ewing, Samuel	Rachael Masterjohn	July 22, 1801

F

Fagins, Joseph	Lydia Fleming	Mar. 15, 1799
Feagins, Henry	Fanny Calvert	May 20, 1802
Feagins, Obadiah	Jane Logan	Dec. 23, 1800
Faulkner, George	Elizabeth Collins	Apr. 18, 1801
Faulkner, William	Anne Mitchell	Aug. 26, 1796
Ferguson, Aaron	Kesiah Price	Dec. 1, 1801
Finney, James	Mary Cochran	Feb. 9, 1797
Fisher, Adam	Sarah Phineas	Jan. 30, 1800
Fitch, Samuel	Elizabeth Martin	Nov. 26, 1801
Fitzgerald, Benjamin	Sally Chamberlin	June 7, 1804
Fitzgerald, Peter	Elizabeth Ackley	Feb. 13, 1792
Fitzgerald, William	Elizabeth Kiger (Keiger)	May 16, 1791
Fleming, Jacob	Naomi Goodwin	May 23, 1801
Fleming, John	Mary Butler	June 12, 1801
Flora, Robert	Freelove McMechen	Dec. 4, 1802
Foreman, John	Catherine Rowe (Roe)	Nov. 21, 1803
Foreman, Samuel	Margaret Smith	Dec. 2, 1801
Fox, Daniel	Nancy Bowman	Nov. 15, 1795
Freeland, Jacob	Pattie Leslie	Dec. 17, 1800
Freeman, Joseph	Elizabeth Higgins	July 25, 1799
Froman, Soloman	Sarah Boone	Sept. 30, 1800
Fruit, Martin	Elizabeth Levington	Nov. 30, 1794

Groom	Bride	Date of Marriage
Fuller, John	Polly Summers	Jan. 5, 1802
Fulton, Hugh	Jane Rogers	Dec. 11, 1798
Fulton, Isaac	Elizabeth Cralle	Aug. 18, 1795
Furr, William	Sinia Edwards	Nov. 8, 1794

G

Groom	Bride	Date of Marriage
Gallant, James	Polly Clay	Apr. 22, 1801
Galligher, John	Elizabeth Beard	Apr. 19, 1798
Galligher, Samuel	Susannah Zorn	Feb. 7, 1797
Galloway, Elijah	Nancy West	Jan. 4, 1799
Garred, John	Elizabeth Porter	Apr. 6, 1797
Gifford, Elisha	Ann Jones	Nov. 26, 1794
Gill, James	Elizabeth Moss	Sept. 20, 1803
Gill, Reuben	E. Chapman	Apr. 26, 1798
Gellespie, (Gillespie), Wm.	Frances Marshall	July 18, 1799
Givens, Samuel	Lucy Taylor	Nov. 14, 1803
Givens, William	Mary Shields	Mar. 8, 1798
Glenn, Isaac	Elizabeth Drake	Apr. 18, 1804
Glenn, Robert	Ruth Dye	Apr. 12, 1797
Glover, Elijah	Catherine Jones	Jan. 6, 1802
Glover, John	Prudence Lamb	Dec. 17, 1800
Gooden, William	Elizabeth Rigdon	Dec. 22, 1802
Gooding, William	Susannah Wood	Dec. 2, 1791
Gorman, William	Jane Henderson	Sept. 11, 1792
Gray, James	Agnes Summers	June 9, 1802
Gray, John	Rachael Ralson	Nov. 5, 1801
Gray, Samuel	Catherine Heflin	Feb. 14, 1803
Grey, Alexander	Lydda Havens	Feb. 3, 1795
Grey, John	Mary Stewart	Feb. 12, 1797
Grey, Joseph	Hannah Bright	Jan. 1, 1796
Gregson, Dick	Sarah Owings	July 14, 1791
Griffith, Leroy	Nancy Kay	Feb. 26, 1799
Grimes, Noble	.... Willett	Feb. 12, 1803
Grimstead, Robert	Elizabeth Bunn	Mar. 29, 1803
Guinn, William	Sarah Thoraman	Jan. 14, 1800
Guthridge, James	Hannah McLaughlin	Feb. 2, 1797
Guthridge, John	Margaret Parkinson	Sept. 27, 1798

H

Groom	Bride	Date of Marriage
Hail, (Hale) Robert	Deborah Bedder	Dec. 11, 1795
Hall, James	Elizabeth Swiser	Mar. 17, 1795
Hall, Sylvester	Anne Downing	Mar. 29, 1797
Hallon, John	Mary Allen	Dec. 25, 1797
Hamar, James	Mary Ann Helms	June 20, 1791
Hammon, Richard	Catherine Payne	Dec. 11, 1802
Hanks, Samuel	Nancy Wiatt	Mar. 16, 1802
Hanson, Samuel	Rachael Waterman	July 2, 1796
Harbough, Phillip	Jennie Pickerell	Mar. 25, 1804
Hardy, Samuel	Lettie Gill	Dec. 5, 1800
Harlan, Nathaniel	Elizabeth Berry	Nov. 14, 1801
Harmon, John	Catherine Miller	Sept. 18, 1799
Harris, Edward	Elizabeth Campbell	Jan. 17, 1799
Harris, Edward	Margaret Jackson	Mar. 8, 1802
Harris, George	Polly Maddox	Oct. 21, 1801
Harrison, Thomas	Margaret Furr	1795 or 1796

Groom	Bride	Date of Marriage
Havens, John	Nancy Heflin	Jan. 2, 1800
Havens, William	Margaret Evans	June 24, 1794
Hawkins, John	Johanna Harrison	Dec. 18, 1803
Haynes, Peter	Mary McDowell	Apr. 22, 1796
Hays, James	Mary Wood	Aug. 27, 1790
Headley, George	Sarah Gordon	Aug. 27, 1790
Hedges, John	Rachael Wells	Aug. 20, 1794
Heflin, Elijah	Elizabeth Crane	Sept. 16, 1796
Heighten, Elijah	Charlotte Hart	Feb. 5, 1803
Helm, Meredith	Elizabeth Drake	Jan. 17, 1804
Helm, Samuel	Pheby Watson	Nov. 2, 1798
Helm, William	Elizabeth Drummons	Dec. 2, 1791
Helman, Joseph	Polly Youngman	Mar. 19, 1800
Herbert, John	Elizabeth Lawrence	Oct. 17, 1803
Herbert, Thomas	Sarah Helm	July 6, 1802
Heth, Peter	Polly Dexter	May 8, 1795
Hiatt, John (Hyatt)	Keziah Hiatt	Jan. 25, 1803
Hiatt, Stephen	Mary Day	Mar. 28, 1803
Highsong, John	Elizabeth Watson	Sept. 13, 1801
Higgins, John	Ruth Wiggins	Dec. 1, 1799
Highland, Andrew	Mary Osborn	Nov. 29, 1794
Hillis, Abraham	Peggy Cowan	May 12, 1803
Hillis, William	Elizabeth McCorkell	Sept. 13, 1796
Hillman, Joseph	Polly Youngman	...., 1799?
Hinton, Vaschel	Nancy Roy	Nov. 21, 1796
Hixon, Nathaniel	Anna Morris	Mar. 24, 1792
Hixon, Thomas	Rachael Jennings	Oct. 31, 1799
Hodges, William	Parmelia Jones	July 21, 1801
Holton, Jesse	Jane Ireland	July 25, 1803
Hord, Elias	Anne Triplett	Sept. 15, 1796
Hoover, Peter	Isabella Graham	May 25, 1803
Horton, John	Letitia Ball	May 16, 1804
Houghton, William	Ann McKay	Oct. 17, 1803
Houston, John	Nancy Wilson	Feb. 18, 1804
Howard, Robert	Mary Black	Apr. 24, 1804
Howard, Thomas	Sally Pattey	Apr. 12, 1796
Howes, Henry	Ann Nichols	June 19, 1800
Howe, Samuel	Isabella Smith	Jan. 26, 1803
Hughey, Charles	Nancy Record	Aug. 17, 1790
Hughey, Humphrey	Lyn Sanders	Feb. 9, 1790
Hughey, John	Elizabeth Records	Nov. 2, 1791
Hull, John	Rebecca Bennett	Feb. 24, 1803
Hunt, Israel	Elizabeth McDonald	Jan. 15, 1802
Hunt, James	Sarah Hickman	Mar. 17, 1800
Hunter, John	Mary Dewitt	June 28, 1794
Hunter, John	Mary McCord	Jan. 4, 1798
Hurst, James	Elizabeth Stapleton	Mar. 13, 1798
Hurst, John	Elizabeth Harper	June 7, 1798
Hurst, John	Patty Poe	Jan. 31, 1797
Hurst, Landon	Sally Crane	Sept. 29, 1796
Hyatt, Jonathan (Hiatt)	Patty Norris	Sept. 9, 1799

I

Inglis, (Ingles) Peter	Hettie Allen	July 28, 1803
Irwin, Gerrard	Eleanor Taylor	Apr. ...., 1799
Israel, William	Martha Price	May 6, 1803

Groom	Bride	Date of Marriage
J		
Jackson, Alexander	Charlotte Asbury	Dec. 18, 1802
Jackson, Andrew	Phoebe Thomas	Aug. 6, 1800
Jackson, Bernard	Milly Chamberlain	June 30, 1795
Jenkins, John	Rachael Turner	Mar. 28, 1796
Johnston, Henry	Clara Day	May 15, 1802
Johnston, James	Alcey Parker	Nov. 27, 1800
Johnston, James	Sarah Early	Feb. 19, 1800
Johnston, James	Keziah Coryell	Feb. 24, 1801
Johnston, James	Nancy McFarland	May 22, 1801
Johnston, John	Abigail Harris	June 24, 1794
Johnston, John	Polly Kelley	June 15, 1798
Johnston, John	Jane Thurman	Feb. 25, 1801
Johnston, Joseph	Prudence Pittinger	Oct. ...., 1800
Johnston, Samuel	Nancy Monohan	July ...., 1803
Jones, Jeffrey	Jane Brown	June 28, 1801
Jones, John	Mary Greene	Aug. 13, 1800
Jones, Samuel G.	Phoebe Coone	Dec. 28, 1801
Jones, Samuel	Elizabeth Reaves	...., 1790
Jones, William	Ephema Earley	June 1, 1797
Journey, Peter	Eleanor Sargent	Apr. 6, 1797
Judd, James	Polly Newland	Jan. 6, 1800
Judd, John	Nancy Henson	July 27, 1801
K		
Kelsey, James	Elizabeth Howell	Sept. 25, 1792
Kenton, John	Elizabeth Thompson	May 5, 1792
Kenton, Simon	Elizabeth Jarbo or Garbo	Mar. 27, 1798
Kenyon, Jonathan	Sarah Stralton (Stratton)	Feb. 23, 1803
Kerchival, James	Nancy Langby (Langley)	Sept. 20, 1802
Key, Alexander	Elizabeth Sawes	Dec. 26, 1801
Key, James, Jr.	Nancy Ireland	Dec. 17, 1802
Key, Zachariah	Catherine McDuffie	Dec. 25, 1799
Kile, George	Anne Marshall	Apr. 24, 1802
Kilgeese, George	Zilpha Burcam	Aug. 26, 1795
Killgore, Robert	Rachael Strode	May 28, 1798
Kint, (Kent) Jacob	Mary Howard	Jan. 16, 1795
Kirk, Nathaniel	Dorcas Madden	Feb. 6, 1800
Kiser, John	Christianna Tupp	Dec. 28, 1792
L		
Langley, Thomas	Jane Osborn	Dec. 27, 1802
Lauderdale, James	Polly Helman	Oct. 14, 1800
Laughlin, William	Mary Thompson	Mar. 17, 1795
Lawson, Jeremiah, Rev.	Matilda Higgins	Mar. 3, 1799
Layton, James	Mary Breeze	Jan. 5, 1804
Leech, Benjamin	Tabia Tennis	Dec. 15, 1797
Lee, Barton	Ruth Smith	Jan. 13, 1804
Lee, Lewis	Mary Hankins	May 7, 1798
Lee, Lewis	Catherine Jones	Nov. 10, 1802
Leepar, James	Margaret Henderson	Sept. 21, 1797
Lee, John	Mary Cantrell	Jan. 28, 1797
Lewis, Thomas	Fanny Bagby	July 24, 1797
LeMarr, James	Rose McGlothlin	Apr. 3, 1800
LeMarr, John	Mary Davidson	Dec. 10, 1800

Groom	Bride	Date of Marriage
Leonard, Valentine	Polly Fowler	Feb. 27, 1794
Lewis, Charles N.	Betsy Bragg	Nov. 17, 1801
Lewis, Thomas	Jemima Lucas	Dec. 3, 1791
Little, Samuel	Margaret Newcomb	Sept. 17, 1797
Littlejohn, John	Ann Taylor	Oct. 28, 1801
Lock, Thomas	Mary Demos	July 17, 1797
Logan, John, Jr.	Ruth Smith	April 4, 1801
Logan, John, Sr.	Mary Thompson	June 30, 1801
Logan, Joseph	Sarah Chambers	Dec. 18, 1794
Logan, Samuel	Phoebe Richards	Nov. 21, 1799
Long, John	Mary Gray	Dec. 26, 1797
Long, Robert	Sarah Burk	Mar. 29, 1798
Low, Isaac	Margaret McClure	Nov. 9, 1797
Lowry, William	Elizabeth Stratton	April 13, 1803
Loyd, Dixon	Clary Berry	June 26, 1791
Lynnville, John	Elizabeth Shehan	Apr. 12, 1797
Lyon, William	Ann Brown	Feb. 10, 1801
Lucas, Edmund	Lucretia Burns	July 11, 1799

M

Madden, Jeremiah	Sarah Barry	Mar. 16, 1801
Maddox, Charles	Sally Kehoe	Jan. 18, 1802
Maddox, Hezekiah	Rhoda Harris	Dec. 26, 1801
Maddox, John	Nancy Hurst	Jan. 8, 1800
Mahan, Abraham	Sarah Reeves	April 11, 1795
Mann, John	Abigail Devour (Devore)	Mar. 8, 1798
Marshall, John	Nancy Key	Feb. 9, 1795
Marshall, Phillip	Margaret Pitts	Aug. 17, 1795
Martin, Beak	Sarah Wilson	Mar. 9, 1795
Martin, Ebenezer	Sidney Long	June ...., 1802
Martin, Elijah	Mary Taylor	Mar. 27, 1800
Maxwell, John	Agnes Boyles	Feb. 18, 1797
Mefford, Andrew	Susannah Burns	Aug. 31, 1802
Metz, Jacob	Judith Martin	June 13, 1804
Miles, James	Elizabeth Murphy	June 3, 1800
Miller, John	Eleanor Highfield	Apr. 7, 1800
Miller, Joseph	Mary Cannon	May 18, 1801
Miller, Robert	Jane Guthridge	Dec. 10, 1793
Miller, William	Mary Hughes	Aug. 21, 1799
Mills, George	Amy Kelly	Nov. 30, 1803
Mills, John	Mary Brooks	Jan. 29, 1795
Mitchell, Sanford	Lydda Shotwell	Feb. 5, 1793
Montgomery, David	Sarah Brooks	June 9, 1802
Moore, Aaron	Sarah Watson	.........., ...
Moore, John	Sarah Carter	Sept. 24, 1802
Moore, Nathaniel	Nancy Welch	Mar. 6, 1799
Moore, Samuel	Sarah Griffith	Jan. 10, 1803
Morris, Thomas	Mary Given	May 23, 1797
Moss, Elijah	Polly Smith	Aug. 8, 1798
Moss, Moses	Mary Pitzer	July 5, 1798
Myers, Alexander	Rebecca Parker	June 7, 1797
Myers, Henry	Sarah Hord	May 24, 1804
Myers, Jacob	Nancy Means	Sept. 14, 1801
Myers, Joseph	Abigail Crane	Apr. 8, 1794
Myers, Joseph	Margaret Walker	Feb. 14, 1799
McAfee, Benjamin	Sarah Hodge	Oct. 25, 1800
McAllister, ...?	Lydia Summers	Mar. 7, 1801

231

Groom	Bride	Date of Marriage
McCane, James	Jane Ewing	Nov. 12, 1795
McCarty, Daniel	Elizabeth Brown	Feb. 6, 1795
McCarty, William	Martha Reibut	Dec. 23, 1799
McCleary, John	Margaret McCorkle	Dec. 8, 1795
McCullough, Robert	.... Ellison	Sept. 23, 1800
McCorkle, William	Jane Gooding	Sept. 13, 1796
McCoy, James	Nancy Flood	June 16, 1793
McCoy, John	Nancy Fitch	Apr. 2, 1793
McCoy, John	Margaret Kern	Dec. 10, 1793
McDermid, Edward	Martha Coryell	...., 1793
McDonald, Samuel	Allie Applegate	Aug. 25, 1803
McFarland, Archibald	Charlotte Donovan	May 9, 1798
McIlvain, Hugh	Mary Brunt	Jan. 15, 1793
McIlvain, John	Jane Hord	Feb. 15, 1799
McIlvain, Robert	Jane Taylor	May 15, 1804
McIlvain, Thomas	Polly Robb	May 16, 1803
McIntire, John	Cassey Freeland	Apr. 7, 1796
McKee, John	Betsy McCleese	Mar. 16, 1797
McKibbon, Hugh	Susannah Hughes	Feb. 21, 1797
McKibbon, Joseph	Ann Lynn	Mar. 14, 1799
McKinley, George	Agnes Arthur	Sept. 16, 1803
McKinney, John	Isabella Crawford	July 16, 1803
McLaughlin, John	Elizabeth Clemmons	Sept. 14, 1801
McMichael, Robert	Jane Hamilton	Sept. 16, 1796
McNabb, William	Sarah Coryell	Mar. 16, 1801
McNary, John	Sarah Tennis	Feb. 22, 1798

N

Nicholas, James	Nancy Whaley	Aug. 31, 1802
Nichols, John	Ann Proctor	June 28, 1798
Nichols, Thomas	Delly Berry	Oct. 3, 1799
Neill, John	Betsey Boyd	Aug. 8, 1799
Newman, John	Nancy Donovan	Sept. 5, 1796
Northcutt, Benjamin	Marsha O'Dell	Nov. 11, 1800
Norris, James	Nancy Gates	Apr. 2, 1804
Norris, John	Anne Lamb	Oct. 10, 1794

O

O'Banion, William	Susannah Asberry	Oct. 12, 1796
O'Conner, Charles	Ann Hutson	Jan. 29, 1795
Oden, William	Sary Metcalf	Jan. 12, 1799
Oliver, Elias	Elizabeth Martin	Dec. 15, 1796
Oliver, John	Polly Ross	July 1, 1802
O'Neal, Daniel	Millie Carr	Jan. 27, 1802
Owings, Thomas	Mollie Carter	Nov. 21, 1800
Owings, William	Jane Dowden	Mar. 14, 1792
Ozburn, (Osborn) James	Patsy Johnston	Jan. 12, 1797
Ozburn, (Osborn) Levi	Hanna Dunnivan	Dec. 8, 1794

P

Palmer, William	Drucilla Flora	Aug. 5, 1801
Parker, Henry	Polly McKee	May 31, 1796
Parker, James	Susannah Donovan	Oct. 21, 1802
Parker, Jacob	Jemoma Campbell	Mar. 31, 1802
Parker, Winslow, Jr.	Sally Lee	Nov. 18, 1800

Groom	Bride	Date of Marriage
Parks, Thomas	Anne Wilson	Oct. 8, 1794
Pattie, Sylvester	Polly Hubbard	Aug. 7, 1802
Patton, John	Mary Peck	May 26, 1803
Peed, Gabriel	Betsy Green	Sept. 4, 1797
Peed, Phillip	Nancy Brumby	Apr. 22, 1801
Peddicord, Nicholas	Cynthia Craighead	Apr. 22, 1801
Pepper, Samuel	Brittania Artis	Mar. 21, 1803
Peters, Thomas	Mary Sparling	Sept. 11, 1803
Peterson, Isaac	Anne Johnston	Jan. 21, 1797
Phillips, Edmund	Milly Phillips	...., ...
Phillips, Gabriel	Milly McDermid	July 27, 1792
Phillips, James	Harriett Bragg	Dec. 27, 1803
Pickrell, William	Sara Ferren	Feb. 26, 1798
Plummer, Benjamin	Polly Shepherd	Mar. 27, 1800
Plummer, Henry	Frances Kerchival	Aug. 23, 1802
Plummer, Kirk	Polly Chapman	Jan. 19, 1797
Plummer, Thomas	Sally Brinton	Sept. 15, 1802
Plummer, Thomas	Jean Ruggles	...., 1800
Plummer, William	Tabitha Chapman	Apr. 3, 1793
Pollard, John	Elizabeth Wallingford	Feb. 3, 1802
Porter, Nathan	Catherine Kennedy	May 11, 1797
Porter, Thomas	Sarah Price	June 4, 1794
Powell, William	Penelope Stout	Aug. 28, 1799
Prather, Erasmus	Betsy McKibbons	Feb. 16, 1797
Prater, Jeremiah	Lucy Hull	May 6, 1803
Preston, Banard (Bernard)	Tabitha Miller	Jan. 20, 1795
Preston, Francis	Elizabeth Stubblefield	...., ...
Preston, John	Jane Ramey	...., ...
Proctor, Jeremiah	Mary Nichols	Aug. 25, 1796
Purcell, George	Peggy Randolph	Sept. 6, 1800
Purcell, Thomas	Elizabeth Powell	Sept. 2, 1802
Putnam, William	Elizabeth Brumby	Oct. 29, 1802
Pyle, John	Mary Poe	Apr. 24, 1798

R

Ragsdale, Drury	Sophy Waller	...., 1792
Rairdon, John	Catherine Slaw (Snow)	May 30, 1800
Rankin, Benjamin	Catherine Stubblefield	Apr. 20, 1796
Record, Laban	Nancy Sellers	Oct. 7, 1789
Record, John	Sarah Stewart	Aug. 23, 1798
Record, Spencer	Elizabeth Elrod	Apr. 9, 1789
Record, William	Lucinda Nash	Jan. 31, 1797
Redman, Gabriel	Sally Levingston	Mar. 8, 1793
Reece, Abel	Elizabeth Purden	Apr. 22, 1801
Reece, Jonathan	Rachael Martin	Apr. 2, 1800
Reed, Hugh	Hannah Goble	Apr. 24, 1800
Reed, Joseph	Susannah Lee	Jan. 30, 1804
Reed, Thomas	Eleanor Lee	Apr. 9, 1804
Reeder, Simon	Elizabeth Boone	Sept. 14, 1795
Reeves, Benjamin	Nancy Reeves	...., 1790
Reeves, Eli	Sarah Ann Redman	...., 1790
Reeves, Samuel	Elizabeth Melton	Apr. 7, 1800
Reeves, Spencer	Susannah Reeves	...., 1791
Reeves, Stace	Sarah Lawrence	Feb. 2, 1802
Rice, Daniel	Rachael Wells	Mar. 17, 1804
Richey, (Richie) David	Mary McIntire	Aug. 15, 1793
Richie, John	Mary Maddox	Sept. 11, 1801

233

Groom	Bride	Date of Marriage
Rigdon, William	Elizabeth Donovan	Oct. 27, 1802
Rigg, Clement	Esther Campbell	Apr. 6, 1803
Riley, Charles	Catherine Houghton	Feb. 1, 1800
Riley, Edward	Elizabeth Garvis (Jarvis)	Nov. 10, 1804
Riley, James	Ruth Wells	Sept. 16, 1792
Riley, William	Mary McIlvain	Oct. 10, 1803
Ritchie, Adam (Richie)	Hetty Loudon	Sept. 18, 1798
Roberts, Silas	Lydia Blue	Jan. 23, 1800
Robertson, Andrew	Anna Wishard	...., 1797
Robertson, John	Sarah Delap	Aug. 2, 1798
Rogers, George	Susannah Phillips	Apr. 7, 1802
Rogers, John	Elizabeth Webb	...., 1796
Rogers, Rowland	Hannah Evans	Feb. 8, 1798
Rowland, Parker T.	Eleanor Botts	Apr. 25, 1796
Rose, Enoch	Lucy Anderson	Sept. 6, 1803
Ross, John	Mary Johnston	Apr. 20, 1800?
Ross, Joseph	Eleanor Wilson	Jan. 31, 1804
Ross, Richard	Elizabeth Fowler	June 20, 1792
Rouse, Levi	Sallie Barns	May 15, 1802
Rowland, Stewart	Mary Jane Miller	Mar. 3, 1803
Ruggles, James	Sarah Conway	Mar. 13, 1804
Rumford, Jonathan	Elizabeth Cox	Sept. 6, 1798
Rush, Elijah	Elizabeth Robertson	Mar. 21, 1804
Russell, Joseph	Mary Parish	May 5, 1792
Rutter, Richard	Sarah Anno	Jan. 4, 1798

S

Groom	Bride	Date of Marriage
Scott, James	Margaret Simms	Jan. 2, 1798
Scott, Thomas	Matty Ralston	Feb. 26, 1797
Scroggs, Alexander	Martha Finney	Mar. 2, 1791
Seeley, John	Jane B. Jannison (Jameson)	May 29, 1800
Shackleford, John	Susan Clarke	Nov. 10, 1801
Shepherd, Charles	Catherine Brandenberg	May 14, 1802
Shepherd, Thomas	Molly McFarland	...., 1793
Sherry, Daniel	Nancy Devour (Devore)	Nov. 24, 1794
Shipley, James	Elizabeth Howell	Sept. 26, 1792
Shipley, Noah	Ann Reed	Feb. 5, 1796
Shockley, Abraham	Nancy Rector	Sept. 10, 1800
Shotwell, John	Rachael Dye	Mar. 1, 1803
Shylock, John	Sarah Monroe	Nov. 25, 1801
Skidmore, William	Mary Criswell	June 23, 1792
Small, Benjamin	Ann Reese	Mar. 15, 1802
Small, Henry	Rebecca Caldwell	July 29, 1800
Small, James	Elizabeth Waller	June 14, 1799
Smith, Henry	Elizabeth Lee	Dec. 28, 1797
Smith, John	Violet Buchanan	Aug. 3, 1799
Smith, Kiah	Anna Rector	Dec. 12, 1794
Smith, Nathan	Easter Waterman	Dec. 29, 1800
Smith, Robert	Susanna Hancock	May 22, 1804
Somers, William	Mary Haven	Nov. 24, 1789
Southard, Hezekiah	Rachael Neely	Aug. 20, 1794
Soward, John	Susannah Jones	Oct. 11, 1794
Sowards, Reuben	Ann Jones	Nov. 16, 1795
Spates, Robert	Nancy Breeding	Nov. 29, 1798
Stagg, Joseph	Sarah McGlone	Aug. 5, 1800
Stagg, Samuel	Malissa Burns	Aug. 11, 1803

Groom	Bride	Date of Marriage
Stanford, Elijah	Rebecca Rouse	June 28, 1803
Starks, David	Martha Rogers	Dec. 18, 1798
Stephens, Samuel	Margaret Chamberlain	Apr. 30, 1800
Stephenson, Francis	Mary Ford	Dec. 24, 1800
Stevenson, John	Polly Prater	Mar. 26, 1802
Stewart, Robert	Rebecca Dunlavy	June 23, 1795
Stockton, Joshua	Phoebe Durrett	Dec. 1, 1801
Stockwell, James	Eleanor Noble	Mar. 9, 1798
Stout, Thomas	Margaret Colvin	Nov. 17, 1789
Sullivan, William	Hannah Donovan	Mar. 29, 1802
Summers, William, Jr.	Elizabeth Bell	Sept. 30, 1800
Sutton, Parker	Pricilla Jones	Nov. 23, 1797
Sweet, Joshua	Jemima Davis	Nov. 16, 1790

T

Groom	Bride	Date of Marriage
Tarvain, Joseph	Martha Cowgill	June 27, 1799
Tarvain, Richard	Sarah Armstrong	Aug. 3, 1796
Taylor, Edward	Nancy Roach	Aug. 24, 1802
Taylor, Henry	Sarah Berry	Feb. 26, 1792
Taylor, James	Elizabeth Rock	Dec. 20, 1798
Taylor, Joseph	Jane Irwin	Aug. 7, 1797
Taylor, John	Rachael Cole	Mar. 20, 1798
Taylor, William	Elizabeth Wise	Dec. 29, 1797
Terhune, Barnett	Ruth Carter	June 24, 1803
Tennant, Richard	Elizabeth Cahill	Aug. 28, 1797
Tennant, Richard	Lydia Shotwell	Aug. 19, 1790
Thomas, Absolom	Catherine Meek	Aug. 1, 1789
Thomas, Israel	Katie Halbert	July 10, 1803
Thomas, Jacob	Elizabeth Case	Mar. 10, 1802
Thomas, Nathaniel	Peggy Highfield	Oct. 29, 1803
Thomas, Robert	Temperance Hiatt	Aug. 27, 1802
Thomas, Thurston	Martha Phillips	Sept. 14, 1797
Thomas, William	Elizabeth Feagans	May 12, 1793
Thompson, John	Esther Dickson	Feb. 13, 1802
Thompson, John	Margaret Barr	May 15, 1795
Threlkill, (Threlkeld) David	Delilah Nichols	Jan. 30, 1796
Threlkeld, John	Sarah Nichols	Sept. 13, 1800
Threlkill, William	Polly Walker	Jan. 9, 1795
Tibbs, Samuel	Sallie Durrett	Dec. 22, 1802
Tivis, Peter	Jane Purcell	Sept. 1, 1802
Triplett, ? John	Mary Yancey	May 16, 1801
Turner, Thomas C.	Rachael Moore	July 30, 1800

V

Groom	Bride	Date of Marriage
Vance, John	Sallie Boyd	Mar. 7, 1804
Van Meter, Absolom	Tabby Harris	Apr. 13, 1801
Vannoy, Francis	Alse Glenn	Mar. 15, 1798
Verden, Hugh	Phoebe Slack	Mar. 1, 1798
Vickers, James	Polly Watson	Apr. 14, 1803

W

Groom	Bride	Date of Marriage
Wakefield, Thomas	Mary Pickerell	Sept. 10, 1801
Walker, Alexander	Charity Bennard	June 27, 1792
Wallace, Michael	Charity McCane	June 30, 1798
Wallace, William	Emily McFarren	Mar. 6, 1799

Groom	Bride	Date of Marriage
Waller, Clement	Susannah Sanders	May 3, 1802
Walters, John	Ailsey Cooper	Apr. 28, 1804
Walters, Michael	Esther Matton	Mar. 28, 1803
Ward, Charles	Elizabeth Waters	Aug. 26, 1794
Ward, James	Peggy Machir	June 9, 1795
Ward, Jeremiah	Polly Fuqua	May 16, 1804
Waters, Richard	Nancy Jones	Apr. 1, 1801
Watkins, Jonathan	Clary Allen	Aug. 31, 1797
Watkins, Joshua	Nancy Colvin	...., 1802
Watkins, William	Polly Davis	Dec. 3, 1797
Watkins, William	Rebecca Case	May 1, 1800
Watts, Thomas	Eleanor Love	Oct. 9, 1794
Watson, James	Mary Thorne	Dec. 14, 1802
Warick, John	Elizabeth Markwell	June 3, 1796
Warren, Edward	Susannah Martin	Sept. 13, 1794
Waring, Francis	Mary H. Waring	Dec. 19, 1799
Waring, Thomas T. H.	Nancy Mefford	Apr. 25, 1799
Washburn, Cornelius	Jemima Masterson	June 3, 1791
Washburn, Joseph	Elizabeth Mann	Mar. 12, 1795
Watson, Amos	Leah Furr	Aug. 10, 1794
Watson, Arthur	Tempy Robertson	Aug. 28, 1798
Webb, Thomas	Ann Shotwell	Apr. 6, 1802
Welch, Abraham	Margaret Shirley	June 9, 1797
Wells, Aaron	Ruth Wiggins	Aug. 3, 1790
Welton, William	Drucilla McDonald	Sept. 27, 1803
West, Thomas	Elizabeth Parker	Dec. 26, 1799
Wharton, John	Sarah Rice	Aug. 17, 1797
Wheatley, William	Mary Castleman	Aug. 23, 1800
Wheeler, Levi	Mary Foster	Apr. 23, 1800
Whips, James	Elizabeth Davidson	Aug. 24, 1800
Whips, William	Celia Finch	...., 1799
White, William	Sally Fisher	Mar. 18, 1797
Whiteman, Benjamin	Catherine Davis	Mar. 2, 1793
Wiggins, Philip	Comfort Covalt	Mar. 25, 1798
Wilkes, John	Elizabeth Lynn	June 26, 1801
Wilcox, John	Comfort Plummer	Jan. 16, 1796
Williams, Archibald	Mary Ross	July 30, 1800
Williams, Morgan	Betsy Bryant	Jan. 15, 1803
Willson, George	Saphira Evans	Oct. 5, 1798
Wilson, Amos	Ann Mills	June 24, 1791
Wilson, James	Hannah Bailey	Dec. 5, 1799
Wilson, John	Polly Smoote	Feb. 8, 1797
Wilson, John	Rachael Plummer	Mar. 22, 1798
Wilson, John	Nancy Boyd	Apr. 16, 1803
Wilson, Moses	Nancy Dean	Sept. 24, 1801
Wilson, Robert	Elizabeth Harris	Feb. 22, 1803
Wilson, Thornton	Elizabeth G. Fife	Dec. 24, 1799
Wilson, William	Judah Hensley	July 29, 1802
Wise, Adam	Margaret Wiley	Nov. 26, 1799
Wise, John	Mary Shotwell	Jan. 21, 1799
Wood, Absolom	Charlotte Shotwell	Sept. 27, 1789
Wood, Allen	Annie Porter	Jan. 12, 1797
Wood, John	Catherine Record	Sept. 10, 1800
Wood, Richard	Catherine Mills	Feb. 24, 1796
Wormsley, Jack	Elizabeth Ginn	Apr. 30, 1797
Wormsley, William	Sarah Wickoff	June 28, 1798
Worthington, Thomas T.	Lydia Whips	June 4, 1799

Groom	Bride	Date of Marriage
Wright, Joseph	Sally Lewis	Dec. 29, 1790
Wright, William	Susanna French	Nov. 10, 1800

Y

Yates, Thomas	Esther Price	Jan. 19, 1796
Yeates, Joseph	Jane Dougherty	Mar. 19, 1797

CHAPTER XV

PIONEER MEMBERS OF THE KENTUCKY LEGISLATURE FROM THE EASTERN AND SOUTHEASTERN SECTIONS OF THE STATE

FLOYD COUNTY — HOUSE OF REPRESENTATIVES

David Morgan, 1813; died, succeeded by
Henry Stratton, 1813, 1815
Alexander Lackey, 1816, 1817, 1818, 1825, 1826, 1830, 1831, 1840
Henry B. Mayo, 1819
David K. Harris, 1820
Richard R. Lee, 1820, May 1822
James Stratton, 1821
Henry C. Harris, 1834, 1835, 1838
Thomas Cecil, 1839
John Martin, 1841, 1843

James H. Lane (Layne) 1845
John M. Elliott, 1847, 1861-63, expelled December 21, 1861, for being connected with, or giving aid and comfort to the Confederate Army; succeeded by
Thomas S. Brown, 1862-63
John M. Burns, 1857-59
Alexander L. Martin, 1867-69
Joseph M. Davidson, 1869-73
Allen C. Higgins, 1875-77

FLOYD AND CLAY COUNTIES

John Hibbard of Clay County, 1809

John Bates of Clay County, 1811

FLOYD AND PIKE COUNTIES

Robert Walker, Peter Amyx, 1822
Jacob Mayo, 1824
Thomas W. Graham, Jacob Heaberlin, 1827

Samuel May, 1832, 1833
Greenville Lackey, 1836

FLOYD, PIKE AND JOHNSON COUNTIES

Bernard H. Garrett, 1850

FLOYD COUNTY — SENATE

Benjamin South, 1814-19
Alexander Lackey, 1819-23
Henry B. Mayo, 1823-27
David K. Harris, 1827-34

Henry C. Harris, 1843-47
John P. Martin, 1855-59
Alexander L. Martin, 1871-75

FLOYD AND PIKE COUNTIES

Samuel May, 1834-39

FLOYD AND MONTGOMERY COUNTIES

Richard Menifee, 1814

KNOX COUNTY — HOUSE OF REPRESENTATIVES

John Ballinger, 1806
.... Herndon, 1807
Thomas Johnston, 1809
Joseph Eve, 1810, 1811, 1815
Gen. George Britton, 1813, 1814
Hiram Jones, 1816
Joseph Parsons, 1817, 1818
James F. Ballinger, 1819
Westley M. Garnett, 1822
Henry Tuggle, 1831, 1832
John P. Bruce, 1837
Green Adams, 1839, 1840

James Hayes, 1841
Silas Woodson, 1842, 1853-55
Radford M. Cobb, 1846
William D. Miller, 1849
James W. Davis, 1857-59; 1863-65
John Word, 1859-61
James W. Anderson, 1861-63
William B. Anderson, 1865-67
Dempsey King, 1867-69
W. W. Sawyers, 1873-75
James D. Black, 1875-77

KNOX AND WHITLEY COUNTIES

Dr. .... Wilson, 1834

KNOX AND HARLAN COUNTIES

Andrew Craig, 1820, 1821

KNOX COUNTY — SENATE

Joseph Eve, 1817-21
Richard Ballinger, 1821-26

John P. Bruce, 1848, 1850
Radford M. Cobb, 1851-55

KNOX, LAUREL, ROCKCASTLE AND WHITLEY COUNTIES

Joseph Gilless, 1842-45

GREENUP COUNTY — HOUSE OF REPRESENTATIVES

Thompson Ward, 1814, 1815, 1817, 1818, 1830
Francis H. Gaines, 1816, 1820
Thomas T. G. Waring, 1819
John M. McConnell, 1822, 1824, 1825
William Conner, 1826, 1827, 1847
John C. Kouns, 1828, 1829, 1831
Samuel Seaton, 1832, 1833, 1845
John Hollingsworth, 1834, 1835
David Trimble, 1836, 1837, 1838, 1839
Basil Waring, 1840
Robinson M. Biggs, 1841
Joseph D. Collins, 1842, 1843

Jesse Corum, 1844
Jefferson Evans, 1846
James W. Davis, 1848
Richard Jones, 1849, 1855-57
Marcus L. Williams, 1850
William C. Grier, 1851-53
Christopher C. Chinn, 1853-55
Joseph Patton, 1857-59
William C. Ireland, 1859-63
Edward F. Dulin, 1863-65
John D. Russell, 1865-69
James L. Waring, 1869-73
Dr. Samuel Ellis, 1873-75
Marshall Baker, 1875-77

GREENUP AND LEWIS COUNTIES

Plummer Thomas, 1809

John Radford, 1811

GREENUP COUNTY — SENATE

Charles Nelms Lewis, 1813
Thompson Ward, 1820, 1826
John M. McConnell, 1826-30
William Connor, 1830-34, 1842-46

William G. Carter, 1834-38
John C. Kouns, 1850
Henry M. Rust, 1857-61
William J. Worthington, 1865-69

CLAY COUNTY — HOUSE OF REPRESENTATIVES

John Hibbard, 1809, 1813, 1814
John Bates, 1811, 1815, 1817, 1824, 1832
John H. Slaughter, 1816
James Love, 1818, 1820
Thomas McRoberts, 1819
Daniel Garrard, 1822
Alexander White, 1825, 1826

James H. Garrard, 1836
William Morris, 1838
Theophilus T. Garrard, 1843, 1844
James T. Woodward, 1850-51
Dan B. Stivers, 1851-53
Daniel Garrard, 1855-57
Alexander T. White, 1861-63
William McDaniel, 1865-67

CLAY COUNTY — SENATE

Daniel Garrard, 1813-17, 1825-29
John Gilbert, 1833-37
Alexander White, 1847-50

Theophilus T. Garrard, 1857-61
David Y. Lyttle, 1867-71
John J. Hyden, 1875-79

PIKE COUNTY — HOUSE OF REPRESENTATIVES

James M. Rice, 1829
Colbert Cecil, 1842, 1855-57
George N. Brown, 1849
John M. Rice, 1859-61
David May, 1861-63, expelled for joining or aiding the Confederate Army, August 29, 1862

John H. Reynolds, 1865-67
Orlando C. Bowles, 1867-71, 1875-77
Nelson Hamilton, 1873-75 (See Floyd and Letcher Counties)

PIKE AND FLOYD COUNTIES — SENATE

Samuel May, 1834-39

LAWRENCE COUNTY — HOUSE OF REPRESENTATIVES

John L. Elliott, 1836, 1837
Green V. Goble, 1838, 1840, 1843
Walter Osburn, 1844
William F. Moore, 1851-53
John J. Jordan, 1853-55
Andrew J. Prichard, 1855-57
Sinclair Roberts, 1857-61

Daniel W. Johns, 1861-64, resigned 1864
D. J. Burchett, 1865-67
John M. Rice, 1867-69
George R. Diamond, 1869-71
George Carter, 1871-73
Ulysses Garred, 1873-75

LAWRENCE AND CARTER COUNTIES

James Rouse, 1841
Samuel Short, 1845

Ulysses Garred, 1848
George Burgess, 1850

LAWRENCE AND MORGAN COUNTIES

Wiley C. Williams, 1824
Elisha McCommas, 1825
Edward Wells, 1826

Rowland T. Burns, 1828, 1829, 1830
Joseph R. Ward, 1832, 1833, 1835

LAWRENCE AND MORGAN COUNTIES — SENATE

James M. Rice, 1838-42, 1846-50
John L. Elliott, 1851-52

Kenas F. Prichard, 1869-73

PIONEER MEMBERS OF THE KENTUCKY LEGISLATURE

CARTER COUNTY — HOUSE OF REPRESENTATIVES

Andrew Kitchen, 1842
Walter Osburn, 1844
George W. Crawford, 1846
George Grubb, 1847
John T. Ratcliff, 1849, 1859-61
John J. Park, 1851-55
Ephraim B. Elliott, 1855-57
Richard B. Whitt, 1857-59

Stephen J. England, 1861-62, re-
signed August, 1862 and suc-
ceeded by
William Bowling, 1862-63
Sebastian Eifort, 1863-65
B. F. Shepherd, 1865-67
James Kilgore, 1869-71
Richard D. Davis, 1873-75

CARTER COUNTY — SENATE

D. K. Weis, 1853-57

William C. Grier, 1861-65

BOYD COUNTY — HOUSE OF REPRESENTATIVES

John D. Ross, 1864-65
John H. Eastham, 1867-69

Mordecai Williams, 1871-73
K. R. Culbertson, 1875-77

BOYD COUNTY — SENATE

Kenas F. Prichard, 1869-73

William W. Culbertson, 1873-77

JOHNSON COUNTY — HOUSE OF REPRESENTATIVES

Samuel K. Friend, 1844
Daniel Hager, 1846
John B. Harris, 1848
Garland Hurt, 1851-53
Henry G. Hager, 1853-1855

John B. Auxier, 1855-57
Samuel Salyer, 1859-61
George H. Whitten, 1863-67 (See
Floyd County)

JOHNSON COUNTY — SENATE

None resident of this county over the period covered by this work.

ELLIOTT COUNTY — HOUSE OF REPRESENTATIVES

William Kitchen, 1875-77, first representative resident of the county.

ELLIOTT COUNTY — SENATE

None resident of this county over the period covered by this work.

MORGAN COUNTY — HOUSE OF REPRESENTATIVES

Thomas F. Hazlerigg, 1827
John S. Oakey, 1831
James P. Kendall, 1834
William Henry, 1839
Eli Lykins, 1841, 1842
Joseph Carter, 1844
Mason Williams, 1847
David N. Cottle, 1848

Caleb Cash, 1849
Stephen M. Farrish, 1853-55
Newton P. Reid, 1857-59
George M. Hampton, 1861-63
John W. Kendall, 1867-71
William Mynhier, 1871-73
Thomas J. Henry, 1875-77

MORGAN AND BREATHITT COUNTIES

Thomas J. Frazier, 1843

James Elliott, 1846 (See Lawrence
County.)

Eastern and Southeastern Kentucky

Morgan and Breathitt Counties — Senate

Mason Williams, 1839-43
William Wallace Brown, 1851-55

Alexander L. Davidson, 1859-63
John E. Cooper, 1871-75

Perry County — House of Representatives

Henry Duff, 1833
John Haddix, 1835
Elijah Combs, 1840

Joseph Eversole, 1848
Zachariah Morgan, 1867-69
Josiah H. Combs, 1871-73

Perry and Clay Counties

Alexander Patrick, 1827, 1828, 1830, 1831
Elnathan W. Murphy, 1829
Robert S. Brashears, 1837

John C. Wilson, 1839 (See Letcher County)

Perry and Clay Counties — Senate

No resident members from these counties over the period covered by this work.

Letcher County — House of Representatives

Hiram Hogg, 1847
Preston H. Collier, 1849
Robert Bates, 1857-59

Alexander E. Adams, 1863-65
James B. Fitzpatrick, 1871-73

Letcher, Clay and Perry Counties

Hiram Begley, 1845

Letcher, Perry and Pike Counties

James H. Hundley, 1851-55

Lewis Sewards, 1853-55

Breathitt County — House of Representatives

Jeremiah W. South, 1840
George Bowling, 1845
Thomas Hagins, 1851-53
John S. Hargis, 1855-57
William Day, 1859-61

Thomas P. Cardwell, 1863-65, 1871-73
John Deaton, 1867-69
Isaac B. Combs, 1869-71

Breathitt County — Senate

Jeremiah W. South, 1843-47

Thomas P. Cardwell, 1865-69

Harlan County — House of Representatives

James Farmer, 1824, 1825, 1826, 1834
Hiram Jones, 1833
John Jones, 1824
James Sparks, 1845
James Culton, 1847, 1855-57

Caro B. Brittain, 1850
Hiram S. Powell, 1861-65
Elijah C. Baker, 1865-67
Elijah Hurst, 1869-71
George B. Turner, 1873-75

PIONEER MEMBERS OF THE KENTUCKY LEGISLATURE

HARLAN AND KNOX COUNTIES

James Love, 1828, 1829, 1830
James Dorton, 1836, 1838
A. G. W. Pogue, 1843

William Word, 1848
Drury Tye, 1851-53

HARLAN, KNOX AND LAWRENCE COUNTIES

Robert George, 1827

HARLAN AND CLAY COUNTIES

Thomas J. Buford, 1835

HARLAN AND CLAY COUNTIES — SENATE

Thomas Jefferson Percifull, 1851-53

HARLAN, CLAY, KNOX AND WHITLEY COUNTIES

Robert George, 1829-33

HARLAN, CLAY, KNOX, WHITLEY AND LAUREL COUNTIES

Franklin Ballinger, 1837-41

LAUREL COUNTY — HOUSE OF REPRESENTATIVES

Jarvis Jackson, 1830, 1831, 1835
Thomas J. Buford, 1838, 1841, 1842, 1843
Mark A. Watkins, 1840
Evan Chestnut, 1844
Granville Pearl, 1846

William Jackson, 1848
George P. Brown, 1850
George W. Miller, 1853-55
E. B. Bacheller, 1861-63
Charles B. Faris, 1865-67
J. Francis Baugh, 1869-71

LAUREL AND WHITLEY COUNTIES

John S. Laughlin, 1829

LAUREL AND ROCKCASTLE COUNTIES

John J. Haley, 1851-53

LAUREL AND ROCKCASTLE COUNTIES — SENATE

Jarvis Jackson, 1849
Robert Boyd, 1867-75

LAUREL, LINCOLN AND ROCKCASTLE COUNTIES

Henry Owsley, 1829-34 (See Knox and Harlan Counties)

ROCKCASTLE COUNTY — HOUSE OF REPRESENTATIVES

Johnston Dysart, 1814
William Carson, 1816, 1826
William Smith, 1817, 1818, 1819, 1820, 1821, 1822, 1827, 1828, 1829
Uriah Gresham, 1824, 1839
John H. Slaughter, 1825
Charles Collyer, 1830, 1833, 1840
Elisha Smith, 1831, 1832, 1842, 1843, 1845
John A. Moore, 1834
Henry S. Langford, 1836, 1837
William H. Kirtley, 1841

William B. Moore, 1847
Jonathan S. Langford, 1849
Milton J. Cook, 1855-57, 1859-61
Jonathan Newcum, 1857-59
E. B. Bacheller, 1861-63
William A. Brooks, 1863-65
John K. McClary, 1867-69
R. D. Cook, 1871-73
R. P. Gresham, 1873-75
John M. Fish, 1875-77 (See Laurel County)

ROCKCASTLE AND LINCOLN COUNTIES

John Withers, 1812   James Dysart, 1814

ROCKCASTLE AND LINCOLN COUNTIES — SENATE

William Smith, 1834-38
John A. Moore, 1841
James S. Henderson, 1845, 1848

Milton J. Cook, 1863-67 (See Knox
and Laurel Counties)

WHITLEY COUNTY — HOUSE OF REPRESENTATIVES

John F. Sharp, 1820
Burton Litton, 1821, 1822, 1824,
1827, 1828
Baker E. Watkins, 1825, 1826
Dempsey White, 1833, 1835, 1838,
1839
Joel Snyder, 1836, 1840
Andrew Craig, 1837
Basil Brawner, 1841
Thomas Rockhold, 1842, 1843
James H. Early, 1844
Jeptha W. Brawner, 1845
Jonathan Foley, 1846
Milton E. White, 1847, 1863-65
Solomon Stevens, 1848

Levi Monroe, 1849
Daniel Cain, 1850
Thomas R. Harman, 1851-53
Squire Gatliffe, 1853-55
Pleasant W. Mahan, 1855-57
W. B. Skean, 1857-59
H. S. Tye, 1859-61
Hugh F. Finley, 1861-62, resigned
August, 1862, succeeded by
James M. Jones, 1862-63
Jackson Veach, 1865-67
Robert Bird, 1867-69
George W. Little, 1869-71, 1871-73
J. T. Freeman, 1873-75 (See Knox
and Laurel Counties)

WHITLEY COUNTY — SENATE

William C. Gillis, 1855-59, 1859-63   Hugh F. Finley, 1875-79

OWSLEY COUNTY — HOUSE OF REPRESENTATIVES

Harvey S. Hensley, 1857-59
Abijah Gilbert, 1859-61
Andrew Herd, 1863-65
Andrew J. Herd, 1867-69

Howell Brewer, 1869-71
Joseph P. Hampton, 1871-73
John S. Herd, 1873-75
E. B. Treadway, 1875-77

OWSLEY AND CLAY COUNTIES

Joseph N. Eve, 1853-55

OWSLEY AND ESTILL COUNTIES

Elisha L. Cockrell, 1847   Morton P. Moore, 1850

OWSLEY AND ESTILL COUNTIES — SENATE

Abijah Gilbert, 1850   James Ewing Gibson, 1859-63

MEMBERS OF THE CONSTITUTIONAL CONVENTION OF 1849

From Breathitt and Morgan Counties—John Hargis
From Carter and Lawrence Counties—Thomas J. Hood
From Clay, Letcher and Perry Counties—James H. Garrard
From Estill and Owsley Counties—Luther Browner
From Floyd, Johnson and Pike Counties—James M. Lackey
From Greenup County—Henry B. Pollard
From Knox and Harlan Counties—Silas Woodson
From Laurel and Rockcastle Counties—Jonathan Newcum
From Pulaski County—Milford Elliott
From Whitley County—Thomas Rockhold

CHAPTER XVI

EASTERN AND SOUTHEASTERN KENTUCKY IN WAR

Revolutionary War Officers and Soldiers who Settled in Eastern or Southeastern Kentucky

Bath County

Ashley, Thomas, Private, Virginia Line
Bailey, John, Captain, Virginia State Troops (Clark's Illinois Regiment)
Botts, Moses, Private, Virginia Line
Burch, John, Private, Pennsylvania Line
Bromigan, Jarvis, Private, Virginia Line
Boyd, William, North Carolina Line
Collins, Josiah, Private, Virginia Line
Deskins, Daniel, Private, Virginia Line
Fosbrook, John, Private, Pennsylvania Line
Gorrell, John, Private, Pennsylvania Line
Griffin, Gordon, Private, Pennsylvania Line
Hasty, John, Private, Virginia Line
Hensley, James, Sergeant, Virginia Line
Hines, James, Private, Virginia Line
Jameson, William, Private, Virginia Line
Kearns, William, Private, Virginia Line
Love, Mark, Private, South Carolina Line
Lynam, Andrew, Private, Virginia Militia
Moore, Michael, Private, Virginia Line
McIlheny, James, Captain, South Carolina Line
McGahee, William, Private, Pennsylvania Line
Mulberry, John, Private, Virginia Line
Nelson, Moses, Private, North Carolina Line
Parker, Edward, Sergeant, Virginia Line
Purvis, William, Private, Virginia Line
Pettit, Matthew, Private, Pennsylvania Line
Rice, Charles, Virginia State Troops (Clark's Illinois Regiment)
Rice, Holman, Captain, Virginia Line
Sims, John, Private, Virginia Line
Smallwood, Beane, Private, Virginia Line
Sorrell, Elisha, Private, Virginia Line
Thomas, Richard, Private, North Carolina Line

Breathitt County

Bowling, Jesse
Bush, Drury
Turner, Rogers

Clay County

Baker, Bowling, Private, North Carolina Line
Benge, David, Private, North Carolina Line
Burge, David, Sr., Private, Virginia Line
Burns, William, Private, Virginia Line
Bowling, Jesse, Private, North Carolina Line
Chandler, John, Private, North Carolina Line

Garland, John
Lewis, Messenger, Private, New York Line
Martin, Azariah, Private, Virginia Line
Phillips, John, Private, South Carolina Line
Ratcliffe, Harper, Private, Virginia Line
Seabourn, Jacob, Private, Virginia Continental Line
Stapleton, Thomas, Private, North Carolina Line
Wood, Samuel, Private, South Carolina Continental Line

FLOYD COUNTY

Auxier, Samuel, Private, Virginia Line
Bouney, Joseph, Private, Virginia Line
Brown, Thomas C. Cornet, Virginia Line
Brown, William
Cains, Richard, Private, Virginia Line
Cameron, James, Corporal, Virginia Line
Connelly, Henry, Captain, North Carolina Line
Castle, Basil
Cassady, Thomas
Conley, David
Dorten, Edward, Private, Virginia Line
Davis, Zachariah
Fairchild, Abuid, Private, North Carolina Line
Fitzgerald, William
Flannery, James
Flatwood, Isaac
Ferguson, William, Private, Pennsylvania Line
Fraley, James, Private, Virginia Militia
Graham, John, Virginia Continental Line
Hamilton, Thomas
Hall, Anthony, Private, North Carolina Line
Hall, John
Harris, James, Private, Virginia Militia
Harris, Samuel
Haney, William, Private, Virginia Line
Hitchcock, Joshua, Private, North Carolina Line
Hopkins, Garner, Private, New York Line
Herrell, Reuben, Private, Virginia Line
Jacobs, Roley, Private, Virginia Line
Jacobs, William, Private, Virginia Line
Jones, Ambrose, Private, Virginia Line
Jones, Gabriel, Private, North Carolina Line
Johns, Thomas
Justice, Simeon, Drummer, North Carolina Line
Justice, John
Kelly, John
Lovelady, Thomas, Private, Virginia Line
Matthews, Reuben
Moore, John, Private, North Carolina Line
Mullins, John, Private, Virginia Line
Murray, Thomas, Private, Pennsylvania Line
Nolen, William, Private, South Carolina Line
Patrick, James, Sr., Private, Virginia Line
Pitts (or Pytts), Jonathan, Private, North Carolina Line
Porter, James, Private, Virginia Line
Porter, John, W., Private, Virginia Line
Preston, Moses, Private, Virginia Line
Preston, Nathan, Private, Virginia Line
Smith, John III, Private, Virginia Line
Stone, Cudbeth, Private, Maryland Line

Sullivan, Peter, Private, Virginia Line
Thacker, Reuben, Private, Virginia Line
Wadkins, Benedict, Private, North Carolina Line
Wells, Richard, Sergeant, Virginia and North Carolina Lines
Williams, Philip, Private, Virginia Line
Young, Alexander, Private, South Carolina Line

GREENUP COUNTY
Burns, Jeremiah, Private, Virginia Line
Chadwick, John, Private, North Carolina Line
Dixon, Thomas, Private, Virginia Line
Hackworth, Thomas, Private, Virginia Militia
Hannon, William, Private, Maryland Line
Howe, John W., Private, Virginia Line
Johnson, John II, Private, Connecticut Line
Lawson, James, Private, Virginia Line
Mayhew, Elisha, Private, Connecticut Line
Patton, James, Private, Pennsylvania Line
Rigg (or Riggs), Charles, Corporal, Maryland Line
Sartin, Claibourne, Private, Virginia Line
Smith, Godfrey, Private, Virginia Line
Shortridge, John, Corporal, Virginia Continental Line
Young, Reuben, Private, Virginia Line
Westlake, Joseph (or Josiah), Private, New Jersey Line
Zornes, Andrew, Private, Virginia Line

HARLAN COUNTY
Ballew, Richard, Private, North Carolina Line
Brock, Jesse, Private, North Carolina Line
Caywood, Berry, Private, Virginia Line
Cozard, Benjamin
Green, Lewis, Private, Virginia Line
Fixworthy, John, Private, Virginia Militia
Hall, James, Private, South Carolina Line
Jackson, James, Sr.
Jones, Stephen, Private, North Carolina Line
Osborne, Ephraim, Private, Virginia Line
Furnish, John, Private, Virginia Militia
Shackleford, Henry, Private, Virginia Line

JOHNSON COUNTY
Auxier, Simon
Clark, Samuel
Davis, Joseph
Flannery, John
Francis, Thomas
Larkin, Prestley
Van Hase (Van Hoose), John, Private, Virginia Line (Clark's Illinois Regt.)
Walker, George R.

KNOX COUNTY
Ballew, Richard, Private, North Carolina Line
Browning, Edward
Blevins, Abraham
Broughton, Job, Private, North Carolina Line
Chick, James, Private, Virginia Line
Cooper, Jacob
Davis, Jesse, Private, Virginia Line

Edwards, Brown, Private, North Carolina Line
Garland, John, Private, North Carolina Line
Hammonds, Obadiah, Private, North Carolina Militia
Hammonds, Peter
Henson, William, Private, North Carolina Line
Horn, Christopher, Private, Virginia Line
Hamlin, Pierce Dant, Private, North Carolina Line
Horton, John Payton, Private, Virginia Line
Hubbs, John, Private, South Carolina Line
Miller, James
Mullens, Joshua
Pearcefield, John, Private, Pennsylvania Line
Patterson, William, Private, Virginia Line
Woodson, Wade M., Private, North Carolina Line

LAUREL COUNTY

Ayres, Nathaniel, Private, North Carolina Line
Clark, Elijah, Private, Maryland Line
Evans, John, Private, Virginia Militia
Fawbush, John
Forbes, John, Private, North Carolina Line
French, James, Private, Connecticut Line
Freeman, John, Private, Virginia Line
Hyde, Jesse, Private, North Carolina Line
Loven, Isaac, Private, North Carolina Line
McHargue, William, Private, North Carolina Line
Mersham, Titus, Private, New Jersey Line
Nix, John, Private, Virginia Line
Pitman, Ambrose, Private, Virginia Line
Simpson, John, Private, North Carolina Militia
Stranberry, [Stansberry], Solomon, Private, North Carolina Line

LAWRENCE COUNTY

Atkinson, David, Private, Virginia Line
Atkin, David, Private, Virginia Line
Bates, William, Private, Virginia Line
Brown, William, Private, Virginia Line
Burgess, Edward, Private, Virginia Line
Blumer, Gilbert, Private, New York Line
Castle, Basil, Private, Virginia Line
Cox, William, Private, Virginia Line
Crum, Adam, Private, North Carolina Line
Childers, Abner, Private, Virginia Line
Davis, Joseph, Private, Virginia Line
Hensley, Joseph, Private, Virginia Line
Hardwick, George Private, Virginia Line
Kitchen, James, Virginia Continental Line
Lee, Samuel, Private, Virginia Militia
Lesley, John, Private, Virginia Line (Clark's Illinois Regiment)
Lyon, William, Private, North Carolina Line
Marcum, Josiah, Private, Virginia Line
Marshall, John, Private, Virginia Militia
Mills, Richard, Private, Virginia Militia
Norton, James, Private, Virginia Militia
Perkins, George, Private, North Carolina Militia
Patrick, James, Private, Virginia Militia
Pratt, James, Private, Virginia Line
Sexton, John, Private, North Carolina Line
Ward, James, Private, Virginia Line
Wooten, Silas P., Private, Virginia Line

MORGAN COUNTY

Barker, George, Private, Virginia Line
Blevins, James, Private, Virginia Line
Butler, John, Private, Virginia Line
Cooke, William, Private, South Carolina Line
Cooper, John, Private, Pennsylvania Militia
Day, John, Private, Virginia Line
Ellington, David, Private, Virginia Militia
Hamilton, Thomas, Private, Virginia Line
Hamilton, Benjamin, Private, Virginia Line
Howerton, William, Private, Virginia Line
Johnson, Jacob, Private, South Carolina Line
Jones, Ambrose
Keeton, Isaac, Private, North Carolina Line
Kelly, Samuel, Private, North Carolina Line
Kulby, John
Lewis, Thomas, Private, Virginia Line
McGuire, John, Private, Virginia Line
McKinzie, Isaac, Private, Virginia Militia
Montgomery, Alexander, Private, Virginia Line
Prewitt, John
Ratliff, Reuben, Private, Virginia Militia
Smothers, John, Private, Virginia Line
Stephenson, Levi
Stevens, Gilbert, Private, Virginia Line
Swanson, Levi, Private, Virginia Militia
Wages, Benjamin, Private, Virginia Line
Walsh, William, Private, North Carolina Line
Williams, Philip, Private, Virginia Line

PERRY COUNTY

Burns, Andrew, Private, Virginia Line
Bush, Drury, Private, Virginia Line
Combs, John, Private, Virginia Line
Caudill, James
Croft, Archelos, Private, North Carolina Line
Cordill, James, Private, North Carolina Line
Cordill, Stephen, Private, North Carolina Line
Cornett, William
Ellis, Charles, Private, Massachusetts Line
Hurst, Hy, Private, Virginia Militia
Hagins, William, Private, North Carolina Line
Harwell, Andrew, Private, Virginia Line
Howard, James, Private, Virginia Line
Howard, Thomas, Private, Virginia Line
Justice, John, Private, South Carolina Line
Justice, Richard, Private, South Carolina Line
Justice, Simon, Private, South Carolina Line
Kelly, John, Private, North Carolina Line
May, David, Private, Virginia Line
Mullins, Joshua, Private, Virginia Line
McDaniel, George, Private, South Carolina Line
Osborne, Ephraim, Private, Virginia Line
Patrick, Ezekiel, Private, North Carolina Line
Pigman, Leonard, Private, North Carolina Line
Polly, Edmund, Private, Virginia Line
Stidham, Samuel, Private, North Carolina Line
Turner, Robert, Private, North Carolina Line

Wadkins, Thomas, Private, North Carolina Line
Williams, William, Private, North Carolina Line
Wooton, Silas P., Private, Virginia Line

PIKE COUNTY

Atkinson, James, Trumpeter, Virginia Line
Blankenship, William, Private, Virginia Militia
Childers, Pleasant, Private, North Carolina Line
Collins, Meredith
Dailey, Dennis, Private, Virginia Line
Ford, Joseph, Private, North Carolina Line
Hall, Rodden
Jackson, James, Private, North Carolina Line
Johnson, John
Mims, Robert
Maynard, James
May, John
Potter, Abram
Stepp, Moses, Private, South Carolina Line
Stewart, Thomas
Trout, Christian, Private, Maryland Line

ROCKCASTLE COUNTY

Abney, William, Private, Virginia Line
Anderson, James, Private, Pennsylvania Line
Bates, Humphrey, Private, North Carolina Line
Chasteen, James, Private, Virginia Line
Cash, William, Private, Virginia Militia
Collier, John
Craig, William, Private, Virginia Militia
Denny, Elijah, Private, North Carolina Line
Dysart, James, Captain, Virginia State Troops
Faris, Moses, Private, Virginia Militia
Frost, Micajah, Private, North Carolina Militia
Gadd, Thomas, Private, Maryland Militia
Gentry, Richard, Private, South Carolina Line
Haggard, Henry, Private, Virginia Militia
Hamm, John, Private, Virginia Line
Harlowe, George
Hawke, Nicholas, Private, North Carolina Militia
Johnson, Thomas, Virginia Militia
Lawrence, William, Virginia Militia
Pew, Reuben C.
Proctor, George, Virginia Militia
Ramsey, E., Sr.
Sigmond, John
Stephens, Jacob
Sweeney, William

WHITLEY COUNTY

Adkins, Thomas
Anderson, John, Private, Fifer, North Carolina Line
Gatliff, Charles, Private, Virginia Militia
Hood, John, Private, North Carolina Line
Laughlin, Thomas, Private, North Carolina Line
Mahan, James, Private, Virginia Militia
Moore, Joseph, Private, New Jersey Line
Moses, Joshua, Private, North Carolina Line
Porch, Henry, Private, North Carolina Line

Although not definitely established, the records of Floyd and/or Johnson Counties would seem to indicate that other Revolutionary War soldiers settled in that area:

Auxier, Michael
Barnett, Jesse
Evans, John
Fitzpatrick, Isaac
Fitzpatrick, James
Fitzpatrick, Solomon
Holt, William

Howe, Samuel
Janes, Stephen
Jayne, William
Johnson, John
Kelly, Jesse R.
King, Oliver
Kirk, James

Ramey, John
Ward, Isaac, Sr.
Ward, James
Wheeler, Stephen
Wiley, Thomas
Wooten, Silas P.

REVOLUTIONARY WAR OFFICERS AND SOLDIERS WHOSE DESCENDANTS SETTLED IN EASTERN OR SOUTHEASTERN KENTUCKY

Burke, William, Private Lee's (Virginia) Legion
Bragg, Thomas, Captain Virginia Line
Brown, George Newman, Virginia Line
Bryson, John, Captain Pennsylvania Line
Castner, Jacob, North Carolina Forces
Chandler, Thomas, Private North Carolina Line
Culbertson, Joseph, Virginia Forces
Connelly, Thomas, 1st Regiment, South Carolina Line
Dupuy, James, Jr., Captain Virginia Militia
Dupy, John, Lieutenant Virginia Militia
Elliott, Richard, Colonel Virginia Line
Fuqua, Peter, Virginia Line
Fuqua, Moses, Captain Virginia Line
Gilbert, Samuel, Private Virginia Line
Grayson, William, Colonel 8th Virginia Regiment Continental Line
Harvie, John, Colonel Virginia Forces
Hager, John, Sr., South Caroline Line
Hampton, Dr. Cary Henry (surgeon) Colonel (?) Virginia Line
Hord, Thomas, Captain Virginia Line
Hord, James, Captain Virginia Militia
Hord, John, Captain Lee's (Virginia) Light Dragoons
Hord, Richard, Captain Virginia Continental Line
Kilgore, Charles T., Virginia Forces (?)
Leftwich, William, Colonel Virginia Line
Means, John, Co. South Caroline line (?)
Meek, Moses, Private South Carolina Light Dragoons
McCarty, Richard, Captain Virginia Line
Nevile, George, Cornet, Virginia Continental Line
Poage, George, Colonel Virginia (Boutetourt Co.) Militia
Poage, George, Captain Virginia (Augusta Co.) Militia
Poage, John, ensign, Virginia (Augusta Co.) Militia
Poage, Robert, Lieutenant Virginia (Rockbridge Co.) Militia
Poage, William, Tate's Company, Augusta County, Virginia Militia
Price, Thomas, Private Virginia Militia
Ramsey, Joel, Virginia Forces (?)
Robinson, James, Virginia Line
Stratton, Solomon, Virginia (Clark's Illinois Regiment)
Salyer, Benjamin, Jr., Virginia Continental Line
Stafford, Thomas, Pennsylvania Line
Salyer, Zachariah, Virginia Continental Line
Smallwood, Samuel, Captain, Maryland Militia
Strother, Robert, Virginia Forces
Waring, Thomas, Lieutenant and Captain Maryland Militia

Witten, Thomas, Sr., Virginia Line
Witten, Thomas, Jr., Virginia Line
Witten, James, Virginia Line
Wells, George, Pulaski Legion
Wells, James, General (?) Maryland Continental Line (?)

WAR OF 1812

SECOND REGIMENT, KENTUCKY MILITIA[1]

Roll of Field and Staff

Lieutenant Colonel: William Jennings
First Major: John Faulkner
Second Major: Joseph Eve
Surgeon: William Craig
Surgeon's Mate: David Nelson
Paymaster: Jonathan Desert (Dysart)
Second Paymaster: Henry Beaty
Adjutant: Samuel Lapsley
Quartermaster Sergeant: James Morrison
Sergeant Major: Barney Young
Adjutant: Thomas McGilton

Captain Daniel Garrard's Company

Captain: Daniel Garrard
Lieutenant: Daniel Cockrells
Ensign: William Cunningham
Sergeants: Thomas Murphy; James Love; Benjamin Blythe; Horatio
   Bruce; John Allen; Lincoln Ames; David Fee
Corporals: Daniel Sibert; John Cane; William Simpson; John Eversidge
Musicians: Valentine Percifield?; Samuel Eldridge

POGUE'S REGIMENT, KENTUCKY MILITIA
COMMANDED BY LIEUTENANT-COLONEL ROBERT POGUE[2]

Field and Staff Officers

Lieutenant Colonel: Robert Pogue
First Major: William Reed
Second Major: David Hart
Surgeon: Ardemus D. Roberts
Surgeon's Mate: Thomas Doniphan
Adjutant: Benjamin Norris
Paymaster: George W. Botts
Quartermaster: Benedict Bacon
Quartermaster Sergeant: John Heddleson
Sergeant Major: Walter Lacey
Drum Major: John Wire
Fife Major: Joab Houghton

Captain Thompson Ward's Company

Captain: Thompson Ward
Lieutenant: George Benaugh
Ensign: Benedict Bacon
Sergeants: James Ward; Thomas Wilson; Jacob Kouns; John Gholson
Corporals: Samuel D. Fishback; Charles Jackson; Charles Craycraft;
   James Gibson

POAGE'S REGIMENT, KENTUCKY VOLUNTEERS, COMMANDED BY COLONEL JOHN POAGE[3]

Field and Staff

Colonel: John Poage
Majors: Aaron Stratton; Jeremiah Morton
Adjutant: John E. McDowell
Quartermaster: Samuel L. Crawford
Paymaster: John Hockaday
Surgeon: Anderson Donaphan
Surgeon's Mate: Thomas Nelson
Quartermaster Sergeant: Edward Brooks
Sergeant Major: William Triplett

Captain Moses Demmitt's Company

Captain: Moses Demmitt
First Lieutenant: Thomas Hord
Ensign: Joseph Thorn

Captain Francis Gaines' Company
(Recruited in Greenup County)

Captain: Francis A. Gaines
Lieutenant: Thomas T. G. Waring
Ensign: Thomas Page, Sr.
Sergeants: Hezekiah Magruder; William Ward; John Poage; James Poage; John Bartley
Corporals: John Evans; James Nichols; David White; Levi Shackles

Captain Aaron Stratton's Company
(Recruited in Lewis County)

Captain: Aaron Stratton
First Lieutenant: Richard Soward
Second Lieutenant: George W. Davis
Sergeants: Elijah Houghton; Charles Parker; Henry Halbert; William Calvert.
Corporals: Charles Alkins (Atkins?); Ashel Brewer; Jacob Frizle (Frizzell?); Daniel Thomas

Captain Stratton's Company apparently was recruited in Lewis County.

KENTUCKY MOUNTED VOLUNTEER MILITIA[4]

Captain Johnston Dysart's Company

Captain: Johnston Dysart
Lieutenant: Charles C. Carson
Ensign: Joseph Henderson
Sergeants: James Wilson; Jacob Frederick; Isaiah Ham; Samuel Vance
Corporals: John Bustle; John Evans; George Watkins; Isaac Dillard

KENTUCKY BATTALION, MOUNTED VOLUNTEERS[5]
Captain Thomas Dollarhide's Company
Captain: Thomas Dollarhide
Lieutenant: John Cowen
Ensign: Jesse Evan
Sergeants: Samuel Hays; Hand Beastard; George M. Gaham; Joel Roberts

Captain Tunstall Quarles' Company
Captain: Tunstall Quarles, Jr.
Lieutenant: Lewellin Hickman
Ensign: Robert J. Foster
Sergeants: William Irvine, Jr; Bird Smith; Jesse Shell; William McCan
Corporals: Joseph Porter; Jesse Stringer; William Chesney; John Nortrip

Captain William Spratt's Company
Captain: William Spratt
Lieutenant: Johnson Dysart
Ensign: James Forsyth
Sergeants: John Bright; James Terrel; William F. Murphy; Weedin Smith
Corporals: Andrew Leeper; David Sutton; John Hand; David Logan
Fifer: Skelton Rentfro

THE CIVIL WAR
UNION ARMY

FOURTEENTH KENTUCKY REGIMENT VOLUNTEER INFANTRY[6]
Roll of Field and Staff
Colonels: Laban F. Moore, John C. Cochran, George W. Gallup
Lieutenant Colonels: Joseph R. Brown, Orlando Brown, Jr., Rhys M. Thomas
Majors: William B. Burke, Drury J. Burchett
Adjutants: John F. Babbitt, Edward J. Roberts
Regimental Quartermaster: James D. Foster
Surgeons: S. J. Yates, Akin C. Miller, Strother J. Yates
Assistant Surgeons: Franklin M. Meacham, Samuel D. Richards, Benjamin A. Stubbins, Cyrus L. Mobley
Chaplains: A. J. McMillan, Robert B. Herron
Sergeant Majors: John Cochran, Jr., Daniel H. Brown, Henry H. Hill, David C. Thomas
Quartermaster Sergeants: John C. Henderson, James F. Dixon
Commissary Sergeants: George B. Patton, George W. Hutchison
Hospital Stewards: Beverly W. Hereford, Charles C. Culver, John Laing

Commissioned Company Officers
Company "A"
Captains: James C. Whitten, Rhys M. Thomas
First Lieutenants: William C. Brown, Henry B. Brodess
Second Lieutenants: John M. Lothere, George W. Hopkins

Company "B"
Captains: Walter O. Woods, James H. Davidson, George W. Green
First Lieutenants: Chilton A. Osborn, James W. Chaffin
Second Lieutenant: Ralph W. Holbrook

Company "C"

Captains: David M. Mims, Oliver M. Frasher
First Lieutenants: William Killgore, David H. McGhee
Second Lieutenant: George B. Patton

Company "D"

Captains: Thomas McKinster, Charles A. Wood
First Lieutenants: John C. Henderson, Henry A. Borders, Russell T. Thompson
Second Lieutenants: Samuel T. Moore, Bluford F. Hale, John S. Thompson, Henry H. Hill

Company "E"

Captains: Archibald Means, Dwight A. Leffingwell
First Lieutenants: William Price, James T. Womack
Second Lieutenant: Jacob M. Poage

Company "F"

Captains: Solomon Davis, David L. Worthington, John Cochran, Jr., Patrick O. Hawes, Henry G. Gardner
First Lieutenants: Dwight A. Leffingwell, Thomas H. Stewart, James H. Sperry
Second Lieutenants: John Murphy, Henry H. Gallup

Company "G"

Captains: John C. Collins, Oliver D. Botner
First Lieutenants: Daniel H. Brown
Second Lieutenants: George H. Roberts, Lawrence P. Davenport

Company "H"

Captains: Isaac Hollingsworth, John F. Babbit, William H. Bartram
First Lieutenants: George R. B. Chapman, George F. Johnson
Second Lieutenants: Francis M. Burgess, James H. Carey

Company "I"

Captains: John Powers, Wiley C. Patrick, John M. Atkinson
First Lieutenants: Henry G. Gardner, Mason H. Power
Second Lieutenants: Richard M. Elam, Andrew B. Fitch

Company "K"

Captains: John M. Smith, Drury J. Burchett, Thomas D. Marcum
First Lieutenant: Andrew J. Fox
Second Lieutenant: James W. Shannon

The Fourteenth Regiment Kentucky Volunteer Infantry was organized in October, 1861, at Louisa, Kentucky, under Colonel Laban T. Moore; was mustered into the United States service, December 10, 1861, and was mustered out at Louisa, January 31, 1865. It participated in the battles at Ivy Mountain, Middle Creek, and Salyersville, Kentucky; Lost Mountain, Georgia; Laurel Mountain, Virginia; New Hope Church, Kenesaw, Peachtree Creek, Cass Station, and Jonesboro, Georgia; Johnsonville, Tennessee; Atlanta and Marietta, Georgia.

Twenty-Second Kentucky Volunteer Infantry[7]

This regiment was organized at Camp Swigert, Greenup County, Kentucky, December 12, 1861, under D. W. Lindsey, as colonel, George W. Monroe, lieutenant colonel, and Wesley Cook, major, by which officers the regiment was principally recruited. Companies "D", "H" and "I" were recruited from Carter County; "B" and "C" from Greenup County; "G" from Carter and Boyd Counties; "F" from Franklin and Greenup Counties; and "E" from Lewis County.

Roll of Field and Staff

Colonels: Daniel W. Lindsey; George W. Monroe
Lieutenant Colonels: William J. Worthington
Majors: Wesley Cook; John Hughes
Adjutants: Orlando Brown, Jr., Joseph W. Roberts; Francis C. Robb
Quartermasters: E. F. Dulin, John Paul Jones; James F. Trueman; Shadrack L. Mitchell; James W. Barbee
Surgeons: Benjamin F. Stevenson, Henry Manfred; William R. Davidson
Chaplain: Samuel S. Sumner
Quartermaster Sergeant: Charles W. Hillerman
Commissary Sergeant: John P. Vance
Hospital Steward: Sidney Van Bibber

Commissioned Company Officers

Company "B"

Captains: William J. Worthington; John L. Godman
First Lieutenants: Henry E. Evans; Daniel W. Steele

Company "C"

Captain: John F. Lacy
First Lieutenant: Francis C. Robb
Second Lieutenant: Robert Montgomery

Company "D"

Captains: James W. Scott; James G. Milligan
First Lieutenant: James W. Barbee
Second Lieutenants: John A. Gilbert, James A. Watson

Company "E"

Captains: Lewis P. Ellis, Alexander Bruce
First Lieutenant: David C. Thoroman
Second Lieutenants: Elijah Scott, William B. Hegan, Jabez Truett

Company "F"

Captains: Daniel Garrard, Jr.; Williamson W. Bacon
First Lieutenant: James Morton
Second Lieutenants: William H. Sneed; Richard J. Frayne

Company "G"

Captains: John Paul Jones; William H. Hegan; Evan D. Thomas; Jacob Swigert, Jr.
First Lieutenant: Charles L. Nevius
Second Lieutenant: Harry B. Litteral

Company "H"

Captains: Edwin Cook; John T. Gaithright; Stephen Nethercutt
First Lieutenant: Thomas P. Harper
Second Lieutenant: John Everman, Sr.

Company "I"

Captains: Jordan Nethercutt; Frank A. Estep; William K. Gray
First Lieutenants: Jeremiah Noland; Charles G. Shanks
Second Lieutenant: William Nethercutt

This regiment rendered most important service in the expedition against the Confederate General Humphrey Marshall in the Big Sandy Valley. A detachment under command of Lieutenant Colonel Monroe, during the battle of Middle Creek, charged and dislodged from a strong position the command of General John S. Williams, Confederate States Army, which movement, as the commanding officer, General Garfield, reports, was "determinate of the day."

The regiment engaged in the following general engagements, besides numerous skirmishes: Middle Creek, Kentucky; Cumberland Gap, Tazewell, Tennessee; Haynes Bluff or Chickasaw Bayou, Mississippi; Arkansas Post, Port Gibson, Champion Hill, Big Black Bridge, Siege of Vicksburg, Jackson, Mississippi, and Red River.

THIRTY-NINTH REGIMENT KENTUCKY INFANTRY[8]

Roll of Field and Staff

Colonels: John Dils, Jr.; David A. Mims
Lieutenant Colonel: Stephen M. Ferguson
Majors: John B. Auxier; Martin Thornsbury
Adjutants: Levi J. Hampton; John F. Stewart; Robert F. Huey
Quartermasters: Martin Fulkerson; Lindsey Layne
Surgeons: James H. Hereford; William E. Phillips
Assistant Surgeons: James N. Draper; James H. Phillips
Chaplain: Marcus S. King
Sergeant Majors: Lewis A. Thornberry; Clinton B. Buskirk; James E. Grace
Quartermaster Sergeants: James W. Allison; Tandy M. Layne
Commissary Sergeant: William N. Randolph
Hospital Stewards: J. S. C. Taylor; Isaac Rice

Commissioned Company Officers

Company "A"

Captains: John B. Auxier; David V. Auxier; Henry R. Brown
First Lieutenant: Isaac Goble
Second Lieutenant: Richard L. Burchett

Company "B"

Captains: William Ford; Jacob S. Eberman
First Lieutenants: Ellington Kilgore; John Breeding
Second Lieutenants: John F. Stewart; Andrew J. Adkins; John Harkens

Company "C"
Captain: Thomas J. Sowards
First Lieutenants: Andrew J. Sowards; James W. Allison
Second Lieutenant: Jacob Helvey

Company "D"
Captains: Martin Thornbury; Isaac E. Gray
First Lieutenants: Alfred C. Hailey; Hughey Plymale
Second Lieutenants: Walter Thornbury; William Weddington

Company "E"
Captains: Lewis Sowards; Alfred C. Hailey
First Lieutenants: James M. Sowards; William T. Berry
Second Lieutenants: Paris L. Reed; Shadle R. Pauley

Company "F"
Captain: Hezekiah Webb
First Lieutenants: George J. Allen; Augustus E. Kendrick
Second Lieutenant: Calvin Preston

Company "G"
Captain: Allen P. Haws
First Lieutenants: John B. VanHoose; James M. Rice
Second Lieutenant: Addison Miller

Company "H"
Captain: William King
First Lieutenants: Richard D. Coleman; James M. Thornbury
Second Lieutenant: James H. Stump

Company "I"
Captains: Joseph M. Kirk; Benjamin A. Rogers
First Lieutenants: William Hagerman; John D. Reinhart
Second Lieutenants: Charles Helton; Simeon L. Payne

Company "K"
Captains: Harrison Ford; Nathaniel Collins
First Lieutenant: Joseph D. Powers
Second Lieutenant: Samuel Keel.

This regiment was organized at Peach Orchard, Kentucky, under Colonel John Dils, and was mustered into the United States service, February 16, 1863, and was mustered out, September 15, 1865, at Louisville, Kentucky. The command was raised entirely in the Big Sandy Valley and the counties adjoining and was stationed in that section of the country for its protection against the frequent incursions of the rebels from Virginia. A portion of the regiment proceeded with other troops to Gladeville, Virginia, and succeeded in capturing Colonel Caudill and his command, who were brought back as prisoners of war.

The regiment participated in many battles and skirmishes: Pond Creek, Pike County, May 16, 1864; boat fight in Johnson County, December 4, 1862; Beaver Creek, Floyd County, June

27, 1863; Marrowbone, Pike County, September 22, 1863; Clark's Neck, Lawrence County, August 27, 1863; Paintsville, Johnson County, April 13, 1864; Half Mount, Magoffin County, April 14, 1864; Mount Sterling, Kentucky, June 9, 1864; Cynthiana, Kentucky, June 12, 1864; Saltville, Virginia, October 2, 1864.

FORTIETH REGIMENT KENTUCKY VOLUNTEER MOUNTED INFANTRY[9]

Roll of Field and Staff

Colonel: Clinton J. True
Lieutenant Colonel: Matthew Mullins
Majors: Thomas H. Mannen; Frederick H. Bierbower
Adjutants: Edward C. Barlow; James B. True
Quartermasters: A. L. Burke; John C. Ball; George W. Littlejohn
Surgeons: Joseph G. Roberts; William B. Bland
Assistant Surgeons: James H. Phillips; Oscar E. Holloway
Chaplain: James A. Snead
Sergeant Majors: John W. Frazer; Benedict F. Dorcey
Quartermaster Sergeants: Robert C. Snead; Luther Krouse
Commissary Sergeants: Alonzo Mateer; Peter U. Weaver
Hospital Steward: Samuel N. Loy
Principal Musicians: James L. Hunt; Charles McLain

Commissioned Company Officers

Company "A"

Captains: Frederick H. Bierbower; Charles R. Curtis
First Lieutenant: Charles Roberts
Second Lieutenant: Alex. W. Lawwill

Company "B"

Captains: Simon Rice; Edward C. Barlow
First Lieutenant: John S. Reed
Second Lieutenants: Noah Johnson; Raphael Tomlinson

Company "C"

Captain: John B. Nipp
First Lieutenants: Robert D. Adams; Warren H. Devore
Second Lieutenant: Robert C. Snead

Company "D"

Captains: John McGuire; Elias P. Davis
First Lieutenant: Middleton McGuire
Second Lieutenant: Alexander Johnson

Company "E"

Captain: Harrison B. Literal
First Lieutenants: George W. Littlejohn; John Foster
Second Lieutenants: James Garvin; John M. Tyree

Company "F"

Captain: James H. Johns
First Lieutenant: William E. Arnold
Second Lieutenant: Zachariah H. Mullins

Company "G"

Captain: Thomas R. Rorer
First Lieutenant: Christopher C. McGinety
Second Lieutenants: Isaac A. Whitaker; Lloyd McGill

Company "H"

Captain: Greenberry Reid
First Lieutenant: Cornelius B. Pettet
Second Lieutenants: John W. Evans; William S. Waugh

Company "I"

Captain: Isaac Kelly
First Lieutenants: Thomas H. Larimore; Mark Wallace
Second Lieutenant: Marshal W. Stubblefield

Company "K"

Captain: Stephen H. Young
First Lieutenants: William Frisby; Henry E. Evans
Second Lieutenants: James McGuire; John W. Frazer

This regiment was recruited and mustered in at Grayson, Carter County, Kentucky, in September, 1863, for twelve month's service and was mustered out at Catlettsburg, Kentucky, December 30, 1864. The State being overrun with guerrillas and the regiment being ordered into active service immediately after, and sometimes before thoroughly organized, it had no time for drill and discipline. Being mounted, it was constantly employed in defending different portions of Eastern Kentucky, and rendered good service. The regiment was with General Burbridge in his expedition against Saltville, Virginia, and participated in all the battles in Kentucky during the frequent raids of Morgan.

FORTY-FIFTH REGIMENT KENTUCKY VOLUNTEER MOUNTED INFANTRY[10]

Roll of Field and Staff

Colonel: John Mason Brown
Lieutenant Colonel: Lewis M. Clark
Majors: Nathan A. Brown; John C. Henderson
Adjutant: James Seaton
Quartermasters: John C. Ball; Harman Conley
Surgeon: Samuel Maguire
Assistant Surgeons: William E. Scobey; Joseph L. Rowland
Chaplain: Elisha Thacker
Sergeant Major: James H. Marcum
Quartermaster Sergeant: John V. Olinger
Commissary Sergeant: A. J. W. Lyons
Hospital Steward: Frank Blanchard

Commissioned Company Officers

Company "A"

Captain: Joseph W. Cottingham
First Lieutenant: Daniel Hendrickson
Second Lieutenant: Pleasant H. Stricklett

Company "B"

Captains: Benjamin R. Haley; William B. Shockley
First Lieutenants: James H. Loh; John W. Thornton
Second Lieutenant: William A. Haley

Company "C"

Captains: George W. Brown; Frank Mott
First Lieutenant: Edwin S. Turner
Second Lieutenant: David W. German

Company "D"

Captain: W. S. Adams
First Lieutenants: J. J. Matney; William P. Cooper
Second Lieutenants: Calvin F. Vaughn; George F. Ratliff

Company "E"

Captain: Thomas Damron
First Lieutenant: Daniel H. Walker
Second Lieutenant: Jasper Hatten

Company "F"

Captain: Thomas Russell
First Lieutenant: Richard Williamson
Second Lieutenant: Mordecai McClure

Company "G"

Captain: William B. Jones
First Lieutenant: William B. Johnson
Second Lieutenants: Erastus M. Gates; Coburn D. Outten

Company "H"

Captain: Jackson J. Matney
First Lieutenant: Calvin F. Vaughn
Second Lieutenant: Horace January

Company "I"

Captain: James H. O'Brien
First Lieutenant: Robert H. Wilson
Second Lieutenant: Milton J. Smith

Company "K"

Captain: Jacob L. Ross
First Lieutenant: Edward W. Brown
Second Lieutenant: John Thompson

This regiment was at first designed as a battalion for local service on the Virginia front and in the eastern counties of Kentucky. In the summer of 1863 four companies were recruited and it was determined to increase the command to a regiment and muster it into the United States service. Recruiting was rapid and the regiment was put on active duty in October, 1863, and the organization effected at Ashland, Kentucky. The regiment was mustered out at Catlettsburg, Kentucky — certain companies on December 24, 1864, and others on February 14, 1865.

The regiment led the pursuit after Morgan in June, 1864, and was the leading regiment of the assaulting column at the battle of Mount Sterling, June 9, 1864. It participated in the battle of Cynthiana, June 12, 1864, in which Morgan's force was finally destroyed, having, up to that engagement, been continuously on duty for twenty-six days and nights, with no halt of as much as four hours.

In November and December, 1864, this regiment was in Stoneman's column at the capture of Bristol, Tennessee, Marion, Abingdon, and Saltville, Virginia, and participated in all the engagements of that campaign.

FOURTEENTH REGIMENT KENTUCKY VETERAN INFANTRY[11]

Roll of Field and Staff

Lieutenant Colonel: Henry G. Gardner
Surgeon: Benjamin A. Stubbins
Sergeant Major: David C. Thomas
Commissary Sergeant: Jonas Burton
Hospital Steward: Levi J. Sparks

Commissioned Company Officers

Company "A"

Captains: Henry G. Gardner; James H. Sperry
Second Lieutenant: Henry H. Gallup

Company "B"

Captain: John M. Atkinson
First Lieutenant: Mason H. Power
Second Lieutenant: Henry H. Hill

Company "C"

Captain: Thomas D. Marcum
First Lieutenant: Russell T. Thompson
Second Lieutenant: James W. Shannon

Company "D"

Captain: George F. Johnson

KENTUCKY STATE TROOPS PROPER
FIRST REGIMENT CAPITAL GUARDS

SANDY VALLEY BATTALION[12]

Company "E"

Captain: Jacob Nelson
First Lieutenant: David L. Evans
Second Lieutenant: William H. H. Callihan

Company "G"

Captain: John Welsh
First Lieutenant: William G. Porter
Second Lieutenant: Robert C. Howard

Company "K"

Captain: Alexander W. Nickell
First Lieutenant: Jackson H. Jacobs
Second Lieutenant: Frederick Stumbaugh

Company "L"

Captain: Irad B. Hutchison
First Lieutenant: John B. Maynard

THREE FORKS BATTALION[13]

Company "C"

Captain: William B. Eversole
First Lieutenant: John B. Campbell
Second Lieutenant: Stephen Stamper

Company "D"

Captain: Shadrack Combs
First Lieutenant: Shadrack Stacy
Second Lieutenant: Samuel Begley

Company "E"

Captain: William Strong
First Lieutenants: William F. Little; Alfred Little
Second Lieutenant: Edward Marcum

Company "F"

Captain: Benjamin F. Blankenship
First Lieutenant: Henry Day
Second Lieutenant: Enoch Blair

KENTUCKY STATE MILITIA
HARLAN COUNTY BATTALION[14]

Roll of Field and Staff

Major: Ben F. Blankenship
Quartermaster: William Dixon

Commissioned Company Officers

Company "A"

Captain: George W. Morgan
First Lieutenant: Abner Lewis
Second Lieutenant: Moses Isom
Third Lieutenant: Joshua B. Hall

Company "B"

Captain: Ambrose Powell
First Lieutenant: Enoch Blair
Second Lieutenant: Elisha Huff
Third Lieutenant: William M. Jenkins

Company "C"

Captain: Joshua C. Perkins
First Lieutenants: Josiah B. Spurlock; Wright Kelly
Second Lieutenant: William Gilbert
Third Lieutenant: Chadwell F. C. Nolen

Company "D"
Captain: Josiah B. Spurlock
First Lieutenant: John J. Lewis
Second Lieutenant: Eli Huff
Third Lieutenant: Sanders Spurlock

Company "E"
Captain: Augustus B. Culton
First Lieutenant: Jesse Mattingly
Second Lieutenant: Larkin Wells
Third Lieutenant: John Campbell

Company "F"
Captain: Henry Day
First Lieutenant: Joseph Wells
Second Lieutenant: Jesse Clay
Third Lieutenant: Joshua B. Singleton

Company "G"
Captain: James Howard
First Lieutenant: James Helton
Second Lieutenant: John Howard
Third Lieutenant: George Helton

TWENTY-SECOND KENTUCKY ENROLLED MILITIA[15]

Roll of Field and Staff
Colonel: Thomas J. Ewing
Major: Job F. Lewman
Adjutant: James P. Castner
Surgeon: James D. Kincaid

Company "A"
Captain: John Faulkner
First Lieutenant: W. O. Hampton
Second Lieutenant: Jesse Eastwood

Company "B"
Captain: James Murphy
First Lieutenant: William J. Poteet
Second Lieutenant: Louis L. Kible

SIXTY-EIGHTH KENTUCKY ENROLLED MILITIA[16]

Roll of Field and Staff
Colonel: Thomas McKinster
Lieutenant Colonel: Martin H. Johns
Major: William M. Jones
Adjutant: Buford F. Hale
Quartermaster: Thomas Wallace
Surgeon: Edmond Osborn
Sergeant Major: James Burk
Quartermaster Sergeant: John M. Rice
Commissary Sergeant: John B. Hatcher

Company "A"

Captain: David Sturgeon
First Lieutenant: Jacob P. Williams
Second Lieutenant: Milton Swetnam

Company "B"

Captain: Samuel Sparks
First Lieutenant: Thomas J. Lester
Second Lieutenant: Linsey Lester

Company "C"

Captain: Ira B. Hutchison
First Lieutenant: Joseph S. Billups
Second Lieutenant: Francis Maynard
Third Lieutenant: A. H. McClure

Company "D"

Captain: Joseph F. Hatten
First Lieutenant: Marshel Dean
Second Lieutenant: Charles R. Neal

Company "E"

Captain: Harris Vaughan
First Lieutenant: James Preston
Second Lieutenant: Lafayette Preston

Company "F"

Captain: Hiram Jordan
First Lieutenant: James Smith
Second Lieutenant: John W. Hensley

Company "G"

Captain: James H. Moore
First Lieutenant: John W. Young
Second Lieutenant: William H. Moore

Company "H"

Captain: J. E. Cassel
First Lieutenant: Francis Fluty
Second Lieutenant: Henderson Branham

Company "I"

Captain: William M. Blankenship
First Lieutenant: Samuel K. Muncy
Second Lieutenant: William Waldack

Company "K"

Captain: William Borders
First Lieutenant: Martin P. M. Davis
Second Lieutenant: John B. Spencer

SIXTY-FIFTH KENTUCKY ENROLLED MILITIA[17]

Roll of Field and Staff

Colonel: Burgess Preston
Lieutenant Colonel: George W. Brown
Major: Peter Daniel
Adjutant: Wiley W. Howes
Quartermaster: James Neibert
Surgeon: Hamilton S. Swetnam
Sergeant Major: John Vanhouse (VanHoose)
Commissary Sergeant: James E. Stewart

Company "A"

Captain: James H. Spradlin
First Lieutenant: Jackson Patrick
Second Lieutenant: Benjamin F. Spradlin

Company "B"

Captain: Thomas Stafford
Second Lieutenant: Lafayette Preston
Third Lieutenant: John S. Miller

Company "C"

Captain: Samuel Spears
Second Lieutenant: Robert Akers
Third Lieutenant: Timothy Cunningham

Company "D"

Captain: Philip Cassaday
First Lieutenant: James Dalton
Second Lieutenant: Anderson Banister

Company "E"

Captain: Peter C. Craise
First Lieutenant: Fleming Litterel
Second Lieutenant: Rhodes Meed

Company "F"

Captain: B. F. Salyers
First Lieutenant: Isom Daniel
Second Lieutenant: W. W. Chandler

CONFEDERATE STATES ARMY

FIFTH REGIMENT INFANTRY KENTUCKY VOLUNTEERS[18]
Roster of Field and Staff

Colonels: John S. Williams; Andrew J. May; Hiram Hawkins
Lieutenant Colonels: Andrew J. May; Hiram Hawkins; George W. Connor
Majors: George W. Connor; William Mynhier
Adjutants: Thomas Benton Cook; R. T. Daniel
Acting Adjutant: Asa M. Swimm
Capt. A.Q.M.: William Wells; William S. Rogers; Thomas Johnson
Acting A.Q.M.: W. W. Cox
Surgeons: Hudson Rutherford; Charles Mann
Asst. Surgeons: Basil C. Duke; N. J. Thompson; R. E. Alexander; J. M. Woodford

Non-Commissioned Staff

Sergeant Majors: Thomas A. Page; William Wallace Hawkins; Abner H. Quillen
Ordnance Sergeants: Samuel Crooks; John B. Lambkin
Quartermaster Sergeant: John E. Poor
Commissary Sergeant: John Tilford Hawkins
Hospital Steward: R. D. Weaver
Chief Musician: Thomas J. Williams

266

Company "A"
Captains: Andrew J. May; William Mynhier
First Lieutenants: William Mynhier; Mason H. P. Williams; William F. Pierce
Second Lieutenants: Mason H. P. Williams; William S. Pierce; Western W. Cox; William H. Taulbee; Daniel J. Lykins; Holly P. Nickel

Company "B"
Captains: James K. Hunter; Henry T. Stanton; Joseph Adkins
First Lieutenants: Henry T. Stanton; Joseph Adkins; Peter M. Fannin; J. Thomas Chenowith
Second Lieutenants: Joseph Adkins; J. Thomas Chenowith; Samuel W. Thompson; Samuel S. Adkins; Peter M. Fannin

Company "B" (Consolidated)
Captain: William T. Barry South
First Lieutenant: Edward C. Strong
Second Lieutenants: Jerry W. South; Hyronimus Jett; Thomas J. Little

Company "C"
Captains: Hiram Hawkins; George R. Diamond
First Lieutenants: George W. Seaman; Asa M. Swimm
Second Lieutenants: Benjamin J. McConias (McComas?); George R. Diamond; Asa M. Swimm; H. R. Dobyns; Richard Morton

Company "C" (Reenlistment and Reorganization)
Captain: Robert Wells
First Lieutenant: Alfred Bascom
Second Lieutenants: John F. Johnson; Jonathan Crouch

Company "C" (Consolidated)
Captain: Thomas J. Henry
First Lieutenants: James M. McGuire; Andrew J. Parker
Second Lieutenants: Milton B. Cox; Robert D. Strother; Walter S. Henry

Company "D"
Captains: Leonidas H. Elliott; Alex C. Casey
First Lieutenants: Alex. C. Casey; Hiram A. Rice
Second Lieutenants: Hiram A. Rice; John T. Horton; Elijah Horton

Company "D" (Consolidated)
Captain: A. C. Cope
First Lieutenant: James K. Polk South
Second Lieutenants: Gabriel Hays; Hiram B. Miller; Hayden Ferguson

Company "E"
Captain: Thomas R. Worsham
First Lieutenants: W. S. Kouns; Edwin Trimble
Second Lieutenants: Elijah Goble; John W. Herrold; Hannan Harris

Company "F" (Became nucleus of Caudill's Battalion)
Captain: R. E. Caudill
First Lieutenants: James E. Sarver; W.T.B. South
Second Lieutenants: Rolin F. Walter; Jesse Amburgey; B. F. Kelly; Hiram F. Stamper

Company "F" (Reenlistment and Reorganization)
Captain: Henry G. Calvin
First Lieutenant: Hayden Ferguson
Second Lieutenants: John W. Ferguson; Dial S. Williams

Company "G"
Captains: James M. Carey; John H. Lair
First Lieutenants: John H. Lair; Anderson Moore
Second Lieutenants: Anderson Moore; James L. Ratliff; James M. Cox

Company "G" (Consolidated)
Captain: John T. Ratliff
First Lieutenant: John W. Sparks
Second Lieutenants: William J. Fields; David J. Catin; Alfred G. Rice

Company "H"
Captains: George W. Conner; George M. Ewing
First Lieutenants: George M. Ewing; James M. Brother
Second Lieutenants: James M. Brother; Marcellus C. Jackson; Thomas
   J. Peters; Thomas J. F. Hargis

Company "H" (Reenlistment and Reorganization)
Captain: Joseph Ratliff
First Lieutenant: William J. Hutton
Second Lieutenants: H. Weddington; William Scott

Company "I"
Captain: Henry C. Swango
First Lieutenant: David F. Swango
Second Lieutenants: G. W. Cox; G. W. Houck

Company "I" (Reenlistment and Reorganization)
Captain: A. C. Cope
First Lieutenant: James K. P. South
Second Lieutenants: Gabriel Hays; Hiram B. Miller; Hayden Ferguson

Company "K"
Captains: Daniel Blevins; Thomas T. Mobley
First Lieutenants: John B. Williams; William M. Peyton; Thomas T.
   Mobley; Henry T. Jayne
Second Lieutenants: Thomas A. Williams; James T. Patterson; Thomas
   T. Mobley; John W. Sparks; Joel Sparks; Thomas A. Frizzell

THIRTEENTH REGIMENT CAVALRY,
KENTUCKY VOLUNTEERS, C.S.A.[19]

Roster of Field and Staff
Colonel: Benjamin F. Caudill
Lieutenant Colonel: David J. (Henry) Caudill
Major: Thomas J. Chenowith
Surgeons: Hiram Strong; George S. Whipple
Captain A.Q.M.: More Newton
Assistant A.Q.M.: J. W. Collier; E. C. Strong; John Craft
Adjutants: Robert A. Hope; J. H. Craft
Ordnance Sergeant: A. J. Booth

Company "A"

Captain: H. H. Stamper
First Lieutenants: J. W. Collier; Wilburn Ambergey
Second Lieutenants: Campbell Pigmon; Wilburn Amburgey

Company "B"

Captains: D. J. Caudill; George Hogg
First Lieutenants: George Hogg, P. M. Duke; William E. Cornett
Second Lieutenants: P. M. Duke; Hiram G. Pratt; William E. Cornett;
Samuel B. Smith

Company "C"

Captain: Anderson Hayse
First Lieutenants: Lewis Grisby; John E. Craft
Second Lieutenants: Austin Richie; Edward Grisby

Company "D"

Captains: Enoch A. Webb; J. T. Rogers
First Lieutenants: Solomon Wright; Samuel Thompson
Second Lieutenants: B. B. Adams; J. L. Craft; John T. Crutchfield

Company "E"

Captains: Archelaus Hammons; William J. Hall
First Lieutenants: Elliott G. Mullins; James B. Fitzpatrick; Alexander
Mullins
Second Lieutenants: Abner Caudill; Henry Caudill; Henry B. Anderson;
Miles Hall; Gilbert Johnson

Company "F"

Captains: Adam Martin; James C. Walker
First Lieutenants: A. Gearhart; Wiley W. Jones; William W. Jones
Second Lieutenants: James C. Walker; John M. Allen

Company "G"

Captains: H. M. Combs; W. S. Landrum
First Lieutenants: J. L. Noble; S. H. Combs
Second Lieutenants: S. H. Combs; William H. Noble; Samuel C. Caudill

Company "H"

Captain: S. R. Brashears
First Lieutenants: Stephen A. Whitaker; A. R. Bentley
Second Lieutenants: A. R. Bentley; H. R. S. Caudill

Company "I"

Captain: William Smith
First Lieutenants: James Gwin; G. W. Houck
Second Lieutenants: John B. Fitzpatrick; Isaac Smith; G. W. Houck

This Regiment was also known as Tenth Kentucky Mounted
Rifles, Tenth Kentucky Infantry and Eleventh Mounted Rifles.

FOURTEENTH REGIMENT CAVALRY
KENTUCKY VOLUNTEERS, C.S.A.

(Formerly May's Battalion Kentucky and Virginia Mounted Rifles — Tenth Cavalry) [20]

Roster of Field and Staff

Colonels: A. J. May; George R. Diamond; Edwin Trimble
Lieutenant Colonels: George R. Diamond; Edwin Trimble
Majors: William R. Lee; A. J. May
Surgeon: B. M. Long
A.Q.M.: Albert G. Smith
A.C.S.: Alexander K. Morgan
Adjutant: J. W. Kendall

Company "A"

Captains: Edwin Trimble; A. J. Harris
First Lieutenant: A. W. Cecil
Second Lieutenants: Green L. Davidson; A. J. Harris; James P. Gearhart

Company "B"

Captains: W. W. Cox; A. R. Colvin
First Lieutenants: A. R. Colvin; J. C. Hensey
Second Lieutenants: J. C. Hensey; B. F. Richmond

Company "C"

Captains: Anderson Moore; William Ratliff
First Lieutenants: William Ratliff; Spencer Adkins
Second Lieutenants: Spencer Adkins; James M. Bevins; Henry May

Company "D"

Captains: George R. Diamond; James Honaker
First Lieutenants: James Honaker; David A. Powell
Second Lieutenants: David A. Powell; John H. Williamson; James W. McFaul

Company "E"

Captains: D. F. Strange; Thomas J. F. Hargis
First Lieutenants: Thomas J. F. Hargis; Fielding S. Helm
Second Lieutenants: T. G. Asberry; William H. Swang; John G. Diamond

Company "F"

Captain: Squire Gibson
First Lieutenant: John Lee
Second Lieutenants: Thomas Fuller; Milburn J. Stiltner

Company "G"

Captain: A. F. Gibson
First Lieutenant: Meshack Ratliff
Second Lieutenants: Squire Adkins; John M. Ratliff; B. F. Shortridge

Company "H"

Captain: Hiram Justice
First Lieutenant: Harrison Fuller
Second Lieutenants: Larkin Justice; James W. Day

Company "I"

Captain: John S. Ratliff
First Lieutenant: John S. Stilton
Second Lieutenant: Isaac Boyd

Company "K"

Captain: Elias G. W. Harman
First Lieutenant: E. G. Harman Harris
Second Lieutenants: John Potter; James H. Potter; W. W. Hatcher

FIRST BATTALION CAVALRY, KENTUCKY VOLUNTEERS, C.S.A.[21]

Roster of Field and Staff

Lieutenant General: W. E. Sims
Major: John Shawhan
Surgeon: John Talbott

Company "A"

Captains: John Shawhan; William H. VanHook
First Lieutenant: James M. Frazier
Second Lieutenant: Charles H. Fowler

FIELDS' COMPANY OF PARTISAN RANGERS, KENTUCKY VOLUNTEERS, C.S.A.[22]

Officers

Captain: William J. Fields
First Lieutenant: John W. Sparks
Second Lieutenants: William K. Elliott; William Horton

Non-Commissioned Officers

First Sergeants: John W. Wills; B. W. Ward
Second Sergeants: John R. Crittenden; Jesse Lyons
Third Sergeants: Henry T. Jayne; John T. Parker
Fourth Sergeant: James T. Johnson
Fifth Sergeants: Elijah Jackson; John M. Chafin
First Corporals: F. M. Thompson; Eli Cook
Second Corporals: H. W. Barker; Jesse Rose
Third Corporals: Reason Lyon; R. M. Clay
Fourth Corporals: Andrew Miner; James M. Green

This organization was recruited principally in Eastern Kentucky and consisted of two hundred and one officers and enlisted men.

FIRST BATTALION MOUNTED RIFLES, KENTUCKY VOLUNTEERS, C.S.A.[23]

Company "A"

Captains: Orville G. Cameron; Joseph Hardin
First Lieutenants: Joseph Hardin; William C. French
Second Lieutenants: William C. French; William W. Burns; G. S. Magee; W. H. VanHook

Company "C"

Captain: Ezekiel F. Clay
First Lieutenant: Thomas S. Lewis
Second Lieutenants: James G. Bedford; James T. Rogers; David H. Bowles; C. Duncan

Company "D"

Captain: John B. Holladay
First Lieutenant: Thomas M. Campbell
Second Lieutenants: William M. Collins; Ro. Kincart; James White

NOTES

Chapter XVI

1. Report of the Adjutant General of Kentucky, Soldiers of the War of 1812, 1891, pp. 59-61.
2. Ibid, 92-100.
3. Ibid, 131-136.
4. Ibid, 182-3.
5. Ibid, 70.
6. Report of the Adjutant General of Kentucky, 1861-1866, Vol. I, pp. 872-893.
7. Report of the Adjutant General of Kentucky, 1861-1866, Vol. II, pp. 96-130.
8. Ibid, 384-424.
9. Ibid, 424-441.
10. Ibid, 443-459.
11. Ibid, 603-610.
12. Ibid, 771-776.
13. Ibid, 780-791.
14. Ibid, 883-887.
15. Ibid, 888-889.
16. Ibid, 889-894.
17. Ibid, 894-897.
18. Report of the Adjutant General of Kentucky, Confederate Kentucky Volunteers, War of 1861-1866, Vol. I, pp. 192-266.
19. Report of the Adjutant General of Kentucky, Confederate Kentucky Volunteers, War of 1861-1866, Vol. II, pp. 142-177.
20. Ibid, 178-206.
21. Ibid, 320-325
22. Ibid, 338-342.
23. Ibid, 346-362.